Rhetorical Analysis

An Introduction to Biblical Rhetoric

Roland Meynet

Journal for the Study of the Old Testament
Supplement Series 256

Historical Analysis

An Introduction to Higher Biblical Criticism

Roland Mushat

JOURNAL FOR THE STUDY OF THE OLD TESTAMENT SUPPLEMENT SERIES
256

Sheffield Academic Press

To Georges Mounin
master and friend

The publishers are grateful for permission to include extracts from
Chiasmus in the New Testament: A Study in Formgeschichte by Nils
Wilhelm Lund. Copyright © 1942 by the University of North Carolina
Press, renewed 1970 by Mrs N.W. Lund. Used by permission of the
publisher.

Published by
Sheffield Academic Press Ltd
Mansion House
19 Kingfield Road
Sheffield S11 9AS
England

Typeset by Sheffield Academic Press
and
Printed on acid-free paper in Great Britain
by Bookcraft Ltd
Midsomer Norton, Bath

British Library Cataloguing in Publication Data

A catalogue record for this book is available
from the British Library

ISBN 1-85075-870-0

CONTENTS

The present work is more than just a simple translation of *L'Analyse rhétorique: Une nouvelle méthode pour comprendre la Bible. Textes fondateurs et exposé systématique* (Initiations; Paris: Cerf, 1989; Italian translation: *L'analisi retorica*, Biblioteca biblica, 8; Brescia: Editrice Queriniana, 1992). It is, in fact, a new, revised, and augmented edition.

The second half of the book has been totally rewritten in order to accommodate particularly the developments in the analysis of the first two chapters of Amos, after the publication of the commentary written in collaboration with Pietro Bovati (*Le Livre du prophète Amos*, Rhétorique biblique, 2; Paris: Cerf, 1994; Italian edition: *Il libro del profeta Amos*, Retorica biblica, 2; Rome: Edizioni Dehoniane, 1995).

The new 'Foreword' includes an article first published in Portuguese, then in French, in Italian and in Arabic: a new method, unknown to the educated layman, is expounded here in accessible form. These few pages have proved to be a precious source of help, particularly to my students at the *Centre Sèvres* in Paris, but also for my students in biblical theology at the Gregorian University in Rome.

As an introduction to the second part, I have added the first half of a study on the presuppositions of rhetorical analysis given as a seminar paper at the Catholic school of theology of the University of Strasbourg and published in a collection of essays entitled *Exégèse et Herméneutique. Comment lire la Bible?* (LD, 158; Paris: Cerf, 1994).

Finally, to conclude the second part, I have included a conference paper that the Roman group of New Testament exegetes had asked me to give: 'I frutti dell'analisi retorica per l'esegesi biblica', published in *Greg.* 77 (1996), pp. 403-36.

It remains for me to wish that this new version of a book, which has as yet no equivalent on the subject, be useful to the English-speaking public.

PREFACE
by Paul Beauchamp

Rhetorical Analysis, Roland Meynet's new book, helps us place the agenda of 'rhetorical analysis' within the context of the multiple operations necessary for biblical exegesis. We are now able to place it within its history, which is essential; indeed, its forerunners are rescued from oblivion, while at the same time a continuity is established with two centuries of building on their discoveries. We might add that, for several decades, the 'rhetorical' method was used on a large number of texts by many researchers, more in Anglo-Saxon and Latin countries than in Germany: witness the index of Angelico di Marco. But it was not always known under the same name. Exegetes have often called 'literary structure' an equivalent result to what is sought by 'rhetorical' analysis. We are shown here how the latter, like structural analysis, finds its model and inspiration in linguistics, or at least can and should do it. But 'rhetorical analysis' limits its field to the distribution of verbal significants, instead of going straight for the relationship between functions, values or symbols. It is therefore a way, among others, of taking into account structures of signification. Would it be more appropriate to speak of stylistics? Yes, it would, if it concerned the characteristics of an author. But such is not the case: inquiry tells us that there are common laws in the ordering of verbal signs within the biblical corpus. American scholars have given to these laws the collective name of 'biblical rhetoric'. It is difficult not to object that classical rhetoric is more prescriptive than descriptive and, more to the point, that its field of inquiry is much larger, encompassing knowledge of man and society. However, it may be more advantageous to conform to a widely acclaimed denomination.

The biblical rhetoric (from now on, without quotation marks) that Roland Meynet invites us to discover puts us straight into the perspective of modern exegesis, insofar as it would be the enactment of a maxim which also outgrows its domain, according to which, 'form is the door to signification'. Romanticism had already been attracted by the ancient and oriental forms of popular expression, anterior to literature, but still perceptible in its most archaic manifestations, including the Bible. This romantic intuition was raised to the status of a system in Germany with research on the 'history of forms', which emphasized the study of lost oral configurations. With the hint of an apologetic concern, the Catholic 'milieu' shifted this tendency towards wider and less sociologically determined 'literary genres', but closer to the biblical texts as they were transmitted. Despite these differences, and thanks partly to the steadfastness of the Catholic magisterial body, everybody agreed that no text could be interpreted outside its own laws, besides those of grammar and logic. Once these laws governing ways to signify, namely the set of processes of communication, were recognized, we had already entered, unwittingly, the era of semiology.

Against this common background, rhetorical analysis distinguishes itself by the stress it puts on the *written* page, per se. It agrees, in this respect, with the recent trend which pays a new respect to writing or to the nobility of *letters*. Or, to be more precise, rhetorical matters deserve to be called such, since they invite us to reduce our reckoning of the differences between the written and the oral. The 'formularity' dear to Marcel Jousse, the regularity of recurrences, and the symmetry of layout pushed to the finest detail, are no longer the prerogative of orality; not unless we admit that our texts are written in 'oral style'. This remark, which was once used to describe fragments of a more degraded whole, fallen from a more noble state of primeval orality, can no longer be applied to this lengthy set of texts following the same rules, which appear to us here. For the method has been applied to the *Epistle to the Hebrews* (A. Vanhoye), and it is certainly applicable to the *Wisdom of Solomon*; the number of texts it is applicable to grows and Roland Meynet's previous work, *L'Evangile selon saint Luc: Analyse rhétorique*, demonstrates its validity throughout the Lukan Gospel. So there have been writing norms directly kindred to oral style, which render the traditional dramatization of their difference less indispensable. That even questions the preconceived idea that orality was derived from the written. Does the '*archi-écriture*' not suggest the encoding, coinciding with the beginning of all meaning, according to which the unfolding of discourse is programed? What we mean is that memory, which plays the leading part in all theories of oral style, necessarily offers a spatial aspect. It is visual. All mnemotechnics are an interior writing, inscribing signs inside the body. Rhetorical analysis shows that the scribe is, if not an orator, at least a traditional 'learner', less detached from the rhythms of memory than we had thought. He draws on them to innovate.

A part of the old rhetoric dealt with *dispositio*, namely the order and the distribution of parts. The method we have here makes *dispositio* its sole preoccupation, but relies on the verbal series. It is important to understand how far this standpoint disturbs old habits. It does more: it seems to go against the immediate impression that the biblical text gives the western reader, who often finds it badly or not at all composed, as if it had been tinkered. What strikes the reader in an almost physical way, luring or repulsing him, is the existence of discontinuities within the biblical texts; these discontinuities are incomparably greater than those found in western writing. The exegesis of the scientific age has registered this shock in its own way by reading into those discontinuities the traces of successive outside interventions: additions; corrections; not always consistent reinterpretations; sometimes simply contradictions. A large part of the exegetical effort has been, and is still being, spent on the detection of this plurality. It is an undeniable fact, to our eyes, that the numerous texts of the Bible present this composite characteristic, especially in the Old Testament, the redaction of which took so long. We should not use the abuse of bold conjectures as a pretext to ironize on the researcher's stabs in the dark. What is more striking is that the conditions of composition which have culminated in so richly stratified documents have not been more studied. What language, which society, lent itself to such manner of collective writing, over a long period of time, and open to such sedimentation? The so-called historical method, the empiricism of which we cannot deny, has done little to develop its own anthropology, and its own ethnography of writing.

Without venturing too far into this territory, we will at least ask ourselves if one should not turn the usual problematic on its head. We believed that we were faced with a text which had originally been a whole, and which had then been disjointed from the outside. Were we not in fact faced with a text open by nature, made of associated, yet distinct, units? Prone, therefore, to be interlaced with new insertions and, shall we say, welcoming them? If this is the case, it follows that the end result—each page of our Bible—even when it is plural, remains *a text* and begs to be treated as a finished product resulting from a long elaboration. Which therefore legitimizes, in any case, the rhetorical analysis approach, along variable lines which have yet to be foreseen. The case of the Lukan Gospel is the most simple example for rhetorical analysis, since it is not necessary to start from the hypothesis of a composite work to study it.

But let us get back to this primary fact, to the sensible intuition of a tinkered-with composition, following a 'parataxis' principle, that is juxtaposition instead of coordination. Used to seeking significants of subordination, of transition and everything which, to us, highlights the inner coherence of discourses, our eyes are blind to other signs, that analysis nevertheless makes out. Visibility is itself their principal characteristic, their inner resource. The words are arranged on the page following a coherent optical disposition. This principle draws its strength from its ability to be reduced to two principal traits, recurrence and contrast, themselves opposed to one another. But we resist recurrence, because we have learnt at school not to repeat the same words twice. And we resist contrast, because nothing seems to prepare us for. . . It is not our role, in this preface, to expose those modes of writing. It should be enough to say that the initial impression of disorder gradually gives way to understanding of the law of the text, with its rigorous constraints, at least where analysis has brought its fruits: enough, in our case, to convince us that the rules are real, and with sufficient failures to keep us searching. . .

Thus, beyond and without transitions, the words speak with one another through what Jousse had called 'verbal rhymes'. One hesitates to resort to the particularities of Hebrew to explain this writing style, since it admirably deploys itself in several biblical writings in Greek, in the Old as in the New Testament. Those writings, however, are evidently fertilized and completely impregnated by Hebrew writings. We must therefore go back to this source. We note that Hebrew tends to stunt the expansion of words, in several ways. Its verbal roots, when we compare them to those of Greek, seldom branch out. The substantive and the verb attract to them the prepositions, possessive and personal pronouns, to make one term. The linking words are very few and brief, the *waw* being particularly multifunctional (on this point, the westernization of modern Hebrew can serve as *a contrario* proof). The subordination ('hypotaxis') is therefore very limited. The vocabulary is very sparse. One should think that there should be a compensation proportional to all those limits, if, according to our belief, the capacity to signify is equal in all languages.

The exiguity of the vocabulary, the condensation in a single term of several grammatical functions, the poverty of the signs of transition, all these limitations call for compensation by resorting to a rich combinative of the verbal positions. Each word signifies, not only through its grammatical or syntactic function, but through its *place*, chosen to put it in relation with other words within an organized whole. For example, each word positioned at the beginning and at the end of a unit (often in its centre as well) exerts, by the same token, an influence on the interpretation. But we are dealing with a combinative, where the constants are here to provide support for the variations. Thus, we can understand that it is the pressure of a law, at the risk of calling up a repulsive rigidity, which provides the indispensable conditions for it to be a play, that is freedom, on the works. This system of echoes always keeps, even in prose, poetical efficacy, and always directs the gaze towards a meaning which can only be 'between the lines'. This is true at the simplest level of the mere parallelism: 'You will tread on the lion and the adder; the young lion and the serpent you will trample under foot' (Ps. 91.13): this leads me to the *idea* of a threat, distinct from its materializations but inseparable from them. Energy is born out of the image, but it has to get free from it. This is probably why the biblical texts offer so much food for thought to the most demanding mind, without doing its thinking for that individual. They propel their readers towards the fearsome moment when they will have to do the interpretation by themselves. And many among those readers, as has been said, have engraved their own inscription on the old tree, before the Book was closed.

The reader will appreciate the progress that Roland Meynet has afforded rhetorical analysis by this unprecedented contribution, which I judge to be indispensable, to a methodological elaboration. It was undoubtedly necessary to face the difficulty that Georges Mounin suggested in his preface to *Quelle est donc cette Parole*? Does the possibility of superimposing several simultaneous arrangements not render illusory the objectivity of the results and the quality of 'law' awarded to biblical rhetoric? The answer is given, in essence, by the principle of the autonomy of levels, which I believe to be solid. But the work which would deal at once with the level of the minimal unity (as it has been studied in detail by Roland Meynet on the basis of the

simplest parallelism) and the level of the coherence of the whole book,
goes beyond the abilities of one researcher; and it is perhaps better
this way. So I would prefer, rather than rally readers to a cause, to
call upon the participation of various researchers in suggesting the
fecundity of the questions addressed in this work, given the actual
state of exegesis.

All method—historical or rhetorical—should go as far as it can.
And it is the condition for the free appearance of the questions it
raises, in relation to the hermeneutic responsibility of the exegete. Let
us be grateful to Roland Meynet for having led his research far enough
to allow dialogue with him in all clarity. Those lines are nothing but
the continuation of such a dialogue, which started between us a long
time ago, and also involved a few others. Some points seem to have
already been made. The symmetries of biblical rhetoric are not an end
in itself: to admire such astonishing structures as one might admire ice
crystals made on window panes does not interest us in the slightest.
The participation of the researcher is far more profound than these
abstractions: has not Lévi-Strauss qualified as 'corporeal' the pleasure
that structures give to those who penetrate them? Roland Meynet has
described successfully the arduous work that was necessary for him to
rewrite the text of Luke in his rhetorical form as an 'incorporation
through the hand'. Opening the door to meaning, this exercise already
preserves from what is purely cerebral and fuels a living attention.
Besides, the remarkable pedagogy that inspires all the expositions
testifies to a real concern for the reader as well as for the text.

It is in this direction, it seems, that the future of the method lies,
and where all the problems that it still addresses will be answered. It
will have to give itself more of a body. This can be done following the
lines of an anthropological study. What education, what physical discipline, what gestures, what conditions of transmission, contributed to
this writing style? The historical method still lacks its anthropology. It
falls to the rhetorical method to be ready, as far as its subject matter is
concerned, to remedy to this flaw. 'Anthropology', one of the strong
key words of Marcel Jousse, who nourished his disciples with insight-
ful inspiration and astonishing drive, while waiting for their work to
merge with his and for the appearance of the social conditions he felt
were lacking for the completion of his undertaking... May all those
who are, after all, his successors (even if they are on different tracks

than his own) now collaborate with each other in order to reach the next stage!

To give a body to the method, also means to build the study of each particular text upon the familiar knowledge of the whole 'biblical corpus', an undertaking without end. One should be well aware that this work should not be the expansion or the confirmation of the method: but that it is rather the central heart that gives it life and rhythm. Indeed, the recurrences are but the hard skeleton on which the verbal series, those more sensitive parts of the structure, are built. To take a rudimentary example, 'sky, earth, sea' form a closed set, thus are able to suggest a structure built upon three distinct units. But how can we know this if not by noticing the recurrence of this ternary list in the whole of biblical literature, while we cannot say the same for 'earth, water, air, fire', a list of four elements which is foreign to the biblical corpus? Thus, all texts speak, not only through the words that they share with other texts, but also through the *groups* of words that are repeated elsewhere without necessarily being contiguous, but sometimes only rhythmically distributed. Roland Meynet has taken this fact into account very seriously, which has led him to make room to accommodate a preliminary stage to what he calls, legitimately, 'interpretation'. This stage is indispensable and at the same time very difficult to systematize, without mentioning the difficulty of execution when dealing with a long text. This recourse to the intertext dispels the temptation to delve into closed texts, at the cost of ignoring their context, but at the same time it calls for a task impossible to achieve. It indicates from afar the analysis of the method's limits, which, far from devaluing it, are essential. It is through them that it communicates with other attempts. This is the wish that I want to formulate, before all others, for the work that is presented here.

ABBREVIATIONS

AJSL	*American Journal of Semitic Languages and Literatures*
AnBib	Analecta biblica
AB	Anchor Bible
ArPh	*Archives de philosophie*
AThR	*Anglican Theological Review*
BetM	*Beth Miqra*
Bib	*Biblica*
BibOr	Biblica et orientalia
BT	*The Bible Translator*
Brot.	*Brotéria*
BTB	*Biblical Theology Bulletin*
CBQ	*Catholic Biblical Quarterly*
CNRS	Centre national de la recherche scientifique
CrozQ	*The Crozer Quarterly*
CivCatt	*La civiltà cattolica*
EeT(O)	*Eglise et théologie (Ottawa)*
ErIs	*Eretz Israel*
ExpTim	*The Expository Times*
EBib	Etudes bibliques
ETL	*Ephemerides theologicae lovanienses*
Greg.	*Gregorianum*
GRBS	*Greek, Roman, and Byzantine Studies*
HSCP	*Harvard Studies in Classical Philogogy*
HSM	Harvard Semitic Monographs
HTR	*Harvard Theological Review*
HUCA	*Hebrew Union College Annual*
ICC	International Critical Commentary
Int	*Interpretation*
JBL	*Journal of Biblical Literature*
JR	*Journal of Religion*
JSOT	*Journal for the Study of the Old Testament*
JSOTSup	Journal for the Study of the Old Testament, Supplement Series
JSS	*Journal of Semitic Studies*
LAPO	Littératures anciennes du Proche-Orient

LB	*Linguistica biblica*
LD	Lectio divina
LiBi	Lire la Bible
MUSJ	*Mélanges de l'Université Saint Joseph*
NCah	*Les nouveaux cahiers*
NRT	*Nouvelle revue théologique*
NTS	*New Testament Studies*
OBO	Orbis biblicus et orientalis
PUF	Presses universitaires de France
RA	*Revue d'assyriologie et d'archéologie orientale*
RB	*Revue biblique*
RdQ	*Revue di Qumran*
RevQ	*Revue de Qumran*
RevPhil	*Revue de philosophie*
RevSR	*Revue des sciences religieuses*
RSR	*Recherches de science religieuse*
SBLDS	Society of Biblical Literature Dissertation Series
SEÅ	*Svensk exegetisk årsbok*
SGKA	*Studien zur Geschichte und Kultur des Altertums*
SSN	Studia semitica neerlandica
ST	*Studia theologica*
SE	Studia evangelica
StPat	*Studia patavina*
TSK	*Theologische Studien und Kritiken*
TPBT	*Technical Papers to the Bible Translator*
TS	*Theological Studies*
UF	*Ugarit Forschungen*
VD	*Verbum domini*
VT	*Vetus Testamentum*
VTSup	Vetus Testamentum Supplement Series
ZAW	*Zeitschrift für die alttestamentliche Wissenschaft*
ZNW	*Zeitschrift für die neutestamentliche Wissenschaft*

PROLOGUE
RHETORICAL ANALYSIS: A NEW METHOD
TO UNDERSTAND THE BIBLE

I have been asked several times to present orally—and in a non-technical way—the 'rhetorical analysis' (also called in French: *structurelle*).[1] At the request of the Portuguese journal *Brotéria*, I wrote down this brief presentation which had taken shape little by little, according to the rules of oral style.[2] The appraising feedback that I got for this article encourages me to use it as a foreword, for want of a better substitute, for the readers seeking a first approach to the method and the fruits that it can bear for a renewal of biblical exegesis. This draft has benefited from the remarks and suggestions of several readers, whom I thank warmly.

The subtitle of these few pages is at once entirely true and completely false. It is true, because so far, this method has only been applied systematically to a relatively small number of texts; moreover

---

1. The method has been used under this appellation by several authors: J. Radermakers, *Au fil de l'Evangile selon saint Matthieu* (Heverlee/Leuven: Institut d'Etudes Théologiques, 1972); *La Bonne Nouvelle de Jésus selon saint Marc* (Brussels: Institut d'Etudes Théologiques, 1974); J. Radermakers and P. Bossuyt, *Jésus, Parole de la grâce selon saint Luc* (Brussels: Institut d'Etudes Théologiques, 1981); M. Girard, *Les Psaumes: Analyse structurelle et interprétation* (I. Ps. 1–50; Montréal: Bellarmin; Paris: Cerf, 1984); *idem, Les Psaumes redécouverts: De la structure au sens* (II. Ps. 51–100; III. Ps. 101–150; Montréal: Bellarmin, 1994; I. Ps. 1–50; Montréal: Bellarmin, 1996).

2. 'A Análise retórica: Um novo método para compreender a Bíblia', *Brot.* 137 (1993), pp. 391-408; also published in Italian: 'Un nuovo metodo per comprendere la Bibbia: l'analisi retorica', *CivCatt* 3 (1994), pp. 121-34 (reproduced in *'E ora, scrivete per voi questo cantico': Introduzione pratica all'analisi retorica, 1. Detti e proverbi* [Retorica biblica, 3; Roma: Edizioni Dehoniane, 1996], pp. 9-21); in French: 'L'analyse rhétorique, une nouvelle méthode pour comprendre la Bible', *NRT* 116 (1994), pp. 641-57; in Arabic: 'Al-taḥlīl al-balāġī, ṭarīqa ğadīda li-'idrāq maʿānī al-kitāb al-muqaddas', *Al-Machriq* 70 (1996), pp. 391-410.

short texts, like psalms, rather than entire books.[3] The method is new
also because it is only recently that it has known an important development: an increasing number of exegetes, indeed, are interested in
the composition of the texts they are studying. One must add that it is
only in its early stages, in as much as very few authors can use it with
true proficiency. However, it would be false to pretend that rhetorical
analysis is new, since its origins date back to the middle of the eighteenth century, with the *Lectures on the Sacred Poetry of the Hebrews*
by R. Lowth (1753), and mostly to the turn of the nineteenth century
with the work of J. Jebb and most of all T. Boys, two major authors
whom a large majority of exegetes have nevertheless never heard of.

Another point needs to be made concerning the subtitle: 'A New
Method to Understand the Bible'. Is the rhetorical analysis truly an
exegetical method? The recent document by the Pontifical Biblical
Commission, *The Interpretation of the Bible in the Church*,[4] introduces 'Rhetorical Analysis' as the first of 'New Methods of Literary
Criticism'; in fact, it distinguishes under this title three different
methods: the 'Classical rhetoric', which is the application of Graeco-
Roman classical rhetoric to biblical texts, the 'biblical literary tradition' and the 'new rhetoric'. 'Classical rhetoric' is what the Americans
call 'rhetorical criticism'; the 'rhetorical analysis' of this book, on the
other hand, is exactly what the document of the biblical commission
calls the 'biblical literary tradition'.[5] It would be perhaps more accurate to say that it is but one of the operations, one of the multiple steps
of the exegetical work, along with the textual criticism, lexicographic

---

3.   A. Vanhoye, *La Structure littéraire de l'Epître aux Hébreux* (Paris: Desclée de
Brouwer, 1963, 1976); R. Meynet, *L'Evangile selon saint Luc, analyse rhétorique*,
I–II (Paris: Cerf, 1988) Italian trans.: *Il vangelo secondo Luca* (Retorica biblica, 1;
Rome: Dehoniane, 1994); P. Bovati and R. Meynet, *Le livre du prophète Amos*
(Paris: Cerf, 1994); Italian edn: *Il libro del profeta Amos* (Rome: Dehoniane, 1995).

4.   Pontifical Biblical Commission, *The Interpretation of the Bible in the Church*
(Rome: Libreria Editrice Vaticana, 1993).

5.   'Other exegetes concentrate upon the characteristic features of the biblical
literary tradition. Rooted in Semitic culture, this displays a distinct preference for
symmetrical compositions, through which one can detect relationships between
different elements in the text. The study of the multiple forms of parallelism and other
procedures characteristic of the Semitic mode of composition allows for a better
discernment of the literary structure of texts, which can only lead to a more adequate
understanding of their message' (*The Interpretation of the Bible in the Church*, pp.
42-43).

enquiry, grammatical and syntactical analysis, history of the text, determination of the literary genres, and so on. This somehow reduces its significance but, on the other hand, acknowledges its importance. In this light, rhetorical analysis is no longer another method, which one can choose among others or discard; but it has become an indispensable step in exegetical research. Should one choose to leave this debate aside, one can always say that it is a new 'approach' to biblical texts.[6]

Like all other exegetical approaches, the aim of rhetorical analysis is to understand the texts. It is convinced that, in order to reach this aim, it is important, almost indispensable, to bring the *composition* of the text to light. And, first of all, to establish its limits. Exactly as a linguist would identify the limits of the sentences of the corpus he is studying. The biblical texts, except from the psalms, have indeed no boundaries marked by either titles or typography (such as returns which would indicate paragraphs). The problem is not new: all exegetes experience the same difficulties in determining the beginning and end of literary units. The only two unquestionable limits of a biblical book are the beginning and end of the book; inside the book, one has nonetheless to divide! One does it, usually, following empirical methods. The historico-critical exegesis, which has ruled unchallenged for a century, tells us that only small units can be considered; 'forms' (miracle story, apophthegm, parable and so on). It has taught us to read these small units distinct from one another; according to this method, the Gospels (and also the books of the prophets) were nothing but rather ill-assorted collections of small units, which circulated among primitive communities, and that an editor (a collector!) decided one day to compile without a true composition. Rhetorical analysis assumes the contrary, if one can reasonably imagine that small stories circulated separately at first, the evangelists were nonetheless genuine authors, who organized their material in intricate compositions. Rhetorical analysis asserts that these compositions do not obey the

---

6. *The Interpretation of the Bible in the Church* distinguishes between the 'methods' and the 'approaches'; in a first draft, only 'The Historical-Critical Method' was considered as an 'approach'; in the definitive draft, 'Rhetorical Analysis' was promoted from the subaltern rank of 'approach' to that of 'method'; see A. Vanhoye, 'L'interpretazione della Bibbia nella Chiesa: Riflessione circa un documento della Commissione Biblica', *CivCatt* 3 (1994), pp. 3-15 (the author is the Secretary of the Pontifical Biblical Commission).

rules of Graeco-Roman rhetoric, but the specific laws of Hebraic rhetoric, of which the authors of the New Testament are the direct inheritors.[7]

But enough generalities and principles! The following examples will speak for themselves. Let us begin at the beginning, which is the minimal unit, the distich, or bimember segment:

For not in	**my bow**	DO I TRUST,	
nor can	**my sword**	SAVE ME.	(Ps. 44.7)

The mere fact that the same thing is repeated twice, in two different ways, 'leads the gaze to a sense which can only exist "between the lines". To hear this, points me to an *idea*, other than its materializations but inseparable from them.'[8] The reader can read the rest of Psalm 44 and see how the whole poem, which contains twenty-eight distichs (or bimember segments), walks on two feet from beginning to end. The 'parallelism of the members', as it is called by Lowth, is the fundamental characteristic of Hebraic poetry; more generally, this bipolarity marks the entirety of biblical literature. Things are always said twice, since truth would not be encapsulated in one affirmation, but given in the interaction of two complementary affirmations, or in the shock of contrasts.

Like this short text of parallel composition (Lk. 11.31-32), chosen among a thousand examples, the second part seems a simple repetition of the first part, what we might call a 'doublet', redundant if not useless. But complementarity adds to the function of insistence which one cannot ignore (repetition is the first figure of rhetoric!), in this case multiple: the double complementarity, sexual, between a woman ('the queen') and the 'men', and geographical, between the 'South' and the North ('Nineveh'), is a way of indicating the whole (all Gentiles will judge this generation). Furthermore, there is also a necessary chronological complementarity between to 'listen to' and to 'repent', and between the 'wisdom' of the king ('Solomon') and the 'proclamation' of the prophet ('Jonas'), which is a way of saying that Jesus is at once king and prophet. Finally, there is the complementarity between

7.   See R. Meynet, 'Présupposés de l'analyse rhétorique, avec une application à Mc 10,13-52', in C. Coulot (ed.), *Exégèse et Herméneutique: Comment lire la Bible?* (LD, 158; Paris: Cerf, 1994), pp. 69-111 (redrafted in part below, pp. 108-17.

8.   P. Beauchamp, preface to R. Meynet, *L'Analyse rhétorique*, pp. 11-12 (see below, p. 26).

the centripetal movement which brings the queen of the South 'from the ends of the earth' to Israel and the centrifugal movement which brings Jonas from Israel to Nineveh. This example shows that when two literary units seem totally similar, one must not forget to spot the differences which perhaps are richer in meaning than the similarities.

```
+ 31 The queen of    the South    will rise            at the judgment
+ with the men of                                      this generation
        -and judge them,

            : because she came from the ends of the earth
            : to LISTEN TO     THE  WISDOM         of    Solomon

                    = and see, there is here more       than   Solomon!
-------------------------------------------------------------------------------
+ 32 The men of      Nineveh      will get up          at the judgment
+ with                                                 this generation
        -and judge it,

            : because
            : THEY REPENTED at  THE  PROCLAMATION    of    Jonah,

                    = and see, there is here more       than   Jonah!
```

The following example is of the same order, but provides a nice concentric construction (Lk. 14.7-14):

The rewriting of this text aims to show how v. 10 is parallel, and opposed in all respects, to vv. 8-9; with the necessary variations, however, to avoid a too-mechanical parallelism. One should note, in v. 10, the opposition 'to fall'—'go up', as well as the variation 'higher' (and not 'at the first place' expected) which prepares for the opposition between 'exalted' and 'humbled' in v. 11.

[7] He was saying to those who were invited a parable,
when he noticed how they chose the first places, saying to them:

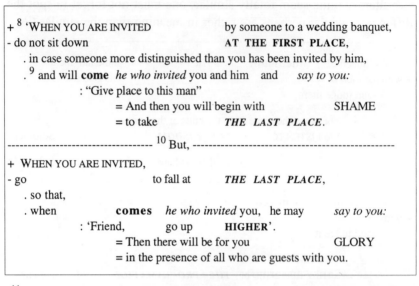

+ [8] 'WHEN YOU ARE INVITED		by someone to a wedding banquet,
- do not sit down		AT THE FIRST PLACE,
. in case someone more distinguished than you has been invited by him,		
. [9] and will **come** *he who invited* you and him and *say to you:*		
: "Give place to this man"		
= And then you will begin with		SHAME
= to take		*THE LAST PLACE.*

-------------------------------- [10] But, --

+ WHEN YOU ARE INVITED,		
- go	to fall at	*THE LAST PLACE,*
. so that,		
. when	**comes** *he who invited* you, he may	*say to you:*
: 'Friend,	go up	**HIGHER'.**
= Then there will be for you		GLORY
= in the presence of all who are guests with you.		

[11] For every one   **WHO EXALTS HIMSELF**   *WILL BE HUMBLED*
and   *WHO HUMBLES HIMSELF*   *WILL BE EXALTED.*[9]

Such are the limits which are assigned to this text by almost every modern edition of the Bible. For the western reader, heir to the Graeco-Romans, it is obvious that a parable should end with the lesson that is drawn from it, as often do the stories of Aesop or La Fontaine. Verse 11 fulfils this function admirably.

It is not the way, however, that biblical texts are organized. Jesus' speech is indeed not over. To cut it short at v. 11 would be like amputating the following segment from its second member:

| Unless the Lord | builds | the house, |
| in vain | labor | the builders   (Ps. 127.1). |

Anyone can see that the sentence is not over! After having addressed the guests (7-10), Jesus now speaks to the host (12-14):

---

9.   The translations, very close to the original texts, are mine.

¹² And he said also to the man who had invited him:

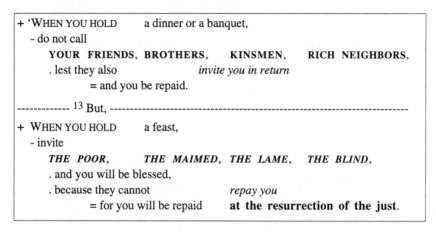

There is here another striking parallelism between the two pieces (12b-e and 13b-e); the four terms enumerating those to be invited answer to the four terms enumerating those who should not be invited. The final addition of 'at the resurrection of the just' should be noted as a major variation.

The parable is double: it is addressed, in a complementary way, to all, to the guests as much as to the host. And v. 11, 'For every one who exalts himself will be humbled and he who humbles himself will be exalted', is not only the conclusion of the first half of the parable; it is also, as a matter of fact, the introduction to the second half. If both halves of the parable are of parallel composition, the whole is of concentric construction. The 'moral', or the proverb which sums up the whole, is not at the end, in conclusion, but in the middle; it is the heart, the keystone of the whole. To my knowledge, only the translation of the New Testament in modern Hebrew[10] has not separated what Luke has joined: it has entitled the whole of Lk. 14.7-14: 'moral lesson to the guests and host'.

Let us take now another example, undoubtedly the most famous text in the New Testament, which any Christian knows by heart and often recites: 'Our Father' (according to Mt. 6.9-13). Everyone knows that this prayer is composed of seven requests; when it is recited by two voices, it is divided in two unequal parts: the first counts the first three

---

10. The Bible Society in Israel, Jerusalem, 1976, 3rd edn, 1995.

requests (which are in 'you'), the second the last four (which are in 'us'):

Our Father in heaven,
+   hallowed be **your** name,
+   **your** kingdom come,
+   **your** will be done, on earth as it is in heaven.

=   Give *us* this day our daily bread,
=   and forgive *us* our debts, as we also have forgiven our debtors
=   and lead *us* not into temptation
=   but deliver *us* from evil.

It is not wrong to note the difference of pronouns between the third person singular in the first three requests, and the first person plural in the last four. But this is no more than one mark of composition. And there are more, as important as this one. If one retains but one mark, there is a risk of missing the genuine organization of the text, and losing much of its meaning.

One should note that the last three requests aim at liberation from negative things, 'debts', 'temptation', 'evil'; on the other hand, the 'bread' of the fourth request is not a negative thing, but a positive thing, like the other first three, namely God's 'name', his 'kingdom', and his 'will'. One can see that, from a morphological point of view, the fourth request is affiliated to the last three (in 'us'), but from a semantic point of view, it is linked to the first three (positive things).

Moreover, the third and the fifth request are the only ones that end with an expansion which, in Greek, start by the same 'as': '*as* on earth as it is in heaven' and '*as* we also have forgiven our debtors'. This provides a nice frame for the fourth request, that is, the numerically central request.

But this is not all: the fourth request is distinct from all the others by the fact that its two members are strictly parallel (if taken literally):

| The bread of | **u s** | *the daily* |
| give | **u s** | *every day* |

The two principal terms of the sentence (the direct object and the verb), are followed by 'us', and then the synonyms 'daily' and 'every day'.

Last, but not least, the request for daily bread is the one which agrees best with the name of him to whom the prayer is addressed. If the first and last three requests were to be preceded by the divine name, it would be 'our King' for the second request ('thy kingdom come'), it would probably be 'our God' for all the others. Strictly speaking, however, only the fourth and central request requires the Father's name: the experience common to all children—at least at the time—is that it is the father who provides the daily bread.

If we take into account all the converging marks of composition, it is no longer a bipolar division, but a concentric organization which appears. One could ponder, undoubtedly with more results, on the relationship between the corresponding requests, like a mirror image, each side of the central request: for example, between the 'hallowed' of the beginning and 'evil' of the end, on the 'kingdom' of God and 'temptation' which, in the Gospel, are two realities in which one 'enters', or does not 'enter';[11] and, in noting the parallel between the two demands which frame the centre, one can wonder what exactly is God's will!

THE PRAYER OF THE LORD (Mt. 6.9-13)

Our	Hallowed be *thy*		NAME			1
Father	Come	*thy*	KINGDOM			2
who	Be done	*thy*	*WILL*	AS in the heaven	so on earth	3
			THE BREAD of *us*	the daily		4
			give	to *us*	this day	
art	And forgive	*us* our	*DEBTS*,	AS we also forgive	our debtors	5
in	And lead not	*us* into	TEMPTATION			6
heaven	But deliver	*us* from	EVIL.			7

The reader will have no doubt noticed that the figure of the Our Father strangely mirrors the shape of the seven-branched candelabra.[12]

11. 'Whoever does not receive the kingdom of God as a little child will never enter it' (Lk. 18.17; also Lk. 18.24-25 and 23.42).
12. The text which describes the candelabra (Exod. 25.31-37 = 37.17-22) is itself a good example of concentrical construction; for its analysis, see R. Meynet,

This type of construction is not uncommon in the Bible—on the contrary. If a number of texts are of parallel composition, a greater number still, especially at the higher level of textual composition, are of concentric construction.[13]

As shown by this example, rhetorical analysis is useful, if not indispensable, in order to analyse short texts—pericopes, that is minimal units of recitation, such as miracle stories, parables, small speeches—and in order to find their limits. Its main use, however, is revealed in the superior levels: ensembles of pericopes which constitute sequences (and sub-sequences); ensembles of sequences which form sections (and sub-sections); and finally the book in its entirety. Without going into detail of the precise analysis of each pericope of Mk 10.35-52 and of Mt. 20.20-34, it will be enough to show how each evangelist used different means to elaborate similar constructions.

The most remarkable fact is that the first passage starts with a question, 'What do you want me to do for you?' (36), which is taken up at the end of the last passage (51). These two questions, which serve as an 'enclosure', indicate that the text they enclose is one whole and that the three passages which compose it are to be read as one. The characters with whom Jesus is talking have therefore something in common: James and John, indeed, both want to be 'seated' at Jesus' sides (37) and, when leaving Jericho,

itself a good example of concentrical construction; for its analysis, see R. Meynet, *Quelle est donc cette Parole? Analyse 'rhétorique' de l'Evangile de Luc (1–9 et 22–24)* (LD, 99 A and B; Paris: Cerf, 1979), vol. A, pp. 135-37; vol. B, pl. 1; *idem*, 'Au coeur du texte: Analyse rhétorique de l'aveugle de Jéricho selon Lc', *NRT* 103 (1981), pp. 696-97.

13. Even in the third gospel, whose author is deemed to be of Greek rather than Jewish culture. See R. Meynet, *L'Evangile selon saint Luc*, I, pp. 260-61.

³⁵ And THEY WENT-to him James and John, the **sons of Zebedee** saying to him: 'Teacher, we want you to do for us what we *ask* of you'. ³⁶ He said to them:

'**W**HAT DO YOU *WANT* ME TO DO FOR YOU?'

³⁷ And they said: 'Grant us to *SIT*, one at your right hand and one at your left, in your glory'. ³⁸ Jesus said to them: 'YOU DO NOT KNOW what you are asking. Are you able to drink the cup that I drink, or to be baptized with the baptism with which I am baptized?' ³⁹ And they said to him: 'We are able'. And Jesus said to them: 'The cup that I drink you will drink; and with the baptism with which I am baptized, you will be baptized. ⁴⁰ But to *SIT* at my right hand or at my left is not mine to grant, but it is for those whom it has been prepared.' ⁴¹ And when the ten heard it, they began to be indignant at James and John.

⁴² Calling them,

Jesus said to them:

'YOU KNOW that		
. those who are supposed to rule over the Gentiles	lord it over them	
. and their great men	exercise authority over them.	
⁴³ It shall not be so among you,		
+ but whoever *WOULD* become great among you	must be	your servant
+ ⁴⁴ and whoever *WOULD* become among you first	must be	slave of all.
⁴⁵ For the **Son of man** also came not		
. to be served	but to serve,	
. and to give his life	as a ransom for many.'	

⁴⁶ And they came to Jericho.

And as THEY WENT-off towards Jericho, he, his disciples and a considerable crowd, the **son of Timaeus**, Bartimaeus, a BLIND-man *asking*-for-alms was *SITTING* by the roadside. ⁴⁷ And when he heard that it was Jesus of Nazareth, he began to cry out and say: '**Son of David**, Jesus, have mercy on me!' ⁴⁸ And many rebuked him to be silent; but he cried out all the more: '**Son of David**, have mercy on me!' ⁴⁹ And Jesus stopped and said: 'Call him'. And they called the blind man, saying to him: 'Take heart; rise, he is calling you'. ⁵⁰ And throwing off his mantle he sprang up and came to Jesus. ⁵¹ And Jesus said to him:

'**W**HAT DO YOU *WANT* ME TO DO FOR YOU?'

And the blind man said to him: 'Rabbuni, let me receive my sight'. ⁵² And Jesus said to him: 'Go your way; your faith has saved you'. And immediately he received his sight and followed him on the road.

the man that Jesus meets is not only blind but he is 'sitting by the roadside' (46). That this detail is important is shown at the end of the passage, since, having recovered sight, 'he followed him on the road' (52). In response to the request of his two disciples, Jesus says: 'You do not know what you are asking' (that is: 'You do not see', as suggests common experience and probably a play on words between the two Greek verbs); and the master applies himself to opening their eyes on condition that they do what is required to obtain what they ask, 'drink the cup' and 'be baptized with the baptism' of the passion.

At the heart of the whole lies the speech to the group of the Twelve (42-42a). Jesus starts with what they know well ('You know that' [42] as opposed to 'You do not know' of v. 38), namely worldly wisdom (42), to which he contrasts his own wisdom (45); at the centre, at last, the Law that they must follow (43), which is reminiscent of 'For every one who exalts himself will be humbled and who humbles himself will be exalted' in Lk. 14.11.

One can see with this example that it is not necessary to artificially impose a 'spiritual' interpretation to the healing of the blind man of Jericho, which would be but a corporeal healing. The Gospel itself indicates it: the blindness of the blind man calls up a comparison with the blindness of James and John; and also with that of the other ten who are 'indignant' at the brothers (41), probably because each of them considers himself as a candidate for the post!

Matthew shares the same set-up (Mt. 20.20-34), but he uses other rhetorical means. Other than those already noted here, Mark uses what we could call a textual curtain-rod to hold up the three passages of his construction together: James and John are indeed called 'sons of Zebedee' at the beginning of the first passage (35); and the blind man is called 'son of Timaeus' at the beginning of the third passage (46);[14] in turn, Jesus calls himself 'son of man' (45; this name designates he who triumphs after having gone through the passion) and is called 'son of David' by the blind man (47 and 48). The text of Mt. 20.20-34[15] is similarly limited by the inclusion formed by the two (almost identical) requests that are also found in Mark; it suggests a similar relationship between extreme passages with the repetition of the word 'sit', but does not use the same 'curtain-rod' as Mark. We know that in the first Gospel, it is not only one blind man that Jesus heals leaving from Jericho, but two. And exegetes have long wondered who, between Mark and Matthew, conveyed the historical truth. As if it mattered! The reasons behind such inconsistencies are rhetorical in

---

14. Only Mark, out of the three synoptic Gospels, mentions the name of the blind man of Jericho; as if he had to for the means of his literary construction.

15. It is not necessary to reproduce it here.

nature (one must add that Matthew likes to pair his characters off): when Mark talks of the 'sons of Zebedee', Matthew has them called by their mother 'my two sons' (Mt. 20.21), and at the beginning of the central passage, it does not say, like in Mk 10.41, that 'the ten became indignant at James and John', but 'at the two brothers' (Mt. 20.30). One can clearly see, with this example, the purpose and use of rhetorical analysis: it provides us with the means to read texts which were meant, by a variety of means, to be read together.[16]

Since we have just seen how Mark and Matthew have integrated their version of the blind man, or men, of Jericho in a series of three passages, it is only natural to ask what the third Gospel does with the same passage. Luke does not deal with the episode of the sons of Zebedee; on the other hand he has linked the story of the blind man of Jericho (Lk. 18.35-43) with that of Zacchaeus, which is particular to this Gospel (Lk. 19.1-10). These two stories take place at Jericho; Zacchaeus 'sought to see who Jesus was' but could not because of his small size. In this way he is similar to the blind man; and both are 'saved'. But the most important point lies in determining the limits and the composition of the sequence in which Luke integrates his version of the story of the blind man. It will be enough here to outline the pattern in broad strokes. The sequence is composed of seven passages (another kind of seven-branched candelabra):

---

16. For more details on the two constructions of Mark and of Matthew, see R. Meynet, *Initiation à la rhétorique biblique, 'Qui donc est le plus grand?'* (Initiations; Paris: Cerf, 1982). The reader will have noted, among other symmetries, that Mark uses two verbs of the same root to start his first and last story. One will find an analysis of the whole sequence of Mk 10.13-52 in R. Meynet, 'Présupposés de l'analyse rhétorique, avec une application à Mc 10,13-52', in C. Coulot (ed.), *Exégèse et Herméneutique: Comment lire la Bible?* (LD, 158; Paris: Cerf, 1994), pp. 88-111.

+ Jesus announces the passion to his disciples who do not understand   18.31-34

= near Jericho, the **son of David**   saves a blind man   18.35-43
= in   Jericho, Jesus   saves a son of Abraham   19.1-10

| PARABLE OF THE **KING** AND THE COINS | 19.11-28

= near the mount of Olives, Jesus   is enthroned on a colt   19.29-36
= near the mount of Olives, Jesus   is acclaimed as a **king**   19.37-40

+ Jesus announces the passion of Jerusalem who does not understand   19.41-46

We will not, needless to say, go into the details. It is enough to note a few of the most striking symmetries. The blind man of the second passage calls Jesus '*son of David*', as the disciples of the penultimate passage praise him saying: 'Blessed be *the King* who comes in the name of the Lord';[17] in contrast, in both passages, there are some who want to shut up the blind man and the disciples, like in the central parable, the citizens of the nobleman who say: 'We will not have this man *to reign* over us'. Similarly, as Jesus had announced in the first passage, the son of man (who is destined to receive *royal* glory) will be rejected and finally killed by his fellow citizens. As regards Zacchaeus, he is like the servants of the king of the central parable: he repents and 'gives' away his goods, like the good servants who have invested their money; like the disciples of the fifth passage who, with a double gift similar to that of Zacchaeus, put their clothes on the colt as well as on the king's path. At the end of the sequence, Jerusalem will succumb to a fate similar to that which the enemies of the king endure, at the end of the central parable. This example shows how the heart of a

17. Luke alone uses the title 'King' at the time of Passover.

construction is the key to its interpretation. Not that it is the most important passage, as one might be tempted to think; the key of a coffer is not more 'important' than the treasure it contains. The key, with which one locks (like a parable, which is always enigmatic, which hides the meaning), allows one to open, without doing violence to the coffer or the text.

We will conclude this tour with a visit to one of the most beautiful pieces of the New Testament and, undoubtedly, of all literature, ch. 15 of Luke. It is usually referred to as 'the three parables of mercy'; the parable of the lost sheep, that of the lost coin, and that of the prodigal son. As long, however, as we consider this text to be formed of three parables, an important aspect of its internal logic will escape us. When Jesus speaks to the Pharisees and scribes who criticize him because he eats with publicans and sinners, it is written that he tells one parable, not two (15.3). And one has to wait until the beginning of the parable of the prodigal son to find another introductory phrase: 'he said' (15.11). One should take Luke seriously and consider that the parable of the lost sheep and the lost coin, lost then found, is one and the same parable. It is a double parable, similar to that of the mustard seed which a 'man' cast into his garden and the leaven that a 'woman' has hidden in three measures of meal (Lk. 13.18-21). Like this last parable, the first double parable of Luke 15 features first a man, and then a woman.

[1] All   THE TAX COLLECTORS AND SINNERS   were drawing near to hear,
[2] but   THE PHARISEES AND THE SCRIBES   murmured   *saying:*
       'This man receives sinners and eats with them!'
       [3] He told them this parable,   *saying:*

+ [4]   'What man of you   having a hundred sheep
  : if he has lost   one of them,
      -does not leave   the ninety-nine in   **the wilderness**
        = and go after   the one which is lost   until he finds it?
          . [5] And when he has found it,
            he lays it on his shoulders, rejoicing, [6] and coming home,
            . he calls his friends and his neighbours, saying to them:
  :: "Rejoice with me,   for I have found my sheep   which was lost!"
      * [7] I tell you, just so   there will be joy   in heaven
      *   over one SINNER   who repents

      ----
      more than over ninety-nine RIGHTEOUS persons who need no repentance.

+ [8] Or   what woman   having ten drachmas,
  : if she loses one drachma,   just one,
      - does not light a lamp   and sweep   **the house**
        = and seek diligently   until she finds it?
          . [9] And when she has found it,

          . she calls her friends and her neighbours, saying to them:
  :: "Rejoice with me,   for I have found my drachma which I had lost!"
      * [10] Just so, I tell you, there is joy   before the angels of God
      *   over one SINNER who repents.'

Even the most inattentive reader will have noticed that the two halves of the parable (4-10) are exactly parallel between them, as the illustration on the next page shows. One will note, however, one initial difference: the end of v. 5 and the beginning of v. 6 have no equivalent in the second half of v. 9. It is true that the scene of the finding of the silver pieces is less spectacular than that of the sheep: and the breathless shepherd, carrying the lost sheep on his shoulders by its legs has inspired more painters and sculptors than the woman with her little silver piece between index and thumb! The second difference lies in the fact that the end of v. 7 is not paralleled at the end of the second half of the parable; which is a way of drawing attention, not to the repentant 'sinners', but to the 'just, which need no repentance'; the word 'just' appears only at this point in the text. One should not forget that the target of the parable is indeed the 'Pharisees and scribes' (2a) and not the 'publicans and sinners' (1)!

But there remains another difference which usually escapes the scrutiny of the reader. It concerns the locations where the sheep and the silver coin are lost: the sheep 'in the wilderness' (4), whereas the silver coin is lost in 'the house' (8); one is lost far away, the other close. To phrase things differently, despite the fact that it did not get out of the house, contrary to the sheep which got lost outside, far away, in the wilderness, the silver coin is nonetheless lost.

This is not dissimilar to the second parable, also a double parable, since it features two sons. The younger indeed got lost 'into a far country', like the sheep; whereas the elder, despite the fact that he never got out of the house, like the silver coin, is nonetheless lost himself. He sins because, like the Pharisees and scribes, he criticizes him who eats with sinners.

One can see, with this example, that when two literary units seem alike in all points, one should look for the dissimilarities, which are likely to be of importance to the understanding of the text. Conversely, when two literary units do not seem to have any similarities, one should look more closely, since it is the similarities which will bring into light their relationship with each other. As regards the two sons, they seem dissimilar in all respects. They are nevertheless alike in some way. Despite his repentance, the younger has not yet understood what it is to be a son, since he ends his apology with the words 'treat me like one of your hired *servants*' (15.19). His father will not let him utter such blasphemy. The elder is no better, since he considers himself one of his father's slaves in saying: 'For all these years I have been working like *a slave* for you' (15.29). When his father has prepared the fatted calf, not only for his brother but also for him, he tells him: 'yet *you have never given* me a young goat' (15.29)! Similarly, his younger brother realizes, when he is in misery, that '*no one gave* him anything' (15.16).

It has long been noted that the story of the two sons is not finished: we do not know indeed if, in the end, the elder accepts the invitation of his father and shares the meal with his brother. The parable is open-ended, for it is addressed, like the first, to those who, like the elder, believe themselves to be just ('I never disobeyed your command': 15.29) and who not only refuse to mix with men whom they still consider as sinners despite their repentance, but criticize Jesus for eating with them (15.2). This opening is the sign of the proposition, the invitation that Jesus makes, like the father in the parable.

Iconography has always liked to represent the lost sheep and has neglected to a large extent the silver piece; in most representations of the second parable, one sees the father who receives the younger son in his arms. The elder does not figure in those representations, unless he is relegated to some obscure corner. Notwithstanding, he is the most important son of the two; since it is to him that Jesus and the evangelist addresses themselves. So why is he so conscientiously rebuked, not only in the iconography but also in our own mental images? It is probably because the reader unconsciously identifies with the character which has the best part, with the one who sinned, indeed, but repented! But in fact it is to the Pharisee that is within the reader that Jesus addresses.

After such an example, should we conclude? Surely not, if only to say that there are many treasures to discover in the Scriptures, and that rhetorical analysis is a key which should not be ignored.

INTRODUCTION

The French appellation 'analyse rhétorique' is a recent one: it only began to be used at the end of the 1970s.[1] It is not much older in the Anglo-Saxon world, since it was only ten years earlier that James Muilenburg proposed the equivalent phrase of 'rhetorical criticism'. In his paper of 18 December 1968, at the annual conference of the Society of Biblical Literature, which met at the University of California (Berkeley), he declared:

> What I am interested in, above all, is understanding the nature of Hebrew literary composition, exhibiting the structural patterns that are employed for the fashioning of a literary unit, whether in poetry or prose, and discerning the many and various devices by which the predications are formulated and ordered into a unified whole. Such an enterprise I should describe as rhetoric and the methodology as rhetorical criticism.[2]

The American rhetorical criticism which flows from Muilenburg is in fact quite different from the one we have called 'rhetorical analysis'. The different stems of 'rhetorical criticism' are characterized by the use of the categories of classical rhetoric of the Graeco-Roman world.[3] What we mean by rhetorical analysis, and what we practice, looks to establishing specific organizational laws of biblical texts. Its

---

1. It appears for the first time in R. Meynet, *Quelle est donc cette Parole? Lecture 'rhétorique' de l'Evangile de Luc (1–9 et 22–24)* (LD, 99A and B; Paris: Cerf, 1979).

2. 'Form Criticism and Beyond', *JBL* 88 (1969), p. 8. Those lines of J. Muilenburg have been quoted often, such that they have now become the one quotation that encapsulates the birth of the new method of 'rhetorical criticism'. This view, however, does away with the fact that E. Black had published in 1965 a book entitled *Rhetorical Criticism: A Study in Method* (New York: MacMillan, 1965).

3. G. Kennedy, the author of three substantial works on the history of classical rhetoric, is without doubt one of the most significant authors of this school; see W. Wuellner, 'Where is Rhetorical Criticism Taking us?', *CBQ* 49 (1987), pp. 448-63.

purpose is to identify the rhetoric which presided over the composition of these texts, a rhetoric which we are entitled to think is distinct from the classical rhetoric of the Graeco-Roman world.

Furthermore, unlike classical rhetoric, inasmuch as it can be summed up by the catalogue of figures that it became, rhetorical analysis is only concerned with the structure of composition of these texts. As if, of the three main parts of classical rhetoric (*inventio* or search for ideas, *dispositio* or organization of ideas in a composition, and *elocutio* or *ornatus*, which is the manner by which a speech can be adorned with figures),[4] rhetorical analysis would only consist of the second, which is *dispositio* or composition of a discourse.

If the term 'rhetorical analysis' is recent, the methodology on the other hand is not new.[5] It is nothing more than the *analyse structurelle* that is practised by Albert Vanhoye,[6] following the tracks of Paul Lamarche[7] and Enrico Galbiati.[8] Many contemporary scholars have adopted the name *analyse structurelle*: thus Marc Girard[9] and Pierre Auffret, whose many articles are almost all entitled after it,[10] to cite only two names among many more. The fact that the two terms, *structurelle* and 'rhetoric', co-exist suggests that the methodologies they respectively describe are still in their infancy.[11]

---

4. For a clear and synthetic approach, see G. Mounin, 'Rhétorique', *Encyclopaedia Universalis* (Paris: Encyclopaedia Universalis, 1985), t. 15, pp. 1107-10.

5. The title of this book is therefore slightly misleading. It nonetheless obeys the commercial imperatives of attracting readership which do nothing more than reproduce the laws of classical rhetoric: the 'captatio benevolentiae' is not the sole domain of the introduction, but starts in the title!

6. *La Structure littéraire de l'Epître aux Hébreux* (Paris: Desclée de Brouwer, 1963, 1976).

7. *Zacharie IX–XIV. Structure littéraire et messianisme* (EBib; Paris: Gabalda, 1961).

8. *La struttura letteraria dell'Esodo* (Rome: Alba, 1956).

9. *Les Psaumes: Analyse structurelle et interprétation* (I. Ps. 1–50; Montréal: Bellarmin; Paris: Cerf, 1984); *idem, Les Psaumes redécouverts. De la structure au sens* (II. Ps. 51–100; III. Ps. 101–150; Montréal: Bellarmin, 1994); I (revd edn, 1996).

10. See a list of his articles in M. Girard, *Les Psaumes redécouverts*, I, p. 24 n. 64.

11. Indeed, when they are born, new realities are often given different names. The work of terminologists is to record them, and advise the use of one word in preference of others, a choice which will always be sanctioned by common use which always decides in the end.

In the meantime, before a decision is taken on which term to use, allow the one who is responsible for introducing the term 'rhetoric' in French to defend his point of view by exposing his arguments! This plea might not lead to the triumph of the preferred terminology, but at least its definition will be that much more precise. One has first to concede that the word *structurel* was not chosen without good grounds. The term is transparent, since there are indeed structures that this kind of analysis brings to light, forms which shape the texts, structures which can be reduced to two basic forms: parallel and concentric. The term '*structurel*', however, has two major flaws. It is too close to the French word *structural* and the risk of mistaking *analyse structurelle* with *analyse structurale*, which caps a very different methodology, is too great.[12] Moreover, the minimal distinction between the two French terms, *structurel* and *structural*, cannot be rendered in other languages like English, Italian or Spanish. Less transparent than *structurel*, the term 'rhetoric', on the other hand, avoids the pitfall of the confusion between *structurel* and *structural*. It also prevents another confusion: the adjective 'literary', even when collated with 'structure', as in 'literary structure of', can suggest 'literary criticism' which is yet another method which purports to establish the various sources of a text.[13]

Others would have surely preferred, instead of the old tarnished word 'rhetoric', the word 'stylistic'. But the latter risks reminding one exclusively of the catalogue of 'figures of style' to which the last treatises of rhetoric had limited themselves in the end. Furthermore, the word 'style' too often calls up that which is characteristic of an author. 'Rhetoric' rings more true, it seems, to what characterizes, not an individual, but a culture and a tradition. 'Rhetoric' has, last but not least, the advantage of denoting the link between this 'modern' method, which is rhetorical analysis, and the great classical tradition of the science of speech-writing which sprang from Greece twenty-five centuries ago.[14]

12. See, for example D. Patte, *What is Structural Exegesis?* (Philadephia: Fortress Press, 1976).

13. See, for example, M.-E. Boismard and A. Lamouille, *La Vie des Evangiles. Initiation à la critique des textes* (Initiations; Paris: Cerf 1980).

14. The work of S. Glass, *Philologia Sacra* (Leipzig, 1725 [1636]) especially the fifth book, entitled 'Rhetorica Sacra', can be seen as a watershed between classical rhetoric, applied to the Bible, and the studies inaugurated by Lowth: everything that

Under the name of rhetorical analysis, of *analyse structurelle*, or no
particular appellation at all, the study of texts, biblical or otherwise,
which employ this methodology has grown spectacularly in number in
the last few years. Certain texts were submitted to this kind of analysis
by several authors; it seems that the prologue of John (Jn 1.1-18)
holds the record, with no less than fifteen concentric structurations, all
more or less different from each other.[15] The disagreement of the
various tenants of exegesis on the composition of the prologue of
John, of the Benedictus, the Magnificat, of the canticle of Hannah and
many more texts, must not surprise us if one considers the obvious
fact that the methodology, although it is being applied by many, is
nonetheless at its beginning. Thomas Boys was writing in 1824 that it
was still 'in its infancy'.[16]

One has to recognize that this observation is still valid today. A few
attempts at systematization were indeed made in the last few years, by
people such as Bailey,[17] Watson,[18] and Girard.[19] In my thesis on the
Gospel of Luke,[20] I had myself taken up, in a more developed and rigorous form, what I had already exposed in two earlier publications![21]
The second part of this book is a new draft of this methodological
'exposé', which has benefited from judicious criticism from the
examiners of my doctoral dissertation, and primarily from the man
who did me the honour of writing the Preface to this book.

was invented in later years already seems to be there, at least in seed: Lowth's
'parallelism of the members', under the name of 'pleonasmus' (col. 1230-35) and
what we call 'figures of composition' in the chapter that he entitles *'De schematibus
seu figuris'* (col. 1990–96).

15. See R. Meynet, 'Analyse rhétorique du Prologue de Jean', *RB* 96 (1989),
pp. 481-510.

16. *Tactica Sacra: An Attempt to Develop, and to Exhibit to the Eye by Tabular
Arrangements, a General Rule of Composition Prevailing in the Holy Scriptures*
(London: T. Hamilton, 1824), p. 11.

17. K.E. Bailey, *Poet and Peasant & Through Peasant Eyes: A Literary Approach
to the Parables in Luke* (Grand Rapids: Eerdmans, 1983).

18. W.G.E. Watson, *Classical Hebrew Poetry: A Guide to its Techniques*
(JSOTSup, 26; Sheffield: JSOT Press, 1984).

19. M. Girard, *Les Psaumes*.

20. *L'Evangile de Luc et la rhétorique biblique* (3 vols.; State dissertation; Faculté
des Lettres d'Aix-en-Provence [section of general linguistics], 1986.

21. *Quelle est donc cette Parole?*, vol. A, pp. 21-68; which has been reproduced
in a more succint form in *Initiation à la rhétorique biblique: Qui donc est le plus
grand?* (Initiations; Paris: Cerf, 1982).

This new presentation of the method has indeed benefited from an increased experience and deeper thinking; in fact, if it has improved at all, it is mainly due to the research that I pursued in parallel on the historical development of the method. Many things that we think of having discovered recently had already been well discussed at the beginning of the nineteenth century. And furthermore, in the best of cases, the majority of contemporary scholars are only familiar with the famous *Chiasmus in the New Testament* of Nils W. Lund.[22] It has to be said in their defence, that the works of his most important predecessors, John Jebb, Thomas Boys and John Forbes, are practically inaccessible.[23]

The present volume would like to remedy this failing by providing the founding texts of the rhetorical analysis for the researcher. One should not be mistaken about the value or the influence of these pages: their author is not a professional historian and has been unable to put the techniques of this science into use to retrace the history of the methodology. This enterprise would definitely deserve to be taken up by a practitioner of the art of history. One should, therefore, take this study for what it is: the genealogical inquiry of an amateur, curious about his origins, happy to be able to meet his ancestors, and most of all, having benefited greatly from the random search into the treasures of past generations, often amazed in finding pearls that he naively thought he had discovered himself!

It remains to enunciate briefly the criteria by which the choice of these texts was made. The older texts have been given priority over others, for several reasons: first, because they are the founding texts and it is always useful to go back to the source of original intuitions; secondly, because these texts are often richer than most contemporaries; lastly because, unlike more recent ones, they are not accessible to a wider readership. The reader will soon realize that the pages that have been retained are essentially presentations and analyses of biblical

22. *Chiasmus in the New Testament: A Study in Formgeschichte* (Chapel Hill: University of North Carolina Press, 1942); repr. *Chiasmus in the New Testament: A Study in the Form and Function of Chiastic Structures* (Peabody, MA: Hendrickson, 1992).

23. I have found them neither in France, Italy, nor in Israel, not even in the best specialized libraries of the 'Institut Biblique Pontifical de Rome' and the 'Ecole Biblique et Archéologique Française de Jérusalem', but only in the Bodleian Library at Oxford.

texts; this choice is not arbitrary, because what characterizes all scholars of what we might call the 'rhetorical school' is precisely the speed of the methodological discourse and, on the other hand, the richness of examples and analyses. Who will be surprised to find that a number of them are erroneous? One should not be surprised either, to find here the texts which have seemed to the author, who had the pleasure to look for them and bears the responsibility of their choice, the most sturdy ones.

Part I

THE FOUNDING TEXTS OF RHETORICAL ANALYSIS

Chapter 1[*]

THE FORERUNNERS
(EIGHTEENTH CENTURY)

The year 1753 can be considered a symbolic date in the history of exegesis. Two books which were at the origin of two ways of approaching the Biblical texts as literary texts were published that year.[1] The French doctor Jean Astruc, with his Coniectures sur les mémoires originaux dont il paroit que Moyse s'est servi pour composer le livre de la Genèse, *is the initiator or the forerunner of the study of sources and of historical criticism. The Reverend Robert Lowth, future bishop of Oxford and London, with the publication of his thirty-four* Lectures on the Sacred Poetry of the Hebrews, *as he gave them at Oxford between 1741 and 1751, was to be recognized as the father of the 'poetical' analysis of the Bible.[2]*

Robert Lowth

In his nineteenth lecture, Lowth presented a description of the biblical parallelism that was to have a considerable success. His classification of 'parallelism of the members' into three categories, synonymous, antithetical and synthetic (or constructive) parallelism, can be found in all dictionaries. Twenty-five years later, in 1778, Lowth published an English translation of Isaiah where the text of the prophet was for the first time disposed in verse, following the principles of parallelism.[3] This translation was preceded by a dissertation wherein the author gave an improved version of his nineteenth lesson. It would have been interesting to give

---

   *   In this part of the book the author's comments are represented as indented and italicized.

    1. G.B. Gray, *The Forms of the Hebrew Poetry* (London, 1915; New York: Ktav, 1972), p. 5.

    2. *De sacra poesi Hebraeorum praelectiones academicae Oxonii habitae* (Oxford, 1753).

    3. *Isaiah: A New Translation, with a Preliminary Dissertation and Notes, Critical, Philological and Explanatory* (London: J. Dodsley & T. Cadelle, 1778).

here a few extracts of this dissertation since, according to the very opinion of the author, it was a marked progress on what had been done a quarter of a century earlier. But although Isaiah had been re-published several times,[4] it is mostly the text of the nineteenth lecture which has influenced his successors, such as it is found, in Latin, in his De sacra poesi hebrae-orum *and very soon in English translation,[5] and French.[6] Here, then, are some large extracts from his nineteenth lesson:*

   After having described

[p. 24]

The psalmody of the Hebrews—The manner of chanting the hymns by alternate choirs: whence the origin of the poetical construction of the sentences, and that peculiar form, in which verses and distychs run parallel or correspondent to each other.[7]

   Lowth moves on to:

[p. 33]

Such appears to have been the origin and progress of that poetical and artificial conformation of the sentences, which we observe in the poetry of the Hebrews. That it prevailed no less in the Prophetic Poetry than in the Lyric and Didactic, to which it was, in the nature of things, most adapted, [p. 34] is evident from those very ancient speci-mens of poetical prophecy already quoted from the historical books; and it only remains to show, that it is no less observable in those which are contained in the volumes of the prophets themselves. In order the more clearly to evince this point, I shall endeavour to illus-trate the Hebrew parallelism according to its different species, first by examples taken from those books commonly allowed to be poetical, and afterwards by correspondent examples from the books of the prophets.

The poetical conformation of the sentences, which has been so often alluded to as characteristic of the Hebrew poetry, consists chiefly in a certain equality, resemblance, or parallelism between the members of

---

4.   The thirteenth edition was published in London in 1843.

5.   By Lowth and Michaelis in 1763.

6.   Two 'first' French translations: *Leçons sur la poésie sacrée des Hébreux traduites pour la première fois en français du latin du Dr Lowth par M. Sicard* (trans. M. Sicard; 2 vols.; Lyon, 1812; Avignon: Segin aîné, 2nd edn, 1839) and *Cours de poésie sacrée par le Dr Lowth traduit pour la première fois du latin en français par F. Roger* (trans. F. Roger; Paris, 1813).

7.   I quote according to *Lectures on the Sacred Poetry of the Hebrews*, II (Hildesheim: Georg Olms, 1969; reprint of the 1787 edition).

each period; so that in two lines (or members of the same period)
things for the most part shall answer to things, and words to words, as
if fitted to each other by a kind of rule or measure. This parallelism
has much variety and many gradations; it is sometimes more accurate
and manifest, sometimes more vague and obscure; it may however, on
the whole, be said to consist of three species.

[p. 35]

1. The first species is the *Synonymous Parallelism*,[8] when the same
sentiment is repeated in different, but equivalent terms. This is the
most frequent of all, and is often conducted with the utmost accuracy
and neatness: examples are very numerous, nor will there be any great
difficulty in the choice of them: on this account I shall select such as
are most remarkable in other respects.[9]

> When Israel went out from Egypt;
> The house of Jacob from a strange people:
>
> Judah was as his sacred heritage:
> Israel his dominion.
>
> The sea saw, and fled;
> Jordan turned back:
>
> The mountains leaped like rams;
> The hills like the sons of the flock. [. . .]   Ps. 114.1-6

[. . .]   [p. 36]

The Prophetic Muse is no less elegant and correct:

> Arise, be thou enlightened; for thy light is come
> And the glory of JEHOVAH is risen upon thee.
>
> For behold darkness shall cover the earth;
> And a thick vapour the nations:
>
> But upon thee shall JEHOVAH arise;
> And his glory upon thee shall be conspicuous.
>
> And the nations shall walk in thy light;
> And kings in the brightness of thy rising.   Isa. 60.1-3

[. . .]   [p. 37]

Isaiah is indeed excellent, but not unrivalled in this kind of composition: there are abundant examples in the other prophets.

---

8.   The decimal numbering of the paragraphs has been added for greater clarity.
9.   To make reading easier, a gap has been added between the 'periods'.

[. . .]   [p. 39]

There is great variety in the form of the synonymous parallelism, some instances of which are deserving of remark.

1.1. The parallelism is sometimes formed by the iteration of the former member, either in the whole or in part:

> Much have they oppressed me from my youth up,
> May Israel now say;

> Much have they oppressed me from my youth,
> Yet have they not prevailed against me.   Ps. 129.1-2

[. . .]   [p. 40]
Thus Isaiah:

> Because in the night Ar is destroyed, Moab is undone!
> Because in the night Kir is destroyed, Moab is undone.   Isa. 15.1

[. . .]   [p. 41]
1.2. There is frequently something wanting in the latter member, which must be repeated from the former to complete the sentence:

> The king sent and released him;
> The ruler of the people, and set him free.   Ps. 105.20

In the same manner Isaiah:

> Kings shall see him and shall rise up;
> Princes, and they shall worship him [. . .]   Isa. 48.7

1.3. Frequently the whole of the latter division answers only to some part of the former:

> JEHOVAH reigneth, let the earth rejoice;
> Let the multitude of islands be glad.   Ps. 97.1

> Arise, be thou enlightened; for thy light is come
> And the glory of JEHOVAH is risen upon thee. Isa. 60.1

[p. 42]
1.4. Sometimes also there are triplet parallelisms. In these the second line is generally synonymous with the first, whilst the third either begins the period, or concludes it, and frequently refers to both the preceding:

The floods have lifted up, O JEHOVAH,
The floods have lifted up their voice;
The floods have lifted up their waves.

Than the voice of many waters,
The glorious waves of the sea,
JEHOVAH on high is more glorious.   Ps. 93.3-4

Come and let us return unto JEHOVAH;
For he hath torn, and he will heal us;
he hath smitten and he will bind us up.

After two days he will revive us;
On the third day he will raise us up
And we shall live in his sight.   Hos. 6.1

1.5. In stanzas (if I may so call them) of five lines, the nature of which is nearly similar, the line that is not parallel is generally placed between the two distychs:

Like as the lion growleth,
Even the young lion over his prey;

Though the whole company of shepherds be
called together against him: [p. 43]

At their voice he will not be terrified,
Nor at their tumult will he be humbled.   Isa. 31.4

Askalon shall see it, and shall fear;
Gaza shall also see it, and shall be greatly pained:

And Ekron shall be pained, because her expectation
                              is put to shame;

And the King shall perish from Gaza;
And Askalon shall not be inhabited.   Zech. 9.5

1.6. Those which consist of four lines generally form two regular distychs; but there is sometimes a peculiar artifice to be perceived in the distribution of the sentences:

From the Heavens Jehovah looketh down,
He seeth all the children of men;
From the seat of his rest he contemplateth
All the inhabitants of the earth.   Ps. 33.13, 14

[...]

the latter members are to be alternately referred to the former.

[. . .]   [p. 45]

2 *The Antithetic Parallelism* in the next that I shall specify, when a
thing is illustrated by its contrary being opposed to it. This is not confined to any particular form: for sentiments are opposed to sentiments,
words to words, singulars to singulars, plurals to plurals, &c. of which
the following are examples:

> The blows of a friend are faithful;
> But the kisses of an enemy are treacherous.
>
> The cloyed will trample upon an honey-comb;
> But to the hungry every bitter thing is sweet.   Prov. 27.6-7

[p. 46]

There is sometimes a contra position of parts in the same sentence:
[. . .]

> I am swarthy but comely, O daughters of Jerusalem;
> As the tents of Kedar, as the pavilions of Solomon.   Cant. 1.5

The last line here is also to be divided and separately applied to the
preceding, 'swarthy as the tents of Kedar; comely as the pavilions of
Solomon.' [. . .]

This form of composition, indeed, agrees best with adages and acute
sayings: it is [p. 47] therefore very prevalent in the proverbs of
Solomon, in some of which the principal force and elegance depend
on the exactness of the antithesis. It is not however inconsistent with
the superior kinds of Hebrew poetry.

[. . .]   [p. 48]

The sublimer poetry seldom indeed adopts this style. Isaiah, however,
by means of it, without departing from his usual dignity, adds greatly
to the sweetness of his composition in the following instances:

> In a little anger have I forsaken thee;
> But with great mercies will I receive thee again:
>
> In a short wrath I hid my face for a moment from thee;
> But with everlasting kindness will I have mercy on thee. [. . .]
>   Isa. 54.7

3. There is a third species of parallelism, in which the sentences answer to each other, not by the iteration of the same image or [p. 49]

sentiment, or the opposition of their contrary, but merely by the form of construction. To this, which may be called *the Synthetic or Constructive Parallelism*, may be referred all such as do not come within the two former classes: I shall however produce a few of the most remarkable instances:

> The law of JEHOVAH is perfect, restoring the soul;
> The testimony of JEHOVAH is sure, making wise the simple:
>
> The precepts of JEHOVAH are right, rejoicing the heart;
> The commandment of JEHOVAH is clear, enlightening the eyes:
>
> The fear of JEHOVAH is pure, enduring for ever;
> The judgements of JEHOVAH are truth, they are just altogether.
>
> More desirable than gold, or than much fine gold;
> And sweeter than honey, or the dropping of honey-combs.
>
> Ps. 19.8-11

3.1. This kind of parallelism generally consists of verses somewhat longer than usual, of which [p. 50] there are not wanting examples in the prophets:

> How hath the oppressor ceased! the exactness
>   of gold ceased!
> Jehovah hath broken the staff of the wicked,
>   the sceptre of the rulers
>
> He that smote the people in wrath with a stroke unremitted;
> He that ruled the nations in anger is perse-
>   cuted, and none hindereth. [. . .]   Isa. 14.4-9

3.2. Triplets are frequently formed of this kind of parallelism:

> The clouds overflowed with water;
> The atmosphere refounded;   [p. 51]
> Thine arrows also issued forth;
>
> The voice of thy thunder was in the skies;
> The lightnings enlightened the world;
> The earth trembled and shook.   Ps. 77.18
>
> I will be as the dew to Israel
> He shall blossom as the lily;
> And he shall strike his roots like Lebanon.
>
> His suckers shall spread,
> And his glory shall be as the olive-tree,
> And his smell as Lebanon.   Hos. 14.6, 10

[...] [p. 52]

3.5. The variety in the form of this synthetic parallelism is very great, and the degrees of resemblance almost infinite: so that sometimes the scheme of the parallelism is very subtitle and obscure, and must be developed by art and ability in distinguishing the different members of the sentences, and in distributing [p. 53] the points, rather than by depending upon the obvious construction. How much this principle pervades the Hebrew poetry, and how difficult of explication it is, may in some degree be illustrated by one example. This appears to consist of a single line, if the sentiment only be considered:

> I also have anointed my King on Sion, the
>   mountain of my sanctity.   Ps. 2.6

But the general form and nature of the Psalm requires that it should be divided into two parts or versicles; as if it were,

> I also have anointed my King;
> I have anointed him in Sion, the mountain of my sanctity.

Which indeed the Masorites seem to have perceived in this as well as in other places.[10]

In this peculiar conformation, or parallelism of the sentences, I apprehend a considerable part of the Hebrew metre to consist; [p. 54] though it is not improbable that some regard was also paid to the numbers and feet. But of this particular we have at present so little information, that it is utterly impossible to determine, whether it were modulated by the ear alone, or according to any settled or definite rules of prosody. Since however this, and other marks or vestiges, as it were, of the metrical art are alike extant in the writings of the prophets, and in the books which are commonly allowed to be poetical, I think there is sufficient reason to rank them in the same class.

Lest I should seem to have attributed too much to this conformation of the sentences, and to have rashly embraced an opinion not supported by sufficient authority, I shall beg leave to quote to you the opinion of Azarias, a Jew Rabbi, not indeed a very ancient, but a very approved author:[11]

---

10. For they mark the word *malkî* with the distinctive accent Athnac, by which they generally distinguish the members of the distichs [. . .] (Lowth's note).

11. *Mantissa Dissert. ad librum Cosri*, p. 418.

Without doubt, says he, the sacred songs have certain measures and
proportions, but these do not consist in the number of the syllables perfect
or imperfect, according to the form of the modern verse; but in [p. 55] the
number of things, and of the parts of things; that is, the subject and the
predicate, ant their adjuncts, in every sentence and proposition.

[...] For instance, 'Thy right hand O Jehovah',[12] according to
Azarias, consists of two terms, or parts of a proposition; to which is
connected, 'is all glorious in power', consisting likewise of two terms;
these joined together make a Tetrameter. The following is constructed
on a similar principle:

Thy right-hand, O Jehovah, hath crushed the enemy.

Exod. 15.6

[p. 56]

Thus in the following propositions there are three terms or measures,

My-doctrine shall-drop, as-the-rain; my-word
        shall-distil, as-the-dew.   Deut. 32.2

'And thus joined together they form an Hexameter.' In fact, what he
has here remarked is neither groundless nor altogether just. For with
respect to many passages, in which the distribution of sentences is
very unequal, and in which the propositions have but little correspondences with each other, as happens frequently in the Psalms, we
must have recourse to some other solution; and when the sentences are
most regular and correct, they cannot at all times be reduced to his
rules. But although the present question does not depend upon this
single point, no man, I think, who reads with attention the poetic
books, and especially what may be properly called the prophetic part
of them, will entertain a doubt that it is of the utmost importance to
distinguish the system of the verses.

[p. 57]

But should all that has been remarked concerning the members and
divisions of the sentences appear light and trifling to some persons,
and utterly undeserving any labour or attention; let them remember
that nothing can be of greater avail to the proper understanding of any
writer, than a previous acquaintance with both his general character,
and the peculiarities of his style and manner of writing: let them rec-
ollect that translators and commentators have fallen into errors upon

12. Exod. 15.6.

no account more frequently, than for want of attention to this article; and indeed, I scarcely know any subject which promises more copiously to reward the labour of such as are studious of sacred criticism, than this one particular.

Predecessors of Lowth

Other Jewish scholars had noticed the existence of parallelism besides R. Azarias, among them, Rashi (1040–1105), his grandson Rashbam, and most importantly David Kimshi (1160–1235).[13] *The awareness of the parallelism of the members goes, in fact, much farther back in time: the Latin word* fasucium *used by Cassiodorus in order to translate the Hebrew* pasûq *seems to describe the same reality indeed.*[14] *Saint Augustine, whom Cassiodorus considers as his master, had noted the phenomenon several times, and calls it* geminatio *or* repetitio.[15] *The habit of writing certain biblical texts according to lines of meaning, a habit which must go back several centuries before our era,*[16] *indicates that a certain awareness of the parallelism of the members is extremely ancient. No author previous to the eighteenth century, however, has presented a typology such as the one elaborated by Lowth.*

Christian Schöttgen

Twenty years before Lowth's first book, however, Christian Schöttgen published two large volumes entitled Horae Hebraicae et Talmudicae.[17] *He added, in an appendix, a few dissertations. The sixth is called* De exergasia sacra. *This dissertation is composed of three parts. In the first chapter, dedicated to* exergasia *in general, the author starts with a definition:*

13. Gray, *The Forms of the Hebrew Poetry*, p. 17-18; J. Kugel, *The Idea of Biblical Poetry: Parallelism and its History* (New Haven/London: Yale University Press, 1981); Kugel explains the 'omission' of parallelism in anterior Rabbinic exegesis by the theological principle of biblical omnisignificance which was then unanimously admitted: the second stich of what Lowth would call synonymous parallelism could simply not be the repetition of the same idea in other words; another meaning was always found, even if what would now seem spurious explanations were resorted to.

14. A. Vaccari, 'Cassiodoro e il pasûq della Bibbia ebraica', *Bib* 40 (1959), pp. 309-21.

15. Vaccari, 'Cassiodoro', pp. 313-14. Several other Church Fathers were aware of the parallelism (Kugel, *The Idea*, pp. 135-36). On this point see L. Alonso Schökel, *Estudios de Poética Hebrea* (Barcellona: Juan Flors, 1963), pp. 197-98.

16. For example, it is in this way that Deut. 32 is written in the manuscripts of Qumran.

17. (Dresden and Leipzig: apud Hekelii, 1733).

All the rhetorical treatises teach that *exergasia* is the 'conjunction of entire sentences of similar signification'. They mark, however, a difference between synonymy and *exergasia*: 'the first consists in repeating in a different way a single word, whereas the second consists in repeating in a different way either several words, either members of entire sentences' (p. 1249). It is what authors like Cicero (*Rhetoric to Herennius*, 4.42) call *expolitio*, or others like Aquila call it *isocolon* (*De figuris sententiarum*, p. 18), or *epexegèsis* (Glassius, *Rhetorica sacra*), *pleonasmus* (Hennischius, *Thesaur. Disput. Loc.* XII, p. 471), *tautologia* (Martianus Capella; Luther). The figure is known to the poets: J.C. Scaliger (*De re poetica*, 3.41-43) enumerates three categories; *repetitio, frequentatio, acervatio*. The Rabbis that have noted the existence of *exergasia* in the Scriptures often use this expression: 'the same sentence is repeated twice using different words' (Kimshi, *ad* Os 2.3; R. Solomon ben Melech, *ad* Ps. 56.5). On the other hand the Christian writers have neglected it, despite the fact that it occurs frequently, not only in the poetical books, but also in the Prophets and Hagiographs.

> *The second chapter which describes the ten laws of* exergasia *should be quoted in full*:

LAW I: *exergasia* is perfect when the elements (*membra*) of the two members (*commata*) correspond to each other perfectly without any more or less text.

Ps. 33.7

| He gathered | | as in a bottle | | the waters of the sea |
| And he put | | in storehouses | | the deeps. |

Num. 24.17

| A star | | shall come forth | | out of Jacob |
| And a sceptre | | shall rise | | out of Israel. |

Lk. 2.47

| My soul | | magnifies | | the Lord |
| And my spirit | | rejoices | | in God my Saviour. |

LAW II: Sometimes, however, the subject is not repeated in the second half of the sentence, but it is omitted in an ellipsis and implied because of the proximity.

Isa. 1.18

| Though your sins | are like scarlet, | | they shall be as white as snow |
| Though — — | they are red like crimson, | | they shall become like wool. |

Prov. 7.19

| For my husband | | is not at home |
| — — | | he has gone on a long journey. |

Ps. 129.3

| Plowed upon my back | | the plowers |
| they made long their furrows. | | — — |

LAW III: One part of the subject only might be missing.

Ps. 37.30

| The mouth of the righteous | | utters | | wisdom |
| And his tongue — | | speaks | | justice. |

Where it is simply part of the subject which is repeated since the pronoun 'his' is not the whole subject.

Ps. 102.28

| The children of your servant | | shall dwell secure |
| And their posterity — | | shall be established before you. |

Isa. 53.5

| But he | | was wounded | | for our transgressions, |
| — | | was bruised | | for our iniquities. |

LAW IV: There are some cases when it is the predicate which is omitted in the repetition of *exergasia*.

Num. 24.5

How fair are	|	your tents,	|	O Jacob
— —	|	your encampments,	|	O Israel!

Ps. 33.12

Blessed is	|	the nation	| whose God is the Lord,
— —	|	the people	| whom he has chosen as his heritage.

Ps. 123.4

Our soul	| has been sated	| with the scorn of those who are at ease,
—	| — —	| the contempt of the proud.

LAW V: Sometimes it is only part of the predicate which is missing.

Ps. 57.10

I will give thanks to you	|	among the peoples,	|	O Lord
I will sing praise to you	|	among the nations	|	—

Ps. 103.1

Bless	|	the Lord,	|	O my soul;
And—	|	all that is within me	|	his holy name.

Ps. 129.7

The reaper	|	does not fill	|	his hand
Or the binder	|	—	—	|	his bosom.

LAW VI: Certain elements are added in a member and cannot be found in the other.

Num. 23.18

Rise,	|	Balak,	|	and hear;
—	|	O son of Zippor	|	hearken to me.

Ps. 102.28

The children of your servants	| —	—	| shall dwell secure
Their posterity	| before thee		| shall be established.

Dan. 12.3

And whose who are wise		—		shall shine	
And those who turn to righteousness		many		— —
	like the brightness of the firmament			— —
	like the stars			for ever and ever.

LAW VII: Sometimes, two propositions describe different things which, explained by 'merism',[18] can and should be referred to a single general proposition.

Ps. 94.9

| He who planted | | the ear | | does he not ear? |
| he who formed | | the eye | | does he not see? |

Ps. 128.3

| Your wife | | like a fruitful vine | | within your house |
| Your children | | like olive shoots | | around your table. |

Sir. 3.16

| Whoever forsakes | his father | is like a blasphemer |
| And whoever angers | his mother | is cursed by the Lord. |

No-one will think that one means that 'the eye' and 'the ear' are the same thing, or 'the father' and 'the mother', etc... But those two propositions express together a more general one; thus the general proposition of the first quote is: *God knows everything.* That of the second quote is: *You will be happy in matrimony.* That of the third: *Woe unto he who offends his parents.*

LAW VIII: There are some cases of *exergasia* where the second proposition means the contrary to the first.

Prov. 15.8

| The sacrifice | of the wicked | is an abomination to the Lord, |
| But the prayer | of the upright | is his delight. |

18. 'Merism' is a way of expressing the whole in coordinating its constituent terms: e.g. 'the sky and the earth', in order to say 'the whole of creation'; 'from dawn till dusk' to say 'incessantly' (author's note).

Prov. 14.1

| Wisdom of women | | builds her house, |
| But folly with her own hands | | tears it down. |

Prov. 14.11

| The house | | of the wicked | | will be destroyed, |
| But the tent | | of the upright | | will flourish. |

LAW IX: We also have examples of *exergasia* where it is entire propositions which answer one another, although the subjects and their predicate are not the same like in the preceding example.

Ps. 51.5

Behold, I was brought forth in iniquity,
And in sin did my mother conceive me.

Ps. 119.168

I keep thy precepts and testimonies,
For all my ways are before you.

Jer. 8.22

Is there no balm in Gilead, is there no physician there?
Why then has the health of the daughter of my people not been restored?

LAW X: There also is an *exergasia* with three members.

Ps. 1.1

Blessed is	the man	who walks not	in the counsel	of the wicked
—	—	nor stands	in the way	of sinners
—	—	nor sits	in the seat	of scoffers.

Ps. 130.5

I wait for the Lord,
My soul waits,
And in his word I hope.

Ps. 52.7

See the man	who would not make God his refuge,
But —	trusted in the abundance of his riches
And —	sought refuge in his wealth.

The third chapter of the sixth dissertation is entitled: 'Of the usefelness of sacred exergasia'. For Schöttgen it is double.

Exergasia *first allows us to better understand the meaning of the Hebraic words. For example in Ps. 34.10, the meaning of the first word has been the focus of a long controversy*:

| kefarîm | suffer want and hunger; |
| but those who seek the Lord | lack no good thing. |

Some have translated it as 'the lions', others as 'the rich'. Law VIII of exergasia *leads us to the hypothesis that this word is opposed to 'those who seek the Lord', which is confirmed by a lexicographic inquiry in other oriental languages as well as in the Bible.*

Exergasia *also makes difficult and corrupted texts easier and safer to interpret; Schöttgen will devote an entire dissertation on the case of Gen. 49.10 (seventh dissertation).*

Predecessors to Lowth other than Schöttgen have been found.[19] But it is nonetheless the Oxford professor who was recognized by all his successors as the father of Hebraic poetic criticism. His De sacra poesi Hebraeorum *has known many different editions,[20] translations,[21] and plagiaries.[22]*

Johann-Albrecht Bengel

Lowth, however, had only discovered, so to speak, half the truth. Indeed he did not limit himself to the analysis of the distych and also studied

19. A. Baker, 'Parallelism: England's Contribution to Biblical Studies', *CBQ* 35 (1973), pp. 429-40; U. Bonamartini, 'L'epesegesi nella Santa Scrittura', *Bib* 6 (1925), pp. 424-44; R. Jakobson, 'Grammatical Parallelism and its Russian Facet', *Languages* 42 (1966), pp. 399-429 (see p. 403-404); reprinted in *Selected Writings* III. *Poetry of Gramar and Grammar of Poetry* (The Hague: Mouton, 1981), pp. 98-135.

20. As early as 1758 (then in 1761 and 1770), the famous Michaelis edition (with additions) of Gottingen.

21. In English, by Lowth and Michaelis in 1763.

22. Du Contant de la Molette, *Traité sur la poésie et la musique des Hébreux* (Paris: Moutard, 1781), pp. 49-50 (Lowth is not quoted except on p. 95); and esp. A. Henry, *Eloquence et Poésie des Livres Saints* (Paris: Lecoffre, 1849), pp. 99-109. Both quote the same examples as Lowth. The latter plagiarizes Lowth in plagiarizing Sicard's translation (pages 99-108 and 108-109 in Henry are exact reproductions of pages 287-305 and 284-87 in Sicard; it is Lowth's nineteenth lecture).

stanzas of five members and more. He even remarked that 'some periods may be considered as making stanzas of five lines, in which the odd line or member [. . .] comes in between two distychs'.[23] But he does not endow any particular significance to this phenomenon. He manifestly missed the relevance of concentric constructions, as the following example clearly shows:

> Askalon shall see it, and shall fear;
> Gaza shall also see it, and shall be greatly pained:
> And Ekron shall be pained,
>   because her expectation is put to shame;
> And the King shall perish from Gaza;
> And Askalon shall not be inhabited   Zech. 9.5[24]

without noticing that the place names answer one another in a concentric fashion around the central member 'Ekron':

Askalon   GAZA   EKRON   GAZA   Askalon

But, a few years earlier, a German exegete, Johann-Albrecht Bengel[25] had discovered the existence of concentric constructions and had noted their importance:

Chiasm is a figure of speech, when two pairs (AB and CD) of words or propositions are disposed in such a way that a relation is obtained between one or the other word or proposition of the first pair and one or the other word or proposition of the second pair.

Chiasm is either *direct* if the relation is found between A and C and between B and D:

A   LOVE
   B   the enemies of   *you*
---------- and ---------------
C   PRAY for
   D   those who persecute   *you*
                    Mt. 5.44 (cf Lk. 6.27)

(Also) Jn 5.26-29[26]

or *inverted* when the relation is between A and D and B and C:

---

23. *Isaiah*, p. xii.

24. *Lectures on the Sacred Poetry of the Hebrews* (Hildesheim, 1969), II, p. 43; other examples in *Isaiah*, p. xii.

25. *Gnomon Novi Testamenti* (Tubingen: Io. Henri Philippi Schranii, 1742).

26. Bengel is content with giving references; it seemed useful to include some of the most demonstrative texts, laid out according to a visualization that he does not use himself but using, for more clarity, the letters which symbolizes the terms of his structures.

Then was brought to him a demoniac
  A blind
    B and dumb;
and he healed him, so that the dumb man
    C spoke
  D and saw

Mt. 12.22

(Also) Jn 5.21-25; 8.25-28; Acts 2.46; 20.21; 1 Cor. 9.1.

  . . . because I hear

    A of your love
      B and of the faith which you have

      C toward the Lord Jesus
      D and all the saints.

Phlm. 5 (cf. Eph. 1.15)[27]

And he adds:

Knowledge of this figure is of the utmost importance in order to perceive the beauty of the discourse and to remark its vigour, to understand the truth and full meaning, to bring to light the genuine and well proportioned structure of the sacred text.[28]

> *When Lowth classifies according to the content, Bengel does it according to form, that is, according to the order of symmetrical elements. The difference between the two pioneers can be explained by the genre of texts that each has studied and by their respective preoccupations. Lowth, studying poetical texts, is concerned with the structures of the verse and his observations on ensembles of verses are but marginal. Bengel works on New Testament texts, almost exclusively in prose, and he is sensitive to the composition of the texts, from the sentence to larger ensembles, where Lowth sees nothing but a string of distychs of synonymous parallelism:*

27. This example will be taken up by J. Jebb, who explains that his 'faith' is adressed to 'the Lord Jesus' in the centre, and that 'love' is aimed at the 'saints' (i.e. the Christian brothers) at the edges (see below, p. 96).

28. *Gnomon Novi Testamenti* (Stuttgart, 1887), p. 1144. Bengel uses 'chiasm' for symmetry; his 'direct chiasm' is not a chiasm, since the elements are not alternated, but a parallelism.

The sea looked, and fled;
Jordan turned back:

The mountains skipped like rams;
The hills like the sons of the flock.

What ails you, O Sea, that you flee;
Jordan, that you turn back:

Mountains, that you skip like rams;
And hills, like the sons of the flock?[29]

Bengel would have noted a 'direct chiasm' between the first four members and the following four:

a	The		sea looked	and FLED,	
	b		Jordan	TURNED	back.
		c	The	MOUNTAINS	*SKIPPED*	*like rams,*
			d the	*HILLS*	*like the sons of the flock.*
a' What ails you,			O sea,	that you FLEE,	
	b'		Jordan,	that you TURN back,	
		c'		MOUNTAINS,	that you *SKIP*	*like rams,*
			d' and	*HILLS,*	*like the sons of the flock?*

In Isa. 60.2, where Lowth sees nothing but a global (i.e. semantic) correspondence between two members of synonymous parallelism,

But upon thee shall Jehovah arise
And his glory upon thee shall be conspicuous[30]

Bengel would have noted an 'inverted chiasm':

a But   *upon thee*   SHALL ARISE
  b Jehovah
          and
  b' his glory
a'   *upon thee*   SHALL BE CONSPICUOUS[31]

Predecessors of Bengel

Bengel is considered by his successors as the discoverer of concentric constructions. The awareness of this structure, however, was already

---

29. Ps. 114.1-6; *Lectures on the Sacred Poetry of the Hebrews*, II, p. 35.
30. *Lectures on the Sacred Poetry of the Hebrews*, II, p. 36.
31. This translation respects the order of words in Hebrew. The 'layout' adopted here in order to make the reading easier is not Bengel's; very rare in his work, it remains rudimentary (the most elaborate is found in 1 Cor. 13.5).

present in the Jewish world, at least since the fourteenth century. A text of the Kabbala[32] interprets Psalm 67 as representing the menorah, *the seven-branch candelabra. The concentric composition of Psalm 67, analogous to that of the* menorah,[33] *was thereon commonly represented visually by oriental Jews: Psalm 67, called 'psalm-menorah', is written in a way to show the seven-branch candelabra (see following illustration). It should be said that this seems to be an isolated occurrence and that it did not provoke the discovery of this structure in other texts.*

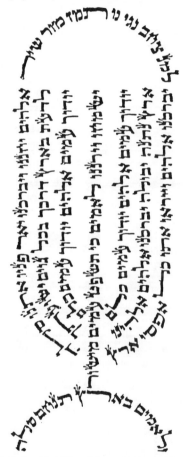

From A. HAKHAM, *Sefer Tehillîm*, Mossad Harav Kook, Jerusalem, I, p. 386.

32. Vatican Manuscript no. 214 (*Encyclopoedia Judaica*, II, 1971, col. 1368).

33. The text which describes it in Exod. 25 is itself a good example of concentrical composition: R. Meynet, *Quelle est donc cette Parole?*, vol. A, pp. 135-37; *idem*, 'Au coeur du texte, analyse rhétorique de l'aveugle de Jéricho selon Lc', *NRT* 103 (1981), pp. 698-710.

Psalm 67[34]

+ [2] May God be gracious to us and *BLESS* us,
+ and make his face to shine upon us,

- [3] that may be known upon   EARTH   your way,
- among   all   HEATHENS   your salvation.

. [4]   Let praise thee   THE PEOPLES,   God,
.   Let praise thee   THE PEOPLES,   all!

for thou dost judge
THE PEOPLES with equity
[5] Let be glad   and
and sing for joy   THE NATIONS upon earth
THE NATIONS   thou guide.

. [6]   Let praise thee   THE PEOPLES,   God,
.   Let praise thee   THE PEOPLES,   all!

- [7]   THE EARTH
gave its fruit:
+   he *BLESSES* us   God
     our   God
+ [8]   he *BLESSES* us   God
and they fear him
-    all the ends of   THE EARTH.

---

34. For the rhetorical analysis of this psalm, see R. Meynet, 'Le Psaume 67: "Je ferai de toi la lumière des natíons"', *NRT* 120 (1998), pp. 3-17.

Chapter 2

THE FOUNDERS
(NINETEENTH CENTURY)

While Lowth's 'parallelism of the members' was largely adopted by exegetes, Bengel's 'direct or inverted chiasm' did not benefit from the same notoriety.[1] Only a few English authors of the 19th century have pursued Bengel's intuitions as well as Lowth's work, although their work was never properly acknowledged.[2] And yet their contribution is far from negligible.

John Jebb

John Jebb published in 1820 a work in which he refers specifically, down to the title, to Robert Lowth: Sacred Literature comprising a review of the principles of composition laid down by the late Robert Lowth, Lord Bishop of London in his Praelectiones and Isaiah: and an application of the principles so reviewed, to the illustration of the New Testament in a series of critical observations on the style and structure of that sacred volume,[3] *but he offers a profound revision of his principles which leans towards Bengel's discoveries.[4]Lowth had showed that the parallelism of passages known as 'poetical' before him was also found in the prophets: Jebb proposed to extend this observation to the New Testament. His most striking contribution is the emphasis on what Bengel called* chiasmus inversus *and that he calls 'introverted parallelism'. Given the importance of this work, it is necessary to quote broad passages of it.*

[p. 1]

It is the design of the following pages, to prove, by examples, that the structure of clauses, sentences, and periods, in the New Testament, is

1. See the translations of the plagiaries of Lowth's *Praelectiones* (quoted above, p. 59 nn. 21, 22); see articles in dictionaries under 'Hebraic poetry', and 'parallelism'.
2. F. Bussby, 'Bishop Jebb, A Neglected Biblical Scholar', *ExpTim* 60 (1948–49), p. 193.
3. London: Cadell & Davis, 1820.
4. Whom he quotes on severall occasions, for example on pp. 70, 358.

frequently regulated after the model afforded in the poetical parts of
the Old: and it is hoped, that, in the course of investigation necessary
for the accomplishment of this design, somewhat may be incidentally
contributed, towards the rectification or establishment of the received
text; some grammatical difficulties may be removed; some intricacies
of construction may be disentangled; some light may be thrown on the
interpretation of passages hitherto obscure; and several less obvious
proprieties of expression, and beauties, both of conception and of
style, may be rendered familiar to the attentive reader: while, if the
thoughts, not hastily or indeliberately submitted to the public, shall
approve themselves to competent minds, a new, and, if my own experience be not deceitful, an agreeable field of enquiry will be opened to
students of the Sacred Volume.

> *In the second section, Jebb recalls and summarizes Lowth's theory on
> the parallelism of the members.*
>
> *He devotes his third section to a criticism of the synonymous
> parallelism:*

[p. 35]

in the parallelisms commonly termed synonymous, the second, or
responsive clause invariably diversifies the preceding clause; and generally so as to rise above it, forming a sort of climax in the sense.

[p. 36]

Within a brief compass, this point probably cannot be more fairly
brought to issue, than by examining Bishop Lowth's own examples, of
what he terms parallel lines synonymous; [...]

> O Jehovah, in thy strength the king shall rejoice;
> And in thy salvation, how greatly shall he exult:
> The desire of his heart, thou hast granted him;
> And the request of his lips, thou hast not denied.

Ps. 21.2

The gradation of member above member, and line above line, in each
couplet of this stanza, is undeniable: 'salvation' is an advance upon
'strength'; and 'how greatly shall he exult', an advance upon 'he shall
rejoice': again, 'the request of the lips', is something beyond 'the
desire of the heart',—it is desire brought into act.

[p. 38]

[...] And if, in any instance, the sense may, at first view, appear to
stand still, a nearer inspection will not fail to disclose some distinction

of meaning; and, in the great majority of cases, an unquestionable climax.

On the whole, therefore, it would appear, that Bishop Lowth's definition of this species of parallelism ought to be corrected; and, that the *name* also, should, at least, not be at *variance* with the *thing*. The term *Progressive Parallelism* would apply in all cases where there is a *climax* in the sense but it may be preferable to use a term that will include other varieties: the *anti-climax* occasionally occurs, and with powerful effect; sometimes there is an accent from *species* to *genus*, for the purpose of generalisation; sometimes a descent from *genus* to *species* for the purpose of particularisation: with these, and other varieties in view, if I might venture to suggest a name, it should be the COGNATE PARALLELISM; in all such cases, there is a close relationship, though by no means absolute identity.

This is no idle disquisition about *words*: if *things* were not intimately concerned, it should [p. 39] assuredly be spared. But it is no trifling object to rescue the language of Scripture from the imputation of gross tautology; an imputation which could not easily be repelled, if the Sacred Volume were admitted to abound in consecutive pairs of lines *strictly synonymous*.[5] But another, and not less important consideration remains. It can, I apprehend, be satisfactorily shown, that a great object of the duality of members in Hebrew poetry, accompanied by a distinction, and, commonly, either a progress or antithesis, in the sense of related terms, clauses, and periods, is, to make inexhaustible provision for marking, with the nicest philosophical precision, the moral differences and relations of things. The *Antithetic Parallelism* serves to mark the broad distinctions between truth and falsehood, and good and evil: the *Cognate Parallelism* discharges the more difficult and more critical function, of discriminating between different degrees of truth and good on the one hand, of falsehood and of evil on the other. And it is probable, that full justice will not be done to the language, either of the Old Testament, or of the New, till interpreters qualified in all respects, and gifted alike with sagaciousness and sobriety of mind, shall accurately investigate these nice distinctions. One

5. The imputation is not new; and the defence has been long since *almost* anticipated: 'Nothing is thought more impertinent in Scripture than the frequent repetitions: but the learned need not to be told, that many things seem to the ignorant *bare repetitions*, which yet ever bring along with them some LIGHT, or some ACCESSION' (*Boyle on the Style of Scripture*, p. 90 [Jebb's note]).

[p. 40] or two specimens shall now be given, of passages exemplifying this moral discrimination:

> Who shall ascend the mountain of Jehovah?
> And who shall stand within his holy place?
> The clean of hands, and the pure in heart.

Ps. 24.3-4

To *ascend* marks progress; to *stand*, stability and confirmation: the *mountain of Jehovah*; the site of the divine sanctuary; *his holy place*, the sanctuary itself: and in correspondence with the advance of the two lines which form the first couplet, there is an advance in the members of the third line: *the clean of hands; and the pure in heart: the clean of hands, shall ascend the mountain of Jehovah: the pure in heart, shall stand within his holy place.* [...]

[p. 41]

> O the happiness of that man,
> Who hath not walked in the counsel of the ungodly;
> And hath not stood in the way of sinners;
> And hath not sat in the seat of the scornful.

Psalm 1

The exclamation with which the Psalm opens, belongs equally to each line of the succeeding triplet. In the triplet itself, each line consists of three members; and the lines gradually rise, one above the other, not merely in their general sense, but specially, throughout their correspondent members. To *walk*, implies no more than casual intercourse; to *stand*, closer intimacy; to *sit*, fixed and permanent connection: the *counsel*, the ordinary place of meeting, or public resort; the *way*, the select and chosen foot-path; the *seat*, the habitual and final resting-place; the *ungodly*, negatively wicked; *sinners*, positively wicked; the *scornful*, scoffers at the very name or notion of piety and goodness.

Section IV

[p. 53]

It is the object of the present section to produce, and sometimes to observe upon, certain varieties in the poetical parallelism, unnoticed as such by Bishop Lowth, or by subsequent writers on the subject.

There are stanzas so constructed, that, whatever be the number of lines, the first shall be parallel with the last; the second with the penultimate; and so throughout, in an order that looks inward, or, to borrow a military phrase, from flanks to centre. This may be called the *introverted* parallelism—

My son, if thine heart be wise;
My heart also shall rejoice;
Yes, my reins shall rejoice;
When thy lips speak right things.

Prov. 23.15-16

Unto thee do I lift up mine eyes, O thou that dwellest in the heavens;
  Behold, as the eyes of servants to the hands of their masters;
  As the eyes of a maiden to the hand of her mistress:
Even so look our eyes to Jehovah our God, until he have mercy upon us.

Ps. 123.1-2

[p. 54]

From the hand of hell I will redeem them;
  From death I will reclaim them:
  Death! I will be thy pestilence;
Hell! I will be thy burning plague.

Hos. 13.14

And I saw as the colour of electrum;
  As the appearance of fire round about within it:
    From the appearance of the loins even upward;
    And from the appearance of the loins even downward:
  I saw as the appearance of fire;
And it has brightness round about.

Ezek. 1.27

And I shall come to pass in that day;
  Jehovah shall make a gathering of his fruit:
    From the flood of the river; [scil. Euphrates.]
    To the stream of Egypt:
  And ye shall be gleaned up, one by one;
O ye sons of Israel.

And it shall come to pass in that day;
  The great trumpet shall be sounded:
    And those shall come, who were perishing in the
                                      land of Assyria;
    And who were dispersed in the land of Egypt;
  And they shall bow themselves down before Jehovah;
In the holy mountain, in Jerusalem.

Isa. 27.12-13

In these two stanzas of Isaiah, figuratively in the first, and literally in the second, is predicted the return of the Jews from their several dispersions. The first line of each stanza is parallel with the sixth; the second with the fifth; and the third with the fourth: also, on comparing the stanzas one with another, it is manifest, that [p. 55] they are constructed with the utmost precision of mutual correspondence; clause harmonising with clause, and line respectively with line: the first line of the first stanza with the first line of the second, and so throughout. It is extraordinary that the peculiarity of construction in this passage should have escaped the penetration of Bishop Lowth: in the first stanza, *his* distribution of the clauses into lines is subversive of the order manifestly designed by the prophet; yet, so indestructible is that order, that it is here exhibited in the precise language of the Bishop's own version, without the translocation of a single word. The stanzas are merely separated; the lines properly distributed, and the parallelism distinctly marked.

A difficult passage in the Psalms may, perhaps, derive some partial elucidation from a simple reduction to this form of stanza:

> Blessed is the man whose strength is in Thee:
>> The passengers in whose heart are the ways;
>>> In the valley of Baca make it a spring,
>>> The rain also filleth the pools;
>> They go from strength to strength;
> He shall appear before God in Zion.

Ps. 84.5-7

The first and sixth lines are here considered, at once, as constructively parallel, and as affording a *continuous* sense [...]: the intermediate four lines may be accounted parenthetical; the second, constructively parallel with the fifth; and the third with [p. 56] the fourth. The first line seems to contain the character of a confirmed proficient in religion,—*his strength is in God*; the sixth line, to describe his final beatification,—*he shall appear before God in Zion*. The intermediate quatrain may be regarded as descriptive of the intermediate course pursued by those who desire to be good and happy: they are passengers; but they know their destination, and they long for it; at a distance from the temple, (the mystical 'sapientum templa serena',) they are anxious to arrive there; the very highways to Jerusalem are in their heart. And what is the consequence? Affection smooths all difficulties: the parched and sandy desert becomes a rich well-watered valley; and they cheerfully advance from strength to strength; from one degree of virtuous proficiency to another.

Whether the above distribution throws any light on the passage, it is for others to determine: commentators have been so perplexed by it, that even a total failure cannot be attended with disgrace; while partial success may be serviceable to those who shall come after. [. . .]

[p. 57]

One more example of the same kind:

> The idols of the heathen are silver and gold:
> The work of men's hand;
> They have mouths, but they speak not;
> They have eyes, but they see not;
> They have ears, but they hear not;
> Neither is there any breath in their mouths;
> They who make them, are like unto them:
> So are all they who put their trust in them.

Ps. 135.15-18

The parallelism here marked out, will, it is presumed, be found accurate:

> In the first line, we have the idolatrous heathen;
> In the eighth, those who put their trust in idols:
> In the second line, the fabrication;
> In the seventh, the fabricators:
> In the third line, mouths without articulation;
> In the sixth, mouths without breath:
> In the fourth line, eyes without vision;
> And, in the fifth line, ears without the sense of hearing.

The parallelism of the extreme members, may [p. 58] be rendered more evident, by reducing the passage into two quatrains; thus;

> The idols of the heathen are silver and gold:
> The work of men's hand;
> They who make them, are like unto them:
> So are all they who put their trust in them.
>
> They have mouths, but they speak not;
> They have eyes, but they see not;
> They have ears, but they hear not;
> Neither is there any breath in their mouths;

The construction of the original passage, though artificial, is easy: the parallelism, though involved, is unembarrassed: and perhaps it may be no unreasonable conjecture, that this, and similar instances of obvious though extended parallelism, may have been provided, among other purposes, as so many moulds and forms, by means of which, shape and consistency may hereafter be given to passages, at present, if not wholly unintelligible, at least, 'hard to be understood'. We have seen (Sect. II) that, in some four-lined stanzas, the sense is not directly, but *alternately* continuous: something not dissimilar, may be analogically expected, in stanzas of eight lines or of ten; and in the introverted, no less than the alternate stanza: the first line and the tenth, for example, of some hitherto obscure passage, may, very possibly, be not only parallel in construction, but consecutive in sense; in like manner, the second line, with the ninth; and so, throughout, in the introverted order. This, indeed, is at present no more than [p. 59] an hypothetical case; but the bare possibility of its real existence may serve to show, that these technical niceties are by no means unimportant. I wish not to recommend *theory*, but *experiment*. And, in this view, that student cannot surely be ill employed, who tries to gain a familiarity with Hebraic stanzas of all descriptions; and to acquire a well-regulated habit of analysing their component members. At the very least, experiments of this kind, if not *immediately* profitable, towards the interpretation of Scripture, and the establishment of sound doctrine, may lay the foundation of *future* profit, to a large extent: [...] Meantime, obscurities in abundance remain in the Sacred Volume; most of all, perhaps, in the books most susceptible of involved versicular arrangements,—the writings of the prophets: and it were presumptuous to conjecture, but more presumptuous to limit, the possibilities of future discovery in the much-frequented, but entangled walks of prophetic interpretation, by those who shall bring along with them prudence, penetration, perseverance, but, above all, a properly chastised imagination, to the study of Hebraic parallelism.

Jebb noted an analogous phenomenon at the level of the distich and attempts to explain it:

There is, in Hebrew poetry, an artifice of construction much akin to the introverted parallelism, [p. 60] which I will endeavour to describe. Distichs, it is well known, were usually constructed with a view to alternate recitation, or chanting, by the opposite divisions of the choir, in Jewish worship; and when one line of the couplet closed with an important word or sentiment, it was often so contrived, that the antiphonal line of the couplet should commence with a word or sentiment precisely parallel: a practice obviously in the order of nature; for, if you present any object to a mirror, that part of it which is most distant from you will appear nearest in the reflected image. This artifice, however, was by no means capriciously employed, or for the sake of mere ornament.

> *Curiously, after having described what seems to give primacy to the centre, for Jebb it is the extremities that are highlighted in the reversed construction of the four elements of the distich:*

Its *rationale* may be thus explained: two pair of terms, or propositions, conveying two important, but not equally important notions, are to be so distributed, as to bring out the sense in the strongest and most impressive manner: now, this result will be best attained, by commencing, and concluding, with the notions to which prominence is to be given; and by placing in the centre the less important notion, or that, which, from the scope of the argument, is to be kept subordinate: an arrangement, not only accordant with the genius of Hebrew poetry, and with the practice of alternate recitation, but sanctioned, also, by the best rules of criticism:—for, an able rhetorician recommends, that we should reserve for the last, the most emphatic member of a sentence; and for this reason, that, if placed in the middle, it must lose its energy. [...]

[p. 61]

But my meaning will be made clearer by an example. In the hundred and seventh Psalm, the wish is earnestly and repeatedly expressed, that the subjects of Jehovah's goodness, would praise him for that goodness, and for his wonderful interposition on behalf of mankind. Special motives to call forth suitable expressions of gratitude are urged; particularly in the ninth and sixteenth verses; which verses are both constructed in the manner just described:

> For he hath satisfied the craving soul;
> And the famished soul, he hath filled with goodness.

Ps. 107.9

Here are two pairs of terms, conveying the two notions of complete destitution by famine; and of equally complete relief, administered by the divine [p. 62] bounty. The notion of relief, as best fitted to excite gratitude, was obviously that, to which prominence was to be given; and this, accordingly, was effected by placing it *first* and *last*: the idea of destitution, on the contrary, as a painful one, and not in unison with

the hilarity of grateful adoration, had the *central*, that is, the less
important place assigned it. [. . .]

> *Abandoning the particular case of the four members distich, Jebb*
> *comes back to the essential of his inquiry; the concentric construction, his*
> *'inverted parallelism'.*

[...]   [p. 65]

The figure of speech, for such it may be called, the grounds and
reasons of which I have here attempted to explain, has not been
unnoticed by commentators and critics; several, indeed, have observed
the *phaenomenon*; but not one, that I am aware of, has hitherto
explored the *rationale* of it. Some are disposed to maintain that it is
purely classical; and it does *sometimes* occur in Greek and Latin
authors; but it is so prevalent, and so peculiarly marked, in the Sacred
Volume, that it may be justly accounted a Hebraism; and, as I am
disposed to believe, a feature of Hebrew poetry. Rhetoricians have
given it various names; for example, *hysterèsis, chiasmus, synchysis,
epanodos*: the last is its most frequent appellation. That, which I have
ventured to call the introverted parallelism, is a species of *epanodos*;
and, in every instance of it, the reasons may be clearly shown, why
this order has been chosen.

> *In the fifth section, Jebb initiates the movement which will lead him to*
> *prove that parallelism, whose existence in the Old Testament he has*
> *shown after Lowth, is also found in the New. First he noticed that the*
> *parallelism of the Hebrew text was kept in the oldest Greek translation*
> *done by the Jews themselves, the Septuagint, and that it was applied in*
> *the Apocryphal books and in the writings of the Rabbis.*

[p. 77]

Now, the question may be confidently asked, is it in any degree
probable, that such a manner should have been abruptly and altogether
discarded in the New Testament?

> *Three reasons are then presented to give a negative answer to his*
> *question: the unity of Scriptures; the fact that the authors of the New*
> *Testament were Jews who had been brought up in the Old Testament*
> *techniques of composition; and moreover the observation of the facts, that*
> *is, of the parallelism which is indeed found in the New Testament.*
>
> *In the next three sections, Jebb is concerned with following up paral-*
> *lelism in the quotations of the Old Testament that are found in the New:*
> *pure quotes in the sixth section (Mt. 2.6 which reproduces Mic. 5.2;*
> *Mt. 2.18 which reproduces Jer. 31.15, etc.); quotations which combine*
> *several passages from the Old Testament in the seventh section (for*

example: Mk 11.17 which combines Isa. 56.57 and Jer. 7.11); lastly quo-
tations which are intimately linked to the text of the New Testament author
(for example, Rom. 10.13-18 which starts with a quotation of Joel 2.32,
and carries on with Paul's question and ends with a distich from Isa.
52.7). In all cases, minutely analysed, the law of biblical parallelism is
scrupulously respected.

The following sections are devoted to the analysis of the original mate-
rial of the New Testament. Jebb follows an approach initiated by Lowth,
that is, by starting with the shorter units, distichs and tristichs (section
IX), quatrains (section X), stanzas of five or six verses[6] *(section XI), and*
finally stanzas of more than six verses (sections XII). He will try to show
how several stanzas form a paragraph or a section (sections XIII and
XIV); nothing of these two sections will be reproduced here since, if
intuition serves, the analyses are less than satisfactory.

Section IX

[p. 143]

I have now sufficiently exemplified the manner, in which the writers
of the New Testament were accustomed to cite, to abridge, to amplify,
and to combine, passages from the poetical parts of the Old Testament; and frequently to annex, or intermingle with their citations,
parallelisms by no means less perfect, of their own original composition. Henceforward, I shall confine myself to parallelisms purely
original; commencing with parallel couplets and triplets; examples of
which, with occasional annotations, will form the present section.

1. In the first place, then I shall give a few plain specimens of
parallel couplets:

My soul doth magnify the Lord;
And my spirit hath exulted in God my Saviour.

Lk. 1.46-47

To him that asked thee, give;
And him that would borrow from thee, turn not away.

Mt. 5.42

[p. 144]

For with what judgement ye judge, ye shall be judged;
And with what measure ye mete, it shall be measured
    unto you.

Mt. 7.2

6. Which, after Lowth, I will call 'members'.

[. . .]
> Unto whomsoever much is given, of him shall be
>   required;
> And to whom they have committed much, of him will
>   they demand the more.

Lk. 12.48

> He who soweth sparingly, sparingly also reap;
> And he who soweth bountifully, bountifully also shall reap.

2 Cor. 9.6

> He who soweth to his flesh, of the flesh shall reap corruption;
> And he who soweth to the spirit, of the spirit, shall reap life eternal.

Gal. 6.8

[. . .]   [p. 149]

2. The next examples to be adduced, are examples of triplet; that is, of three connected and correspondent lines, at least constructively parallel with each other; and forming, within themselves, a distinct sentence, or significant part of a sentence:

> The foxes have dens;
> And the birds of the air have nests;
> But the son of man hath not where to lay his head.

Mt. 8.20

[...]

> And I will give unto thee the keys of the kingdom of
>   Heaven;
> And whatsoever thou shalt bind on earth, shall be bound
>   in heaven;
> And whatsoever thou shalt loose on earth, shall be loosed
>   in heaven.

Mt. 16.19

[. . .]   [p. 156]

> Ask, and it shall be given to you;
> Seek, and ye shall find;
> Knock, and it shall be opened unto you:
>
> For every one who asketh, receiveth;
> And every one who seeketh, findeth;
> And to every one who knocketh, it shall be opened.

Mt. 7.7-8

These triplets are closely connected, not merely in their subject-matter, but by their form of construction; [p. 157] the first, second and third lines of each, being respectively parallel to the first, second, and third lines of the other: the parallelisms will be obvious, by reducing the passage to a stanza of six lines, thus:

> Ask, and it shall be given unto you;
> For every one who asketh, receiveth:
> Seek, and ye shall find;
> For every one who seeketh, findeth:
> Knock, and it shall be opened unto you;
> For to every one who knocketh, it shall be opened.

The existing order, however, is incomparably preferable. [. . .]

[p. 159]

Commentators have variously explained the terms *ask*, *seek*, *knock*. The explanation of Euthymius Zigabenus is worthy of attention: 'He commanded us to ASK, and promised the gift: not, however, simply to ask, but with perseverance and alacrity; for this is indicated by the word SEEK: and not only with perseverance and alacrity, but with fervour also, and vehemence; for this is the force of the word KNOCK.' An interpretation, it must be observed, which Euthymius extracted and abridged from S. Chrysostom. See this Father's twenty-third homily on S. Matthew.

Perhaps, without doing any violence to the moral meaning, the continuity and progress of the metaphor may be thus exhibited:

> Ask the way, and information shall be given to you;
> Seek the house, and ye shall find it;
> Knock at the door, and it shall be opened unto you.

[. . .]

Section X

[p. 168]

I proceed with examples of the quatrain; that is, of two parallel couplets, so connected, as to form one continued and distinct sentence; the pairs of lines being either directly, alternately, or inversely parallel:

> I, indeed, baptize you with water, unto repentance;
>   But he who cometh after me, is mightier than I;
>   Of whom I am not worthy to carry the shoes;
> He will baptize you with the Holy Spirit and with fire.

Whose fan is in his hand;
And he will throughly purge his floor:
And will gather the wheat into his granary;
But the chaff he will consume with unquenchable fire.

Mt. 3.11-12

[p. 170]

For since by man came death;
By man also came the resurrection of the dead;
For as in Adam all die;
Even so, in Christ shall all be made alive.

1 Cor. 15.21-22

[...]   [p. 191]

It will be recollected, that, in the second section of this work, some specimens were produced of alternate quatrains, in which, by peculiar artifice of construction, the third line form a continuous sense with the first, and the fourth with the second. This variety occurs also in the New Testament; for example:

Being darkened in the understanding,
Being alienated from the life of God:
Through the ignorance which is in them;
Through the blindness of their hearts.

Eph. 4.18

That is, adjusting the parallelism:

Being darkened in the understanding,
Through the ignorance which is in them;
Being alienated from the life of God,
Through the blindness of their hearts.

Again:

And they sought to seize him;
And they feared the people:
For they knew, that against them he spake the parable;
And having left him, they departed.

Mk 12.12

That is:

And they sought to seize him;
For they knew, that against them he spake the parable;
But they feared the people;
Therefore, having left him, they departed.

Section XI

[p. 193]

I propose, in this Section, to exemplify stanzas consisting of five lines; and those also which contain six.

1. The five-lined stanza admits considerable varieties of structure: sometimes the odd line or member commences the stanza; frequently, in that case, laying down a truth to be illustrated in the remaining four lines: sometimes, on the contrary, after two distichs, the odd line makes a full close; often containing some conclusion deductible from what preceded: sometimes the odd line forms a sort of middle term, or connective link, between two couplets: and occasionally the five-lined stanza begins and ends with parallel lines; a parallel triplet intervening. Of all these varieties, some exemplification shall be given:—

> Are there not twelve hours in the day?
>> If a man walk in the day, he stumbleth not;
>>> Because he seeth the light of this world:
>> But if a man walk in the night he stumbleth;
>>> Because the light is not in him.

Jn 11.9-10.

[. . .]   [p. 195]

>> By their fruits ye shall thoroughly know them:
>>> Do men gather from thorns the grape?
>>> Or from thistles the fig?
>>> Thus, every sound tree beareth good fruit;
>>> But every corrupt tree beareth evil fruit:
>
>>> A sound tree cannot bear evil fruit;
>>> Nor a corrupt tree bear good fruit: [p. 196]
>>> Every tree not bearing good fruit,
>>> Is hewn down and cast into the fire:
>> By their fruits, therefore, ye shall thoroughly know them.

Mt. 7.16-20.

[. . .]

These two connected stanzas are distributed with masterly skill. In the first stanza, the odd line commences the paragraph; laying down a proposition to be proved, or illustrated; 'by their fruits ye shall thoroughly know them'. In the second stanza, on the contrary, the odd line makes a full close, re-asserting with authority the same proposition, as undeniably established by the intermediate quatrains—'by their fruits, *therefore*, ye shall thoroughly know them'. The entire illative force of the particle *arage*, it is impossible to convey in any single English word. This passage unites the most exact logic, with the most beautiful imagery: the *repetition*, too, is no less poetical than it is argumentative.

[...]   [p. 199]
> For he is not a Jew, who is one outwardly
> > Neither is circumcision that which is outward in the flesh:
> But he is a Jew, who is one inwardly;   [p. 200]
> > And circumcision that of the heart, in spirit, not in letter:
> Whose praise is not from men, but from God.

Rom. 2.28-29

In this specimen, it will be observed, the first, third, and fifth lines not only are parallel, but keep up a continuous sense, though that sense be twice suspended, by the intervention of the second and fourth lines. I shall hereafter have occasion to show, that this alternation of distinct and incommiscible senses is sometimes carried to a far greater extent in the New Testament.

> Consider the ravens:
> > They neither sow, nor reap;
> > They have neither store-house nor barn;
> > And God feedeth them:
> How much are ye superior to those birds?

Lk. 12.24

[...] The habit of observing such niceties is far from trifling; every thing is [p. 201] important which contributes to illustrate the *organisation* of Scripture.

2. The six-lined stanza sometimes consists of a quatrain, with a distich annexed: sometimes of two parallel couplets, with a third pair of parallel lines so distributed, that one occupies the centre, and the other the close: and occasionally, of three couplets alternately parallel; the first, third, and fifth lines corresponding with one another; and in like manner, the second, fourth, and sixth. The parallelism in this form of stanza is also frequently introverted; a variety, which, for the most part, comes under the description of *epanodos*; and which will hereafter, in that character, be more largely exemplified.

Specimens of the six-lined stanza must now be given:

When it is evening, ye say, 'A calm!
    For the sky is red:'
And in the morning, 'to-day a tempest!
    For the sky is red and lowering:'
Hypocrites! The face of the sky ye know how to discern;
But ye cannot [discern] the signs of the times!

Mt. 16.2-3

[p. 204]

The first man, from earth, earthy;
    The second man, the Lord from heaven:
As the earthy man, such also the earthy men;
    And as the heavenly man, such also the heavenly men;
And as we have borne the image of the earthy man;
    We shall bear also the image of the heavenly man.

1 Cor. 15.47-49

[p. 205]

Fear not them who kill the body,
And after that have no more that they can do;
    But I will show you whom ye shall fear:
Fear him, who after he hath killed,
Hath power to cast into hell;
    Yea, I say unto you, fear him.

Lk. 12.4-5

[p. 208]

Come unto me, all ye who labour, and are burdened:
    And I will give you rest:
        Take my yoke upon you, and learn of me;
        For I am meek, and lowly in heart;
    And ye shall find rest unto your souls:
For my yoke is easy, and my burden light.

Mt. 11.28-30

The parallelism here marked, will, it is presumed, appear both unquestionable and intentional, when the related lines are brought into contact with each other; thus:

[p. 209]

Come unto me, all ye who labour, and are burdened;
For my yoke is easy, and my burden light:
And I will give you rest;
And ye shall find rest unto your souls:
Take my yoke upon you, and learn of me;
For I am meek, and lowly in heart.

[p. 212]

Section XII

It frequently happens, that more than six parallel lines are so connected, by unity of subject, or by mutual relationship, as to form a
distinct stanza. Examples of this kind of distribution shall be given in
the present section.

[p. 213]

Whosoever, therefore, heareth these my words, and doeth them,
I will liken him to a prudent man,
Who built his house upon the rock:
  And the rain descended,
  And the floods came,
  And the winds blew,
  And fell upon that house;
And it fell not; for it was founded upon the rock.

And every one hearing these my words, and doing them not,
Shall be likened to a foolish man,
Who built his house upon the sand;
  And the rain descended,
  And the floods came,
  And the winds blew,
  And struck upon that house;
And it fell; and the fall thereof was great.

Mt. 7.24-27

[p. 223]

The princes of the nations lord it over them;
And the great ones exercise harsh authority over them;
It shall not be so among you;
  But whosoever would among you become great,
   Shall be your servant;
  And whosoever would among you be chief,
   Shall be your slave;
Even as the Son of Man
Came not to be served, but to serve,
And to give his life a ransom for many.

Mt. 20.25-28[7]

---

7. Jebb's analysis, reproduced here, illustrates at once the keenness of his mind,
and the intelligence of the text that the method enables. See the study of the same
text, done before I could benefit from Jebb's hindsight: R. Meynet, *Initiation*, p. 82
and pl. 10.

[p. 226]

The whole construction of this passage is eminently beautiful; the several divisions of it are linked together by a close, but neither 'obvious nor obtrusive' correspondence of related members; which correspondence must be strictly examined, and clearly exhibited, in order to a just disclosure of [p. 227] the sense. The central quatrain may be regarded as the key of the whole paragraph or stanza: it stands connected, antithetically, with the commencing, and homogeneously, with the concluding triplet: which triplets again, by the explanatory intervention of the same central quatrain, will approve themselves antithetically parallel with each other, in the introverted order.

The antithesis to be first noticed, is that between the first two lines of the first triplet, and the two distichs of the central quatrain: the lines in question, are severally taken up in the introverted order; the second line first:

> And the GREAT ONES exercise harsh authority over them:

which is provided with its antithetical relative in the first couplet of the adjoining quatrain:

> But whosoever would among you become GREAT,
> Shall become your SERVANT.

The first line of the first triplet is next referred to:

> The PRINCES of the nations lord it over them:

antithetical to which, is the second couplet of the central quatrain:

> And whosoever would among you be CHIEF;
> Shall become your SLAVE.

In the first couplet of the stanza at large, there is an anticlimax, or descending scale of dignity:

[p. 228]

> The princes of the nations lord it over them;
> And the great ones exercise harsh authority over them:

the *archontes* being kings or autocrats, who rule over their subjects with supreme dominion; *katakurieusousin*: and the *megaloi*, only lords or satraps, who exercise over those entrusted to their charge a delegated sway; *katexousiazousin*.

In the quatrain, on the contrary, there is a climax, or ascending scale of dignity:

But whosoever would among you become great,
    Shall be your servant,
And whosoever would among you be chief,
    Shall be your slave:

The *megas*, or *great one*, is here correspondent to the lords or satraps; and the *prōtos*, or *chief*, is equivalent to the *archontes*, kings or autocrats. This change from anti-climax to climax, is subservient to a high moral purpose: it shows us, 'by due steps', how Christians are to attain the first dignity of the Christian character; 'he that would become *great*; let him be as a *servant*; but he that would become CHIEF, let him be as a SLAVE'. In the religion of our crucified Redeemer, the deepest humiliation, is the path to the most exalted pitch of glory: it is thus, in that true sense, of which Stoicism was but the mockery, that men may become not only '*priests*', but 'KINGS *unto God*'. See Rev. 1.6.

[p. 229]

The third line of the first triplet,—'it shall not be so with you',—though not brought into parallelism with any part of the central quatrain, is by no means inactive, or inefficient; that it is provided with a correspondent or parallel member, we shall presently see: meantime, considered in itself, and independently of parallelism, it serves as a most apt transition, from the case of Gentile kings and satraps, to the case of aspirants after Christian greatness and perfection. 'It shall not be so among you.'

The connection between the central quatrain and the concluding triplet, is, as I have already intimated, not of the antithetical, but of the homogeneous kind; in other words, the parallelism is, what I term cognate. Into this parallelism, the first line of the last triplet does not, strictly speaking, enter: it is the turning point, or connecting link, between the couplets of the preceding quatrain, and the other two lines of the same triplet: and with the last line of the first triplet, it forms an antithetical parallelism, thus:

It shall not be so with you;
Even as the son of Man:

that is, in other words:

You shall not resemble the ambitious heathen;
But you shall resemble the meek and lowly Saviour of mankind.

The cognate parallelism between the central quatrain, and the last two lines of the concluding [p. 230] triplet, is not in the reversed, but in the direct order: the first couplet of the quatrain, is first provided with its homogeneous relative:

> But whosoever would among you become great,
> Shall be your *servant*:
> [Even as the Son of Man]
> Came not to be served, but to *serve*.

The second couplet of the quatrain, is then similarly provided:

> And whosoever would among you be chief,
> Shall be your *slave*:
> [Even as the Son of Man came]
> *to give his life a ransom for many.*

In the first of these parallelisms, the relationship is brought out with strict verbal identity: *diakonos—diakonēsai*; a *servant*, to *serve*. In the second parallelism, the *verbal* coincidence is not equally striking, but the *reality of agreement* is, if possible, more strong. It is not said, that Christ became a slave; but much more; *that he gave his* LIFE A RANSOM *to redeem many from the* SLAVERY *of sin and death.*

[p. 231]

Finally, the commencing and concluding triplets, especially after the above explanatory intervention, approve themselves antithetically parallel, in the introverted order: the last line of the first triplet, we have already seen, is opposed to the first line of the last triplet. The second line of each are, in like manner, antithetical:

> The great ones exercise harsh authority:—
> Came not to be served, but to serve:

The authority of the oppressive noble, opposed to the voluntary obedience of the servant: while the first line of the commencing, is antithetical to the last line of the concluding triplet:

> The princes of the earth lord it over them:—
> To give his life a ransom for many:

The tyranny of early potentates, opposed to the humiliation, even to the death of the cross, of Him who is KING OF KINGS, AND LORD OF LORDS.

[p. 335]

Section XVI

In the fourth section of these observations it was intimated, that, when I should have proceeded some way in the examination of New Testament parallelisms, I would resume the subject of the epanodos. That engagement I am now about to fulfil.

The Epanodos is literally *a going back*; speaking first to the second of two subjects proposed; or, if the subjects be more than two, resuming them precisely in the inverted order; speaking first to the last, and last to the first. The *rationale* of this artifice in composition, I ventured to explain. [. . .][8]

[p. 336]

>No man can serve two masters:
>>For, either he will hate the one, and love the other;
>>Or he will adhere to the one, and neglect the other:
>Ye cannot serve God and mammon.

Mt. 6.24

In this quatrain at large, there is a clear *epanodos*: in the first line, the impossibility is, in general terms, asserted, of serving two masters; that is, two masters of opposite tempers, issuing opposite commands: in the fourth line, this impossibility is re-asserted, and brought personally home to the secular part of our Lord's hearers, by the specification of the two incompatible masters, GOD and MAMMON. These two assertions, as the leading [p. 337] members of the passage, are placed first and last; while, in the centre, are subordinately given the moral proofs by which the main propositions are established. But the two central members are so disposed, as to exhibit an epanodos yet more beautiful and striking. In a divided service, the dispositions and conduct of the servant, towards the opposite powers who claim his obedience, are distributable into two classes; each class containing two degrees: on the one side *love*, or at least, *adherence*: on the other side, *hatred*, or at least, *neglect*.

[p. 338]

>Give not that which is holy to the dogs;
>>Neither cast your pearls before the swine;
>>Lest they trample them under their feet;
>And turn about and rend you.

Mt. 7.6

---

8.   See above page 60 [Jebb's note]; in the present work, pp. 73-74.

The relation of the first line to the fourth, and that of the second to the third, have been noticed by almost all the commentators. A minor circumstance, is not altogether undeserving of attention: [p. 339] the equal lengths, in the original, of each related pair of lines; the first and fourth lines being short, the second and the third lines long. The sense of the passage becomes perfectly clear, on thus adjusting the parallelism:

> Give not that which is holy to the dogs;
> Lest they turn about you and rend you:
> Neither cast your pearls before the swine,
> Lest they trample them under their feet.

[. . .] The more dangerous act of imprudence, with its fatal result, is placed first and last, so as to make, and to leave, the deepest practical impression.

[p. 342]

> Behold therefore the gentleness,
>   And the severity of God;
>   Towards those indeed who have fallen, severity;
>   But towards thee, gentleness.

Rom. 11.22

Gentleness at the beginning; at the close gentleness: this epanodos speaks for itself.

[p. 344]

> We are a sweet odour of Christ;
>   To those who are saved;
>   And to those who perish;
>   To the one, indeed, an odour of death, unto death;
>   But to the other, an odour of life, unto life.

2 Cor. 2.15-16

[p. 345]

The painful part of the subject, is here kept subordinate; the agreeable, is placed first and last.

> Hearing of thy love;
>   And of the faith which thou hast,
>   Toward the Lord Jesus,
>   And to all the saints:

Phlm. 5

that is, the epanodos being reduced:

> Hearing of thy love,
> To all the saints;
> And of the faith which thou hast,
> Toward the Lord Jesus:

An arrangement of the same thoughts, elsewhere afforded by S. Paul himself, only that he places *faith* first, and *love* last:

> Having heard of your faith, in the Lord Jesus;
> And of your love, to all the saints.

Eph. 1.15

*After three sections which deal with secondary questions, there are five more sections devoted to the analysis of entire passages (*Magnificat, Benedictus, Nunc Dimittis, *most important the Sermon on the mount in Mt. 5–7, and lastly Rev. 18) which cannot be reproduced here, partly for lack of space, but mostly because these analyses are so shallow that they have very little to offer.*

It would not be an exaggeration to say that Jebb is the genuine inventor of 'rhetorical' analysis of the biblical texts. He was the first to carry out the synthesis of all the discoveries of his predecessors, in a large volume dedicated to the question.

But he was to be followed and amplified by a number of other scholars, mostly English, but also German and French.

Thomas Boys

Tactica Sacra

Four years after Jebb, Thomas Boys published his first book.[9] From the very beginning, Boys pays a tribute to his immediate predecessor, John Jebb:

[p. 1]

I was but little acquainted with Bishop Lowth; and it is to 'Sacred Literature' that I stand indebted for some of my lights on the subject upon which I am now writing.

Only to immediately add, and that is how he defines his own contribution:

---

9. *Tactica Sacra: An Attempt to Develope, and to Exhibit to the Eye by Tabular Arrangements, a General Rule of Composition Prevailing in the Holy Scriptures* (London: T. Hamilton, 1824).

Those principles which previous writers on parallelism have applied to short passages, are applied by me to long ones; and I arrange chapters and whole epistles as they arrange verses.

In fact, Jebb had already completed his study by presenting a series of long texts. But, for the Magnificat, *the* Benedictus *or the* Nunc Dimittis, *he had failed to grasp their general composition; as for the last two texts he analysed, he had merely provided an elementary page layout. Boys is therefore the first to analyse the composition of complete texts (four epistles: 1 and 2 Thess., 2 Pet., Phlm.). He is also the first to organize his work in two parts; the first describing and justifying the composition of the epistles, completed by a page layout (in Greek and English) in the second half. Before this, he gives a summary description of the principles of parallelism in his introduction, where he reproduces Jebb's presentation, but synthesizes it. He particularly insists on 'introverted parallelism', and provides new examples of it. He goes on to show that the parallelism, and particularly introverted parallelism, can largely be found in the four analysed epistles.*[10]

Given that Boys did not reproduce in his second book any of the 29 examples of introverted parallelism that he had himself found in the New Testament, it will be useful to cite a few here, with the analysis that he provided.[11]

[p. 4]

a. { Follow not that which is evil,
   b. { But that which is good.
   b. { He that doeth good is of God:
a. { He that doeth evil hath not seen God.[12]

3 Jn 11

Here we have evil in the extreme, and good in the central members.

[p. 5]

10. In fact, the two Epistles to the Thessalonians, for example, are of parallel construction, according to his analysis: the very brief dedication and final formula, which frame the body of the epistle, are not enough to make it a concentrical construction.

11. Boys has arranged them along the order of the books in the New Testament. Brief examples are alternated with longer ones. The five examples that were chosen here are true to this order, with preference given to the longer ones.

12. Boys is the first to emphasize the correspondences by the use of the letters a a, b b, etc (on top of the indentation of the margins that had also been used by Jebb).

	And now also the axe is laid unto the root of the trees:
a.	therefore every tree which bringeth not forth good
	fruit, is hewn down, and cast into the fire.

| | b. | I indeed baptize you with water unto repen- |
| | | tance; |

| | | c. | But he that cometh after me is mightier than I, |

| | | *c.* | Whose shoes I am not worthy to bear. |

| | *b.* | He shall baptize you with the Holy Ghost, and with |
| | | fire. |

	Whose fan is in his hand, and he will throughly purge
a.	his floor, and gather his wheat into the garner; but he
	will burn up the chaff with unquenchable fire.

Mt. 3.10-12[13]

Here, in a., the Lord is referred to under the similitude of a hewer of trees; and in *a.*, under that of a winnower of corn. In a., we have the axe, the instrument of the hewer; in *a.*, the fan, the instrument of the winnower. In a., we have the distinction between the good and the bad trees; in *a.*, the distinction between the wheat and the chaff. In a., the unproductive trees are consigned to the fire; and in *a.*, the chaff. In a., we have the immediate danger of the trees, 'the axe is laid to their root'; in *a.*, that the chaff, 'his fan is in his hand'.

In c. and *c.*, we have our Lord's superiority to John: in b. and *b.*, the superiority of our Lord's baptism to John's.[14]

13. The four central members are here disposed as above in *Sacred Literature*, p. 168 [Boys' note].

14. I have reproduced here, for the two preceding examples, the system used by Boys. For reasons of convenience, I will replace from now on the letters in italics (*a. b.*) by the same letters followed by an apostrophe (a', b'). For the same reasons, the full stop after each letter will be omitted.

[p. 5]

```
A   | a        And when he was come into his own country,
    |   b           He taught them in their synagogue.

  B   | Insomuch, that they were astonished, and said,

    C   | Whence hath this man this wisdom
        | and these mighty works?

              | c       Whence hath this man this wisdom
              |         and these mighty works?
        D   | d             Is not this the carpenter's
              |             son?

              | c'      And his brethren, James, and Joses,
              |         and Simon, and Judas?
        D'  | d'            And his sisters, are they not
              |             all with us?

    C'  | Whence then hath this man all
        | these things?

  B'  | And they were offended in him.

    | a' But Jesus said unto them, A prophet is not
    |        without honour, save in his own country,
A'  |        and in his own house.
    |   b'          And he did not many mighty works there,
    |               because of their unbelief.
```

Mt. 13.54-58

Here, in D, we have the father and mother of Christ; in D', his brethren and sisters: that is, his father and brethren in c and c'; his mother and sisters in d and d'—In C and C', we have the corresponding inquiries, 'Whence hath this man', &c. 'Whence then hath this man', &c.: in B, the people 'astonished' at Jesus; in B', 'offended in him'.

In A and A', the extreme members, the correspondence is two-fold, as it is in the central ones: a' answering to a, and b' to b—With regard to a and a', a relates to our Saviour's coming 'Into his own country'; a' to the treatment he there met with.—With regard to b and b', these refer to two things which generally went together in our Lord's ministrations; namely, teaching and the working of [p. 6] miracles. In the present instance, 'He taught them in their synagogue', (b) but 'He did not many mighty works there, because of their unbelief', (b')

[p. 7]

a If he does not give him,
   b having risen,
      c   because he is his friend;

      c' because of his importunity,
   b' he will get up,
a' and give him as many as he needeth.[15]

Lk. 11.8

Here observe that b' means more than b—*Anastas* ('having risen')
merely implies getting up. *Egertheis* ('getting up') implies being
roused, or rousing himself up.
[. . .]

a   Jesus saith unto him, Rise, take up thy bed, and walk.
   b   And immediately the man was made whole,
      c   And took up his bed, and walked.
         d   And on the same day was the sabbath.
         d'   The Jews therefore said unto him that was cured,
            It is the sabbath day.
      c'   It is not lawful for thee to carry thy bed.
   b'   He answered them, He that made me whole,
a'   The same said unto me, Take up thy bed, and walk.

Jn 5.8-11

In d and d', the sabbath; in c and c', the bed carried; in b and b', the
man made whole; in a and a', the words of our Lord.

> *A Key to the Book of the Psalms*
> *It is necessary to spend more time on Boys' second book, published a*
> *year later*, A Key to the Book of the Psalms,[16] *since his methodological*
> *presentation is remarkably more elaborate*:

[p. 4]

As the present work may fall into hands of some readers who are
not acquainted with my former publication, [. . .] it may here be
proper to go over some of the preliminary ground a second time. This
I shall now attempt to do with rather more regularity than before; yet
I would not be understood as attempting to offer any thing like a
complete theory, or a perfect view: the subject is still in its infancy.

Let us begin, as before, with the *parallel couplet*, which is the

---

15. Boys quotes the Greek text; a translation is here given, for the convenience of
the reader who is not a classicist.

16. T. Boys, *A Key to the Book of Psalms* (London: L.B Seeley & Sons, 1825).

simplest form of parallelism. In examining a verse, or other small portion of Scripture, we very commonly find that it falls into two equal, or nearly equal, lines, which mutually correspond: as in the following examples:—[17]

a   Seek ye the Lord, while he may be found;
a'   Call ye upon him, while he is near.

Isa. 55.6 (1)

a   Have mercy upon me, O Lord, for I am weak:
a'   Heal me, O Lord, for my bones are vexed.

Ps. 6.2 (2)

a   They provoked him to jealousy with strange gods,
a'   With abominations provoked they him to anger.

Deut. 32.16 (3)

a   Ye shall eat the flesh of your sons,
a'   And the flesh of your daughters ye shall eat.

Lev. 26.29 (4)
[p. 5]

a   Put away from thee a forward mouth,
a'   And perverse lips put far from thee.

Prov. 4.24 (5)

In each of these instances the reader will readily perceive that a', the second line, corresponds to a, the first.

The examples here given, however, have one material difference. They all admit a subdivision, but not all a subdivision of the same kind. The first and second examples, on being subdivided, may be best exhibited in an *alternate* form.

a | b   Seek ye the Lord,
    | c   While he may be found;

a' | b' Call ye upon him,
    | c' While he is near. (1)

a | b   Have mercy upon me, O Lord,
    | c   *For* I am weak.

a' | b' Heal me, O Lord,
    | c' *For* my bones are vexed. (2)

17. The numbers in parenthesis that follow the biblical references correspond to the order set out by Boys.

In each of these examples, a, the first line of the parallel couplet, is subdivided into the two portions, b and c; and a', the second, into the two corresponding portions, b' and c': b' answering to b, and c' to c; and therefore the whole b' c' or a', to the whole b c or a, as before. (The reader will excuse the technicality with which these arrangements invest the Sacred Text. Their object will appear as we proceed.)

In the two preceding examples, then, the correspondence is *alternate*: b', the third number, answering to b, the first; and c', the fourth, to c the second. But if we pass on to the three next parallel couplets, we find the case is altered. Here we shall in vain attempt an alternate arrangement. The composition is now no longer alternate, but *introverted*: the last portion answering to the first, the last but one to the second.

a	b	They provoked him to jealousy
	c	With strange gods:
a'	c'	With abominations
	b'	Provoked they him to anger.

[p. 6]

a	b	Ye shall eat
	c	The flesh of your sons,
a'	c'	And the flesh of your daughters
	b'	Ye shall eat.

a	b	Put away from thee
	c	A forward mouth
a'	c'	And perverse lips
	b'	Put far from thee.

In these *introverted* parallelisms the construction is somewhat more artificial than in the alternate arrangements previously exhibited. The clauses do not follow here, as there, in what might be called their natural order. 'Put away from thee—a forward mouth, and put far from thee—perverse lips.' The sacred writer inverts that order: so that we have no longer an alternate correspondence; but the last member, b', answering to the first, b, and the third, c', to the second, c; yet still, as before, the whole c' b', or a', answering to the whole b c, or a.

Thus the parallel couplet contains the principle both of the alternate and introverted parallelism. Whether the subdivision of a passage give us the alternate form, b c b' c', or the introverted form, b c c' b', the passage is equally reducible to the simplest couplet; that is, in the former instance, to the couplet,

a | b .... c ....

a' | b'.... c'....

in the latter, to the couplet

a | b .... c ....

a' | c'.... b'....

   Not, indeed, that every parallel couplet admits of one or other of these arrangements. Some, as couplets, are arranged as far, perhaps, as they can be. Others, again, fall into other forms, not at present to be considered. It is to the alternate and the introverted parallelism that I am now desirous to call the reader's attention; and both these may be reduced, [p. 7] whatever be their length, and, indeed, whatever be their variety, to the character of the simple couplet.

> *Boys moves on to show that the parallelism is not only found in the so-called 'poetical' books but also in the prose. For example:*

[p. 9]

a | Then the children of Ammon were gathered together
    b | And he encamped in Gilead:
a' | And the children of Israel assembled themselves together,
    b' | And encamped in Mizpeh.

Judg. 10.17 (11)

We have nothing here out of the simplest style of narrative.

[p. 14]

A   [12] To deliver thee from the way of the evil man, from the man that speaketh froward things;

        B   [13] Who forsake the paths of uprightness to walk in the ways of darkness; [14] Who rejoice to do evil, and delight in the frowardness of the wicked; [15] Whose ways are crooked, and they froward in their paths.

A'   [16] To deliver thee from the strange woman, even from the stranger that flattereth with her words;

        B'   [17] Who forsaketh the guide of her youth, and forgetteth the covenant of her God. [18] For her house inclineth unto death, and unto the dead her paths.

Prov. 2.12-18 (20)

Here we have a twofold object set before us in A and A': 'To deliver thee from the way of the evil man', (A); 'To deliver thee from the strange woman'. (A'). [. . .]

The evil man and the strange woman are characterized, in A and A', respectively, by their speech or words. 'From the man that speaketh forward things'; 'From the stranger that flattereth with her words'. Thus the end of A' answers to the end of A, as well as the beginning of A' to the beginning of A.

In B and B', the persons spoken of in A and A' respectively, are described at length. 'Who forsake the paths of uprightness,' &c. (B) 'Who forsaketh the guide of her youth', &c. (B'). The conclusions of B and B' correspond, as well as the beginnings; both referring to the ways, or paths, of the persons described. Thus at the end of B, we [p. 15] have, 'Whose ways are crooked, and they froward in their *paths*'; and at the end of B' (following the order of the Hebrew), 'And unto the dead her *paths*'. Thus, the end of B' corresponds to the end of B, as well as the beginning of B' to the beginning of B.

The terms at the beginning of A, B, A' and B', may be called *leading terms*; and it is important to observe the use of these leading terms in making out to us the beginnings of corresponding passages. Something of this kind I have already had occasion to point out more than once; but the present instance is, perhaps, more remarkable than any of the preceding.

A | [12] To deliver thee, &c.
         B | [13-15] Who forsake, &c.
A' |16 To deliver thee, &c.
         B' | [17,18] Who forsaketh, &c.

Thus the beginnings of A and A' correspond, and also those of B and B'; and adopting the division, of which these leading terms give us an intimation, we discover two objects proposed in A and A', 'To deliver thee from the way of the evil man,' 'To deliver thee from the strange woman'; and two descriptions given in B and B' 'Who forsake the paths of uprightness', &c. 'Who forsaketh the guide of her youth', &c.

As we proceed, we shall become more and more convinced of the importance of these leading terms. The leading term serves as a kind of catchword to introduce the whole clause or member; and a correspondence in leading terms often serves to distinguish corresponding members, and thus helps us to discover them.

Nor it is of less importance that we should attend to the *final* terms and phrases. In these also there is often a correspondence, of great assistance to us in determining the limits [p. 16] of corresponding members. Somewhat of this correspondence in final terms and phrases, I have pointed out in the passage from Proverbs now under consideration.

A | [12] .... from the man that speaketh froward things.
    B | [13-15] .... and they froward in their paths.
A' | 16 ....from the stranger that flattereth with her words.
    B' | [17,18] .... and unto the dead her paths.

Thus A and A', B and B', respectively, correspond in their final, as well as in their leading terms; and, adopting the division thus marked out for us, we find a twofold object or design in A and A', and a twofold description in B and B'.

[p. 19]

A   [8] My son, hear the instruction of thy father, and forsake not the law of thy mother:
        B   [9] *For* they shall be an ornament of grace unto thy head, and chains about thy neck.

A'   [10] My son, if sinners entice thee, consent thou not. [11] If they say, 'Come with us, let us lay wait for blood, let us lurk privily for the innocent without cause; [12] Let us swallow them up alive, as the grave, and whole, as those that go down into the pit; [13] We shall find all precious substance, we shall fill our houses with spoil; [14] Cast in thy lot among us, let us all have one purse:' [15] My son, walk not thou in the way with them, refrain thy feet from their path:
        B'   [16] *For* their feet run to evil, and make haste to shed blood.
            [17] (Surely in vain the net is spread in the sight of any bird.)
            [18] And they lay wait for their own blood; they lurk privily for their own lives. [19] So are the ways of every one that is greedy of gain; which taketh away the life of the owners thereof.

Prov. 1.8-19 (23)

Here in A and A' we have a twofold exhortation, and in B [p. 20] and B' a twofold motive for compliance. The exhortation in A is, 'My son, hear the instruction of thy father, and forsake not the law of thy mother'. Then follows in B the motive or inducement to comply, 'FOR they shall be an ornament of grace unto thy head, and chains about thy neck'. The exhortation in A' is, 'My son, if sinners entice thee, consent thou not,' (beginning),... 'My son, walk not thou in the way with them, refrain thy foot from their paths', (end). Then follows in B' the inducement to comply with this second exhortation; 'FOR their feet run to evil, and make haste to shed blood' &c. The beginning of A and A' correspond; 'Hear, my son, the instruction of thy father', 'My son, if sinners entice thee, consent thou not',: and the beginnings of B and B' have the particle 'For'. 'FOR they shall be an ornament', &c.; 'FOR their feet', &c.

[p. 21]

It will be objected, perhaps, to these alternate arrangements, that, after all, they exhibit nothing more than we are likely to meet with in every regular composition; an orderly succession of ideas expressed in orderly terms. For instance, in the passage already cited,

> a Then the children of Ammon were gathered together,
>   b And encamped in Gilead:
> a' And the children of Israel assembled themselves together,
>   b' and encamped in Mizpeh.[18]

It may be said, What have we here but a sentence constructed with rather more than the usual attention to regularity? I answer, If we met with only one such a sentence, and that in any book, we should think it a remarkable one, but if we meet with many such, and that in a book which we are bound to study with particular attention, then their frequent occurrence can but be a circumstance deserving our express notice and regard.

[p. 22]

It may be said, such arrangements are obvious. No doubt they are obvious when pointed out. But I believe, in the ordinary reading of the Scriptures, they are constantly overlooked. It is certain they have been, in many instances, overlooked by the translators; for we frequently find the corresponding or identical terms of parallel members translated with so little regard to their mutual reference, that the correspondence, however obvious in the original, in the altered garb of the version is completely lost; and that, in some instances, to the no small detriment of the sense and import of the passage. Nor will I allow that even in the original the arrangement is always so obvious. On the contrary, it is only to be discovered, in many instances, by study and examination. In such cases, our knowledge of the force and purport of a passage often depends upon our knowledge of its

18. Jdg. 10.17 (11.); quoted p. 9 [Boys' note; see above, p. 95].

arrangement; and it is not till we are in possession of the arrangement that we are really in possession of the sense. The idea that such alternate correspondences as I have been exhibiting, are obvious of themselves, and therefore need no exhibition, has certainly been carried too far. With regard to some shorter passages of Scripture it may be correct; though even there the regular construction of periods, for want of being exhibited, has been by no means sufficiently attended to. But in many longer passages, I believe, there exists a demonstrable arrangement, which, so far from being obvious, has perhaps *never* been noticed. The first chapter of Proverbs is a well-known passage of Scripture, being the first evening lesson for the twenty-first Sunday after Trinity: yet how many of my readers, I will ask, have noticed the methodical arrangement, just pointed out, prevailing in a considerable portion of this very chapter; two exhortations, with motives or inducements for each? And similar questions might be asked respecting other passages.—But I will not confine myself to these longer portions. I allege, that in shorter passages, passages consisting of only a single verse, or less than [p. 23] a verse, there sometimes exists an alternate arrangement of no very obvious kind till it be pointed out; but, when it is pointed out, of material, nay, of essential use, in developing the writer's meaning. And, be it observed, since this is the case, it is also necessary to point out similar arrangements in passages where they are more obvious: in order that we may not be charged with inventing a peculiar kind of arrangement for the sake of clearing up a difficulty; and in order to show that we are only exhibiting that kind of arrangement, which commonly prevails.

Various passages have been adduced by preceding writers, in which the alternate mode of arrangement clears up the meaning; and lays open a complicate [sic] idea, if I may so say, by disentangling or unravelling it. On this subject let me be permitted to quote, entire, a passage from which I have partly borrowed in my former work:—

'Sometimes, in the alternate quatrain, by a peculiar artifice of construction, the third line forms a continuous sense with the first, and the fourth with the second. Of this variety a striking example occurs in Bishop Lowth's Nineteenth Praelection. Its distinguishing feature, however, is not there sufficiently noted: more justice has been done to the passage by Mr Parkhurst, (Heb. Lexicon, *voce para'*), whose translation follows:

> I will make mine arrows drunk with blood;
>> And my sword shall devour flesh:
> With the blood of the slain and the captive;
>> From the hairy head of the enemy.

Deut. 32.42

That is, reducing the stanza to a simple quatrain:

> I will make mine arrows drunk with blood;
> With the blood of the slain and the captive:
> And my sword shall devour flesh;
> From the hairy head of the enemy.

[p. 24]

Again,

> From without, the sword shall destroy;
>> And in the inmost apartments terror;
> Both the young man and the virgin;
>> The suckling, with the man of gray hairs.

Deut. 32.25

The youths and virgins, led out of doors by the vigour and buoyancy natural at their time of life, fall victims to the sword in the streets of the city: while infancy and old age, confined by helplessness and decrepitude to the inner chambers of the house, perish there by fear, before the sword can reach them.' (Sacred Literature, p. 29, 30. See also p. 378).

We are then referred to a similar hyperbaton in Isaiah.

> a The sword of the Lord is filled with blood;
>> b It is made fat with fatness:
> a' With the blood of lambs and goats;
>> b' With the fat of the kidneys of rams.

Isa. 34.6

Here we have the same connection between the first and third lines, and between the second and fourth, as in the two preceding examples; that is, in a and a', the blood; in b and b' the fat.

The same sort of alternate correspondence seems to have been discovered by Bishop Lowth in Isaiah 51.20; the first part of which verse points and renders thus:—

> Thy sons lie astounded; they are cast down;
> At the head of all the streets, like the oryx taken in the toils.

That is, connecting the corresponding portions:

> Thy sons lie astounded, at the head of all the streets;
> They are cast down, like the oryx taken in the toils.

Not that it would be right actually to make this transposition [p. 25] in the Sacred Text. The object in making it here is to show the alternate connection. [. . .]

[p. 26]

Let us now pass on from the alternate to the introverted [p. 27] arrangement.—The reader will remember that I began by pointing out a very remarkable difference in the construction of the parallel couplets. Some admit of an *alternate* arrangement; and the consideration of these introduced us to the various alternate correspondences which we have now been examining. But others, on being subdivided, were found to fall into an *introverted* form. Such was the case with the couplet,

> They provoked him to jealousy with strange gods;
> With abominations provoked they him to anger.

Deut. 32.16

That is,

a	They provoked him to jealousy	
	b	With strange gods;
	b'	With abominations
a'	Provoked they him to anger.	(1)

Here the arrangement is no longer alternate, but introverted: a', the last member, answering to a, the first; and b', the third, to b, the second. It is, then, to these introverted arrangements that our attention is now to be directed.

Constructions of this kind are much more common in the Hebrew Scriptures than many persons are aware. In general, the extreme fidelity of our translators has preserved the arrangement of the original.

a	For the vineyard of the Lord of Hosts	
	b	Is the house of Israel;
	b'	And the men of Judah
a'	His pleasant plant.	

Isa. 5.7 (2)

The house of Israel and the men of Judah appear in the centre; the vineyard of the Lord of Hosts and his pleasant plant, in the extremes.

> *Boys gives here twelve other examples of introverted parallelism, in short texts.*

[p. 30]

I proceed to other examples, in which the corresponding members are somewhat longer, and not always symmetrical. The character of the arrangement, however, still continues the same; that is, introverted.

a For my thoughts are not your thoughts,
    b   Neither are your ways my ways, saith the Lord.
    b'   For as the heavens are higher than the earth, so are
         my ways higher than your ways,
a' And my thoughts than your thoughts.

Isa. 55.8-9 (15)

This passage is longer than the preceding ones; and there is not that symmetry, in its corresponding members, which we connect with the idea of parallelism. Still the correspondence is evident. We have 'My thoughts' and 'Your thoughts', both in a and in a'; 'My ways' and 'Your ways', both in b and b'.

[p. 34]

I am speaking [now] of those particular cases of introversion, in which two distinct topics are proposed, and afterwards resumed. Sometimes the two topics thus proposed, are two kinds or classes of persons. [. . .]

[p. 35]

a   Now there was long war between the house of Saul,
    b   And the house of David.
        b'   But David waxed stronger and stronger,
a'   And the house of Saul waxed weaker and weaker.

2 Sam. 3.1 (26)

Saul in a and a'; David in b and b'.

The next passage is much longer, but it partakes of the same character.

A   [3] Neither let the son of the stranger, that hath joined himself to the Lord, speak, saying, 'The Lord hath utterly separated me from his people':

      B   Neither let the eunuch say, 'Behold, I am a dead tree'.

      B'   [4] For thus saith the Lord unto the eunuchs that keep my sabbaths, and choose the things that please me, and take hold of my covenant: [5] Even unto them will I give in mine house and within my walls a place and a name better than of sons and of daughters: I will give them an everlasting name, that shall not be cut off.

A'   [6] Also the sons of the stranger that join themselves to the Lord, to serve him, and to love the name of the Lord, to be his servants, every one that keepeth the sabbath from polluting it, and taketh hold of my covenant: [7] Even them will I bring to my holy mountain, and make them joyful in my house of prayer: their burnt-offerings and their sacrifices shall be accepted upon mine altar; for mine house shall be called an house of prayer for all people.

Isa. 56.3-7 (27)

Here we have the sons of the stranger, in a and a'; the eunuchs in b and b'. The leading terms sufficiently mark the arrangement.

a   (3–) Neither let the son of the stranger, that hath joined himself to the Lord, &c.
   b   (–3)   Neither let the eunuch, &c.
   b'   (4-5)   For thus saith the Lord unto the eunuchs, &c.
a' (6-7) Also the sons of the stranger, that join themselves to the Lord, &c.

Here we may make the same remark as on a former occasion. Two kinds of persons are set before us in a and b; the son of the stranger in a, the eunuchs in b. Reading on, we find a promise first given to the latter: 'For thus saith the Lord unto the eunuchs', &c. This leads us to expect [p. 36] that we shall afterwards find a promise to the former. Nor are we disappointed: the promise to the sons of the stranger follows; 'Also the sons of the stranger', &c.

[p. 37]

The instances of introverted arrangement which have hitherto been given in the present work, consist of no more than four members each. There are, however, similar ones of six members, or more. Take, for instance, the following example:—

a   Ashkelon shall see it, and fear;
   b   Gaza also, and be very sorrowful;
      c   And Ekron:
      c'   For her expectation shall be ashamed;
   b'   And the king shall perish from Gaza;
a'   And Ashkelon shall not be inhabited.

Zech. 9.5 (32)

Here we have Ashkelon in a and a', Gaza in b and b', Ekron in c and c'.

It is also, I believe, by having recourse to the introverted and six-membered form, that we must arrange the following catalogue of Abraham's riches. 'And he had sheep and oxen, and he asses, and menservants, and maidservants, and she asses, and camels.' (Gen. 12.16.) Can any thing appear less methodical, at least according to our ideas of method, than this catalogue? Why mention the asses before the menservants, then the maidservants, and then the she asses? But arrange the passage according to the scriptural method, and every thing appears in its place.

a   And he had sheep and oxen,
   b   And he asses,
      c   And menservants,
      c'   And maidservants,
   b'   And she asses
a'   And camels. (33)

Here we have maidservants in c' answering to menservants in c; she asses in b' answering to he asses in b; and camels in a' answering to sheep and oxen in a.

In one respect there seems to be some little want of symmetry; namely, that we have two particulars, 'sheep and oxen', in the first member, a; but only one in each of the [p. 38] succeeding members, b, c, &c. In the Hebrew, however, sheep and oxen here go together as one kind of property; and therefore the two words are coupled together by a makkaph or hyphen, [. . .] (as if we were to write them 'sheep-and-oxen'). Thus we have one sort of property in a, and another sort of property, corresponding to it, in a': and a' answers to a, as well as b' to b, and c' to c.

[p. 39]

Various instances, also, might be given, of arrangements extending to eight members. Let the four following suffice.[19]

a   And he shall take the cedar wood, and the hyssop, and the
       scarlet;
  b   And the living bird;
    c   And dip them in the blood of the slain bird, and
                    in the running water,
                        d   And sprinkle the house seven times.
                        d'   And he shall cleanse the house,
    c'   With the blood of the bird, and with the running
                    water,
  b'   And with the living bird,
a'   And with the cedar wood, and with the hyssop, and with the
       scarlet.

Lev. 14.51-52 (36)

Here, in a and a', we have the cedar wood, the hyssop, and the scarlet; in b and b', the living bird; in c and c', the blood of the slain bird, and the running water; in d and d', the house.

[p. 41]

If those who have but loose notions on subjects connected with the Sacred Text, should be disposed to say of the alternate arrangements, previously considered by us, that they are merely casual, they will not probably hazard a similar assertion respecting these introverted forms. Here we have the most evident traces of art, contrivance, and design. It has been said, respecting the specimens which have been adduced from one, in particular, of the sacred writers, namely, St. Paul, that these specimens must be imaginary, because that writer composed hastily and was unmethodical. But this is perhaps as bare a *petitio principii* as was ever employed to put down the truth.—I would only observe, at present, that the introverted, as well as the alternate ar-rangement, is sometimes of considerable service to us, in the expla-nation of difficult passages, and in the [p. 42] unravelling of such as are complicated. A few examples it will be well to offer.

19. Only the first of these four examples is reproduced here; the others are Num. 15.35-36; Isa. 60.1-3; Lev. 24.16-22.

a   The incense that ye burned in the cities of Judah, and
        in the streets of Jerusalem,
    b   Ye, and your fathers, your kings, and your
                princes, and the people of the land,
    b'   Did not the Lord remember them,
a'   And came it not into his mind?

Jer. 44.21 (40)

Here we immediately perceive that the 'them', in b', refers to b. But
if, passing on to a', the last member, we were to ask a person what it
was that 'Came into the Lord's mind', he would probably answer, in
general terms, The idolatry of the Israelites, their bad conduct, spoken
of in the preceding members; not perceiving that a' has a particular
reference to the *incense* spoken of in a.—'Did not the Lord remember
them?' that is, 'Your fathers', &c. (b): 'And came it not into his mind?'
that is, 'The incense that ye burned', &c. (a). This is clear from the
Hebrew of a', *watta‘ᵃleh ‘al-libbô* [lit. 'came it not into his mind' in a']:
ta‘ᵃleh ['came'] evidently referring to *kiṭṭēr*, the incense, in a.

[p. 43]

a   And ye shall make no league with the inhabitants of this land;
    b   Ye shall throw down their altars.
    b'   But ye have not obeyed my voice;
a'   Why have ye done this?

Judg. 2.2 (42)

In a we have a thing forbidden, 'Ye shall make no league', &c.; in b
a thing commanded, 'Ye shall throw down their altars'. The guilt of
the Israelites, in each particular, appears in b' and a'. They had done
that which was forbidden, ('Why have ye *done* this?' a'). They had left
undone that which was commanded, ('Ye have not obeyed my voice,'
b'). Thus a' answers to a, and b' to b.

[p. 44]

Let us take another example.

a   And he called the name of the place Massah,
    b   And Meribah,
    b'   Because of the chiding of the children of Israel,
a'   And because they tempted the Lord.

Exod. 17.7 (44)

The place was called Massah (*massâ*) because of their tempting the
Lord (*nassōtām*) and Meribah (*mᵉrîbâ*) because of their chiding (*rîb*).
—Thus, in order to discover the sense of the passage, it is necessary to
observe the correspondence of a and a', and also that of b and b'.

Thus an attention to the arrangement of a passage will often help us to discover its sense or purport.—'These alternate and introverted arrangements', it will be said, 'are not peculiar to the sacred writings, but are to be met with in every regular composition'.

And Boys goes on to quote several examples in other languages.

[p. 46]

Though these forms of composition, then, are neither so frequent nor so extensive in uninspired writings as in the Sacred Scriptures, it cannot be denied that, even in uninspired writings, they are sometimes to be found. But when we do find them, it appears, we must not neglect them, unless we would also neglect the sense. Their occasional occurrence, then, in [p. 47] uninspired works, is no reason whatever why we should disregard their constant occurrence in the Word of God.

[p. 48]

It was my endeavour, in my former work, to show that whole Epistles are composed, and admit of a division, according to the principles here laid down. The attempt is now to be made, with reference to whole Psalms. [. . .]

[p. 50]

With regard to the technicalities of the present work, the term parallelism is still sometimes used, even with reference to the more extensive arrangements. This term was originally employed, only for the purpose of expressing the correspondences prevailing in couplets, clauses, parts of verses, and members of sentences. The doctrine, however, has been since extended, and with it the use of the term. Nor will any serious evil arise from this wider application, if we are aware of the sense in which it is made. Even when two corresponding members of an arrangement do not strictly resemble each other in every part, still, if their correspondence be evident, appearing in their leading topics, in their relative situations, and, in addition to these, perhaps, in their leading and final terms, to express that correspondence I employ the term parallelism. The word may not be thought, in these cases, so strictly applicable, as where the corresponding passages are shorter, and their resemblance more exact. Still the two cases are, in their nature, the same; and a paragraph may be parallel to a paragraph, as well as the end of a verse to its beginning.

I wish to say a few more words on the kind of correspondence, which we may expect to find in the parallel members of longer passages. If, in my former work, I was not sufficiently explicit upon this subject, let me now take to myself the whole blame of any apprehensions, or misapprehensions, that may have arisen from my neglect. The resemblance, I say, in the corresponding members of the larger parallelisms, will not always be found exact in every point; yet still it may be an evident, a demonstrable, and a designed resemblance. On examining, for instance, a Psalm, A B A' B', I find it falls into two parts, A B, and A' B'. Here, A and A' may be two prayers, and B and B' two Thanksgivings; or A and A' two exhortations, and B and B' two reasons or inducements in support of the exhortations; or A and A' may be addresses to the Almighty, B and B' no addresses, but merely descriptions [p. 51] of his attributes, operations, or judgements: then I say, in each of these cases, A and A', and B and B' respectively, though they may not exactly resemble each other in every particular, do certainly correspond. They correspond in their topics; they correspond in their relative situations; and on examination, probably, it will further be found that they correspond in their leading terms; I mean, that A and A' begin with the same or similar words or phrases, and also B and B'. If, on examining further, we find that they also correspond in their final terms; that A and A', and B and B', respectively, not only begin, but end alike; and if, on a still closer comparison, we find other corresponding terms besides those at the beginnings and the ends: then, taking all these particulars together, the correspondence in respect to topics, the correspondence in respect to relative situations, the correspondence in respect to leading terms, in respect to final terms, and also in respect to other and intervening terms, this is as strong a case of parallelism as in most instances we now have to offer. Nor do I allege that there is a concurrence of even all these circumstances in every case. This, indeed, would be too much to expect.

Such is the character of the correspondences and resemblances which I profess to exhibit in the Psalms. The advantages of knowing and observing them are, I conceive, indisputable. They will not always tell us, indeed, whether David wrote the Psalm at Gath or at Mahanaim: but they will tell us what he was writing about; what was the plan of the composition, and what its drift or purport; where its various topics begin, where they terminate, and at what point they are resumed. And on these grounds it is that I call my theory a key to the interpretation of the Psalms.

It will also, I trust, appear evident to the candid reader, that the arrangements which I offer exist in the Psalms considered; that they are not my own, but those of the Sacred Writer: and [p. 52] this, even in those cases where is little more than a general or relative correspondence, and where the resemblance of particular members is the least obvious. Let me be allowed to illustrate my views on this subject. There is no *absolute* likeness between a crown and a sceptre, between a camel and an elephant, a mattock and a ploughshare, a lily and a rose. There is, however, a *relative* likeness, or a correspondence; that is, if on one side we had a crown, a camel, a mattock, and a lily, and on the other side, a rose, a ploughshare, an elephant, and a sceptre; and if we were desirous to arrange these objects, after the most suitable method, in four pairs, it is evident that the sceptre would go with the crown, the elephant with the camel, the ploughshare with the mattock, and the rose with the lily. And further, this would not only be an allowable arrangement: it would be *the* arrangement, (for this is the point we are now to bear in mind), there would be a manifest correspondence in the various objects on each side, which would demand this arrangement and no other. And the moment we made it, its propriety would appear. We should have the two emblems of royalty, the two quadrupeds, the two instruments of agriculture, and the two flowers of the garden. Moreover, in point of order, the arrangement would be attended with great advantage. The four first objects, the crown, the camel, the mattock, and the lily, by themselves present a mere jumble of incongruous images. So also do the four second. But the four couples go off in regular order. We have now arranged our Noah's ark in pairs, and the jumble exists no longer. Hence the advantage of attending to that relative likeness, or correspondence, of which I am now speaking. At the same time, however, it must be observed, that I here understate the question as far as the Psalms are concerned; for in most instances, as we shall find, there is not only this relative likeness in the corresponding members, but a greater or less degree of actual resemblance; a resemblance [p. 53] sometimes of a very striking kind, though not always amounting to that exact symmetry or conformity, which we occasionally observe in the corresponding members of shorter passages.

These remarks have been offered, in explanation of the sense in which I employ the term parallelism. [. . .]

[p. 54]

It being the main object of the present work to exhibit the construction of the whole Psalms, the niceties of arrangement in shorter passages will not always be noticed. Single members of the longer parallelisms often admit of subdivision, as couplets, triplets, or even as alternate or introverted parallelisms in themselves. This is in some measure a separate subject, though the principle of the arrangement is much the same in both cases. In referring to the more delicate task of subdivision, 'Sacred Literature' is the work to which our attention is naturally directed: a work to which we are particularly indebted, for exhibiting with so much originality, power, and conviction, the important doctrine of the introverted parallelism. This is the grandest step, perhaps, that has yet been made, towards the recovery of the true principles of biblical composition.

CHAPTER 1   [p. 55]

ALTERNATE ARRANGEMENTS OCCURRING IN THE PSALMS

One instance of a parallel couplet from the Psalms, admitting of an alternate division has been already given.[20]

[p. 56]

[. . .] Perhaps, it will be best to begin with those cases, in which the corresponding members take up two distinct subjects. For instance:[. . .]

[p. 57]

   a   They that sow in tears,
               b   Shall reap in joy.

   a'   He that goeth forth and weepeth, bearing precious seed,
               b'   Shall doubtless come again with rejoicing, bringing
                       his sheaves with him.

                                   Ps. 126.5-6 (4)

Two topics are here set before us, in a and in b; and afterwards taken up in order and expounded, in a' and b'. First comes the sowing in tears, in a. This subject is resumed in a' 'He that goeth forth and weepeth', (here we have the 'tears',) 'bearing precious seed', (here we have the 'sowing'.)—Then comes the reaping in joy, in b; and this part of the subject is resumed in b' 'Shall doubtless come again with

---

20. *A Key*, p. 4 (quoted above, pp. 92-93).

rejoicing', (here we have the 'joy',) 'bringing his sheaves with him', (here we have the 'reaping'.)—Thus a' answers to a, and b' to b.—A very observable distinction seems also to be intended in the following passage; though it may not immediately strike us.

a Mine enemies speak evil of me, 'When shall he die, and his name perish?'
b   And if he come to see me, he speaketh vanity: his heart gathereth iniquity to itself: when he goeth abroad, he telleth it.

a' All that hate me, whisper together against me; against me do they devise my hurt: 'An evil disease', say they, 'cleaveth fast unto him; and now that he lieth he shall rise up no more'.
b'   Yea, mine own familiar friend, in whom I trusted, which did eat of my bread, hath lifted up his heel against me.

Ps. 41.6-10 (5)

The distinction appears to be, that a and a' refer to the enemies of the Psalmist, b and b' to a false friend.—The persons, spoken of in a and a', are described as enemies at the beginning of those members. 'Mine enemies', (beginning of a): 'All that hate me', (beginning of a')—But the individual who appears in b and b' is evidently a false *friend*. In b', indeed, we find the term employed: 'Yea, mine own familiar *friend*'. But friendly intercourse is intimated both in b and b' 'If he come to see me', (b): 'Which did eat of my bread', (b').

[p. 58]

Neither let us neglect the circumstance of our finding the plural number in a and a', but the singular number in b and b' —In a and a', I say, we have the plural number. 'Mine *enemies*', (a): 'All that hate me', '*They* devise', '"An evil disease", say they', (a')—But in b and b', the singular number appears throughout. 'If *he* come', '*He* speaketh', 'His heart', 'He goeth', 'He telleth', (b): 'Mine own familiar friend ... hath lifted up his heel', &c. (b')—This alternation of the plural and singular numbers is an additional proof of the correspondence of a and a', and b and b', respectively.

a and a' correspond in their leading terms. 'Mine enemies speak evil of me,' 'All that hate me whisper together against me'. Both in a and a', also, the Psalmist tells us what his enemies say; that is, he gives us their words. 'Mine enemies speak evil of me, "When will he die?"' &c. 'An evil disease', they say, 'cleaveth fast unto him', &c. (a') The subject of their conversation is his expected dissolution, in both instances.

Rhetorical Analysis

There is a reason, in the nature of things, for the change from plural to the singular number, in passing from a to a', and from b to b'. The Psalmist complains of numerous enemies, but only one false friend. This is a rarer, as it is a more odious character.—There were many Pharisees, Scribes, and priests, but only one Judas. And it is with reference to Judas, that our Saviour quotes the conclusion of the very passage now before us (Jn 13, 18).

These are instances, in which the alternate numbers treat of two distinct subjects. There are other alternate arrangements, in which the distinction lies between assertion and negation; or in which one pair of members has a positive, and the other a negative character.

[p. 59]

[...] In the following instance, the negative members take the precedence.

> a He will not suffer thy foot to be moved: he that keepeth thee will not slumber: behold, he that keepeth Israel shall neither slumber nor sleep.
>
>> b The Lord is thy keeper, the Lord is thy shade, upon thy right hand.
> a' The sun shall not smite thee by day, nor the moon by night.
>> b' The Lord shall keep thee from all evil, he shall keep thy soul, the Lord shall keep thy going out and thy coming in, from this time forth and even for evermore.

Ps. 121.3-8 (7)

Here a and a' are negative; b and b' positive.—The negative character pervades the whole of a, in which we have three clauses, all of this description. (1) 'He will not suffer thy foot to be moved.' (2) 'He that keepeth thee will not slumber.' (3) 'Behold, he that keepeth thee will not slumber nor sleep.'—In a', again, we have negation. 'The sun shall not smite thee by day, nor the moon by night.'—But, passing from a and a' to b and b', we discover the negative character no longer. Here the whole is positive. First b:

The Lord is thy keeper,	
	Upon thy right hand.
The Lord is thy shade,	

Then b', similar in construction as well as character,

[p. 60]

The Lord shall keep thee from all evil,	From this
He shall keep thy soul,	time and
The Lord shall keep thy going out and thy	for
coming in,	evermore.

Thus the positive character prevails in b and b', as well as the negative in a and a': a' answering to a, and b' to b—The leading terms also of b and b' are similar, especially in the Hebrew: *YHWH Šōmrekā, YHWH yišmār^ekā* [...]

The next example, which is very similar, extends to a whole Psalm.

[p. 61]

PSALM 101

A   [1] I will sing of mercy and judgment; unto thee, O Lord, will I sing. [2] I will behave myself wisely in a perfect way. O, when wilt thou come unto me? I will walk within my house with a perfect heart.

     B   [3] I will set no wicked thing before mine eyes: I hate the work of them that turn aside; it shall not cleave to me. [4] A froward heart shall depart from me; I will not know a wicked person. [5] Whoso privily slandereth his neighbour, him will I cut off: him that hath an high look and a proud heart will not I suffer.

A'   [6] Mine eyes shall be upon the faithful of the land, that they may dwell with me: he that walketh in a perfect way, he shall serve me.

     B'   [7] He that worketh deceit shall not dwell within my house: he that telleth lies shall not tarry in my sight. [8] I will early destroy all the wicked of the land; that I may cut off all wicked doers from the city of the Lord.

(1)

The whole of this Psalm is a promise, or a declaration of the Psalmist's resolutions and intentions. There is, however, a distinction of an obvious kind. In A and A', the first and third members, the Psalmist sets forth what he will do, and whom he will encourage; in B and B', the second and fourth, what he will avoid, and whom he will discourage and destroy.

In order to perceive the truth of this representation, it will be necessary for the reader to examine the several members for himself. In A the Psalmist says, 'I will sing', &c. 'I will behave myself wisely',

&c. 'I will walk', &c.—So again, in A', 'Mine eyes shall be upon the faithful', &c. 'He shall serve me'.—But B and B', on the contrary, set forth what the Psalmist disapproves, and whom he will avoid, discountenance, or suppress. 'I will set *no* wicked thing', &c. 'I *hate* the work of them', &c. 'Whoso privily slandereth will I *cut off*'. 'Him that hath an high look will I *not suffer*.' 'He that worketh deceit *shall not dwell* within my house', &c. 'I will *destroy* all the wicked', &c. 'That I may *cut off* all wicked doers'.

A 'perfect way', (*dērek tamîm*), is spoken of both in A and A'—The reader will also observe many correspondences in B and B'. In each of these members the Psalmist describes the persons whom he will discountenance or destroy. Thus in B he speaks of 'The work of them that turn aside', (*'aśōh sēṭîm*) [p. 62] in B', of him 'That worketh deceit', (*'ōśēh rᵉmiyyâ*). In B he says, 'I will set no wicked thing *before mine eyes*', in B', 'He that telleth lies shall not tarry *in my sight*'. The Hebrew expression is the same in both instances, *lᵉneged 'ênay* (3, 7)— It is also the same Hebrew word, *'aṣmît*, which is rendered in B to 'cut off', (5.) and in B', to 'Destroy', (8.) In the Hebrew, too, there is something very symmetrical in the opening clauses of B and B', though it would be difficult to preserve the resemblance in a translation.

Lō' 'āśît lᵉneged 'enay dᵉbar-bᵉliyyā 'al
Lō' yēšēb bᵉqereb betî 'ōśēh rᵉmiyya

[. . .]

It sometimes happens, in the alternate arrangement, that the distinction is of a nicer kind, and lies in a change of persons; as in the following instance.

[p. 63]

a   For thou wilt lighten my candle:[21]
   b   The Lord my God will enlighten my darkness.
a' For by thee I have run through a troop:
   b'   And by my God have I leaped over a wall.

Ps. 18.29-30 (9)

Here the distinction is, that the Psalmist, in a and a', the first and

---

21. The translation follows the partition of the two stychs by Boys. Most people use the partition of the masoretic text:

For thou wilt lighten my candle, Lord;
my God will enlighten my darkness.

third members, speaks *to* the Almighty; and in b and b', the second and the fourth, speaks *of* him. It will be said, perhaps, that b and b', are, in reality, as much an address to the Almighty as a and a'. But what I mean is, that in a and a' the Psalmist employs the second person, 'For *thou* wilt lighten my candle', 'For by *thee* I have run through a troop'; but in b and b' the third, 'The Lord my God will enlighten', &c. 'By my God have I leaped', &c. Thus, though there is a change of persons, there is no irregularity: the change taking place twice in order; and the result being a regular arrangement; a' answering to a, and b' to b.

'*Mira est personarum confusio*' is, I believe, the remark of Bishop Hare, on a passage in the forty-ninth Psalm. With this Psalm I do not at present meddle. But where there is this marvellous confusion, we are sometimes able to reduce it, by the help of our brackets and parallels, to as marvellous a regularity. And the change of persons, which often appears to be needless, and sometimes to perplex the sense, is, in many cases, the key to an arrangement, which lays open the whole plan and purport of the passage in which it occurs.

This change of persons we have already traced in a passage of two verses. Let us now proceed to consider it as the principle of composition in entire Psalms.

PSALM 128 [p. 64]

A   ¹ Blessed is every one that feareth the Lord; that walketh in his ways.

    B   ² For thou shalt eat the labour of thine hands: happy shalt thou be, and it shall be well with thee. ³ Thy wife shall be as a fruitful vine by the sides of thine house: thy children like olive plants, round about thy table.

A'   ⁴ Behold, thus shall the man be blessed, that feareth the Lord.

    B'   ⁵ The Lord shall bless thee out of Zion: and thou shalt see the good of Jerusalem all the days of thy life. ⁶ Yes, thou shalt see thy children's children, and peace upon Israel. (II)

In this Psalm we have an alternate parallelism of four members, A, B, A', B': the third member, A', answering to the first A; and the fourth, B', to the second, B.

The principle of the arrangement is this. In A and A', the first and third members, the man 'that feareth the Lord', is spoken *of*; in B and B', the second and fourth, he is spoken *to*. Thus A and A' go together; and also B and B'.

On casting the eye over the above arrangement, its propriety becomes obvious. In the first and third members, A and A', the blessedness of him that feareth the Lord is simply *declared*. 'Blessed is every one that feareth the Lord', &c. (A) 'Behold, thus shall the man be blessed that feareth the Lord', (A') But in the second and fourth members, B and B', the nature of the blessing is *particularized*. 'Thou shalt eat the labour of thy hands: happy shalt thou be', &c. (B) 'The Lord shall bless thee out of Zion: and thou shall see the good of [p. 65] Jerusalem', &c. (B') 'Children' are promised in B, and 'Children's children' in B'. But I would principally justify the arrangement given, by the circumstance first alleged; namely, that in the first and third members, the person in question is merely spoken *of*, or described; while, in the second and fourth, he is spoken *to*, or addressed. In one instance, the Psalmist uses the third person; in the other, the second person throughout, as may be seen by casting the eye over B and B'. The following arrangement, then, will represent the plan upon which the Psalm is composed:

$$A^1 \text{ Third person.}$$
$$B^{2-3} \text{ Second person.}$$
$$A'^4 \text{ Third person.}$$
$$B'^{5-6} \text{ Second person.}$$

This distinction of person, I say, is particularly worthy of our attention: as it is a key that will open to us, wholly or in part, the arrangement of several of the Psalms. The advantage is, to be able to see an arrangement where none was before observed. This, surely, must be satisfactory to all who read the Scriptures, and wish to understand what they read. To those whose office it is to preach from the Scriptures, it is not merely matter of satisfaction, but of bounden duty, to ascertain, as far as possible, whatever arrangement prevails in the passages which they select

[p. 69]

It happens, in some instances of alternate arrangement, that the second and fourth members offer two reasons, confirmations, or inducements, in support of what is advanced in the first and third respectively. [. . .]

*After a series of brief examples (Pss. 6.2; 142.6; 143.8; 86.3-4), Boys
moves on to the analysis of entire psalms: first Psalm 96, then Psalm 98:*

PSALM 98   [p. 74]

A   O sing unto the Lord a new song.

   B   *For* he hath done marvellous things: his right hand, and his holy arm,
           hath gotten him the victory. 2 The Lord hath made known his
           salvation, his righteousness hath he openly shewed; in the sight of the
           heathen. 3 He hath remembered his mercy and his truth toward the
           house of Israel: all the ends of the earth have seen the salvation of our
           God.

A'   4 Make a joyful noise unto the Lord, all the earth: make a loud noise, and
        rejoice, and sing praise. 5 Sing unto the Lord with the harp, with the harp and
        the voice of a psalm. 6 With trumpets and sound of cornet make a joyful
        noise before the Lord, the King. 7 Let the sea roar, and the fulness thereof,
        the world, and they that dwell therein. 8 Let the floods clap their hands, let
        the hills be joyful together, 9 Before the Lord.

   B'   *For* he cometh to judge the earth: with righteousness shall he judge
           the world, and the people with equity.[22]

The construction of this Psalm so nearly resembles that of the last
[Psalm 96] that the same arrangement will serve for both.

   A 1— Exhortation to glorify God.
           B —1—3 Inducements.

   A' 4—9— Exhortation to glorify God.
           B' —9 Inducements.

Here the first and third members begin with the corresponding
expressions, 'Sing unto the Lord', 'Make a joyful noise unto the Lord'.
And the second and fourth commence with the particle *kî*, as before
[in Psalm 96]: 'FOR he hath done', 'FOR he cometh'.
[...]

22. Boys separates the first two stychs of the psalm, spreading them between A
and the beginning of B; and he does the same for the two stychs of the beginning of
verse 9, spreading them between the end of A' and the beginning of B'.

[p. 96]

CHAPTER 2
INTROVERTED ARRANGEMENTS OCCURRING IN THE PSALMS

There are some couplets in the book of Psalms, as well as in other parts of the Bible, in which any attempt at *alternate* arrangement would be useless. For instance:

> We are consumed by thine anger,
> And by thy wrath we are troubled.

Ps. 90.7

[p. 97]

Here the arrangement must be *introverted*.

    a   We are consumed
     b   By thine anger,
     b'   And by thy wrath
    a'   We are troubled. (1)

[p. 98]

    a   Blessed be the name of the Lord,
     b   From this time forth and for evermore.
     b'   From the rising of the sun unto the going down of the same,
    a'   The name of the Lord be praised.

Ps. 113.2-3 (6)

The worship due to God's holy name is enjoined in a and a'; the extent to which it is to be rendered, both of time and space, appears in b and b'.[23]

[p. 101]

I have dwelt, in former parts of the present work, upon those examples in which the arrangement turns upon two distinct subjects. Many such are to be found in the Psalms. In some instances, the distinction lies between the righteous and the wicked; as in the following examples:

---

23. In fact, the concentric construction can even be taken a step further, since the last two members answer one another in chiasm:

    THE NAME OF THE LORD
          be blessed
              [...]
          be praised
    THE NAME OF THE LORD.

a   Better is a little that the righteous man hath,

b   Than the riches of many wicked:

b'   For the arms of the wicked shall be broken,

a'   But the Lord upholdeth the righteous.

Ps. 37.16-17 (15)

Similarly in Ps. 11.5-7 (16)

Here we have the righteous in a and a', the wicked in b and b'.

[p. 104]

The next example, though not much longer than this, is an entire Psalm:[24]

PSALM 70

A   Make haste, O God, to deliver me; make haste to help me, O Lord.

B   [2] Let them be ashamed and confounded, that seek after my soul. Let them be turned backward and put to confusion, that desire my hurt. [3] Let them be turned back for a reward of their shame, that say, Aha, Aha.

B'   [4] Let them rejoice and be glad in thee, all that seek thee. And let them say continually, Let God be magnified, that love thy salvation.

A'   [5] But I am poor and needy: make haste unto me, O God. Thou art my help and my deliverer; O Lord, make no tarrying. (1)

I have arranged the Psalm before us as an introverted [p. 105] parallelism of four members, A, B, B', A', for the purpose of intimating that the fourth member, A', answers to the first, A, and the third, B', to the second, B.

The whole of the seventieth Psalm is prayer; but there is this distinction: that the prayer of the Psalmist refers, in the two extreme members, A and A', to himself; and in the two central members, B and B', to others.

In the extreme members, A and A', the Psalmist prays, and that in corresponding terms, for *himself*: saying in A, 'Make haste, O God, to

---

24. The preceeding example was Ps. 18.3-6 (20.). The numbering that Boys added, in between brackets after the references of his examples, is still being used here, so that the reader can appreciate their considerable number; the fact that all these examples cannot be reproduced here might weaken his demonstration, which is for a large part due to the numerous examples that he brings to the attention of his reader.

deliver me; make haste to help me, O Lord'; and in A', 'But I am poor and needy: make haste unto me, O God. Thou art my help and deliverer; O Lord, make no tarrying.' Thus the Psalmist prays for himself, and prays for *speedy* deliverance, both in A and in A'. In A, we have *ḥuša* 'Make haste'; in A', *ḥuša* 'Make haste', *'al-tᵉʻaḥar* 'Make no tarrying'. In both A and A' he speak for help. In A' we have *'ezrî* 'My help', answering to *lᵉʻezrāti* 'To help me', or rather, 'To my help', in A. Such is the mutual correspondence of A and A', in each of which members the prayer of the Psalmist refers to himself.

In B and B', however, his prayer refers to *others*; that is, to the wicked, or his enemies, in B, and to the righteous, or his friends, in B'. 'Let them be ashamed and confounded, that seek after my soul', &c. (B) 'Let them rejoice and be glad in thee, all that seek thee', &c. (B') (*mᵉbakšê nafši* 'That seek after my soul': *mᵉbakšèkā* 'That seek thee'.)

The peculiar and very regular construction, however, of B and B', deserves our attention.

[p. 106]

B	a Let them be ashamed and confounded,
	    a' That seek after my soul.
	b Let them be turned backward, and put to confusion,
	    b' That desire my hurt.
	c Let them be turned back, for a reward of their shame,
	    c' That say, Aha, Aha.

B'	d Let them rejoice and be glad in thee,
	    d' All that seek thee.
	e And let them say continually, Let God be magnified,
	    e' That love thy salvation.

Here we have the Psalmist's petitions, with great regularity, in the five members, a, b, c, d, e; and the persons to whom they refer, with equal regularity, in a', b', c', d', e'. Thus a regularity of construction prevails throughout B and B'; with this distinction, however, that B relates to the enemies of the Psalmist, B' to the righteous, his friends.

Thus A and A' relate to the Psalmist himself, B and B' to others. And, moreover, B and B' are properly separated from one another, because they refer to two different classes of persons. The following, then, is the plan of the Psalmist's prayer:

[p. 107]

A 1 Himself.
> B 2,3 His enemies.
> B' 4 His friends.

A' 5 Himself.

Here the correspondence of the extreme members, A and A', is homogeneous; but that of the central ones, B and B', is antithetical.

Boys moves on to the analysis of Psalm 15 (pp. 107-10), Psalm 89 (pp. 111-17), and Psalm 148 (pp. 117-22), which will not be reproduced here.

PSALM 25 [p. 123]

A [1] Unto thee, O Lord, do I lift up my soul. [2] O my God, I trust in thee. Let me not be ashamed, let not mine enemies triumph over me. [3] Yea, let none that wait on thee be ashamed. Let them be ashamed which transgress without cause. [4] Shew me thy ways, O Lord; teach me thy paths. [5] Lead me in thy truth and teach me: for thou art the God of my salvation; on thee do I wait all the day. [6] Remember, O Lord, thy tender mercies and thy loving-kindnesses; for they have been ever of old. [7] Remember not the sins of my youth, nor my transgressions. According to thy mercy remember thou me, for thy goodness' sake, O Lord.

B [8] Good and upright is the Lord: therefore will he teach sinners in the way. [9] The meek will he guide in judgment; and the meek will he teach his way. [10] All the paths of the Lord are mercy and truth, unto such as keep his covenant and his testimonies.

> C [11] For thy name's sake, O Lord, pardon mine iniquity, for it is great.

B' [12] What man is he that feareth the Lord? Him shall he teach in the way that he shall choose. [13] His soul shall dwell at ease; and his seed shall inherit the earth. [14] The secret of the Lord is unto them that fear him; and he will shew them his covenant.

A' [15] Mine eyes are ever toward the Lord; for he shall pluck my feet out of the net. [16] Turn thee unto me, and have mercy upon me; for I am desolate and afflicted. [17] The troubles of my heart are enlarged: O bring thou me out of my distresses. [18] Look upon mine affliction and my pain, and forgive all my sins. [19] Consider mine enemies; for they are many; and they hate me with cruel hatred. [20] O keep my soul, and deliver me: let me not be ashamed: for I put my trust in thee. [21] Let integrity and uprightness preserve me; for I wait on thee. [22] Redeem Israel, O God, out of all his troubles.

[. . .]

This Psalm partakes of the introverted form: A' the last member, answering to A the first; and B' the last but one, to B the second. The reader, however, will have observed one peculiarity; namely, that in the centre there stands a member, C, with nothing to correspond to it. I have met with similar instances in other parts of the Scriptures. In such cases, there is no want of regularity; as there would be if the single member stood in any part of the arrangement, except the centre. A stone in one side of an arch, must have a corresponding stone in the other side. The keystone alone may [p. 124] be single. I have remarked, that where a solitary member stands thus in the heart of a parallelism, it is usually parenthetical: but this does not appear to be the case in the present instance.

The correspondence of A' to A, and of B' to B, appears in a circumstance, which we have more than once noticed in other examples. In A and A' the Psalmist speaks *to* the Almighty; in B and B' he speaks *of* him.—The whole of A and A', with the exception of one verse to be noticed presently, is an address. Thus, in A, the Psalmist says, 'Unto thee, O Lord, do I lift up my soul', (1.); 'Shew me thy ways, O Lord', &c. (4.); 'Remember, O Lord, thy tender mercies', (6–); and so throughout. In A' the Psalmist begins by saying, 'Mine eyes are ever toward the Lord; for he shall pluck my feet out of the net', (15.) This verse is certainly not, strictly speaking, an address, like the rest of A': but it so evidently corresponds to the beginning of A,

> 'Unto thee, O Lord, do I lift up my soul', (beginning of A)
> 'Mine eyes are ever toward the Lord', (beginning of A')

that I have placed it where it stands, rather than at the end of B'—The whole of the remainder of A' is, like A, an address. 'Turn thee unto me', &c. (16.) 'O bring thou me out of my distresses', (17.) 'Look upon mine affliction', &c. (18.) 'Consider mine enemies', (19.) 'O keep my soul', (20.) 'I wait on thee', (21.) 'Redeem Israel, O God', (22.).

In B and B', on the contrary, the Lord is the Subject of the Psalmist's discourse, no longer the Object of his address. The particular design of the Psalmist, in these two members, is not, as in A and A', to obtain blessings, but to set forth God's general dealings with his people: so that A and A' are supplicatory, B and B' didactic or declaratory. Thus, at the beginning [p. 125] of B, we have, 'Good and upright is the Lord: therefore *will he teach sinners in the way*': and corresponding to this, at the beginning of B', 'What man is he that feareth the Lord? *Him shall he teach in the way* that he shall choose:' So again, at the end of B, we have, 'All the paths of the Lord are mercy and truth, unto such as keep his covenant and his testimonies': and corresponding to this, at the end of B', 'The secret of the Lord is unto them that fear him, and he will shew them his covenant'.—Thus the beginning and end of B' correspond, respectively, to the beginning and end of B.

C, the central member, is supplicatory, like A and A', the extreme ones. In this character, it stands between B and B', partaking of the nature of neither, and separating them on from the other.—The following, then is the arrangement of the Psalm:

> A 1-7 Supplicatory.
>   B 8-10 Didactic.
>   C 11 Supplicatory.
>   B' 12-14 Didactic.
> A' 15-22 Supplicatory.

Boys also analyses Psalms 30, 105 and 135 (pp. 127-43).

Of his long conclusion (pp. 144-65), it will be useful to retain a few short passages. First, it is interesting to note his standpoint on an issue which does not cease to be brought up nowadays, that of the conscience of the author. The first lines of the six pages that he devotes to this problem summarize adequately his position:

[p. 147]

with regard to the correspondences exhibited in the present work, there seem to be several ways of accounting them. We may say that they are merely accidental; we may say that they are evidently designed; or, steering a middle course between these two opinions, we may say, that at the time of composing, there was indeed a degree of perception in the mind of the Author; but that, on the one hand, there was no absolute intention to pursue a peculiar mode of arrangement, while, on the other hand, there was not absolute unconsciousness. For my own part, I see no way of accounting for [p. 148] the various phenomena exhibited, but by supposing positive design and actual intention somewhere.

The following point, what he calls 'the independence of the proofs', is worth quoting in full:

[p. 153]

How far the tokens of arrangement which I have offered, whether in flanks or centre, will be deemed satisfactory, it is not in my power to divine. On one circumstance, however, I may be allowed to insist; namely, that the proofs which I allege are independent one of another. Take, for instance, the following form: —

[p. 154]

```
A {......
    B {.....
        C {.....
            D {......

A' {......
    B' {......
        C' {......
            D' {......
```

Here, perhaps, I am guided to my arrangement, in the first instance, by the *leading terms*; that is, I discover that A and A', and B and B', C and C', D and D', respectively, begin alike: and upon the hint thus furnished me, I place A' in correspondence with A, B' with B, C' with C, &c. But having done this, I next discover a farther correspondence; namely, in the *final terms*; that is, I find that the several pairs of members, A and A', B and B', &c. not only begin, but also end alike. This, then, is a new, and what I call an *independent* proof of the propriety of my arrangement. Presently, however, I make a farther discovery; namely, that there is a correspondence not only in leading and final, but also in *intervening terms*; that is, I find correspondences not only in the opening and final clauses respectively, of the various pairs of members, but also in some of the intervening clauses; A' containing words and phrases answering to words and phrases in A, B' to those in B, &c. Thus, in regard to corresponding terms alone, without coming to the general meaning and purport of the passages, I am able to produce three distinct classes of evidence, attesting the propriety of my arrangement, under the character of leading, final, and intervening terms. I then pass on from terms to *topics*. And on examination it appears, that the same topic appears in A' as in A, the same in B' as in B, &c. Here we have a fourth kind of proof, then, independent of all the preceding. Then also comes the consideration, that the four topics in A, B, C, D, and the four corresponding [p. 155] topics in A', B',

C', D', succeed one another in the same order. Here, then, we derive a farther confirmation and argument from *relative situation*. And then, perhaps, in the last place, I discover, a final evidence, in regard to *corresponding transitions*; that is, there is a transition in passing both from A to B, and from A' to B', from the second to the third person, or *vice versa*; from the singular to the plural, or *vice versa*: there is a corresponding change of speakers again, in passing from B to C, and from B' to C'. In B and B', the Almighty speaks; in C and C', the Psalmist speaks. Thus do I derive my proofs from five or six independent sources; leading, final, and intervening terms; leading topics; relative situation; and corresponding transitions of various kinds. Not that all these proofs meet in every arrangement. It generally happens, however, that where there is less proof of one kind, there we find more of another; and also, that when we have been conducted to the true arrangement of our passage by one sort of proofs, then others come to our aid, and confirm us in the arrangement previously made. In Psalm 128, for instance, we are led, as we have seen, page 64,[25] to make our arrangement, in the first instance, by the change of persons, (the *mira personarum confusio*, as it has been called, but I should rather call it the *lucidus personarum ordo*) the third person appearing in A and in A', and the second in B and B'. But, having made an arrangement upon this principle, we immediately discover, in justification of it, a circumstance of a totally independent character; namely, that A and A', the members in which the person who feareth the Lord is spoken *of*, merely declare his blessedness; while B and B', the members in which he is spoken *to*, particularize the circumstances in which his blessedness consists. And in other cases we find similar confirmations.

> *Boys then insists (pp. 156-58) on the importance of these analyses with regard to understanding and making others understand the sacred texts; in the same way that knowledge of the original language is indispensable, knowledge of the parallelism can be of great use.*
>
> *His conclusion ends with a list of the advantages of parallelism. The first of these is that a study of this type often enables the grasping of otherwise unsuspected relationships between different parts of the text; the second is that knowledge of the true construction of a text is a major trump for the translation, which should respect the formal traits of the original; the third advantage concerns textual criticism, because a serious*

25. In the present work, pp. 115-17.

analysis of the construction enables one to take a standpoint, often critical,
in the face of proposed corrections; the last advantage mentioned is the
ability to refute the frequent allegation that the sacred texts are ill-
composed.

Boys adds, in the end of his book, five appendices. In the first one,
which includes 52 pages (pp. 167-219), he attempts to find external
proofs which would confirm the existence of the uncovered structures.
But from the start he relativizes the scope of his inquiry:

[p. 167]

Since we allege that peculiar modes of arrangement prevail in the
Scriptures, it may be asked, what external evidence we are able to
produce in support of our allegation; whether we have discovered any
intimations of such a circumstance, either in the Scriptures themselves, or in other authentic sources of information?

I would by no means agree to rest the question upon these grounds.
The fact which we allege is only to be proved by the production of
examples, and by the moral and ocular demonstration thus afforded.
And it is upon such evidence that I rest my cause.

From the second appendix, one must quote the following passage
where Boys is manifestly aware that the texts are organized on different
levels:

[p. 220]

Another topic of inquiry is that which relates to Subordinate Parallelism. When I have arranged an integral passage, [p. 221] such as an
Epistle or a Psalm, this, technically speaking, may be called a parallelism of the first order. But if, as we have seen in some instances, any
one member of this parallelism of the first order admits of a separate
and internal arrangement, we have then what I call a parallelism of
the second order. Nay, there may be minor divisions and subdivisions,
down to the arrangement of single verses and couplets. All these, then,
I call by the common name of subordinate parallelisms.

After two more appendices devoted to the analysis of some Jewish
texts and a few Latin sentences where the laws of parallelism are found,
the work ends with a final appendix wherein Boys offers a few exercises
to those who would want to train in the art of discovering how the biblical
texts are composed.

If we can say that Jebb was the inventor of rhetorical analysis, one has
to concede that it is Boys who founded it: he knew how to systematize the
method that he applied, in a remarkably organized long piece of work
(which should be re-edited in full), particularly in detailing all the criteria
that he used.

Friedrich Köster

> Lowth's 'discovery' did not only bear fruit in England. Parallelism of the
> members also gave rise to new developments in Germany. A very few
> years after the work of Jebb and Boys, in 1831, Friedrich Köster[26]
> published a large article where, as Condamin writes:

he exposed, following Lowth's book, what we call the parallelism of
the members; and in a paragraph entitled 'The parallelism of the
verses', he writes: 'We have found that the parallelism of the members
of the verse was probably linked to the double choirs of the oriental
circles (Exod. 15.20). But it is safer to derive it from the great law of
symmetry' (p. 45). Were entire verses and groups of verses, as well as
the members of the verse, not ruled by the law of parallelism? We
have never asked ourselves this question, he writes, and we were
contented with an arbitrary grouping of verse without rule. 'However
it is not only plausible in itself, but it can become self evident by a
careful study *that the verses of Hebrew poetry are subject to the same
rules of symmetry as the members of the verse; and, by the same
token, that this poetry is essentially of the nature of stanzas, i.e. that it
arranges the verses in symmetrical groups*' (p. 47; Koester's emphasis).[27] As Koester has justifiably seen, a hundred years ago, it is the
law of parallelism which rules the groups of verse to form stanzas, as
well as the groups of stichs to form verses. Two or three stichs are
united to form verses; the verses are united, by twos or threes; those
groups, in turn, often in twos or threes as well, are combined to form
stanzas; at last, the arrangement of stanzas makes the poem. *It is
always the meaning which rules those groups.*[28]

> And this is how the 'stanza theory' would know a great success east of
> the Rhine. It is out of the question to follow in detail the development of
> the 'stanza theory' here.[29] Partly because this school, wanting so much to
> find models related to Greek poetry in Hebrew poetry, had finally come to
> a dead-end; also because what was to become 'rhetorical method' did not

---

26. 'Die Strophen oder der Parallelismus der Verse der Hebraischen Poesie',
TSK (1831), pp. 40-114.

27. This is how A. Condamin would present it a century later, in *Poèmes de la
Bible, avec une introduction sur la strophique hébraïque* (Paris: Beauchesne, 1933),
pp. 1-2.

28. Condamin, *Poèmes*, pp. 19-20.

29. See the historical account that Condamin gives of it in *Poèmes*, pp. 2-3.

receive Lowth's heritage through this strand, but through Jebb's and Boys'.[30]

   The starting point of the stanza theory, however, was in fact remarkable: the extension of the laws of parallelism of the members to the superior levels is, indeed, the key to the composition of the texts. The only flaw of Köster's stanza theory—but it is a considerable one and would corrupt the whole system—was to consider that the verse was composed of two or three members (distichs and tristichs), and not to have noticed that there were also verses which are only composed of one member (monostich); also, that the level superior to the verse could be formed of one, two or three verses, and so on and so forth. But such an observation would have in fact ruined the stanza theory and would have by the same token avoided an avenue of research which led to a dead-end.

   Before abandoning this avenue for good to go back to the English tradition, it is nonetheless necessary to acknowledge two German authors of the turn of the century who brought in elements which rallied the discoveries of Jebb and Boys.

David Heinrich Müller

In 1896, David Heinrich Müller, lecturer at the University of Vienna, published a book entitled: *The prophets in their primitive form*, with a subtitle full of promises: *Fundamental laws of primitive Semitic Poetry, established and demonstrated in the Bible, cuneiform inscriptions and the Koran, and found in the choruses of Greek tragedy where their influence was felt.*[31] The essential characteristics of ancient Semitic poetry were, according to Müller, 'the structure of the stanzas and the *responsio*'. [. . .] The stanza is defined as 'a group of lines or verses which, in itself, or in relation to other groups, forms a complete unit' (p. 1). The *responsio* resides in the fact that the stanza and the anti-stanza answer one another by the metre, division of the sentences, the disposition of the members, and frequently also by the thoughts, by identical words or words of similar assonance (p. 2). Add to this, still according to the same author, *concatenatio* repetition, at the beginning of a stanza, of one or more words from the end of the preceding stanza; and *inclusio*, a kind of frame for a stanza,

---

30. On the difference between the two schools, anglo-saxon and continental, see H. Van Dyke Parunak, 'Transitional Techniques in the Bible', *JBL* 102 (1983), pp. 525-48.

31. *Die Propheten in ihrer ursprünglichen Form* (Vienna: Hoebder, 1896).

formed of the repetition of the same words at the beginning and at the end (pp. 3, 200).[32]

Johannes Konrad Zenner

In the same year, 1896, Johannes Konrad Zenner invented what he calls 'the alternating stanza' which will be called by Condamin the 'intermediary stanza'.[33]

John Forbes

But it is necessary to go back some forty years in time to re-integrate the English lines of inquiry inaugurated by Jebb and Boys. In 1854, John Forbes, taking after his predecessors,[34] *wanted to 'introduce a new element, a parallelism of numbers'.*[35] *What he meant was that the inter-related textual units are often of the same length or, for example, that the number of certain lexical recurrences can be relevant. The weakness of several of his demonstrations would by no means jeopardize the truth of his intuition. Following Boys,*[36] *he notes that the function of concentric construction is to heighten the value the centre of the construction: as he would also say in a second publication, 'the central idea may, like a heart, be the* animating centre *of the whole, sending its vitalizing energy and warmth to the very extremities'.*[37] *Like Boys, he notes that the extremities of a unit are often in direct relation with the centre.*

Ethelbert William Bullinger

One should finally note Ethelbert William Bullinger, who publishes in 1890 an analysis of the Psalms based on Boys's notes which completes

32. The above paragraph is taken from Condamin, *Poèmes*, p. 3. Those terms are not Müller's inventions; even if *inclusio* is not his innovation, since it is also found in Donat and Rufin, it remains nonetheless true that it is to Müller that we owe its modern use.

33. We will come back to this theory when we deal with Condamin's work (see below, pp. 136-37).

34. *The Symmetrical Structure of Scripture: Or the Principles of Scripture Parallelism exemplified in an Analysis of the Decalogue, the Sermon on the Mount and Other Passages of the Sacred Writings* (Edinburgh: T. & T. Clark, 1854).

35. *The Symmetrical Structure*, p. 82.

36. Boys was the first to compare the centre of a text to the keystone of an arch (the only stone which is unique and does not have another parallel to it, since it is the one which holds the whole; *A Key*, p. 123 [see above, p. 122]).

37. *Analytical Commentary on the Epistle to the Romans Tracing the Train of Thought by the Aid of Parallelism* (Edinburgh: T. & T. Clark, 1868), p. 82.

them.[38] *All the psalms are thus laid out, accompanied by the diagram of their composition. He ends his book by attempting to find the structure of the* Book of Psalms *as a composed whole. His analyses are often, to say the least, questionable, and his contribution seems to be limited to a better visualization of the page layout: he is the first one to play with typography in order to highlight the symmetries (bold characters, capital letters, italics).*[39]

---

38. *A Key to the Psalms Being a Tabular Arrangement, by which the Psalms are Exhibited to the Eye According to a general rule of Composition Prevailing in the Holy Scripture by the late Rev. Thomas Boys* (London, 1890).

39. Bullinger would also publish a layout of the Book of Job: *The Book of Job* (London: Eyre & Spottiswoode, 1903). K.E. Bailey said the following words about Bullinger which seem totally justified: 'E.W. Bullinger, wrote *The Companion Bible*, in which he discredited the discipline for a full generation' (*Poet and Peasant and Through Peasant Eyes*. II. *Through Peasant Eyes*, p. xix).

Chapter 3

REDISCOVERY AND EXPANSION
(TWENTIETH CENTURY)

*As regards the structure of the Hebrew verse, the theory of the parallelism
of the members presented by Lowth in the middle of the eighteenth century did not see any major development in the next century. If Jebb had
already noted that his 'introverted parallelism' could be found inside the
distichs, we were left, with the work of those who followed Lowth, with
the distinction between synonymous, antithetical and synthetic parallelism, which takes the distich as a whole, solely from a semantic point of
view.*

George Buchanan Gray

*George Buchanan Gray was to turn the problem on its head.[1] He first
classified the distichs according to a purely formal criterion, that of the
number of elements, from those which are composed of only two elements in each stich to those which are composed of six. He then systematically studied the various arrangements used by the poet, which he held
to be measures to bring variety into the text. In the shorter parallel distich,
which contains four elements, the possibilities are reduced to two:*

ab / a'b'   and   ab / b'a'

*The higher the number of elements, the higher the number of possibilities
which are enabled by permutations of symmetrical elements. He then went
on to examine the incomplete parallelism that Schöttgen had already
sketchily described;[2] he makes a distinction between the incomplete
parallelism with compensation and the one without. He concludes his
study by showing the interest of such a thorough analysis for understanding the text and, first of all, for establishing it. It seems that Gray did not
know of the work of Jebb and his successors.*

---

1. *The Forms of Hebrew Poetry* (London, 1915).
2. See above, pp. 55-56.

Charles Souvay

> *Gray's book was to draw the attention of modern-day scholars, since
> David N. Freedman insisted on having it re-edited.[3] This was not the case
> for Charles L. Souvay who, a few years before Gray, published in the
> United States, in French, an* Essai sur la métrique des Psaumes.[4] *Souvay,
> despite a overt independence, is in a straight line with the work inaugu-
> rated by Lowth which was pursued by the German scholars. The image of
> parallelism that he offers is worth quoting here:*

[p. 11]

Very rarely, outside the case where the text has suffered, a stich is
found on its own in the work of the Hebrew poets. So it is possible to
compare the pieces of verse of our holy Books with those necklaces
and tiaras made of coins that the Syrian women used to wear. The
thoughts conceived of by the artist, his spirit beats them on both sides,
and their value is judged as much by the double imprint that they
received as by their true and clear sound of pure metal.

> *As the first words of this quotation seem to suggest, one of the major
> contributions of Souvay is the stress he puts on the monostich verse. He
> acknowledges no less in his preface:*

[p. ii]

Among the conclusions which seem to impose themselves despite
current opinion, I would point out the precisions which were brought
to the question of the mutual relations of the verse and the stich or
colon; the doctrine which is sustained in these pages is the logical con-
sequence of the fact—undeniable in my opinion—of the existence of
the monostich verse.[5]

> *The second point of the work is the remarkable systematization of what
> he calls 'stylistic devices'; that is, the marks of composition of the texts.
> Like Lowth, he starts from the careful examination of alphabetical poems
> in order to establish the existence of the verse (Chapter II, pp. 30-91);
> after a chapter devoted to the 'Rhyme and assonance' (pp. 92-143), he
> goes on to study the 'stylistic devices of the Hebrew verse':*

[p. 144]

The alphabetical and the rhyming pieces are far from constituting
all the poetical literature of the Hebrew. Thanks to them we can find a

---

3. New York: Ktav, 1972.
4. C. Souvay, *Essai sur la métrique des Psaumes* (St-Louis: Séminaire Kenrick,
1911).
5. See also *Essai sur la métrique*, pp. 43, 277.

few traces of the laws which presided over the Hebraic versification; but despite their undeniable importance, they are not the only means at our disposal in our enquiry. The poetical style, indeed, makes use of not only a nobler, rarer and more researched vocabulary, than that of prose, and of more numerous figures of words or thought; but also of certain literary devices destined to produce a special effect on the reader. We have little to do with the vocabulary and figures which pertain to the vivacity and colour of the style, and the harmony of the language. But we should not leave aside the stylistic devices to which we have just alluded.

Let us explain ourselves through a concrete example. One knows the famous piece by André Chénier: *The young 'Tarentine'*. A few verses will suffice, the first two and the beginning of each stanzas:

> Weep, sweet Halcyons, O you, sacred birds,
> Birds dear to Thetys, sweet Halcyons, weep.

> She lived, Myrto, the young 'Tarentine'!
> A ship bore her to the edge of Camarine. . .
> . . . She falls, she shouts, she is in the bosom of the waters.

> She is in the bosom of the waters, the young 'Tarentine'!
> Her beautiful body has rolled under the marine wave. . .

[p. 145]

We realize straightaway that the second verse ends with the word which opens the second: *Weep*. In the first verse, this initial word is followed by a vocative: *sweet Halcyons*; in the second, the final word is preceded by the same vocative: *sweet Halcyons*. Furthermore, there is an obvious parallelism between the two expressions: *O you, sacred birds*, and: *Birds dear to Thetys*. Such that the two verses are each formed by three members which reproduce each other and answer one another following this order: 1, 2, 3 = 3, 2, 1:

> Weep, **sweet Halcyons**, *O you, sacred birds*,
> *Birds dear to Thetys*, **sweet Halcyons**, weep.

From the beginning to the body of the poem, one notes the artistic effect produced by the repetition, at the beginning of the second paragraph, of the last verse of the preceding paragraph:

> She falls, she shouts, *she is in the bosom of the waters*.
> *She is in the bosom of the waters*, the young 'Tarentine'!

Moreover, one will be struck by the verbal correspondence between the first verse of the first stanza:

She lived, Myrto, **the young 'Tarentine'**!

and the first verse of the second:

She is in the bosom of the waters, **the young 'Tarentine'**!

Even if we did not enjoy the help of the typographical processes which have been introduced in the writing of verses in recent years (especially the space between the lines), we would still be able, thanks to the device employed, to find the stanza division of Chénier's poem. For the attention of the analyst would be drawn to the similitude of those two verses, and he would soon count the number of verses which followed and notice that each of those two verses are accompanied by eleven other verses, thus forming two well defined stanzas of twelve verses each.

[p. 146]

One would draw similar conclusions from the analysis of the two initial verses: the peculiar correspondence which flows from it would suggest that, since we are dealing with poetry, we are faced in each of those two lines with one verse. The division of verses in French poetry is undoubtedly shown by the rhyme; but one will concede that in languages where the rhyme is rare or unknown, the study of these literary devices can be of some use to the metricist. [. . .]

[p. 147]

These processes were carefully registered by the grammarians and the patient collectors of stylistic forms. It is not necessary to reproduce this statistical work: it will be enough to choose among these lists, compiled particularly by Mr E. König, the cases which fit our needs.[6] We do not think it is pedantic to accept these categories, which sound learned, under which the various literary devices that can be of use for the metric analysis have been catalogued.

> *He then enumerates a catalogue, with examples, of these 'literary devices' which describe, following a more traditional terminology, the same phenomenon that Boys had called, a century earlier, 'leading terms' and 'final terms':*[7]

6.   E. König, *Stilistik, Rhetorik, Poetik.* . . (Leipzig, 1900) [Souvay's note].
7.   See above, p. 96.

[p. 147]

Anaphora, also called *epanaphora* is the repetition of one or more words at the beginning of several consecutive sentences.

[p. 178]

Epiphora, or *epistrophē*, is the opposite of *anaphora*. One can thus define it as 'the repetition of one or more words at the end of several consecutive members'.

[p. 190]

Symplokē is the combination of *anaphora* and *epiphora*. Mr. E. König gives to this figure the characteristic name of *symploke*; it consists in the repetition, at the beginning and at the end of several members of sentences, of one or more words respectively answering one another.

[p. 193]

Plokē. 'This term ordinarily describes, says Mr. E. König, the repetition of the same words at the beginning and at the end of one or two successive sentences.'

[p. 199]

Regressio. To all the devices described above, Mr E. König adds another one, which he calls *epanodos* or *regressio*: that is the repetition, in the inverted order, of the members of an enumeration.

[p. 199]

Anadiplosis. One of the most commonly used literary devices among biblical writers, especially by the authors of the Psalms, is the repetition at the beginning of a member of sentence the last words [p. 200] of the member of the preceding phrase.

[p. 216]

Anadiplosis iterata or *catena*. As the name suggests, *anadiplosis iterata* is an *anadiplosis* which is followed through to several members of successive sentences.

> *Through the several examples that he presents and discusses, it seems that Souvay has clearly grasped the function of the marks of composition of his 'literary devices'. He will not, however, be content with using those marks to identify the limits of the verses, as the title of his book seems to suggest, since, after having devoted his fifth chapter to 'Poems with choruses', he comes back in the next chapter to 'The stylistic devices and the stanza' (pp. 280-362):*

[p. 280]

In the same way that one can use certain stylistic devices to discover the rhythm of a good number of passages of the Psalter, it seems possible to use the same process to find the division in stanzas.

[p. 281]

The most widely used devices are: *anaphora*—by far the most frequent, because it is the easiest to use and it produces the best results—, *epiphora*, and *concatenatio*—sort of *anadiplosis* whose first member ends a stanza, and whose second, identical to the first, opens the next—, *inclusio*, which is to the stanza what the *plokē* is to the verse. All these devices tend to give the stanzas to which they are applied an inkling of resemblance, or parallelism, which is the principal element of what has been named the *Responsio*. In truth, the *Responsio* can exist independently from these devices: the thoughts, indeed, can answer one another (or be opposed) without a single word being repeated.

> *Despite the fact that Souvay's book, it seems, has had no influence so far, it was necessary to bring into the light this isolated scholar who, on the particular issue of the identification of the Hebrew verse, has made an almost complete list of the marks of composition of the biblical texts.*

Albert Condamin

> *Souvay mentions in his bibliography a work which was published shortly before his own*: Le Livre d'Isaïe *by Albert Condamin.[8] Like his compatriot from across the Atlantic, Condamin makes references to Lowth but completely ignores his English successors. On the contrary, this French Jesuit depends largely upon the German tradition. From the beginning of the century,[9] he adopts the theory of the 'alternating stanza' of Johannes Konrad Zenner[10] which corresponds more or less to Jebb's introverted parallelism such as it was applied by Boys to entire texts or even books. In 1933, he took up his observations in* Poèmes de la Bible, avec une introduction sur la strophique hébraïque.[11]
>
> *It is from Lowth's parallelism of the members that Köster had drawn his stanza theory: for him, the text is organized on several levels: that of the distichs, which are bound in twos or threes; those groups are then organized to form a stanza, and the group of stanzas in turn constitute the*

---

8.   Paris: Victor Lecoffre, 1905.

9.   'Un psaume d'imprécation (Ps CVIII, hébr. 109)', *Revue Théologique Française* (1901), pp. 246-52; and in 1905, in *Le livre d'Isaïe*; and again in 1920, in *Le livre de Jérémie* (Paris: Gabalda, 1920).

10.   See above, p. 111.

11.   Paris: Beauchesne, 1933.

poem. The leading principles of these successive groupings are the meaning first, and then the rhythm. While underlining the primacy of meaning, Condamin adds 'a few clues which help distinguish the stanzas':[12] apart from the chorus, which is very rare, he notes verbal repetitions that he organizes in a remarkable system: in one paragraph, which should be quoted in full, everything, or almost everything, is set out very clearly:

The *parallel* repetition, not only of the thought, but of *words*, is that which takes place at parallel emplacements, more often in different and consecutive stanzas: for example, at the beginning of the stanza and at the beginning of the anti stanza, or at the end of one and the other.[13] The *symmetrical* repetition[14] is that which takes place at symmetrical emplacements, either, most often in the same stanza, at the beginning and at the end, or sometimes in successive stanzas, at the beginning of the stanza and at the end of the anti stanza, or in the middle of one and the other.[15]

His Chapter 6 is devoted to the famous alternating stanza, which he calls the 'intermediary stanza' ('because it occupies, very often, an intermediary place between two pairs of equal stanzas'). He describes its proper characteristics: it distinguishes itself in its shape from the surrounding stanzas; it expresses a stronger thought, in a lighter tone; it is found in the centre, and sometimes at the mathematical centre, of the poem; it cannot be divided in two since it is generally composed of an uneven number of verses. The analyses of the texts he then provides are not all convincing, because of their imprecision, because of the habit, shared with a number of the exegetes of his times, of re-styling the text; the stanza theory no doubt inconvenienced him in his search for the genuine organization of the texts; it remains nonetheless true that he accumulated notations which can still be of use to readers today.

Condamin's theory and discoveries thus met with Jebb's and Boys's and their successors'. The two traditions, English and German, both

12. *Poèmes*, Chapter 5, pp. 23-26.

13. One recognizes what Boys called 'leading terms' and 'final terms' (see above, pp. 106-107).

14. The opposition that Condamin makes between 'parallel' and 'symmetrical' is similar to Bengel's distinction between chiasmus directus and chiasmus inversus; Condamin's symmetry is close to Jebb's introverted parallelism. In fact, he does not describe Bengel's or Jebb's figures as such, but only what we might call partial symmetries.

15. *Poèmes*, p. 26; one can recognize here successively inclusion (which determines short units, longer ones, sometimes the whole text) and the symmetry of the centres.

inheritors of Lowth, nevertheless developed respectively in complete reciprocal ignorance of the other.[16] *Although Condamin's results are largely less assured and less convincing than those of his colleagues from across the Channel, rather than regret it one should note the correspondences.*

Marcel Jousse

During the second quarter of the century, another French Jesuit will have a stronger impact than Condamin, if not on the exegetical world, at least in the French intellectual circles. The notoriety that he has enjoyed in recent years does not allow us to omit him from this survey. Marcel Jousse published Etudes de Psychologie Linguistique: 'Le Style oral rythmique et mnémotechnique chez les Verbo-moteurs' *in 1924.*[17] *Its success was immense. 'A prestigious and inspired book!', exclaimed Henri Bremond who compared Jousse to Christopher Colombus and Copernicus.*[18] *The wide readership that Jousse enjoyed is probably due to the fact that, in a period of virulent historical criticism, he claimed the origin of the words of Christ in the Gospel to Jesus of Nazareth himself: the recitations in 'formulaic oral style' of the Galilean Rabbi had been, according to him, faithfully transmitted thanks to the virtue of a flawless oral tradition, down to the script of the gospel.*

His major contribution lies in bringing the public, his numerous readers and auditors, to the understanding of the oral, living, characteristic of the texts which were too often dissected as a dead letter in his time, and to have highlighted the value, and demonstrated through his system of recitation by gestures, the nourishing function of the Word. Several 'Jousse groups' continue to memorize and recite in 'rhythmic melody' some biblical texts, at least in France and Quebec; in the Christian communities which have kept alive the oral tradition, Jousse's legacy seems to be perpetuated and enriched.[19]

Besides, he has insisted on the importance, for those whose culture is definitely marked by writing, of a possible transposition of the rhythm of

16. This is what we can surmise from the reading of Condamin himself. It is true that Lowth was very well known in Germany, but his English successors were not.

17. *ArPh*, 2.4 (Paris 1925), pp. 436-674; reprinted *Le Style oral* (Paris: Fondation Marcel Jousse/Flammarion, 1981).

18. See the appraisal made by G. Fessard, 'Une nouvelle psychologie du langage. *Le Style oral*, du P. Marcel Jousse', *Etudes* 192 (1927), pp. 145-62. One of the best representations of *Le Style oral* is that of H. Fleisch, 'Etudes de psychologie linguistique' [on M. Jousse, *Le style oral*], *RevPhil* (1931), pp. 623-41; (1932), pp. 147-83.

19. See J. Fédry, 'L'Afrique entre écriture et oralité', *Etudes* 346 (1977), pp. 581-600.

*the texts in 'rhythmic typographies' which gives their composition, hith-
erto physically transmitted in oral recitation, visually.*[20] *However, not
only is he not concerned with justifying his rhythmic typographies, but he
too often forces into a parallel frame texts which had manifestly been constructed along concentric lines. Here is, for example, his rhythmic typography of Lk. 12.24-28:*

Recitation I

a
Consider the ravens of heaven

b   c
they do not sow   they do not reap

d
they do not have a storehouse

e   f
And yet he feeds them   Are you not
your Father of the heavens   much more than them?

g
And which of you

h   i
by being anxious   can add

j
to his span of life one cubit?

k   l
If then you are not able to do   why are you anxious
as small a thing as that   about the rest?

20. See his *Rythmo-mélodisme et rythmo-typographisme pour le Style oral
palestinien* (Paris: Librairie orientaliste Paul Goethner, 1952).

Recitation II

a
Consider the lilies of the fields

b   c
they do not toil   they do not spin

d
and yet how they grow!

e   f
Actually   Actually

g
yet I tell you

h   i
Solomon in all his glory   was not arrayed like one of these

j
But if the grass of the fields

k   l
which stands today   and tomorrow is thrown into the oven

m
God so clothes

n   o
How much more for you   will he do

p
O men of little faith!

Not only the whole of this passage is of concentric composition,[21] but the central piece (12.25-26) is itself constructed along concentric lines:

a **Which** of you,		by being	ANXIOUS
b			**CAN**
	c		*to his span of life add one cubit?*
	c' If then		*the smallest thing*
b' you			**CAN** NOT
a' **why** about the rest		are you	ANXIOUS?

21. See R. Meynet, *L'Evangile selon saint Luc*, I, p. 124.

> *Jousse did not make any progress on the analysis of the texts, among other reasons because, like Condamin, he knew Lowth but completely ignored his English successors. The following extract from his lesson of 17 December 1935 at the 'Ecole des Hautes Etudes' (p. 117 of the typed class notes) gives us an idea of the knowledge that Jousse had of his predecessors:*

There are sometimes discoveries which are apparently valuable for science, but which are the source of posterior blindness.

For perhaps 18 centuries, Latin translations of the Palestinian works were recited in the choirs of monks and nuns, and it was necessary to wait until the 18th century for an Oxford professor of poetry, Lowth, to notice a strange phenomenon which had not been noticed before, which he called the 'Parallelismus membrorum'. It is in the Psalms that he had noticed this parallelism of the members because it was customary to recite them.

A century later, someone noticed that this parallelism of the syntactic members was found elsewhere and the method of dividing the text along typographical lines was used. This method was applied to the prophets because it sprang from a discovery made by a professor of poetry. Since in reality we almost invariably find only what we want to see, the poeticists only sought Parallelism in what they considered poetry. This remained true until the year of the Lord 1925.

> *Lowth's observations are not limited to the Psalms and it was not necessary to wait for a century to note the parallelism of the members in the prophets: Lowth's famous nineteenth lesson was entitled 'The Prophetic Poetry is sentencious'. At the end of his introduction, just before describing the three sorts of parallelism, Lowth clearly announces his purpose:*

Such appears to have been the origin and progress of that poetical and artificial conformation of the sentences, which we observe in the poetry of the Hebrews. That it prevailed no less in the Prophetic Poetry than in the Lyric and Didactic, to which it was, in the nature of things, most adapted, is evident from those very ancient specimens of poetical prophecy already quoted from the historical books; and it only remains to show, that it is no less observable in those which are contained in the volumes of the prophets themselves. In order the more clearly to evince this point, I shall endeavour to illustrate the Hebrew parallelism according to its different species, first by examples taken from those books commonly allowed to be poetical, and

afterwards by correspondent examples from the books of the prophets.[22]

> *As early as 1820, some one hundred years before 'the year of our Lord 1925' when Jousse's* Le style oral *was published, Jebb wrote: 'It is the design of the following pages, to prove, by examples, that the structure of clauses, sentences, and periods, in the New Testament, is frequently regulated after the model afforded in the poetical parts of the Old' (*Sacred Literature, p. 1)
>
> *It must be said in Jousse's defence that those quoted lines are extracted from a lesson which was written in shorthand and typed.*

> *'Marcel Jousse the Prophet'[23] nonetheless marked his era: his voice continues to be heard,[24] calling, against the historical criticism which ruled unmatched in his day, to take the text as it is, and to let oneself be taken by it through the Word of life. In this trend, all those who today devote themselves to the analysis of the texts by placing the history of their formation aside can recognize themselves.*

Nils Wilhelm Lund

> *The link with the English scholars of the nineteenth century was made by an American, Nils Wilhelm Lund, who published from 1930 onwards the result of his analyses of the texts of the New as of the Old Testament.[25] Like many of his predecessors, especially Bengel, Lowth, Jebb, Boys and Forbes, to whom he refers to at the beginning (pp. 35-40), Lund wanted to show that*

for the understanding of the meaning of some passages, for the check-
ing of some old problems of the text and the raising of new questions,

22. *Lectures on the Sacred Poetry of the Hebrews*, II, pp. 33-34.

23. C. Pairault, 'Le prophète Marcel Jousse', *Etudes* 359 (1983), pp. 231-43.

24. Through the re-edition of his *Style oral* and through the gradual publication of several of the classes he taught in Paris which were taken in shorthand by his faithful collaborators: see *L'Anthropologie du geste* (Paris: Gallimard, 1974); *La Manducation de la parole* (Paris: Gallimard, 1975); *Le Parlant, la Parole et le Souffle* (Paris: Gallimard, 1978).

25. 'The Presence of the Chiasmus in the Old Testament', *AJSL* 46 (1929–30), pp. 104-28; 'The Presence of Chiasmus in the New Testament', *JR* 10 (1930), pp. 74-93; 'The Influence of Chiasmus upon the Structure of the Gospels', *AThR* 13 (1931), pp. 27-48; 'The Influence of Chiasmus upon the Gospel according to Matthew', *AThR* 13 (1931), pp. 405-33; 'The Literary Structure of Paul's Hymn to Love', *JBL* 50 (1931), pp. 260-76; 'Chiasmus in the Psalms', *AJSL* 49 (1933), pp. 281-312; *Outline Studies in the Book of Revelation* (Chicago: Covenant Press, 1935).

and for literary appreciation of the New Testament writings themselves a study of chiasmus is likely to yield some important results.[26]

In 1942, he reproduced and synthesized his anterior studies in Chiasmus in the New Testament.[27] *Lund defines his aim in this way*:

[p. 28]

The following pages [. . .] are devoted to the tracing of the Hebrew literary influence on the Greek text of the New Testament; more definitely, they discuss one particular Hebrew form, namely, the extensive use of the inverted order commonly called [p. 29] chiasmus. Since no satisfactory preliminary work exists dealing with the Old Testament material, a study of characteristic passages from the law, the prophets, and the psalms will be made in order to establish the laws governing chiastic structures. A survey will then be made of the epistles and the gospels in order to ascertain how far the chiastic arrangement of ideas recurs in the writings of the New Testament. The scope of our investigation will be restricted to that residue of form which has resisted all attempts to find a place for it in any of the Greek categories, but which, nevertheless, is of a literary character and therefore may not be dismissed as being merely poor Greek or careless writing.

Lund's great originality lies in the fact that he was the first to attempt to ascertain the organizational laws of the concentric structures:

[p. 40]

In the work of attempting to ascertain and classify these laws the present writer has had no help from his predecessors. The fact remains, however, that when a great many passages have been studied and compared, certain recurring features impress themselves upon the reader. They are so definite and recur in so many different combinations, that one is justified in calling them the laws of chiastic structures. These laws are the following:

1. *The centre is always the turning point.* The centre, as we shall see, may consist of one, two, three, or even four lines. [p. 41]
2. At the centre there is often a change in the trend of thought, and an antithetical idea is introduced. After this the original

26. 'The Significance of Chiasmus for Interpretation', *CrozQ* 20 (1943), pp. 105-23 (105).

27. The title of this book is somewhat misleading: indeed, although the accent is put on concentric constructions (called 'chiasm'), parallel structures are not neglected either.

trend is resumed and continued until the system is concluded. For want of a better name, we shall designate this feature *the law of the shift at the centre.*

3. Identical ideas are often distributed in such a fashion that *they occur in the extremes and at the centre* of their respective system, and nowhere else in the system.

4. There are also many instances of ideas, occurring at the centre of one system and recurring in the extremes of a corresponding system, the second system evidently having been constructed to match the first. We shall call this feature *the law of shift from centre to the extremes.*

5. There is a definite tendency of certain terms to gravitate towards certain positions within a given system, such the divine names in the psalms, quotations in central position in a system in the New Testament, or such terms as 'body' when denoting the church.

6. Larger units are frequently introduced and concluded by *frame-passages.*

7. There is frequently a mixture of chiastic and alternating lines within one and the same unit.

> *In order to illustrate those seven laws, Lund analyses 28 texts, of greater or lesser length, from the Old Testament. Only the most demonstrative and the most certain among his examples will be used here.*

[p. 41]

Examples illustrating these laws will be introduced in order to familiarize the reader with them, and references will be made to them from time to time as occasion arises. The reader is asked to accept these attempts to formulate a law *tentatively*, in the light of such evidence as is here briefly presented, awaiting supplementary data which from time to time will be introduced and discussed. We shall then first give a few examples which show clearly how *the centre was regarded as a turning point.*

> *Ashkelon* shall see it and fear;
>> *Gaza* also and be very sorrowful;
>>> And *Ekron*:
>>> For *her* (i.e. Ekron's) expectation shall be ashamed,
>> And the king shall perish from *Gaza*;
> And *Ashkelon* shall not be inhabited.
>
> (Zech. 9.5)

Boys has given this passage as an example of how these forms occur in passages 'where poetry, according to our idea of it, is out of question'. The chiastic form of the passage is clear, but it shows just as clearly how the centre becomes the turning point. Three statements predict the fate of the Philistine cities, but when [p. 42] the centre is passed, the fourth line, introduced by 'for', begins an *elaboration* of the prediction. This is continued until the end of the system is reached. In whatever way one chooses to describe the difference between the first and the last half of the system, the difference is clearly marked.

We may now take another example, showing similar characteristics, except that there is a *single central line*.

> *Seek* ye me, and ye shall *live*.
>> But seek not after *Bethel*,
>>> Nor enter into *Gilgal*,
>>>> And pass not to *Beer-sheba*:
>>> For *Gilgal* shall surely go into captivity,
>> And *Bethel* shall come to naught.
> *Seek* Yahweh, and ye shall *live*.[28]

(Amos 5.4b-6a)

The first line of this system Harper unites with the words that precede, in order not to make 'the prophet give two exhortations in practically the same language'.[29] He also suggests the removal of the central line to some place before the second line, so as not to interrupt the chiasmus formed by the names Bethel and Gilgal. Neither of these changes is needed, nor is it necessary to assume that a line parallel to that dealing with Beer-sheba has fallen out of the centre, for the system runs true to form as it now stands in our arrangement. There are many instances of chiastic systems with single lines at the centre. We observe, however, that while the first and last lines carry an invitation and a promise, the intervening five lines are of a different nature. Of these five lines, the first three give a warning, but the last two, introduced by 'for', as in Zech. 9.5, carry a threat. Consider also the following passage:

28. This example had already been used by T. Boys, *A Key*, p. 126 (author's note).

29. W.R. Harper, *Amos and Hosea* (I. C. C.), *in loco*.

And Yahweh said unto Moses:
> He shall surely be put to death, the man,
>> They shall stone him with stones,
>>> All the congregation without the camp.
>>> And they brought him,
>>> All the congregation without the camp,
>> And stoned him with stones
> To death
As Yahweh commanded to Moses.[30]

(Num. 15.35-36)

[p. 43]

In this passage the first four lines are devoted to the command, and the last five to its execution. In the previous passage from Amos, including seven lines in all, the first four formed the first half and the next three the last half of the system. It is not impossible that we are touching a subtle system of *numerical* symmetry in such arrangements to which we shall have occasions to call the reader's attention in other passages. The present writer is convinced from his observation of a great number of passages that the Hebrew writers have certain numerical designs woven into their writings. These are found not only when numerical adjectives, like three, seven, etc., are expressed, but also where conspicuous words are grouped in clusters in an artistic fashion so as to express designs. Of this we shall see more presently. The three passages already discussed illustrate one way in which the centre is marked off as the turning-point of a system.

The following passages will show another way in which the centre is emphasized for the same reason. The following verse reads like an inventory but is, nevertheless, chiastic in form, a fact which shows how wrong it would be to relate these forms to poetry only.

And he had sheep and oxen,
> And he asses,
>> And men servants,
>> And maid servants,
> And she asses,
And camels.[31]

(Gen. 12.16)

This passage, simple as it is, illustrates a principle of construction

---

30. This example had already been used by Boys, *A Key*, p. 40 (author's note).
31. This example had already been used by Boys, *A Key*, p. 37 (author's note).

which frequently occurs in such systems, namely, *a sudden shift from one subject to another* when the centre is reached, after which the former subject is *resumed* and adhered to until the end of the system. In the inventory of Abraham's wealth we observe that the first two and the last two lines enumerate *animals*, while the two central lines enumerate *human beings*. There are, of course, much elaborate and artistic expressions of the law of the shift—if we may call it so for want of a better name—as may be seen from the following passage: [p. 44]

> Arise,
>   Shine,
>   For thy light is come,
>   And the glory
>   Of Yahweh
>   Upon thee is risen.
>
>   For, behold, darkness shall cover
>   the earth
>   And gross darkness the peoples.
>
>   But upon thee will arise
>   Yahweh,
>   And his glory upon thee be seen,
>   And nations shall come to thy light,
>   And kings to the brightness
> Of thy rising. (Isa. 60.1-3)

In the first two and last lines, as well as in the two central lines, we have a parallelism of *ideas*, but not of words. This condition our English versions do not reveal. In all the other lines of the system, however, there exists, not only a parallelism of ideas, but also a parallelism of *words*. And yet the most striking feature is that the system opens with a beautiful description of the future light and glory of Israel, that the scene suddenly shifts from light and glory to darkness and gross darkness when the centre is reached, and that finally the note of hope and joy is heard once more, amplified now to include all the nations. One who is thinking merely in terms of *parallelismus membrorum* and rhythm, would proceed to arrange such a passage in a strophe of four couplets, or eight lines. However acceptable such an arrangement might be, it is clear that we have in this passage something more than ordinary parallelism and rhythm; here there is a *thought-pattern*, which is chiastic in form and obeys the laws of such constructions.[32]

Under the discussion of the law of the shift at the centre one may include all those passages which show an artistic and closely knit combination of chiastic and alternating lines. These systems are of two kinds. One kind begins with chiastic order, shifts to alternating at the centre, then resumes the chiastic order once more, maintaining this order until the end of the system is reached. The other kind, beginning with a series of alternating lines, shifts [p. 45] to chiastic order at the centre; then it resumes the original alternating order after the centre is passed, retaining this order till the system is completed.

> Let the wicked forsake his *way*,
>> And the unrighteous man his *thoughts*;
>
>> And let him return to Yahweh
>>> And he will have mercy upon him;
>> And to our God,
>>> For he will abundantly pardon.
>
>> For my thoughts are not your *thoughts*,
> Neither are your ways my *ways*, saith Yahweh. (Isa. 55.7-8)

This passage is a sample of the first kind of combination of chiastic and alternating lines. How spontaneous such forms are may be gathered from the last two lines of the structure, in which an extra chiastic feature is discovered in the forms, 'my—your and your—my', a minor piece of ornamentation, a final flourish. The next passage, far more elaborate and extensive, is the exact reversal of the former passage; here we have chiastic lines in the centre and alternating lines in the extremes.

---

32. See the criticism of Lund's translation in R. Meynet, *Quelle est donc cette Parole?*, pp. 67-68.

Because ye have said,   15
We made a covenant with death,
   And with Sheol are we at agreement;
A   When the overflowing scourge shall pass through,
          It shall not come unto us;

   B   For we made lies our refuge,
        And under falsehood have we hid ourselves.

         Therefore, thus saith the Lord Yahweh,   16

		a stone, a stone tried,
C	Behold, I lay in Zion	a corner precious
		a foundation well founded

      D   He that believeth shall not be in haste.   17

   C'   And I will make justice the line,
         And righteousness the plummet.

  B'   And hail shall sweep away the refuge of lies,
       And the waters shall overflow the hiding-places;

And your covenant with death shall be annulled,   18
   And your agreement with Sheol shall not stand;
A'   When the overflowing scourge shall pass through,
        Then shall ye be trodden down by it.

                     (Isa. 28.15-18)

[p. 46]

The lines printed in italics in this structure represent introductory statements designating as speakers the rulers, on the one hand, and the Lord, on the other. What is vital for our present purpose is the observation that, while the *extremes* of this passage describe the plans by which the rulers intended to obtain security for Zion (AB) and the frustration of these plans (B'A'), the *centre* carries by way of contrast a description of the refuge provided by the Lord himself. In C the laying of the corner stone is described in a line which branches off into a triplet (of this more will be said presently); in C' the references to the 'line' and the 'plummet' also point to building operations. The very core of the message is found in the central line, 'He that believeth shall not be in haste'. Thus, the climax is at the centre, not at the end, where we should expect it. It is remarkable also that it is the centre which is quoted in the New Testament where we often meet with the

'corner stone' and the demand for belief in Him. How consciously and
minutely the sense of contrast between the centre and the extremes is
maintained may be seen in a comparison between the 'justice' and
'righteousness' with which the Lord himself builds, and the 'lies' and
the 'falsehood' in which the rulers seek their security (BB'). It will
not be necessary to point out in detail the parallelism which every
reader may be trusted to discover for himself. One new feature, however, calls for some brief remarks. The reader who has observed the
alternating order of the lines in AB and passed over the centre (CDC')
feels disturbed, when he encounters the couplet B' in its present
position. He would perhaps attempt to obtain regularity by moving B'
from its present position and by placing it after A'. The puzzle will be
solved for him in a much simpler way, since in many passages there
are lines which are alternating, while the *clusters* into which these
lines are gathered often follow the chiastic order with [p. 47] reference to one another. In this particular case the clusters ABB'A' form a
chiastic structure, but their lines alternate.[33]

> In the third chapter, Lund studies some texts of the Torah. Only one
> such text will be reproduced here.

[p. 51]

Any reader of the legal portions of the Pentateuch has observed
how repetitious its language is in many sections. He has probably
explained the nature of the laws be references to modern legal documents which are also repetitious. A closer examination of the structure of some of these laws will show, however, that the reiterations
follow certain verifiable literary patterns, and that mere legal for-
mality is not sufficient to explain their form.

---

33. All this discussion on the combination of chiasm and parallelism will be
elucidated by the distinction between the levels of organization of the text (see our
methodological presentation).

[p. 57]

And *Yahweh* spoke unto *Moses*, saying,   13
    Bring forth him that hath *cursed* without the *camp*;   14
A   And let all that heard him lay their hands upon his head,
     And let all the congregation *stone him*:
       And thou shalt speak unto the *children of Israel*, saying   15

B   Whosoever curseth his *God* shall bear his sin.

                                                    16
     And he that blasphemeth the name of Yahweh, he shall surely be put to death;
C   All the congregation shall certainly stone him;
      As well the *sojourner*, as the *home-born*,
    When he blasphemeth the Name shall be put to death.

     And he that smiteth any *man* mortally shall surely be put to death,   17
D   And he that smiteth a *beast* mortally shall make it good, life for life;   18
      And if a man cause a *blemish* in his *neighbor*, as he hath done so
                   [shall it be done unto him.   19

     Breach for breach,
   E   Eye for eye,
     Tooth for tooth.

     As he hath caused a *blemish* in a *man*
               [so shall it be rendered unto him;   21
  D'   And he that killeth a *beast* shall make it good;
     And he that killeth a *man* shall be put to death.

C' Ye shall have one manner of law,   22
    As well for the *sojourner*, as for the *home-born*.

[p. 58
B' For I am Yahweh your *God*.

And *Moses* spake to the children of Israel: 23
A' And they brought forth him that had *cursed* out of the *camp*,
    And *stoned him* with stones.
    And the *children of Israel* did as Yahweh commanded Moses.

                                  (Lev. 24.13-23)

This passage contains two separate laws: the one against blasphemy, which fits into the historical context; the other against violence, which has nothing to do with the historical situation. The preceding verses (24.10-12) tell the story of a son of an Israelite woman and an Egyptian father who blasphemed the Name and cursed; this event gives rise to the law. The central part of this passage however, dealing with violence against man and beast (DED'), is well-knit unit by itself. In the centre we find a triplet stating the law of retaliation (E), while on either side there is a threefold application of the law to man, beast, and man (DD'). We need not discuss in detail the extremely interesting symmetry of this passage in which a great number of parallel terms are found, but it would seem that source criticism of Leviticus would, in this instance at least, receive help from a study of the chiastic form. On either side of this centre are found two sections, one a little more elaborate than the other, but both stating that the law is uniform to both sojourners and home-born (CC'). In BB' we have the only instances in which the name Elohim occurs in the structure. A introduces the command to stone the offender, while A' describes how the command was obeyed. For our present purpose the threefold occurrence of a triplet at the centre of a structure is the most interesting feature. There can be no doubt that the frequent recurrence of triplets in the writings of the New Testament looks to such passages as this for their models.

A systematic search for structures of this kind in the legal sections of the Pentateuch would, very likely, be abundantly rewarded and would contribute not a little to our understanding of the disposition of the material. The critical study of the Pentateuch has nearly always taken account of *sequence*, and when there has been little or no sequence in the arrangement of sections, scholars have turned to the hypothesis of dislocation or redaction [p. 59]. But why should logical considerations alone be permitted to determine the organization of the material in a book, when we have such abundant evidence that its writers were influenced by a well-developed aesthetic interest? May it not be, after all, that blocks of material were arranged in accordance with chiastic or alternating patterns or a combination of both, and that in the mind of the writer and the informed reader similar sections, though far apart in these books, were connected with one another? May it not be also that the language is artistic, although at times it appears to be exceedingly prolix and discursive, the style of 'a jurist rather than an historian' in whose interest it is to be 'circumstantial, formal, and precise'.[34] No doubt legal writings are the least imaginative of all prose, but after a close study of some of these structures we are not ready to deny them certain aesthetic qualities. There is repetition, to be sure, but a measured and orderly repetition according to fixed literary patterns.

> Chapter 4 (pp. 63-93) is devoted to the Prophets; the following chapter to the Psalms (pp. 94-136).

---

34. S.R. Driver, *Introduction to the Literature of the Old Testament* (Edinburgh: T. & T. Clark, 1910 [1891]), p. 12.

[p. 104]

PSALM 115

A	Not unto us, O Yahweh, not unto us,	1
	But unto thy name give glory,	
	Because of thy grace,	
	Because of thy truth.	

B

Wherefore should the nations say,   2
Where, now,/is their *God*.
But our *God*/is in *the heavens*,   3
Whatsoever pleased him he *hath done*.

C

Their *idols* are silver and gold,   4
The *work* of the hands of men.
A *mouth* have they,/but they do not *speak*.   5
Eyes have they, but they do not see.
Ears have they, but they do not hear.   6
A nose have they, but they do not smell.
They have hands, but they do not handle.   7
They have feet, but they do not walk
They cannot *make a sound*/with their *throat*.
Like unto them shall all those that *wrought* them be,   8
Every one that trusteth *in them*.

O Israel, trust in Yahweh,   9
Their help and their shield is he.
O house of Aaron, trust in Yahweh,   10
Their help and their shield is he.
O ye that fear Yahweh, trust in Yahweh, 11
Their help and their shield is he.

C'

Yahweh hath remembered us,   12
He will bless.
He will bless the house of *Israel*,   [p. 105]
He will bless *the house of Aaron*,
He will bless *them that fear Yahweh*,   13
The small,
And the great.

B'

May Yahweh increase you, you and your *children*.   14
Blessed be ye of *Yahweh,*/who *hath made the heavens* and the earth.   15
The heavens, *the heavens*/are *Yahweh's*,
But the earth he hath given to the *children* of men.   16

A'

Not the dead praise Yah,   17
Nor all they that go down into silence.
But we, we will bless Yah,   18
From this time forth and forever.
Hallelujah.

Psalms 113–118 in our Bible are called the Hallel, or praise; they were sung at the Passover meal (Mt. 26.30, Mk 14.26). Psalm 115 presents in a striking contrast the futility of the idols and the all-sufficiency of the living God to all who trust in him. There is a remarkable literary symmetry in this ancient hymn, which is expressed, not only in separate terms and lines, but in the arrangement of the strophes. In A we are told that glory belongs to God, and not to man, and in A' we find that the living, and not the dead, are to render God his praise. In B the taunting challenge of the nations, 'Where, now, is their God?' is answered with the affirmation that God is exalted in the heavens and that his will is supreme. In B' the faithful children of God are introduced in contrast to the hostile nations in B, and God's sovereignty is reaffirmed. Observe the parallel terms which are printed in italics, some of which are found in these two strophes only.

The central strophes of the psalm are antithetical: in C the futility of trusting in idols is set forth and in C', the security given by God. The first of these strophes is *chiastic* in form, while the second is *alternating*. In C there are two introductory lines of a general nature declaring that idols, though made of the best material, silver and gold, are nevertheless 'the work of men's hands'. The two closing lines again declare the futility of the idols and their makers, but refer to them in the *inverted* order. The intervening *seven* lines are very interesting because of the intricate [p. 106] artistic pattern they display. In six of the seven lines the verb is placed at the *end* of the line; the poet departs from this rule in the seventh line only for a very good reason. The first and the seventh lines form a *chiasmus*, by which the group of lines describing the futility of the idols are knit together in a cluster separated from the two introductory and concluding lines of the strophe. The first four lines begin in Hebrew: 'Mouths to them', 'eyes to them', etc. This structure continues till the centre is reached, when it changes to 'Their hands', 'their feet'. In this cluster of seven lines, it should be further observed, features of the body that usually come in pairs (like eyes and ears, hands and feet) appear in couplets. This arrangement gives us a pattern in which single lines alternate with couplets.

In strophe C' we have Israel's great confession of trust in Yahweh. The futility of trusting in other gods is the closing note of the previous strophe. Its opposite is now stated emphatically in three different ways, and is followed by a triple refrain, 'Their help and their shield is he'. The first half of the strophe ends in the words, 'Yahweh hath remembered us, he will bless'. The idea of the divine blessing is again taken up in the last half of the strophe and gone over in a triple statement, 'He will bless', in which the terms of address from the first half of the strophe are repeated. But whereas the first half of the strophe carries these terms in the beginning of each line where they occur, the second half carries them at the end; and whereas the first half of the strophe is made up of couplets, the last half consists of single lines. Thus we find that the principle of mingling single lines with couplets, which is utilized in one way in C, is expressed in another manner in C'. There is an infinite tenderness in the short closing lines of the two halves of strophe C'. There are no divine names in C, but in C' they are placed mostly in the first half of the strophe. The psalm ends in jubilant peal of praise, and with a profusion of divine names in strophes B'A', not less than three in each. This feature finds its explanation in the desire to make the affirmation of faith in the living God against the idolatry of the nations more effective. Eighteen times a year during the continuance [p. 107] of the temple and twenty-one times during the exile was the Hallel repeated at the Jewish feasts in conformity to the law, and at the new moons also according to custom (cf. Sopherim, XVIII.2).

After all these details have been discussed, there still remains an indefinable something, a mood which comes through the reading of the psalm. This mood must be felt rather than expressed. The contrasts of the psalm are overwhelmingly strong. On the one hand we have the biting satire on idolatry and the idol makers, which reminds us of passages in Isa. 44.9-20; 40.19, 20; 41.6, 7; 46.6, 7; on the other hand, we have the deeply emotional appeal to trust in Yahweh. When Israel was oppressed by the empires and surrounded on all sides by idolatry, the hope of the faithful remnant found expression in the words of this psalm. Through the liturgical use of such forms they became familiar in the early church, and were carried over, almost unconsciously, into the early Christian writings.

The chiastic arrangement of strophes is only one of the typical structures in the psalms. There are also several instances in which the alternating arrangement prevails. The following is typical.

Psalm 126

A When *Yahweh* turned back the captivity of Zion,   1
    We were like dreamers.

    B   Then was filled with laughter/our mouth,   2
                    And our tongue/with singing.

                    Then said they among the Gentiles,
        C   *Yahweh* hath done great things for them.
                    Yahweh hath done great things for us;   3
                    We are glad.

A'   Turn back, O *Yahweh*, our captivity,   4
    Like the brooks in the Negeb.

    B'   They that sow/with tears,   5
                    With singing/shall reap.

                    He that goeth forth and weepeth,   6
        C'   Bearing his measure of seed,
                    Shall surely come again with joy,
                    Bearing his sheaves.

In this poem the principle of an equal number of lines in each strophe would lead us to arrange the lines in four quatrains. Such [p. 108] a procedure, however, would hide from the reader some important symmetries in the psalm. The two strophes AA' are obviously parallel, and should be treated as strophes, though they contain only two lines. They both carry the divine name, the verb 'turn', the 'captivity', and a comparison (cf. 'like') in the second line. The jubilant strains of B are only partially repeated in B', for a note of sorrow here mingles with the joy. That the two are to be regarded as parallel, however, is indicated, not only by the common idea of joy, but by the chiastic arrangement of the two. While the laughter and singing occupy the extremes of the chiasmus in B, their counterparts are placed in the centre in B'. We have already observed another instance of such a shift from centre to the extremes of two phrases in strophes BB' in Psalm 101. There is a similar distribution of the ideas of joy and sorrow in CC'; in C there is only a joyful mood described among Gentiles as well as among Israelites because of the 'great things' done by Yahweh, while in C' joy and weeping are distributed in alternating lines. In regard to CC' the ideas are so definitely set off from the rest of the lines, that there can be no possible way of treating them except as parallel quatrains. The ideas of the psalm seem to be evenly divided between the two halves. The first half describes the return from the captivity, and is an occasion for unmixed joy; the second sets forth the missionary task of Israel among the nations, progressing amidst hardships and weeping, but with the assurance of a joyous termination in a harvest. What Yahweh has done is the message of C. What Israel is about to do is the content of C'. [. . .]

[p. 109]

We have described psalms that are in their structure either chiastic or alternating. We shall now give some examples of psalms whose structure is a combination of these two forms. The following psalm is perhaps one of the clearest examples of such a combination of forms; in addition, it is a good illustration of the [p. 110] futility of insisting upon an arrangement in quatrains. Each couplet in this psalm is a separate strophe, and only such an arrangement will bring out the literary pattern used by the poet.

Psalm 114

A		When Israel went forth out of Egypt,			1
		The house of Jacob from a people of strange speech,			
	B		Judah became his sanctuary,		2
			Israel his dominion.		
		C	The sea saw it, and fled,		3
			The Jordan turned back.		
			D	The mountains skipped like rams,	4
				The little hills like lambs.	
		C'	What aileth thee, O sea, that thou fleest?		5
			Thou Jordan, that thou turnest back?		
			D'	Ye mountains, that ye skip like rams.	6
				Ye hills, like lambs?	
	B'		At the presence of **Adon** tremble, thou earth,		7
			At the presence of the **God** of Jacob,		
A'		Who turned the rock into a pool of waters,			8
		The flint into a fountain of waters.			

This psalm is composed of eight equal parts, four of which are alternating (CDC'D'), and four chiastic (ABB'A'). In the construction of these eight strophes a regular scheme is followed, introducing a verb in the first line but not in the second. The result is that the second line becomes a sort of echo to the first, which by continued repetition becomes very effective. There are two exceptions to this rule, for in CC' the second line also carries a verb. The two verbs in C change the effect of this strophe, making it different from the two preceding. Thus the reader is made aware of the fact that he passes now from one part of the poem to another part in which a different literary structure prevails. When he has read through D, he is again arrested by the same kind of change, for C' also carries two verbs. Thus the arrival at the centre of the poem is signalized. In addition, the question, 'What aileth thee?' etc., serves further to emphasize this fact. The sudden changes from 'sea' and 'Jordan' to 'mountain' and 'hills', and the recurrence of these in the following questions (C'D'), are too striking to be missed by any reader; they serve to set off the four central strophes from the rest of the psalm. A new line of thought is introduced but not concluded [p. 111] in B' but is carried to its completion in A'. In other words, the performance in AB is repeated in B'A'. All other strophes in the psalm bring the thought they contain to a conclusion within the strophe (cf. Ps. 58).

A word may now be said in regard to the content of the psalm. Commemorating the Exodus and the settlement of Israel in Canaan, it is a festival psalm sung on the eighth day of the Jewish Passover ritual. The psalm begins with the time of the Exodus and concludes with a reference to an event of the Exodus (cf. Exod. 17.6; Num. 20.11). The next strophe takes us to the settlement in Canaan and the establishment of Yahweh's dominion (B). It is to be observed that the *name* of the deity is nowhere introduced until we reach B'. To speak of the chief actor in the psalm long before he has been introduced would be a fault under ordinary circumstances, but becomes very natural, perhaps even conducive to suspense, once the scheme of the poet is understood. That BB' really are parallel is seen first of all in 'Israel' and 'Jacob', but also in the fact that 'the presence' is naturally expected in his 'sanctuary' and in his 'dominion' (cf. Pss. 33.8; 96.9; Hab. 2.20).

It would not be beyond the ingenuity of the poet to take a final glance at the four alternating strophes in the centre as he closes the poem. These deal with water and with land, and it may be this fact that prompts him to place in sharp contrast in A' rock and flint, on the one hand, and pool and fountain, on the other. The psalm is a combination of the chiastic and the alternating patterns. The ingenuity with which the poet acquaints the reader with the change of the pattern, namely, by the introduction of double verbs in CC' and by the striking question, 'What aileth thee?' when the centre is reached, is an exhibition of the finest art. To write so artistically that one achieves an impression of simplicity is, after all, the highest art.

From chapter 6, Lund touches upon the texts of the New Testament: he starts with Paul.

[p. 139]

The earliest literary deposit of the Christian tradition consists of the epistles of Paul. [. . .] Paul of Tarsus was born in a centre of Greek culture. [. . .] Paul, however, was much more than a Greek; he was also a Hebrew of the Hebrews, who in Jerusalem acquired the training given to scholars of his own race. If, therefore, we should discover in his writings a residue which may not under any circumstances be made to conform to the patterns prevalent in the Greek rhetorical schools, this is merely what we should expect from a writer of his training and circumstances. Unless we feel free to assume that Paul took his Jewish training less seriously than his Greek education, we should naturally expect to find some traces of this training in his writings. Strange to say, these traces have been sought in his Rabbinical method of argument, of Scripture quotation, of allegorization, and the like, but rarely in his literary style. Whenever Paul does not measure up to Greek rhetorical standards, it has been assumed either that he is not interested in or that he is unable to write a literary style. Few students of his style have made the most of the observation, that his writings represent a 'middle-type'.

Now, the epistles of Paul have always presented a great many problems to the interpreter. Not only are they full of allusions to situations with which we are little acquainted, and they present modes of thought which seem strange to us, but they suffer also from a diffuse and repetitious style, which, at times, makes it [p. 140] difficult to construe his sentences. Even when there is no difficulty in following this thought, his literary style appears heavy and cumbersome. From the earliest times to our own days, we meet with writers who find Paul difficult to follow. [. . .]

[p. 141]

There seems to be unanimous agreement among scholars that the style of Paul is exceedingly verbose and repetitious, and that his sentences are loosely put together and hence difficult to understand [p. 142]. Blass, however, emphasizes the central point of the whole matter by directing our attention to the Semitic models of Paul. But neither Blass nor any other scholar has questioned whether it is fair to judge the style of writings, which for their models have Semitic patterns, by the canons of classical Greek writers. Much of the Pentateuch is likewise verbose and repetitious, but, as we have already seen in the leprosy laws, the repetitiousness may easily be reduced to a system, to a literary style, which is just as fixed and determinable as any style of the Greeks or the Romans, and which has just as much claim to our appreciation as any other forms that may come before us in the literature of the human race. The literary patterns which were followed by the writers of the New Testament have not been known, and modern writers on the style of the New Testament have measured it altogether by Greek standards.

[. . .]   [p. 143]

As soon as we approach his epistles with the standards provided for us by the *chiastic* and *alternating* order of ideas, so conspicuous a feature of Hebrew style, we have a new instrument for the investigation and appraisal of Paul's style.

[p. 147]

In 1 Cor. 9.19-22 we have a passage which contains a personal confession of Paul, yet even this autobiographical section of the epistle is wrought in literary form. This has not escaped Weiss,[35] although he does not observe the alternating order of the ideas in the chiastic form of the whole passage.

---

35. Johannes Weiss, *Das Urchristentum*, p. 310.

A
> For though I was free from all,   19
> > I brought myself under bondage to all,
> > > That I might gain the more.

B
> I became   20
> > To the Jews,
> > > As a Jew,
> > > > That I might gain Jews.

C
> To them that are under the law,
> > As under the law,
> > > Not being myself under the law,
> > > > That I might gain them that are under the law.

C'
> To them that are without law,   21
> > As without law,
> > > Not being without the law of God,
> > > > but under the law of Christ,
> > > > > That I might gain them that are without law.

B'
> I became   22
> > To the weak,
> > > Weak,
> > > > That I might gain the weak.

A'
> To all
> > I have become all things,
> > > That I might by all means save some.

This is a good example of passages in which the sections are chiastic while the lines are alternating. Paul shows how in dealing with his converts he has always adapted himself to the stage of maturity in which he found them. The purpose, which in all six instances is expressed in the last line of each section, was to gain [p. 148] them for Christ. Only in A' is the verb 'save' substituted for 'gain', but the meaning remains unchanged. Line by line the same ideas recur without variation until the passage is completed, unless it be in C' where the reference to 'the law of Christ' is made, probably to save Paul from the charge of being a lawless person. This passage is of the same type as Isa. 28.15-18; Lev. 11.24-28; 14.21-32.

[p. 151]

We need not to continue to give any greater number of the briefer passages, which may be found almost anywhere in the epistles of Paul, but shall proceed to analyze some of the *longer sections* into whose structure the chiastic and alternating parallelisms have entered. The seventh chapter of Paul's First Epistle to the Corinthians is long; it deals with some social problems which arose when Christians attempted to apply the ideals of Christianity in a pagan society. We shall first give a general outline of the main parts of this chapter and later give the separate parts. This is done with a view of helping the reader to grasp the main features of the chapter from the start before we enter into details.

A Literary Analysis of Chapter Seven

I. Introduction: A man is not to touch a woman, vs. 1.

  II. The Sexual Problem in the Married State and its Solution, vss. 2-5.

    III. Rules Governing Married Couples and some Unmarried, vss. 6-17.

      IV. Circumcision or Uncircumcision, vss. 18-20.

      V. Bond or Free, vss. 21-24.

    VI. Rules Governing Virgins and some Married Couples, vss. 25-35.

  VII. The Sexual Problem in the Virgin State and its Solution, vss. 36-39.

VIII. Conclusion: A woman is happier as she is, vs. 40.

It will be seen at a glance that the first three parts and the last three deal with the sexual problem, while parts IV and V deal with classes in the church, and what their attitude ought to be. No one can read through the chapter without sensing the radical change of subject at the centre (vss. 18-24). This is nothing else than the law of the shift at the centre, of which several instances have been noticed in the Old Testament. We shall now give a detailed arrangement of Part II (vss. 2-5):

Part II, vss. 2-5

A   But because of fornications,   2

   B   Let each man have his own wife,
      And let each woman have her own husband.

                                                                     [p. 152]
      C   Let the husband render unto the wife her due;   3
         And likewise also the wife unto the husband.

      C' The wife hath not power over her own body, but the husband;   4
         And likewise also the husband hath not power over his own body,
                                           [but the wife.

   B' Defraud not one the other, except it be by consent for a season,   5
      That ye may give yourselves unto prayer, may be together again,

A' That Satan tempt you not because of your incontinence.

This passage does not contain Paul's preference in regard to marriage, which he has expressed in the introduction and conclusion of this chapter (cf. v. 1 with v. 40), but rather his concessions because of weak human nature (cf. v. 6). The members of the church were confronted with temptations because of fornication (A) and because incontinence (A'). They should live in monogamy (B) and they should have marital relations, unless by consent they denied themselves for a season and for specific reasons (B'). The rights of each party are stated in CC'. Paul follows the principle of expediency in the face of human weakness.

> The analysis of 1 Corinthians 7, and of other texts by Paul continues until p. 225. Of Lund's studies of the evangelical texts (pp. 229-319) and on Revelation (pp. 323-411), nothing will be reproduced here, because they bring nothing new from the methodological point of view.

A Few Contemporaries

> From the mid-1950s, studies of short texts, and also of entire books, are legion.
> First of all, it is fitting to mention Enrico Galbiati who published in 1956 La struttura letteraria dell'Esodo.[36] He begins with the 'state of affairs' of research:[37] other than Jousse and Condamin, on whom he

---

36. Rome: Alba, 1956.
37. *La struttura*, pp. 15-37.

spends some time (along with a disciple of the latter), the other thirteen authors he introduces are German; the same ones Condamin refers to. Like Condamin, he ignores the English scholars,[38] as well as Lund. He then formulates fifteen canons which regulate the composition of the narrative texts of the Bible. He provides a catalogue of the first ten, which are those that his predecessors had already noticed: they essentially concern the parallel reproduction of the same story (canons I and VI); under different forms (II);[39] and its various degrees (V); marked by fixed formulas (IV); with complementary cycles (III and IX), which can make progress towards the last repetition (VII); only canon VIII features 'symmetrical or concentric series'.[40] The other canons are those he discovered himself: the distinction (XI) and the alternation of the forms of narration (XII; he distinguishes between narration, formed of several sections, and notices or summaries). In the last three, he opposes 'the total concentric symmetry' (XIII) to 'regression' (XIV): in the first, it is the scenes which are arranged in a concentric manner, whereas it is the sentences in the second. The last canon (XV) is entitled 'supplementary cycles of concentric symmetry' (combination of IX and XIII). Galbiatti admits that his canons XI to XV are similar to the preceding ones (VIII and IX), but whereas Condamin and the others had found them in poetical texts only, Galbiati finds them in narrative texts.

A few year later, in 1961, Paul Lamarche published an analogous study on Zacharias.[41] He establishes a careful hierarchy of his criteria for the delimitation of the pieces (pp. 25-31):

—'First and foremost, *meaning*,
—then certain *clues* which enable the recognition of the beginning (or the end) of a unit (imperatives and certain expressions such as 'so', 'because', 'for', 'thus speaks the Lord'),
—at last, and as a last resort, the *internal structure* of the piece.'

For the internal structure of the pieces, he maintains that the only guide is parallelism in all its forms; he distinguishes:

---

38. Even Lowth is not mentioned in the author's index!

39. An event told by a narrator and reproduced by a character; order and execution; prediction and realization. . .

40. Canon X contemplates the particular case of the insertion of a narration within another.

41. *Zacharie IX-XIV: Structure littéraire et messianisme* (EBib, Paris: Gabalda: 1961).

. 'The structure by simple repetition of a theme, of a formula, or a chorus (in a parallel position or as a form of inclusion),
. the structure of parallel type following the formula a b c a'b'c',
. the structure in the shape of chiasm following the formula a b c c'b'a',
. the complex structure which mixes the preceding two.'[42]

> *Then in 1963 Albert Vanhoye gave an analysis of the Epistle to the Hebrews, which enjoyed some acclaim.*[43] *Vanhoye devoted his work to the explanation of the literary clues which mark the structure of the Epistle: criticizing one of his predecessors, he makes a distinction between the 'hook word', 'a mechanical device of transition' which 'lies in linking two consecutive paragraphs by the repetition of a single word', from the 'announcement of the subject', 'an intelligent device of composition' which 'consists in indicating in advance the theme of a development to come'. He adds to these two devices inclusion, 'the most frequently used and the most important clue' which 'consists in framing a development by the use of the same word or formula', the variations in vocabulary from a section, or part, to the next, the alternation of the genres, from the exposition to the exhortation in the case of the Epistle studied, and at last the symmetrical dispositions (i. e. parallel, concentric and alternated).*[44] *Vanhoye shows how the Epistle obeys, from beginning to end, and at all levels of organization of the text, to the laws of parallel and, above all, concentric composition.*
>
> *Since then, studies of a rhetorical nature have not ceased to multiply, especially on short texts, and there is scarcely an issue of the most important journals of biblical exegesis which do not contain one. Certain researchers have made rhetorical analysis a speciality of sorts.*[45] *To present*

42. In a study of the Epistle to the Romans (P. Lamarche and C. Le Dû, *Epître aux Romains V–VIII: Structure littéraire et sens* [Paris: Editions du CNRS, 1980]), lacking any systemization, other clues appear, such as the alternation of pronouns (p. 11), vocabulary (p. 15) and mainly, although it is not explained, syntaxic parallelism (pp. 23, 29, 56).

43. *La Structure littéraire de l'Epître aux Hébreux* (Paris: Desclée de Brouwer, 1963, 1976).

44. *La Structure* (1976), pp. 33-37; 'Les indices de la structure littéraire de l'Epître aux Hébreux', *SE* 2 (1964), pp. 493-509 (the quotations are taken from this article). Also in the same vein D. Minguez (*Pentecostés: Ensayo de Semiotica narrativa en Hch 2* [AnBib, 75; Rome: Biblical Institute Press, 1976], pp. 22-29) which enumerates, in conjunction with the figures of classical rhetoric, the inclusion, the hook word, the chiasm and the concentric structure.

45. Among others, Y. Radday, A. Ceresko, W. Holladay, A. Wright, D.N. Freedman, P. Auffret and J. Radermakers.

a panorama of the actual situation would grow beyond this work's limits.
A systematic bibliography of all the studies of this kind would already be
an impressive task: Angelico di Marco attempted it and John Welch has
completed it.[46]

But what is most urgently lacking here is a systematic presentation of
biblical rhetoric. The reader will surely have felt a slight discomfort while
reading the texts of the pioneers of rhetorical analysis. Indeed, their
terminology is not always precise and unequivocal. Furthermore, if Jebb,
Boys and Lund, to quote but the greatest, make a distinction between
micro and macro structures,[47] *a clear and coherent exposition of the levels*
of organization of the text is found nowhere. In rhetorical analyses, even,
and perhaps above all, recent ones, this last point is particularly neglected.
Symmetries and relationships of all kinds are very numerous in a text; the
whole problem resides in knowing at which level of organization of the
text they are relevant. It is this flaw that the rest of this work is intended to
contribute to correcting.

---

46. A. di Marco, *Il chiasmo nella Bibbia, contributi di stilistica strutturale* (Torino: Marietti, 1980; reproduction of 'Der Chiasmus in der Bibel', *LB* 36 (1975); 37 (1976); 39 (1976). J. Welch (ed.), *Chiasmus in Antiquity* (Hildesheim: Gerstenberg, 1981).

47. To use the expressions used by M. Girard, *Les Psaumes*.

Part II

EXPOSITION OF RHETORICAL ANALYSIS

Chapter 4

PRESUPPOSITIONS OF RHETORICAL ANALYSIS[*]

I would like to take this opportunity to explain the 'Presuppositions of rhetorical analysis'. It seemed appropriate to start by looking up the meaning of the word 'presupposition' in a current dictionary. According to *The Shorter Oxford English Dictionary*, 'to presuppose' is defined as 'to suppose beforehand or *a priori*'. The understanding of 'to presuppose' presupposes therefore the understanding of 'to suppose'. The same dictionary gives the following as one of the definitions of the verb 'to suppose': 'to substitute by artifice or fraud'. I would not want my discourse to be found within this definition! I therefore choose the modern understanding of 'presuppose', from the scholastic Latin *suppositivus*, the literal translation of the Greek *hupotheticos*, which means as anyone can guess, 'hypothetical'. The two meanings of this word are: first, 'to give as an hypothesis'; secondly, 'to think, admit as a probable thing, or as a plausible explanation, without being able to say for sure'. More than a simple working hypothesis, I allow myself to think that the principles of rhetorical analysis are within the order of the 'plausible explanation'. But it is not only a case of 'supposing' but of 'presupposing'. And, as we have seen, 'to presuppose' is defined as 'to suppose beforehand'. Consequently the question 'before what?' emerges. In other words, can one make presuppositions before making any observations at all? Is it possible to submit a pure hypothesis, gratuitous, without any pre-emptive study of the object of research? In other words, are the principles of rhetorical analysis pure *a priori* or *a posteriori*, presuppositions or postsuppositions?

I would like to paint a panorama of the 'postsuppositions' which,

[*]   This chapter reproduces the seminar paper I delivered on February 14, 1991 at the Catholic school of theology of the University of Strasbourg and published in the first half of my article, 'Présupposés de l'analyse rhétorique, avec une application à Mc 10,13-52'.

little by little, have become mine, and work for me like they were 'presuppositions' in my current work and could be considered as such by those to whom I have offered them and who would like to use them and verify them. What I would call my presuppositions are not general, cultural, ideological, theological *a priori*, which impermeate, along with many others, my thought, and that I received from my formation, my teachers, or simply because I live in the second half of the twentieth century. I leave the analysis of these presuppositions to the men of the arts, philosophers or historians of thought. My purpose is much more modest. What I would call my presuppositions are what I believe to be the firm points of the analysis I practise and that I have tried to formulate, particularly thanks to the linguistic training that I received.

If it were necessary to synthesize in one formula the whole of those presuppositions, I would say that *the biblical texts are well composed, if they are analysed according to the laws of biblical rhetoric, and the study of their composition enables one to understand them better, as far as the analysis brings to light their inner logic.*

First Presupposition:
The Biblical Texts are Composed and Well Composed

The first presupposition of rhetorical analysis is that *the biblical texts are composed*. And, should one say from the beginning, that they are for the most part well composed. It is true that the first impression of the modern western readers is completely to the contrary to this affirmation. The Gospels, the Prophets, and so many other texts seem to them loose and inorganic. It seems to them that they are dealing with scattered collection of pieces with very little links between them. For the contemporary readers, their feeling is reinforced by the sub-heading of the modern translations of the Bible. By reading these sub-headings in succession, the biblical books seem to be more a hodge-podge than a genuine composition. Herewith an example: *Cure of a paralytic, The call of Levi, Eating with sinners in Levi's house, Discussion on fasting, Picking corn on the sabbath, Cure of the man with a withered hand, The choice of the Twelve, The crowds follow Jesus, The inuagural discourse. The Beatitudes, The curses, Love of enemies, Compassion and generosity, Integrity, The true disciple, Cure of the centurion's servant, The son of the widow of Nain restored to life...*

This impression of disorder is gradually replaced, thanks to biblical rhetoric, with an often extremely elaborate construction. At least this is what I think I have demonstrated for the portion of the text of Luke from which the list of titles I have just enumerated was drawn, and, I dare hope, demonstrated for the whole of the third Gospel.[1]

When confronted with any text, any book, rhetorical analysis presupposes that it is constructed or composed, following a logic which is yet to be discovered, at various levels of organization of the text. The construction of the units of the first level of a poetical text—distichs and tristichs—is unanimously recognized, even if it does not present the same regularity everywhere. Let me add immediately that the regularity of a text can be very obscure at one level but reveal itself clearly at the next. For example in this distich from Isa. 43.2:

> When you pass though the waters, I will be with you
> and the river will not overwhelm you;

One can hardly say that the parallelism of the members is obvious; but, as soon as it is seen from the superior level of organization of the text (that of the 'piece' according to my terminology), the parallelism between these two segments and the following is evident:

When	YOU PASS		*the waters,*	*I WILL BE WITH YOU*
		and	*the rivers*	shall not overwhelm you;
when	YOU WALK through		*fire,*	you shall not be burned
		and	*the flame*	shall not consume you.

The phenomenon that I have just illustrated on a short unit is also true for higher levels of textual organization. This is but one aspect of the principle of organicity of the text. Hence the need to analyse the text systematically at all levels of its organization.

To go on to another aspect of the same principle, as well as to a superior level, that of the pericope, rhetorical analysis is concerned with highlighting the proper figure of the passage it studies, and is not concerned—at least initially—in its form, in the sense implied by the history of forms. It is not interested in the recurrence of identical or similar elements in a series of texts, but in the particular realization, in the specificity of each as individual texts. Biblical rhetoric holds that what makes the unique character of an individual text is not to be

---

1. R. Meynet, *L'Evangile selon saint Luc: Analyse rhétorique*. I. *Planches* (Paris: Cerf, 1988); II. *Commentary* (Paris: Cerf, 1988).

found in a differential study, that determines in what ways a text is distinct from all those that have been identified as belonging to the same group or form. Rhetorical analysis prefers to bring its attention to the particular text, without comparing it to others, because it believes that in bringing to light the composition of the pericope it enables the discovery of its own distinctness. Each pericope possesses its own organization, independently from the texts it resembles in content. The internal links between each of its units and all the others form a specific system or figure that resembles no other. Besides the rhetorical organization of the pericope does not necessarily correspond to the partition into elements such as are individualized in the study of forms. The repetitions within a single pericope, the series of terms belonging to the same semantic field, the symmetries that they create through their position in the text, form a system, the knowledge of which enables a better understanding of the text.

In order to step up in the organization of the book, one can say that the most specific contribution of rhetorical analysis is the bringing to light of textual units composed of several pericopes, which I call 'sequences'. Let me add that rhetorical analysis, at least such as I understand and practise it, does not seek to solely identify or extract a sequence or another from the book, but to see how the whole of the book is organized in sequences which cover the entirety of the text. The sequences are then organized in sections and the whole of the sections form the book. This is as far as the first presupposition of the method goes. In other words and to be more precise, biblical rhetoric does not pretend that all biblical books were composed in one stroke, or with the same rigour. It posits it as a reasonable hypothesis because it verified it in more that one book, and can therefore presuppose it for others.

I will conclude this first point in enunciating the three necessary conditions in order to discover the organization of the texts. The first condition to find the composition of a biblical text is very simple. One must look for it. And that demands *much* time, and patience. Because the most undeniable facts have the remarkable propriety of staying long hidden from one's gaze, even from the keen observer's, despite the fact that they are self-evident. The correlation of this premise is that, when after a long period of scrutiny, the text continues to resist and one has not found a convincing construction, it is good practise to attribute this failure, not to the faulty composition of the text, but to

172 *Rhetorical Analysis*

the incompetence of the researcher. Tenacity, in this domain, is profitable. To say things differently, when one has so often experienced texts which turned out to be constructed in a manner beyond all expectations, it is very difficult not to 'presuppose' that other texts which resist explanation will eventually yield the secret of their composition, no matter what it takes. I do not pretend to say that all texts are composed with the same skillful art, or with the same regularity; what I am saying is that on one hand they are composed, and on the other that one should not think it easy to find their organization with any speed. The second condition is that it is necessary to be experienced, and that comes only with a long time of practise and trial and error. Amateurs and people in a hurry, abstain! Why insist on this second condition, which is valid for all arts, if not to warn the beginner against precipitation as well as discouragement. The third condition is to recognize the laws of biblical rhetoric.

Second Presupposition:
There is a Specifically Biblical Rhetoric

Which brings me to the second presupposition, namely that there is a biblical rhetoric. For most westerners, there is only one rhetoric, the 'classical' or Graeco-Roman rhetoric. It dominated learning for about twenty-five centuries, including our own, despite its apparent execution by Romanticism. After an eclipse, it comes back in strength, not only among specialists, but also in teaching, for example under the name of 'techniques of expression', either at university, or in continuing education. In the domain of exegesis, everyone knows that since Antiquity there have been attempts to measure the biblical texts by the canons of the only known rhetoric, the Graeco-Roman rhetoric. Flavius Josephus was only the first of many to look for hexameters, pentameters and other Greek meters in biblical poetry.[2] And the same holds true for the current expounders of American 'rhetorical criticism'.[3]

2. *Ant.* 2.16.4; 4.8.44; 7.12.3 (see C. Souvay, *Essai sur la métrique des Psaumes*, p. 1).
3. For example, G. Kennedy, *New Testament Interpretation through Rhetorical Criticism* (Chapel Hill: University of North Carolina Press, 1984); see my criticism: 'Histoire de l'analyse rhétorique en exégèse biblique', *Rhetorica* 8 (1990), pp. 291-320 (especially, pp. 312-13).

Since the middle of the seventeenth century, Robert Lowth has shown that the Hebrew poetry followed other paths than those of western poetry, antique or modern. The discoveries of John Jebb and Thomas Boys, to mention but the pioneers, have proven that the texts of the New Testament obey the same rules as those of the Old. It is therefore with a biblical rhetoric, and not only Hebraic, that we are dealing. Its laws were not formulated at the time when the biblical texts were composed, and they were only discovered recently, two and a half centuries ago. This second presupposition is therefore divided in two: first, that there is an Hebrew rhetoric, distinct from the Graeco-Roman rhetoric; secondly, the Greek texts of the Old Testament and those of the New Testament obey the same organizational laws as those of the Hebrew Bible.

I would identify three characteristics of the Hebrew rhetoric that distinguish it from classical rhetoric: *it is more concrete than abstract, it uses parataxis more than syntax, it is more involutive than linear.*

First of all, Hebrew literature is essentially *concrete*. When Greek rhetoric looks to illustrate or prove abstract ideas, through examples, Hebrew rhetoric tends to follow the opposite path: it describes reality, leaving the reader to conclude. The Jew shows, the Greek wants to demonstrate.[4] The Greek seeks to lead his reader to the bottom of his thoughts, while the Jew shows the way and encourages him to follow it.

It is in this concrete characteristic, it seems, that lies the principal reason for the strong binary organization of Hebrew literature. Everyone knows that such binary expressions as 'heaven and earth' and 'night and day' are ways of saying 'everywhere' and 'always'; it is less than certain that everyone is aware that one of the major functions of synonimic parallelism is to 'direct the gaze towards a meaning which can only be "between the lines"... "You will tread on the lion and the adder; the young lion and the serpent you will trample under foot" (Ps. 91.13): this leads me to the *idea* of a threat, distinct from its materializations but inseparable from them. Energy is born out of the image, but it has to get free from it. This is probably why the biblical texts offer so much food for thought to the most demanding mind,

---

4. It is impossible to translate the play on the words of the original: 'Le Juif *montre*, le Grec veut *démontrer*'.

without doing its thinking for him';[5] fewer still are those who remark the extension of this manner of speech, for example when Jesus addresses first 'those who were invited' and then to 'the man who had invited him' (Lk. 14.7-14), which is a way of targeting the whole of his auditors.[6]

One should be careful to note that concrete does not mean simple and that binary does not necessarily mean repetition. A reading exclusively sensitive to what is identical in the two halves of a binary unit will miss the core of the argument, what is the aim of the repetition. This is what happened to Augustin George, when he said about the double parables of Luke: 'It is a technique which enables the gaze to enter the essential of a parable. What the parable means, is what is kept in parallel in both parables. [. . .] The parallels help to discover what the fundamental theme of the parable is. This theme is what is parallel; the rest is but decoration, or image.'[7] In the parable of the lost sheep and the lost silver piece, to take once more this demonstrative example,[8] the difference between the two halves of the parable is not decoration at all, it is on the contrary all the more relevant, it constitutes the focal point of the message, the spring of the thought process: although they have stayed *in the house* as the silver piece, the pharisees and the scribes to whom Jesus speaks are nonetheless as lost as the publicans and the sinners represented by the lost sheep *in the wilderness*, far from the house: the binary aspect is redoubled, since if the younger son is lost far from his father's house, like the sheep in the wilderness, the elder is no less a sinner than his brother, despite the fact that he always stayed with his father and had never contravened any of his orders. The difference between the story of the elder and of the silver piece which is parallel to it is as relevant: if the silver piece has been found, it means that the forgiveness and the joy are also offered to the elder son and to the pharisees and scribes. But will they accept it?

---

5.   P. Beauchamp, preface to *L'Analyse rhétorique*, pp. 11-12 (see above, pp. 25-26).

6.   See above, pp. 19-20.

7.   *Lecture de l'Evangile selon St Luc* (Lyon: Profac, 1971), p. 53.

8.   R. Meynet, 'Deux paraboles parallèles; analyse rhétorique de Lc 15,1-32', *Annales de Philosophie de la Faculté des Lettres et des Sciences Humaines de l'Université Saint-Joseph* (Beyrouth) 2 (1981), pp. 89-105; reproduced in *L'Evangile selon saint Luc*.

The second characteristic of Hebrew rhetoric is that is is *paratactic*. That is to say that it juxtaposes or coordinates more than it subordinates. In other words, it does not always expresses the logical relations in the same way that the Greek rhetoric does, using words such as are used in a syllogism or a enthymeme: 'Given that. . . it follows that. . . ', 'whereas', 'therefore', 'consequently'. This is verified mostly at the superior levels of textual organization: such expressions as 'on the one hand. . . on the other' are seldom found to mark a relationship of opposition between two great units.[9] The absence of these verbal marks does not mean that biblical rhetoric is devoid of means to convey logical relations, but the means it uses are from another source: they lie essentially in the disposition of the units and in the repetitions, mostly lexical, between symmetrical units. One of the simplest example would be the proverb: 'The door turns on his hinges, the sluggard on his bed' (Prov. 26.14), where the relation of comparison is not marked by the words 'as' and 'so', but by the sole morpho-syntactic parallelism. In Lk. 8.40-56, there are only the disposition and the lexical repetitions that indicate the complementary resemblances between Jairus's daughter and the haemorrhagic: both tales are intertwined, both women are called 'daughter' and most of all the number 'twelve' is repeated for the one and the other: Jairus's daughter dies at the moment she reaches the age of becoming a bride and a mother, the other woman has been denied motherhood since the age of twelve.[10]

The third characteristic of Hebrew rhetoric is the specific manner in which it composes parallel dispositions and most of all concentrical arrangements. Instead of developing its argumentation in a linear way, in the Graeco-Roman fashion, to a conclusion which is the point of resolution of the discourse, it is organized most of the time in an involutive manner around a centre which is the focal point, the keystone, through which the rest finds cohesion. The centre of a concentric construction most of the time presents certain specific characteristics: it is often of a different shape and genre than the rest of the text, it is very often a question, or at least something which is problematic, which in all cases is enigmatic. Among so many examples, I will mention Moses'

---

9.   Like in the speech of Charles de Gaulle which was broadcast on the radio and television on 17 December 1965 (see R. Meynet, *L'Evangile selon saint Luc*, II, p. 10).

10.   See R. Meynet, *L'Evangile selon saint Luc*, II, pp. 95-96.

canticle, in Exodus 15, constructed around the redoubled question of
v. 11: 'Who is like you, O Lord, among the gods? Who is like you,
majestic in holiness, terrible in glorious deeds, doing wonders?',
because the same structure is reproduced, in shortened form, in the
Canticle of Moses and the Lamb, in Rev. 15.3-4, also centered on a
similar question: 'Who shall not fear and glorify your name, O
Lord?'[11]

This said, I would not want to avoid the question of the relationship
between classical and Hebrew rhetoric. This question is particularly
relevant for the texts of the New Testament, written in Greek, and not
in Hebrew, in a middle-eastern world which was influenced, at least in
certain sections of its population, by Greek civilization and learning.
It is therefore perfectly legitimate to look for what would denote this
influence in the New Testament. Rhetorical analysis, however, poses—
'presupposes', in the sense outlined at the beginning—that the authors
of the New Testament, being impregnated to the bone with the literature of the Jewish Scriptures, have followed—consciously and/or
unconsciously—the laws of composition of Hebrew rhetoric. Consequently, we are perfectly in our rights to speak not only of Hebraic
rhetoric, but more broadly of a biblical rhetoric. I do not deny the
possibility of a Greek influence, if only on the Greek writings of the
Old Testament, but for now, I will limit myself to studying the texts
solely from the point of view of Hebrew rhetoric. To speak only of
my own practise, I found the same kind of construction in the Psalms,
Prophets and the Torah, as in the Gospels and even in the Gospel
according to Luke of whom it is said that he was Greek and whom I
have said, quite provokingly, to be a Jew, for this reason.

The second presupposition, namely that there is such a thing as a
biblical rhetoric, strengthens and complements the first presupposition, namely that the texts are composed, and generally well composed. It is true that, according to the rules of Graeco-Roman rhetoric, the biblical texts seem badly constructed or not at all, but when
analysed with the right tools, according to their own proper rules,
they turn out to be cleverly composed. It is simply that one should not
analyse a language with the grammar of another, especially when the
two languages belong to two families that bear no resemblance whatsoever. What can be misleading in the case of the New Testament, is

11. See R. Meynet, 'Le cantique de Moïse et le cantique de l'Agneau (Ap 15 et
Ex 15)', *Greg.* 73 (1992), pp. 19-55.

that Hebrew thought was dressed in the Greek language the same way that so many contemporary Jews wore the 'chiton'; we know the problem of those who went to the gymnasium to hide their Jewry. The texts of the New Testament are marked in their flesh, in an indelible way, by the covenant of Abraham. And this is not only an image.

Third Presupposition:
The Review of a Certain Method of Historical Criticism

From the first two presuppositions unfolds, logically if not chronologically, a third presupposition, the critical aspect of which is as apparent as that of the preceding two. The third presupposition could be called the principle of trust, trust in the text and in its own internal logic. It is therefore directly in opposition to the customary principle of mistrust which modern criticism rates so highly. One can tax rhetorical analysis of being naïve and uncritical. I have, for my own part, the weakness of thinking that if the analysis called today 'rhetorical' was born before historical criticism,[12] it has become, through the ages, post-critical, or to put things more clearly and more frankly, a criticism of the criticism, especially literary criticism.

Of course, it is possible to preach the principle of irenics in saying that the opposition of the two methods is complementary in nature: it would be a proof of courtesy and toleration which would leave everyone where he started, avoiding all contact which would provoke hostilities that nobody wants. To take a no more war-like metaphor but an agrarian one, everyone should cultivate one's own garden with one's own tools and rigourously limit oneself to one's own field of inquiry. Indeed, each approach should keep its methodological autonomy and to mix them hastily would be disastrous. On the other hand oecumenical irenics which would ignore the problems if not the differences, could turn out to be nothing more than an easy way out. Let us take today a more audacious attitude, even if, here is Strasburg, it is not exempt from any risks! I was led to believe that your project looked for confrontation. I would therefore fail my duty as a guest if I withdrew from it.

The first aspect of the criticism of the criticism: a maximum respect for the Massoretic Text. Although it is much more moderate nowadays, historical criticism has taken for more than a century too many

---

12. Or at the same time (see above, p. 44)

liberties to propose, if not to impose, corrections which for the most part were totally uncalled for. Those corrections not only interfere with the vocalization of the text, but even to the consonantal text, and very often to the order of the verses, when it does not simply eliminate whole portions of the text, for example *metri causa*. The so-called 'critical apparatus' of the Stuttgartensia is filled full of those emendations several of which have unfortunately been reproduced in translation in the vernacular, and have even found a place in the texts and the liturgical hymns, and therefore in the memory of the faithful. Thankfully, the variety of the translations and their speedy obsolescence should mean that the wrong can be amended! The Massoretic Text is indeed sometimes obscure, even unintelligible, but it needs nonetheless to be translated, hence the inevitable conjectures when the older translations are of no avail. It is sometimes faulty and it is possible to correct it.[13] What I simply want to say is that rhetorical analysis, through its knowledge of the organizational laws of the biblical texts, often offers solutions to problems with which those who ignore those laws are confronted. Experience has indeed revealed that it was better to instinctively refrain from all corrections. Rather than doubt the text and the manuscript tradition, rhetorical analysis would more readily be suspicious of the criticism. It has so often verified that the *delenda metri causa* revealed a profound ignorance of the laws of Hebraic poetry, that the displacements resulted from a notable misunderstanding of semitic logic, that it has chosen to ignore them when following the path of research and to combat them vigorously when teaching. I will never forget the very first operation that my master, Paul Beauchamp, would have us do, when we did not know enough Hebrew to work without a translation, was to put the text back in order, where the Jerusalem Bible had changed it![14]

Another aspect of the same presupposition is that the text as it is obeys a certain logic, which, all different from our own as it may be,

13. For example, Ps. 145, an alphabetical acrostic where the distych starting with the letter *noun* is missing from the Massoretic Text which can nevertheless be corrected thanks to the LXX and to a manuscript from Qumran; see R. Meynet, 'Le psaume 145', *Annales du Département des lettres arabes (Institut de lettres orientales)*, Festschrift Maurice Fyet, 6B (1991–92), pp. 213-25.

14. The second edition of the *Jerusalem Bible* (1977) has thankfully corrected certain excesses of the first edition (1956), for example for Hos. 2–3 (unfortunately not for Ps. 146.8-9; see below, pp. 226 n. 32).

is nonetheless real. The word 'logic' is to be understood as the reverse of the word 'rhetoric', as its signifying side. To consider the text as possessing its own logic leads us to be wary of anything that interprets the singularities of the text as the traces of the story of its redaction. One does not deny that there has been, for those texts as of all texts— including this one—a work of composition, sometimes at several hands. What is being questioned is the unilateral interpretation as an indication of sources, and therefore of diverse time periods, of facts that fall within the laws of composition of the texts. What literary criticism calls 'doublets', where it sees posterior adjunctions, seem to be usually explained, most of the time, by the binary law which is sel- dom questioned at the level of the distich. Or, in order to be coherent, literary criticism would have to consider all the second members of bimember segments of synonymic parallelism as doublets, that is as secondary adjunctions! The 'contradictions' and 'logical disruptions' that it seeks are only so, most of the time, to our western logic. To biblical rhetoric and logic, a lot of these indications of redactional nature do not hold. Need the divine names which serve as distinctions between the Yawhist and Elohist documents in the Pentateuch be always held as redactional indications? Could they not, for example in the Psalms, play the part of a mark of composition, used by the poet to build his text, in conjunction with other marks? If, in a list of similar oracles, the form of an oracle differ from that of the others, is it necessarily the sign that this oracle is from a different time period and by a different author than the others? Could it not be the result of the wilful composition of one and the same author instead? Is it cer- tain that in Proverbs 9 the verses 7-12, 'which interrupt the develop- ment and break the Folly–Wisdom diptych (1–6; 13–18), constitute a posterior addition'?[15] Even if it were true—rhetorical analysis thinks it very doubtful, having noticed elsewhere this type of concentric construction—does it bring new light to the understanding of the text in its final version? To qualify, as does the Jerusalem Bible, those central verses of 'aphorisms subsequently inserted as a commentary on v. 6'[16] clearly shows that neither their unity nor their function, as a focal reflection on what a man caught between wisdom and folly should do, was understood. On the other hand, to ignore the concen- tric construction of the central passage around the proverb 'The fear

15. The Osty Bible, *ad loc.*
16. Both editions.

of the Lord is the beginning of wisdom; and the knowledge of the
Holy One is insight' (9.10) is to deny its true interpretative key.

This being said, it nonetheless remains for me to note the points of
correspondence between rhetorical analysis and historical criticism.
The first one concerns the history of composition: it is clear that the
concern it shows for finding traces of the redactor's interventions
indicates that it considers the final text as a composition. The history
of forms, the more so when it tends to individualize literary genres
and their components, seeks—like rhetorical analysis—to make out
the units from the continuum of the text; rhetorical analysis does not
deny its contribution, when for example it notes that the difference of
literary genres can be relevant as an element of the sequence's construction. Many facts brought to light by literary criticism—disruptions, differences, oppositions—are also noted by rhetorical analysis,
even if the interpretation that the two approaches make of those facts
are opposed, sometimes radically.

Such are the three presuppositions of rhetorical analysis: the biblical
texts form well composed wholes, they are organized according to
laws of a specific, semitic and not western, rhetoric, and one should
therefore trust the texts as they are because they have their own
internal logic.

By way of a conclusion, I will attempt to say briefly to what school
of thought, or to what science, rhetorical analysis could be linked. It
will allow me to specify certain notions and certain operations to
which rhetorical analysis pays special attention. Before showing in
what way rhetorical analysis can be linked or be said to be part of
modern or structural linguistics, it is necessary to recall that at the
beginning it was not born out of linguistics. Let us say, to cut a long
story short, that it was marked from its very origins by anglo-saxon
empiricism, that of its true founders, R. Lowth in the middle of the
seventeenth century and mostly J. Jebb and T. Boys at the beginning
of the nineteenth century, even if Lowth makes references to the
Italian rabbi Azarias dei Rossi and if Jebb and Boys take after the
remarks of the German J.A. Bengel on the parallel and concentric
structures. Born long before structural linguistics, rhetorical analysis
can be considered, not only as being linguistic, but also as being part
of linguistics, as constituting the last degree of linguistic organization.

I have explained all of this elsewhere and I will not repeat myself here.[17]

Outflowing from the first presupposition, namely that a biblical book constitutes an organic whole, one of the major operations of rhetorical analysis will be to identify the relevant literary units, at all levels of organization of the text. In other words, as for the identification of phonemes, morphemes and lexemes, propositions and sentences, in linguistics, rhetorical analysis resides in finding procedures which will enable the cutting up, in a more scientific or at least more objective manner, of the text in its diverse units and to determine the function of each of those units in the whole. These procedures give exegesis the means to sharpen the capital notion of context: for example the context of a pericope is not necessarily the pericope, or pericopes, which precedes and follows it, but the whole of the units which constitutes the superior unit to the envisaged pericope: it will therefore be either the units which surround it, either only those which precede it, or only those which follow it. As in the word 'follow' the graphic context of the letter 'f' is constituted only by the five letters which follow it, and that of the 'w' only by the five letters which precede it. If I have chosen to end my exposition by this last point, it is because I want to underline this: if rhetorical analysis is obviously not the only exegetical method, even if one did not consider it an indispensable operation of the exegetical work, like textual criticism or lexicographic enquiries, it is not forbidden to think that it can nonetheless be useful.

17. *L'Evangile selon saint Luc*, II, pp. 8-11.

Chapter 5

RELATIONSHIPS BETWEEN LINGUISTIC ELEMENTS

The marks of composition of a text in prose can be external, at least in part: parts, chapters, paragraphs are often individualized by all sorts of titles and sub-titles following a hierarchy of numbers or various letters, or different types. Ancient world texts, such as those of the Bible, are often devoid of those marks which would have taken too much space at a time when it was necessary to save up as much of the valuable medium of writing as possible. In this case, the marks of composition are all within the text, that is linguistic in nature.[1]

But in order for linguistic elements to have a rhetorical function, as marks of composition, they have to form figures through their position in the text. And so they have to be in a relationship with one another.[2]

1. The 'Capitulation', or the division of biblical books into chapters, which is used nowadays, was done by Etienne Langton, when he was a professor at the University of Paris, in the very first years of the thirteenth century. Given a few reworkings, it was adopted rapidly and replaced the numerous capitulations in use up till then. The oldest known capitulation, that of the Vaticanus (B), dates back to the fourth century (C.-M. Martini, *Novum Testamentum e Codice Vaticanus Graeco 1209*, Vatican, 1968, pp. xii-xiii). From this time, each chapter (*kephalaion = capitulum*) bears, in the margin of the text, a title (is it necessary to recall that the titles of the pericopes of our modern translations of the Bible are no more part of the biblical text than are the ancient *titloi*?). The Gospel of Luke, for example, counts, in B, 152 sections and 83 in the Alexandrinus (A; fifth century). The division of the chapters into verses was introduced by Robert Etienne in 1551 (*Dictionnaire de la Bible*, 'Chapitres de la Bible' and 'Estienne Robert'; B. Metzger, *The Text of the New Testament: Its Transmission, Corruption and Restoration* (Oxford: Clarendon Press, 1964), pp. 22-23. These divisions in chapters and verses are obviously not done haphazardly and correspond, each at their own level, to a certain semantic and syntactic organization of the text. Their primary function is nonetheless practical in nature. Analysis should therefore not give to these divisions any undue importance.

2. For an analysis of rhetoric in the field of linguistics, R. Meynet, *L'Evangile selon saint Luc*, II, pp. 8-11.

Before presenting the basic figures of biblical rhetoric, it is therefore necessary to establish an inventory, as exhaustive as possible, of the relationships which can exist between linguistic elements, at the successive organizational levels of language.

The relationship between the linguistic elements which serve as marks of composition can either be of identity or opposition.

1. *Relationships of Identity*

Identity can either be total or partial; in the latter case, some would prefer to speak of a resemblance, or analogy, rather than identity.

1.1. *At the Lexical Level*

1.1.1. **Identical Lexemes*[3]

1.1.1.1. *Totally Identical Lexemes*
Two lexemes (or lexical *monemes) are totally identical when their *significant[4] and their *significatum[5] are the same.

Thus in Psalm 96, the first three sentences:

Sing *to the* LORD	a new song!
Sing *to the* LORD,	all the earth!
Sing *to the* LORD,	bless his name!

share two identical lexemes, 'sing' and 'Lord'.

In the parable 'of the prodigal son', in ch. 15 of Luke, three occurrences of the same verb 'to give' have a structuring function:

and no one	**GAVE**	him	16
	GIVE	a ring to his hand	22
Yet you never	**GAVE**	me a kid	29

---

3. Or lexical *moneme: a moneme is the minimum significant unit (called 'unit of the first articulation'; A. Martinet, *Elements of General Linguistics* (trans. E. Palmer; London: Faber & Faber, 1964) §§1-9, pp. 15-16); Lexical monemes or lexemes are distinguished from grammatical monemes or morphemes. 'Lexical monemes are those which belong to unlimited inventories' (*Elements*, §§4-19, p. 110); they are the monemes which 'are listed in the lexicon and not in the grammar' (*Elements*, §§1-9, p. 25).

*   The definition of the terms preceded by an asterix are reproduced in the glossary of technical terms, at the end of the book (pp. 372-76).

4. Phonetic form of a linguistic sign.

5. Meaning or value of a linguistic sign.

None of the consulted translations (French, English, Italian, Arabic, Hebrew) respects this identity; the central occurrence is translated by 'to put' in English, and by an equivalent in the other languages.

1.1.1.2. *Partially Identical Lexemes*
1.1.1.2.1. *Homonymous lexemes*. Two lexemes are homonymous[6] when their significant is identical but their significatum different.

In Jeremiah 31, where the same *tamrûrîm* is understood by the commentators as meaning 'very bitter' in v. 15 and 'milestone' (in the sense of 'road sign') in v. 21.[7]

In Amos 2.7-8, both occurrences of the verb *yaṭṭû* are interpreted as two verbal forms of the same root (*hiphil* the first time, and *qal* the second):

And the way of the afflicted	**THEY-TURN-ASIDE**	7
And upon garments taken in pledge	**THEY-LAY-DOWN**	8

1.1.1.2.2. *Synonymous lexemes*. Two lexemes are synonymous when their significatum is the same[8] and their significant different. At the beginning of Psalm 2

Why	**do conspire**	THE NATIONS	
and	THE PEOPLE	**plot**	in vain?

where 'conspire' is synonymous with 'plot' and 'Nations' with 'People'.

In the Prologue of the Gospel of John (Jn 1.12-13; current critical edition),

---

6. In vocalised Hebrew and in Greek (academic pronunciation), where there are no problems of spelling, there is no difference between homography (graphic identity) and homophony (identity of sound). Contrary to English, where 'bread' and 'bred' are not homographic.

7. Albert Condamin gives to these two homonyms the status of mark of composition (he prints them in bold characters): 'signals': 'this word, with this meaning, is not found anywhere else in the Bible. Targ. and Vulg. have translated it 'bitterness' mistaking it for a word of identical form, also rare (found three times in the Bible), which is found in v. 15 of the same chapter. Note the use of these two characteristic words, the one in the first verse of the stanza, the other in the first verse of the anti-stanza' (*Le Livre de Jérémie*, pp. 226-27).

8. Absolute synonymy is rare; it presents degrees which cannot be discussed here.

But to all who received him,
he gave power to   **BECOME CHILDREN**   of God,
    who believed in his name,
who, not of blood nor of the will of the flesh,
nor of the will of man, but   **WERE-BORN**   of God.

the *syntagm[9] 'become children' and the verb 'were-born' can be syn-onymous since they have the same significatum.

1.1.1.2.3. *Paronomastic lexemes.* There is paronomasia between two lexemes when they have different significatum but partly similar sig-nificants.

In the canticle of Hannah (1 Sam. 2.1-10) there is paronomasia in v. 5

The *sated*, for bread engaged themselves
The hungry fattened themselves of food
The barren has borne *seven*
She who has many children is forlorn.

between 'sated' ($\check{s}^e b\bar{e}\hat{i}m$) and 'seven' ($\check{s}ib\text{'}a$) because, apart from the suffix /-îm / and /-a/, all their consonantal *phonemes[10] are either identical (/b/ and /'/) or only differ through their articulation point (/š/ and /š/) and they follow each other in the same order.[11]

In the Prologue of John (Jn 1.12-13), there is paronomasia between *genesthai* ('become') and *egennēthēsan* ('were-born') which end seg-ments 12a and 13 (see above, §1.1.1.2.2).

1.1.1.2.4. Lexemes that belong to the same semantic field. Despite not being synonymous, two or several lexemes can belong to the same semantic field.

9.   All combination of monemes; a syntagm which starts with a preposition is called a 'prepositional syntagm'.

10.   Distinctive phonic unit (called 'of the second articulation'; Martinet, *Elements*, §§1-9, pp. 24-25).

11.   On paronomasia and its varieties, L. Alonso Schökel, *Estúdios de Poética Hebrea*, pp. 71-117 (bibliography: pp. 72-77); *idem* and A. Strus, *Nomen–Omen, la stylistique sonore des noms propres dans le Pentateuque* (AnBib, 80, Rome: Biblical Institute Press, 1978). On paronomasia as a structuring principle of a text, by the same authors: 'Salmo 122: canto al nombre de Jerusalén', *Bib* 61 (1980), pp. 234-50.

In Sirach 24, Wisdom declares:

> [12] So I took root in an honored people
> in the portion of the Lord, who is their inheritance.
> [13] I grew tall like a **cedar** in LEBANON
> and like a **cypress** on the heights of HERMON.
> [14] I grew tall like a **palm-tree** in EN-GEDI,
> and like **rose plants** in JERICHO,
> like a beautiful **olive-tree** in the field;
> and like a **plane-tree** I grew tall.
> [15] Like CASSIA and CAMEL' THORN
> I gave forth the aroma of spices;
> and like choice MYRRH I spread a pleasant odor,
> like GALBANUM, ONYCHA, and STACTE,
> and like the fragrance of FRANKINCENSE in the tabernacle.
> [16] Like a **terebint** I spread out my branches,
> and my branches are glorious and graceful.
> [17] Like a **vine** I caused loveliness to bud,
> and my blossoms became glorious and abundant fruit.

where 'cedar', 'cypress', 'palm-tree', 'rose plants', 'olive-tree', 'plane-tree', 'terebint' and 'vine' belong to the semantic field of trees, where 'Lebanon', 'Hermon', 'En-Gedi' and 'Jericho' belong to that of place names (countries, mountains and cities), where 'cassia', 'camel' thorn', 'myrrh', 'galbanum', 'onycha', 'stacte' and 'frankincense' belong to that of the perfumes. And although less apparently and more mechanically, 'take root' (12), 'grow tall' (13a, 14a, 14d) and all the syntagm 'spread out branches' belong to the same sequence, progressive, of the development of a tree.

Semantic fields can be natural (or universal) like those of tree names (even if species can vary from one continent to the next); they can be cultural, or particular to a people or a culture: in the Bible, 'heart' and 'understand' belong to the same semantic field, which is not the case in English where the heart is not the seat of understanding but of feelings.[12]

---

12. Unfortunately there is no systematic dictionary of synonyms and antonyms of the Bible, even the most widespread. To initiate oneself to the semantic fields of the Hebrew, H.W. Wolff, *Anthropologie des Alten Testaments* (Munich: Kaiser, 1973); ET *Anthropology of the Old Testament* (Philadelphia: Fortress Press, 1974).

1.2. *At the Morphological Level*

1.2.1. *Identical *Morphemes*[13.]

Two or more morphemes are identical when their form and their significatum are identical.

In the canticle of Hannah (1 Sam. 2.2):

+		**there is no**	holy	LIKE	the Lord
	- Yes,	**there is none**		beside	you
+ and		**there is no**	rock	LIKE	our God

the three members contain the same negation; the first and third have the same preposition 'like'.

Also in the canticle of Hannah, the last two members:

And **he** will-give	strength	to	HIS king
he will-exalt	the horn	of	HIS anointed

1 Sam. 2.10

contain two identical personal pronouns: not only because their significant 'he' (*y*- in Hebrew) is the same and because their significatum (third person + singular + masculine + subject) are identical, and also because they have the same *referent,[14] meaning that it designates the same person, 'the Lord'. It is also the case for the pronoun 'his' (possessive in English, personal suffix in Hebrew).

1.2.2. *Morphemes with Significatum in Common*

These morphemes have evidently different significants but have in common one or more significatum.

Also in the canticle of Hannah:

The sated, for bread **THEY**-engage (themselves)
The hungry **THEY**-are-fattened of food
The barren **she**-bears seven
She who has many children **she**-is forlorn.   1 Sam. 2.5

the four pronominal morphemes of the four verbs have in common the significatum of 'third person' and 'subject', but, whereas the first

---

13. Morphemes (or 'grammatical monemes' or 'word-tools') are monemes which belong to limited inventories (pronouns, prepositions, conjunctions, articles, modalities, etc.).

14. The object designated by a moneme; e.g., 'And he taught in their synagogues' (Lk. 4.15), the referent of the pronoun 'he' is Jesus.

two are also 'masculine' and 'plural', the last two are 'feminine' and 'singular'.

In the following verses:

⁶ The LORD	**brings-to-life**	and **brings-to-death,**
he	**brings-down** to Sheol	and **brings-up**;
⁷ The LORD	**makes-poor**	and **makes-rich,**
he	**brings-low**	and **brings-up**

1 Sam. 2.6-7

all the verbs of the original are in the factitive (hiphil), which was translated as 'brings' in v. 6 but could not be translated so in v. 7.

1.3. *At the Syntactical Level*

1.3.1. *Identical Syntactic Functions*

1.3.1.1. *Lexemes*
Two lexemes can be identical in their syntactic function.
In Psalm 15:

⁵ His	MONEY	he does not put out at interest
the	BRIBE	against the innocent he does not take

'money' and 'bribe' are both 'direct objects'.

In the Prologue of John:

¹ In the beginning was THE WORD. . .
¹⁴ And THE WORD became flesh. . .

'the Word' is also subject at the beginning of v. 1 and v. 14.

1.3.1.2. *Morphemes*
Two morphemes can be identical in their syntactic function.
In Psalm 15:

and the speaking truth	IN	his heart.
³ He did not slander	ON	his tongue

both prepositions 'in' and 'on' serve the function of complement of 'his heart' and 'his tongue'.

So in the Prologue of John:

³ *Everything*	**THROUGH him**	was made
	and	
WITHOUT him	was made	*nothing*

1.3.2. *Identical Syntactic Constructions*

1.3.2.1. *Identical syntagms*

Two syntagms can have the same syntactic construction, whether this syntactic identity be joined with an identity of lexemes or morphemes or not.

In Psalm 96, the three syntagms, 'sing to the Lord' (see above, §1.1.1) are identical through their lexemes, morphemes and syntactic construction: (verb + subject) + (preposition + object).

On the other hand, in Psalm 15, the two members:

and the speaking truth	ON	HIS HEART.
[3] He did not slander	IN	HIS TONGUE

end with syntagms which have the same syntactic construction, although the prepositions and lexemes are different (only the pronouns are identical: in Hebrew the suffix pronoun -*ô*, 'of him').

In the Prologue of John, v. 15:

. He who	**after**	ME	comes
.	**before**	M E	ranks
. for he	**before**	M E	he was

the three syntagms 'after me', and 'before me' (repeated twice) have the same construction, preposition + pronoun.

1.3.2.2. *Identical proposition*

The construction can be totally identical:

Like at the beginning of the canticle of Hannah (1 Sam. 2.1):

Exults	my heart	in the LORD
is exalted	my horn	in the LORD

with verb + subject (= substantive + personal pronoun) + complement (preposition + name).

Also in the Prologue of John:

[9]	COMING	*to the world*
[11]	*to his own people*	HE CAME

with the verb and complement of place.

The construction can be partially identical.
Like in Psalm 15:

. [1] O Lord,	WHO shall-sojourn	**in** *your tent?*	
.	WHO shall-dwell	**on** *the mount*	of your holiness?

Both sentences are interrogative sharing the same subject, synonymous verbs with the same modalities, and complements introduced by the same preposition (in Hebrew), but the apostrophe 'O Lord' is not reproduced in the second, the same way that the *expansion[15] 'of your holyness' does not have its equivalent in the first. On the other hand, the two sentences end (in the original) with a suffix pronoun of the second person masculine singular (translated by the possessive 'your').

Similarly in the Prologue of John:

[8] *That-one*	[John]	was not	THE	LIGHT
[9] *He*	[the Word]	was	THE true	LIGHT

'that one' does not have its equivalent in v. 9 and 'true' does not have anything which corresponds to it in v. 8; however both sentences have the same copulative verb 'was' and the same *predicate[16] 'light'.

1.4. *At the Level of Rhythm*

Despite the fact that biblical poetry, mostly Hebraic but also Greek, is not founded on a rigorous rhythm (regular alternation of long and brief as in Greek and Latin poetry, or number of syllables like in French poetry), it is not altogether devoid of a certain quantitative balance. Very often, the relations, for example between two members of a segment (the two stychs of a distych), are firstly semantic but also rhythmic.

For example, in the canticle of Hannah:

He will-give	strength	to-his-king	
he-will-exalt	the-horn	of-his-anointed	1 Sam. 2.10

or that of Mary:

The-hungry	he-has-filled	with-good-things
and		
the-rich	he-has-sent-away	empty

Lk. 1.53

where each member counts three words (that is three accents).

---

15. 'Every element added to an utterance which does not modify the mutual relationships and the function of the pre-existing elements' (Martinet, *Elements*, §§4-30, p. 119).

16. 'The predicative moneme is the element around which the sentence is organized, the other constituent elements marking their function by reference to it' (Martinet, *Elements*, §§4-29, p. 119).

In some cases, mostly in the segments whose members are 'complementary' (to take Lowth's distinction), the relation between the members is above all quantitative or rhythmic in nature.

So in Ps. 113.3:

| From-the-rising | of-the-sun | to-its-setting, |
| is-to-be-praised | the name | of-the-Lord. |

More frequent in what is convenient to call 'poetry', the rhythmic identity can sometimes be found in narratives in 'prose'.

For example, at the beginning of the third Gospel (Lk. 1.5):

There was	in the days	of Herod	king	of Judea
a priest	named	Zechariah	of the division	of Abijah
and his wife	of the daughters	of Aaron	and her name	Elizabeth

1.5. *At the Level of Discourse*

Two textual units are said to be identical if they have in common one or more characteristic of discourse.

In the Judgment of Solomon (1 Kgs 3.22):

THE OTHER WOMAN		SAID:	
	'No,	the living	child is mine
	and	the dead	child is yours.'
AND THAT ONE		SAID:	
	'No,	the dead	child is yours
	and	the living	child is mine.'

alternate sentences of 'narrative' and of 'dialogue'.

2. *Relationships of Opposition*

There cannot be a relationship of opposition between two linguistic objects if they do not partially have a relationship of identity. Opposition, like synonymy, bears degrees. To simplify things, it is possible to make a global distinction between partial and total opposition.

For a total opposition to exist, it is necessary that only one of the constituting elements of the linguistic objects be different. In English, the phonemes /d/ and /t/ are in total opposition since they are opposed but by one of their relevant traits:

	/d/	versus	/t/
identical elements:	consonant		
	occlusive		
	dental		
different elements:	voiced		not voiced

It is this opposition which allows the opposition of the *minimal pair[17] 'dense' versus 'tense'.

But the opposition can be partial if two traits differ at the same time, like between /d/ and /k/:

	/d/	versus	/k/
identical elements:	consonant		
	occlusive		
different elements:	dental		palatal
	voiced		not voiced

This opposition, without being total, nonetheless allows the distinction between the two substantives 'din' and 'kin'.

One could not speak of an opposition between /i/ and /m/ because those two phonemes have no relevant trait in common: /i/ is an oral, front, closed, not rounded vowel, whereas /m/ is an occlusive, bilabial, nasal and voiced consonant.

2.1. *At the Lexical Level*

Lexemes which are opposed necessarily have a different significant, but they only differ through a part of their significatum.

For example in the following sentences:

–[3] Blessed	shall you be	in the **city**,
– and blessed	shall you be	in the **field**.

:: [6] Blessed	shall you be	when you ENTER
:: and blessed	shall you be	when you LEAVE.

Deut. 28.3, 6

17. A pair of monemes which are distinguished only by a relevant trait of a single of their phonemes.

'city' is opposed to 'field' and 'enter' to 'leave'. These last two lexemes can be decomposed in elements of signification: 'movement' + 'between inside and outside' are common to 'enter' and 'leave'; only the direction of the movement changes, 'from outside to within' in 'enter', 'from within to outside' for 'leave'. This kind of opposition can be said to be direct.

In the Prologue of John 1.4:

> The **light** in the **darkness** shines.

The opposition is direct between 'light' and 'darkness'. Oppositions are often less direct.

In Psalm 15.4:

Is **DESPISED** in whose eyes	the *REPROBATE*
and *WHO FEARS THE LORD*	he **HONORS**

if 'despised' is directly opposed to 'honors', the opposition between 'reprobate' and 'who fears the Lord' if indirect is nonetheless there.

In the Prologue of John 1.13:

who, not	of **blood**,	nor of the will	of **flesh**,
nor of the will	of MAN,	but of GOD	were-born.

'God' is directly opposed to 'man' and indirectly to 'flesh' and 'blood'.

Similarly to the case of the semantic fields, the oppositions can be natural or universal: 'come in' and 'go out' for example. They can also be cultural, particular to a nation, a language, or a civilization: such is the opposition characteristic of the Bible between 'Israel' and 'the Nations', which is reproduced in Paul in the form of 'Jews' versus 'Greeks'.

When two opposed lexemes add up to a whole the opposition can be said to be complementary or bipolar: In Proverbs 1.8:

Hear,	my son,	the instruction	of your	**father**
reject not		the teaching	of your	**mother**

where 'father' and 'mother' are a complementary pair which designates the two parents. Similarly when it is said that God created 'heaven and earth', the bipolar opposition signifies the totality of creation.

2.2. *At the Morphological Level*

2.2.1. *The Pronouns*

The opposition can bear on only one of the significatum.
  In the Canticle of Hannah (1 Sam. 2.1, 10):

[1] Exults   **MY** heart   in the Lord;
is exalted   **MY** horn   in the Lord.
Derides   **MY** mouth   **MY** enemies
because I rejoice in your salvation.

----

[10] He will give strength   to   **his** king,
he will exalt the horn of   **his** anointed

the opposition between the pronouns of the introduction (except the
last one) and those of the conclusion bear on the 'person', first person
at the beginning, third person at the end.
  Still in the Canticle of Hannah:

[1] Exults   **MY** heart   in the Lord;
is exalted   **MY** horn   in the Lord.
Derides   **MY** mouth   **MY** enemies
because I rejoice in your salvation.
[3] ...

And there is no rock like   *OUR* God.

there is an opposition of 'numbers' between the pronouns of the first
person singular of v. 1 and that of the first person plural of v. 2 ('our
God').

2.2.2. *The Verbal *Modifiers*[18]

In Psalm 15:

[2] The WALKING   in perfection
and the MAKING   justice
and the SPEAKING   truth   in his heart

[3] **He did not slander**   on his tongue
he did not make   to his neighbor   evil
and an insult   **he did not take up**   against his neighbor

the verbs of v. 2 are doubly opposed to those of v. 3: they are in the
past participle and are in the affirmative whereas the next ones are

18. Grammatical determinants of the lexemes (modes, voices, persons, number
of verbs; gender, number of substantives etc.).

in the perfect tense and in the negation.

In the Prologue of John, the beginning of v. 8 and v. 9 are opposed in their verbal modality, negation versus affirmation:

| [8] That-one | was | NOT | the light |
| [9] He | was | | the light |

and in the last verse, the verbs are similarly opposed:

| NO ONE | has EVER | seen |
| that-one | has | made him known |

2.2.3. *The Nominal Modalities*

Nominal lexemes (substantives and adjectives) can be in opposition in their modalities.

In the Canticle of Hannah, v. 5:

– THE SATED,	for bread	*ENGAGE* (themselves),
THE HUNGRY	*ARE-FATTENED*	of food.
– **The barren**	***bears***	seven,
she-who-has-many	children	***is forlorn***.

'the sated' and 'the hungry' are opposed to 'the barren' and 'she-who-has-many' (lit.: 'the numerous') in number ('plural' versus 'singular') as well as in gender ('masculine' versus 'feminine'). Those oppositions are evidently found in the verbs as well.

2.2.4. *The *Functionals*[19] *(Prepositions and Conjunctions)*

The functionals are numbered among the word-tools or empty-words (that is morphemes) because their main function is to mark the function of the lexemes between one another; some of them have nonetheless their own significatum, which makes them akin to lexemes. They can therefore be opposed through their significatum.

In the Prologue of John:

| [3] Everything | THROUGH | him | was made |
| and | WITHOUT | him | was made nothing |

the prepositions 'through' and 'without' are opposed; the same way that are opposed in v. 15 'before' and 'after':

| . He who | AFTER | me | comes |
| . | BEFORE | me | ranks |

19. For 'functional moneme'.

2.3. *At the Syntactical Level*

There can be opposition between the modalities of the sentence, for example between an interrogative and declaratory sentences.

In Psalm 15, vv. 2-3 (see above §2.2.2) are opposed to the double interrogative at the beginning:

> . O Lord, who shall sojourn in your tent?
> . who shall dwell on the mount of your holyness?

like the answer to a question.

The length and syntactic complexity can be in opposition. Also in Psalm 15:

. The walking	in perfection	
. and the making	justice	
+ and the speaking	truth	*in his heart*

where the third member is longer than each of the first two.

In the Prologue of John, one can speak of a syntactic opposition between the two members of v. 17:

| – For | the Law | through Moses | was given |
| + | Grace *and Truth* | through Jesus *Christ* | came |

because the second member is longer than the first (doubling of the subject and doubling of the proper noun).

One should bear in mind that, in all these examples, it would not be possible to speak of opposition if there was not a relationship of identity in the first place. Opposition can be identified and is relevant only on the background of identity.

2.4. *At the Level of Speech*

Two passages are in opposition if they differ in a characteristic proper to speeches alone.

In Sirach 24, the long speech of Wisdom, in the 'direct style' (vv. 3-32) is introduced by a passage of narrative:

---

[1] Wisdom will praise herself
and will glory in the midst of her people.
[2] In the assembly of the Most High she will open her mouth,
and in the presence of his host she will glory:

> [3] *'I came forth from the mouth of the Most High*
> *and covered the earth like a mist. . . '*

The opposition can be in the content:

Like between the two great passages devoted in Deuteronomy 28 to blessings (vv. 1–14) and curses (vv. 15–68). At the beginning, the opposition is marked in a very precise way at the lexical and morphological levels, on a broad background of identity:

---

[1] And if you obey   the voice of the Lord your God
observing to practice
all his commandments   which I command you today. . .
   = [2] all these BLESSINGS
   = shall come upon you and overtake you:
        :: [3] BLESSED shall you be in the city
        :: and BLESSED shall you be in the field

----

[15] But if you will NOT obey   the voice of the Lord your God
NOT observing to practice
all his commandments...   which I command you today
   = all these CURSES
   = shall come upon you and overtake you:
        :: [16] CURSED shall you be in the city
        :: and CURSED shall you be in the field

The opposition can be that of literary genre:

In Mk 10.35-52, two narratives (vv. 35-41 and vv. 46-52) surround a teaching (vv. 42-45);[20] in the sequence C7 (Lk. 18.31-19, 46) are opposed prophecies, narratives and parable (see below, p. 328).[21]

20. Analysed in Meynet, *Initiation*, I, pp. 71-81; II: pl. 7.

21. When two elements have no relationship of identity or opposition, neither from the lexical, morphological, syntactical nor speech point of view, but if they share an identical position in a construction, one can speak of a relationship of homology. In:

        a Why
            b *do conspire*
                c **the nations**
                   and
                c' **the people**
            b' *plot*
        a' in vain?   Ps. 2.1

if the relationship between b and b' are clear on one hand and between c and c', on the other hand, a and a' only have their position in common: I will call them homologous.

This long enumeration has aimed at showing that the linguistic elements at their different organizational levels can have a rhetorical function, on top of their semantic and syntactic functions. Rhetorical analysis will have to be careful not to pay too much attention to one or the other elements, for example to the pronouns or the tense of the verbs, but to take into account the whole ensemble of elements in order to detect those that are relevant on the rhetorical level, that is to say those that serve as marks in the composition of the text.

Chapter 6

THE FIGURES OF COMPOSITION

The linguistic elements in a relationship of identity or opposition are not distributed at random. Their position in the text does not only obey the syntactic and semantic rules and constraints; at all organizational levels of the text, it follows the structuring laws of discourse. The *position* of the related elements can confer on them a function of indication or mark of *composition*. Their disposition forms figures of composition which all obey the great law of symmetry. The two basic forms of symmetry are parallelism and, at the cost of creating a neologism, *concentrism*; parallelism when the related elements are reproduced in the same order, concentrism when they are reproduced in the reversed order.

This demonstration will be increasingly complex, describing phenomena following the different levels of organization of the text, starting from the simpler ones. Few researchers have a clear vision of the successive levels of composition; not to mention the fact that they often mix them up in their analysis. Albert Vanhoye is one of the few who has really given some thought to the problem and adopted a coherent and univocal terminology to describe the textual units of the *Epistle to the Hebrews* at their different levels. He distinguishes, in decreasing order: part, section, paragraph, subdivision, small paragraph (also called point).[1] It seemed necessary to add to the number of the levels and to consequently adopt another terminology, paying special attention to transparency.

A systematic exposition has to find its way between two equally

---

1. *La Structure de l'Epître aux Hébreux*, pp. 138-52, 244-47. Also his article 'La composition de Jn 5,19-30', in *Mélanges bibliques en hommage au R.P. Béda Riguaux* (Gembloux: Duculot, 1970), pp. 259-74, where the structure of each of the text's eight sentences is first analysed in detail (pp. 263-68) before the structure of the whole is analysed (pp. 268-69).

dangerous pitfalls: an extreme simplification which would not do justice to the complexity of the phenomena on one hand, and a worry of exhaustivity which would do away with any organizational principle on the other. Simplification giving precedence to the chosen system would be obtained in choosing hand-picked examples to illustrate the demonstration. Exhaustivity which prefers a harvest of facts would be the result of the analysis of a corpus chosen at random.

In order to avoid Charybdis and not to fall into Scylla, the only possible way is to join the advantages of one and the other solutions: systematization will clearly appear in a plan of exposition rigorously progressive; exhaustivity, and submission to facts, diverse and complex, will be guaranteed by the choice of a limited corpus, no elements of which will be discarded in the analysis. Two psalms will be studied at different levels of their composition. The advantage of most of the psalms, is that, unlike passages of all the other books of the Bible, they are defined by tradition and it is not necessary to justify the limits of the chosen text, which is always a long and difficult operation. Why Psalms 113 and 146? Because their length and their complexity (they correspond to what we call 'passage') are in agreement with the first pages of the exposition. A third text (Amos 1.3–2.16), noticeably longer, since it counts three sequences, will provide an example of the organization at the levels superior to the passage, namely that of the sequence and of the 'section'.[2] When these three texts cannot provide clear examples of certain constructions, I will resort to other texts in the New Testament as in the Old. A methodological exposition is necessarily difficult. The progressive discovery of three beautiful texts will soften its dryness, at least one can hope so, without slackening its rigor.

---

2.   The choice of those three texts might surprise the reader: they are all poetical texts, written in Hebrew, from the Old Testament. Of texts written in prose, in Greek, and of the New Testament, only a few short examples will be given, at the level of the segment, the piece and of the part. The first reason for this choice is that the so-called poetical texts, are, by definition, more rhythmic than texts written in prose and consequently more fitting, especially at the level of the segment, for an exposition which seeks to be as clear as possible. The second reason is that the reader who would like to see more examples from the New Testament, written for the most part in prose, can refer to my analysis in *L'Evangile selon saint Luc*, where the twenty-four chapters of the third Gospel were analysed at all levels of textual organization, from the 'segment' to the 'book'.

1. *The Member*

The member is the smallest unit of rhetorical organization. It is not easy to give a precise definition for it. From the purely external and quantitative point of view, one can describe it as a syntagm* generally composed of two to five terms*[3] which form a syntactical unit.

'I-(am)   the-Lord   your-God'   Exod. 20.2

is a member which counts three terms: *'ānōkî*, an isolated pronoun, first person singular (translated 'I-[am]'), the lexeme 'the-Lord' ('YHWH'), the lexeme 'God' which forms a single word with the suffix pronoun (*'elōhekā*; those three terms are linked with each other by relationships which make them a single proposition.

2. *The Segment*

The segment is the superior unit to the member. There are several segments which have only one member: they are called 'unimember'. The great majority of the segments are composed of two members and are called 'bimembers'. At last some segments are composed of three members and are called 'trimember' segments.[4] Beyond three members, we reach the superior organizational level of the 'piece'.

2.1. *The Unimember Segment*

It is impossible to speak of rhetorical composition of the unimember segment: in order to have a composition, there has to be a symmetry and there is no symmetry without duality or plurality. Examples of unimember segments:

---

3. Lexeme or even morpheme of more than one syllable.
4. For example, herewith the distribution of the three categories of segments in the three texts that are analysed in this exposition:

	Ps. 113	Ps. 146	Amos 1.3–2.16	TOTAL
unimembers	3	3	15	21
bimembers	8	7	39	54
trimembers	0	3	6	9

Amos 1.3–2.16 counts numerous unimembers; this number which seems a lot higher than average, is due to the great number of introductory formulas and conclusions of oracles.

Praise Yah!	Ps. 113.1 and 9c (see §5.2.1)
	Ps. 146.1 and 10c (see §5.2.2)
He-keeps faith for-ever.[5]	Ps. 146.6c (see §5.2.2)
Who (is) like-the-Lord our-God?	Ps. 113.5 (see §5.2.1)
On-that-(very)-day perish his-plans.	Ps. 146.4c (see §5.2.2)

In Amos 1.3–2.16, most of the formulas of introduction and conclusion of oracles are considered to be unimember segments: 1.3a, 5e,
6a, 8e; 1.9a, 11a; 1.13a, 15c; 2.1a, 3c; 2.4a; 2.6a, 16b. Besides, 1.5d;
1.8d are also unimember segments.[6]

2.2. *The Bimember Segment*

2.2.1. *The Bimember Segment of Less than Four Terms*

Although it is rare, there are bimember segments of less than four
terms.

Luke 6.30 has two bimember segments the second members of
which have but one term:

+	To everyone	who BEGS from you,
=	—	*GIVE*;
+ and	of who TAKES	yours,
=	*DO NOT ASK*	— .

One could think that these two sentences are but a single bimember
segment with six terms:

: To everyone	who BEGS from you,	*GIVE*,
: and of who TAKES	yours,	*DO NOT ASK*.

But one should note that each of the two sentences coordinated by
'and' is composed of two propositions, of one protasis ('To everyone
who begs'; 'who takes yours') and one apodosis in the imperative
('give'; 'do not ask'). Furthermore, the parallelism of this verse with
the preceding one (which is formed of two bimember segments of
four terms) is another argument in favour of the partition of v. 30 in
two bimembers:

---

5.   Hyphens indicate that it is a graphic word in Hebrew.
6.   The letters following the verse numbers indicate the lines of rewriting.

+ [29]	To him	who STRIKES you	on the cheek,
+	*OFFER*	also	the other.
= and	OF WHO TAKES		your cloak,
=	your coat	also	***do not** REFUSE.*

+ [30]	To everyone	who BEGS from you,	
+	*GIVE*;		
= and	OF WHO TAKES		yours,
=			***do not** ASK.*

The four segments have the same syntactic structure; one will note the repetition of 'of who takes' in symmetrical positions (29c, 30c), and the alternation of positive imperatives (29b, 30b) and of negative imperatives (29d, 30d). Note that what we have here is a classical phenomenon of abbreviation and economy (the second verse dispensing with one term in each of its second member, 30b and 30d).

Sometimes, some bimember segments have but two terms, one term each (which is very rare).

So in Lk. 6.37-38:

– [37]	Judge not	*and you will not be judged*	
– and	condemn not	*and you will not be condemned.*	
+	Forgive	*and you will be forgiven;*	
+ [38]	give	*and it will be given*	*to you.*

If the last segment (38a) can be considered to be formed of three terms, the preceding three have but one term per member.[7]

In Amos 1.3–2.16, there are two bimember segments the second member of which has only one term:

+ because they had threshed	with (threshing) sledges	of iron
+ the (land of) Gilead,		

Amos 1.3de

+ because they burned	the bones	of the king	of Edom
+ to (make from them) lime,			

Amos 2.1de

---

7. The symmetry between Lk. 6.37-38 and 6.28-30 confirm this analysis (R. Meynet, *L'Evangile selon saint Luc*, I, p. 60; II, pp. 79-81).

2.2.2. *The Bimember Segment of Four Terms*

This segment allows the presentation of the two basic figures of all biblical rhetoric.

2.2.2.1. *Parallel symmetry (or parallelism)*
When the order of the two terms of the second member is the same as the first member (ab/a'b'), one can speak of parallel symmetry (or parallelism):

+ Old Testament
```
. I-will-divide-them      in-Jacob
. I-will-scatter-them     in-Israel.
```
Gen. 49.7

```
    +           I-hate        the-divided
    + and       I-love        your-law.
```
Ps. 119.113

```
        – For-your-voice    (is) sweet
        – and-your-face     (is) comely.
```
Cant. 2.14

```
            : Departs       his-breath:
            : he-returns    to-its-clay.[8]
```
Ps. 146.4

+ New Testament

```
. The-harvest      (is)    plentiful,
. the-laborers     (are)   few.
```
Lk. 10.2

```
    + And it [the wine]     will-be-spilled
    + and the-skins         will-be-destroyed.
```
Lk. 5.37

Not all the bimember segments of four terms are as regular as these.

2.2.2.2. *Alternated symmetry (or chiasm)*
When the order of the two terms of the second member is different from the first member (ab/b'a'), one can speak of an alternate symmetry, or chiasm (from the Greek *chiasmos* or figure which reproduces the shape of the Greek letter *chi*: χ):[9]

---

8. For the use of the signs / . / + / - / = / : / etc., at the beginning of the members, see below, pp. 342-43.

9. J.C.T. Ernesti, *Lexicon technologiae Graecorum rhetoricae* (Leipzig, 1795), 'χιάζεσθαι'.

+ Old Testament:

```
a For      they-observed
    b             your-word
    b'            and-your-covenant
a'         they kept.
```

Deut. 33.9

```
a    The-sowers
    b      in-tears
    b'     in-songs
a'   will-reap.
```

Ps. 126.5

```
        a            I (am)
            b             my-beloved's
            b'            and-my-beloved
        a'           is-mine.
```

Cant. 6.3

+ New Testament:

```
    a    In the heaven
      b         PEACE
                        and
      b'        GLORY
    a'   in the highest.
```

Lk. 19.38

```
        a      Others
          b      HE-SAVED,
          b'     LET-HIM-SAVE
        a'     himself.
```

Lk. 23.35

The relations between the terms are not always as clear as in the preceding example. In the following segment:

```
      a       to set him
        b       WITH-PRINCES
        b'      WITH-THE-PRINCES
      a'      of his people.
```

Ps. 113.8

the repetition of 'with-the-princes' makes what would otherwise be a single member with three terms ('to set him | with-princes | of his people'), a bimember segment with four alternated terms. But there is no particular relation between a and a' besides their position with b and b'; they are homologous.

2.2.2.3. *Five methodological remarks*

2.2.2.3.1. *The order of terms is independent from meaning.* Classical rhetoric saw in the chiasmus a specific type of antithesis.[10] For Pierre Fontanier, in the last century, chiasmus or 'reversion', was an antithesis: 'Reversion is the reversal, with a different and often contrary meaning, of all the words, at least the essential ones, of a proposition. We can see it as a specific type of antithesis.' Among others, he quotes the following example: 'the wise man is often mad, the mad man is often wise'.[11] For Ignace de la Potterie, parallel symmetry is the development of synonymous parallelism and concentric symmetry the extension of antithetical parallelism.[12]

The examples from the Old Testament provided above are respectively synonymous (Gen. 49.7 and Deut. 33.9), antithetical (Ps. 119.113 and Ps. 126.5) and synthetic or complementary (Cant. 2.14; 6.3; Ps. 146.4), according to Lowth's classification. Those of the first class are of parallel construction, those of the second of chiastic construction. We can therefore see that the order of terms is not linked to meaning, that is synonymity or antonymy.

2.2.2.3.2. *Composition is complex.* The precise analysis of Cant. 6.3:

> \+ I (am)   my beloved's
>   and
> \+ my beloved   is mine

shows that symmetries are complex: if at the words' level the construction is alternated, at the syntactic level the construction is parallel:

> \+ subject   PREDICATE (prepositional syntagm)
>   co-ordinating conjunction
> \+ subject   PREDICATE (prepositional syntagm)

It would be convenient to say that this segment is globally chiastic, but

---

10. H. Lausberg, *Elemente der literarischen Rhetorik* (Munich: Max Hueber, 1949), §392; Italian trans. *Elementi di retorica* (Bologna: Il Mulino, 1969); B. Mortara Garavelli, *Manuale di retorica* (Milan: Bompiani, 1988, 5th edn 1991), pp. 247-49.

11. *Les Figures du discours* (Paris: Flammarion, 1968 [1818–30]), pp. 381-82.

12. *Exegesis quarti evangelii. Prologus S. Johannis*, teaching notes, Roma 1974–75 and 1979–80, p. 16; *idem*, 'Structure du Prologue de Saint Jean', *NTS* 30 (1984), p. 356.

it is necessary to be aware of the complexity of the phenomenon. I will therefore continue to speak of parallel symmetry and alternate symmetry taking into account the order of words only.

2.2.2.3.3. *The function of symmetry.* Despite what one might think,[13] the function of parallelism and chiasm, even at the most elementary level, is not only esthetic; or even rhythmic.[14] It is already rhetoric: the symmetry marks the unity of the two members, it indicates that they form a whole, and determines its limits. This is obvious in the case of antithetic, synthetic or complementary symmetries: it is the voice and the face of the beloved that the woman finds soft and charming (Cant. 2.14); the relationship between the loved and the lover is reciprocal (Cant. 6.3). Sowing and reaping are indissociable from tears and joy (Ps. 126.5); hatred of the divided is correlative to love of the law (Ps. 119.113). In the case of synonymous symmetry, the unity of the two members is not necessary through logic; the insistence of repetition, with other terms, however, is enough to justify their relationship. The function of those two forms of symmetry is obviously not to mark the composition of the whole text; their rhetorical function of composition, at their level, should nonetheless be acknowledged.

2.2.2.3.4. *Symmetry and interpretation.* Finally, it is necessary to see that the function of these two forms of symmetry is to pose the question of interpretation. To say that the function of symmetry is to mark the unity of two members, is to say that a relationship of meaning is established between two parts which are at once similar and different. A few remarks will be enough to show that the question of meaning is relevant even at this level. The understanding of the relationship of the parallel elements of the first example

| . I-will-divide-them | in-Jacob |
| . I-will-scatter-them | in-Israel |

not only implies the knowledge of the code of Hebrew language (or English in translation) but also knowledge of the culture and history

---

13. It was my own point of view, expressed in *Quelle est donc cette Parole?* (pp. 110-11): 'Those chiasms, are rhetorical flowers rather than figures; they adorn the sentence, but they don't structure the discourse. They fall within the remit of *elocutio* and not of *dispositio* . . . The stylistic or sentence chiasmus is of no use for the study of the composition of texts.'

14. *Quelle est donc cette Parole?*, p. 50.

of the people of Israel: if we admit that 'scatter' is commonly perceived as synonymous to 'divide', the relationship of identity between 'Jacob' and 'Israel' will be perceived only by someone who knows the history of the patriarchs, and knows that 'Israel' is another name for 'Jacob' son of Isaac, a name given to him by God (Gen. 35.10), and that both names became those of the Hebrew people, the people of God. Thanks to knowledge of history, the enlightened reader might perhaps perceive, beyond the relationship of identity (identity of the referent), an antithetic or, at least, complementary relationship: first of all a relationship of chronological succession, because 'Israel' is the second name of 'Jacob', given long after the first one;[15] and also a relationship of theological order because if 'Jacob' is the natural and human name of the son of Isaac, 'Israel' is the name that God gave him in view of his mission, of his new life, of the new birth that this mission implies. In order to be fully understood, this first segment requires historical and theological notions from the reader. What is familiar to a Jew or a Christian, will have to be explained to those who are not familiar with biblical texts and culture.

The second example:

| . I-hate | the-divided[16] |
| . and-I-love | your-law |

also implies linguistic and historical notions, but it also, one could say, stimulates thought. The relationship of opposition between 'hate' and 'love' does not constitute a major obstacle for comprehension, or if it does, it lies in knowing what really signifies 'love': not so much a feeling as a commitment, which in the Bible, is an equivalent of 'observe' or 'obey'. On the other hand, the fact that 'law' (*Tôrâ*) as opposed to 'divided' creates a problem of interpretation, especially arduous in this case, since from a purely lexicographical point of view the meaning of this last word (which is an hapax) is not self-evident. It is necessary to note first of all the opposition of the plural and the singular which is probably not fortuitous. The opposition of the verbs

15. It is also the usual order of the names in the texts; in the Book of Psalms, Ps. 14.7; 22.24; 53.7; 78.5, 21, 71; 105.10; 135.4; 147.19. The order is reversed in Ps. 81.5; 114.1-2; 105.23 (because of a superior concentric construction in the first two cases).

16. Or the 'unsteady', 'staggering'; or even 'divided' meaning 'half-hearted' (in opposition, for example, to Ps. 139.22: 'I hate them with perfect hatred'); in this last case, 'half-hearted' would be opposed to loving 'whole-heartedly'.

forces us to understand 'the divided' as opposed to 'the law' (of God). It is of course the bare minimum that we can draw from it from the point of view of interpretation, but it is already a lot. Any philological research that would make synonyms of those two words would be unacceptable simply from a rhetorical reason. Supposing that the meaning of the second word is indeed 'the divided', the opposition between 'the divided' and 'your law' would draw the reader to think about the enigma of this opposition: would the Law of the Lord be the one thing that unites mankind in itself, which brings inner harmony, and brings men together? Would it be what unifies mankind in the worshiping of the one God, in opposition to the division that polytheism implies?

In conclusion, one has to concede that this segment which is said to be antithetical, is not so if we understand that loving the Law of God is the equivalent of hating the divided, that the two members are two complementary formulations of the same attitude and indissociable from one another. The same idea is expressed in the negation of the contrary as in:

. *I hasten*	—	—	
. *and do NOT delay*	to keep	your commandments.	

Ps. 119.60

or in the Prologue of John:

+ ALL (things)	*by Him*	was made
and		
+ *without Him*	was made	NOTHING.[17]

Jn 1.3

2.2.2.3.5. *The path of interpretation*. Each text is an enigma. The enigma, in the simplest form is the puzzle, which is often formulated thus: 'What is the difference between X and Y'? The one who can find either the resemblance between X and Y if they seem totally different, or the difference if they seem totally similar, will solve the puzzle. The same balance between the relationship of identity and opposition that is found on a formal level is found at the level of interpretation. Except that here we have to find what is different between two identical elements and what is identical between two opposed elements. Oedipus deciphers the enigma of the Sphynx when he identifies the animal that

17. 'Him' refers to 'the Word'.

walks on four in the morning, on two legs at noon and on three in the evening. The babylonian enigma, 'there are four kinds of students: the pipe, the sponge, the filter and the van', will be deciphered by someone who will have discovered the relationship of identity and opposition between the first two, the last two, between the first two and the last two and finally between the first three and the last one; and who might conclude that there are three times as many bad students as there are good ones! To go back to the Bible, in ch. 15 of Luke, the enigma of the parables of mercy, the lost sheep and silver piece on one hand and the two sons on the other, could be formulated in this way: 'Is there a difference between the lost sheep and the lost silver piece ?' and 'Is there a difference between the younger son and the elder son?'. The answer to the first question will be necessarily positive, since the two parables seem identical. The answer to the second question will be necessarily negative because the two brothers seem opposed in all respects. The question will then feed back: 'What is the difference between the two sons on one hand and between the sheep and silver piece on the other?'[18]

2.2.3. *The Five Terms Bimember Segment*

The five terms bimember segment can be a six terms bimember segment with a deleted one, for example:

by an ellipse of the verb:

| . THAT-MAY-BE-KNOWN | *upon-earth* | your way, |
| . — | — | *all heathens* your salvation.[19] |

Ps. 67.3

| + and I DESTROYED | *his-fruit* | above |
| + and   — | *his-roots* | beneath. |

Amos 2.9de

| —And-I-RAISED-UP | *from-amid-your-sons* | prophets |
| —and   — | *from-amid-your-young-men* | Nazirites. |

Amos 2.11ab

18. The answer to this enigma is given at the end of the foreword (see above, pp. 38-40).

19. One can consider that 'all' compensates from a rhythmical point of view the lack of repetition of the verb in the second member.

by the lack of repetition of any other element:

| . *Your-people,* | Lord, | they-crush |
| . *your-heritage* | — | they-afflict. |

Ps. 94.5

| + EXALTED | *above* ALL | nations | *THE LORD* |
| + | — *above* — | the-heavens | *HIS-GLORY.* |

Ps. 113.4

| - because | *he-pursued* | with-the-sword | HIS-BROTHER |
| - | *suffocating* — | — | HIS-BOWELS. |

Amos 1.11de

: *For-three*	TRANSGRESSIONS	of Damascus
and		
: *for-four*	—	I-will-not-come-back.

Amos 1.3bc

The following segments are exactly constructed on the same model as the preceding one: Amos 1.6bc, 1.9bc (p. 266); 11bc (p. 267); 1.13bc (p. 268); 2.1bc (p. 269); 2.4bc (p. 270); 2.6bc (p. 256).

| – | *'Get-up* | and stand | IN THE MIDDLE' |
| – And | *rising* | he stood | — — . |

Lk. 6.8

When the unique term is found in third position,

For **Jacob** has chosen   YAH **Israel**   for his possession.[20]

Ps. 135.4

it can be syntactically linked with the first member as well as the second, even if the normal tendency is to link it with the first:[21] the pronominalization is indeed more frequent in the second member than in the first.[22]

We will thus have five terms segments of concentric construction (or concentrism):

: for	*Jacob*		has-chosen
	+	YAH	
:	*Israel*		for-his-property.

Ps. 135.4

20. 'Yah' is the subject, 'Jacob' and 'Israel' the objects.

21. This phenomenon is called 'pivot pattern' (or 'Double duty modifier' or 'two-way middle') by M.J. Dahood ('A New Metrical Pattern in Biblical Poetry', *CBQ* 29 [1967], pp. 574-79; *Psalms* [AB 17A; 1970], pp. 439-40).

22. See for example Amos 1.7, at the end of §2.2.4.

where, apart from the central term, the two members are parallel.
Similarly with:

. *I-will-thank-you*	among-the-peoples
+ LORD	
. *I-will-sing-to-you*	among-the-nations.

Ps. 108.4

The concentrism can be more extreme, term by term:

+ *Deliver-me*
    – from-my-enemies
        MY-GOD
    – from-my-aggressors
+ *save-me.*

Ps. 59.2

+ Because   *they-have-rejected*
        – the-Law
            of-THE LORD
        – and-his-precepts
+   *they-have-not-kept.*

Amos 2.4de

or in the New Testament:

+ *Become*
    – merciful
        AS YOUR FATHER
    – merciful
+ *is.*

Lk. 6.36

All the five terms segments are not as regular as these:

| Do NOT trust | *in-princes* |
| *in-a-son-of-Adam* | in whom there is NO   salvation. |

Ps. 146.3

At the extremities, the terms 'trust' and 'in whom there is no |
salvation' belong to the same semantic field and are affected with the
same negation. The relationship between 'princes' and 'son of Adam'
(Hebrew considers the two words as a single term, since it unites them
with a *maqqeph*) can be said to be one of opposition, the 'princes'
being supposed to provide 'salvation', when 'a son of Adam' is
incapable of doing so. Similarly for:

He-makes	*HEAVENS*	*AND-EARTH*
AND-THE-SEA	and-all that-(is)-in-them.	

Ps. 146.6

where the three terms of the canonical enumeration are spread over the end of the first member and the beginning of the second member. The extreme terms are homologous.

The relationship between the two members is sometimes global and it would be vain to look for special relationships between the terms and the two members. For example, in Amos 1.3–2.16:

: because-they-deported	in-a-total	deportation
: to-deliver (them)	to-Edom.	

Amos 1.6de[23]

– And-have-misleaded-them	their-lies	
– which-went	their-fathers	behind-them.

Amos 2.4fg

. And-upon-garments	taken-in-pledge	they-go-to-lay
. beside	every-altar.	

Amos 2.8ab

Unless one considers in this last case that the unique verb is the central element of a concentrical construction, framed by the two complements of place:

. And-upon-garments	taken-in-pledge
THEY-GO-TO-LAY	
. beside	every-altar.

Similarly for the following segment (object + verb + complement of place):

. And-the-wine	of-the-fined
THEY-DRINK	
. in-the-house	of-their-gods.

Amos 2.8cd

The symmetry which is very discrete at the level of the segment will clearly appear at the superior level (see below, §3.4.1.2).

2.2.4. *The Six Terms Segment*

When the four terms segment only had two possible arrangements, there are six different possibilities with the six terms bimember

---

23. See also Amos 2.11c.

segment. If we combine these six arrangements with the relationships of identity, synonymy, opposition, paronomasia, etc., which can exist between the corresponding terms, one can imagine that there will be many more combinations possible. This is no place to embark on an exhaustive study of the six terms segment, but only to illustrate, by a few chosen examples, an attempt at classification of the phenomena of composition, the relevance and operating character of which will become apparent later on. All the possibilities are listed under two headings which have been outlined with the four terms segments: parallel and concentric symmetry.

2.2.4.1. *Parallel symmetry*

2.2.4.1.1. *Total symmetry*. When the three terms of the second member correspond to those of the first member in the same order:

$$a\ b\ c\ /\ a'\ b'\ c'$$

whether one or two of the terms are identical:

| . PRAISE | O-servants | OF-THE-LORD |
| . PRAISE | the-name | OF-THE-LORD. |

Ps. 113.1

| – with-shouting | IN-THE-DAY | of-battle |
| – with-a-tempest | IN-THE-DAY | of-whirlwind. |

Amos 1.14cd

+ BLESSED	you	among women
and		
+ BLESSED	the fruit	of your womb.

Lk. 1.42

synonymous:

| . *I-will-praise* | THE-LORD | in-(all)-my-life |
| . *I-will-sing* | MY-GOD | in-(all)-my-duration. |

Ps. 146.2

complementary:

| = *I-will-send* | fire | upon-TEMAN |
| = *and-it-shall-devour* | the-palaces | of-BOZRAH.[24] |

Amos 1.12

---

24. See also 2.2ab (p. 240); 2.5 (p. 270).

| + *Sitting* | at-the-feet | OF-THE-LORD |
| + *she-listened* | the-word | OF-HIM. |

Lk. 10.39

or when the two members are opposed:

. *The-glory*	OF-YOUNG-MEN:	their-strength
and		
. *the-beauty*	OF-OLD-MEN:	their-gray-hair.

Prov. 20.29

or when only two terms are in direct relationship and the others more loosely:

+ *The-simple*	BELIEVES	everything
and		
+ *the-prudent*	UNDERSTANDS	his-steps.

Prov.14.15

where the identity of the syntactic constructions allows us to speak of parallelism.

| . And-shall-go | their-KING | into-deportation |
| . he | and-his-PRINCES | altogether. |

Amos 1.15ab

When the relationship is global, and not term by term, one can still speak of parallelism, which will have to be called rhythmic in the following cases:

| . From-the-rising | of-the-sun | to-its-setting |
| . praised (be) | the-name | of-the-Lord. |

Ps. 113.3

| - And-will-die | amid-uproar | Moab |
| - amid-shouting | at-the-sound | of-the-horn. |

2.2.4.1.2. *Partial symmetry.* When two of the six terms correspond to each in the same position:

+ parallelism of the initial terms:

whether the initial terms are identical:

| . IN-GOD | I-praise | his-word |
| . IN-GOD | I-trust | I-do-not-fear. |

Ps. 56.5

```
+ HE-WHO-KEEPS        his-mouth          and-his-tongue
        (is)
+ HE-WHO-KEEPS        out-of-trouble     his-soul.
```
Prov. 21.23

or synonymous:

```
. APPLAUD     God             all-the-earth
. SING        the-glory       of-his-name.
```
Ps. 66.1-2

+ parallelism of the final terms:

```
. Because-of       David            YOUR-SERVANT
. do-not-turn-away the-face-of      YOUR-ANOINTED.
```
Ps. 132.10

```
= He-reigns        the Lord         FOR-EVER
= your-God,        O-Sion,          FROM-AGE-TO-AGE.
```
Ps. 146.10

```
+ And-I-will-cut off   the-ruler    from-the-midst-of-HIM
+ and-all-his-princes  I-will-kill  with    —        HIM.
```
Amos 2.3ab

When the six terms correspond to each other:

either in the a b c / a' c' b' order:

```
+ GIVING
                  to-wisdom        your-ear
+ YOU-INCLINE
                  your-heart       to-understanding
```
Prov. 2.2

or in the order a b c / b' a' c':

```
+ He-raises        from-the-dust
                                   THE-WEAK
+ from-the-dumb    he-exalts
                                   THE-POOR.
```
Ps. 113.7

it is possible to consider the alternated terms as a whole:

  A (b c) / A'(c'b')   and   (a b) C / (b'a') C'

and one can note that the symmetry of the initial terms (Prov. 2.2) or final terms (Ps. 113.7) is particularly relevant.

2.2.4.2. *Concentric symmetry*

2.2.4.2.1. *Total symmetry.* when the three terms of the second member correspond to those of the first member, in reverse order:

$$a\ b\ c\ /c'b'a'$$

whether two of the terms are identical:

a	*I-pour-out*		
	b	BEFORE-HIM	
		c	my-complaint
		c'	my-trouble
	b'	BEFORE-HIM	
a'	*I-tell.*		

                                                                Ps. 142.3

identical two by two:

a	In the beginning		
	b	*WAS*	
		c	THE WORD
			and
		c'	THE WORD
	b'	*WAS*	
a'	with God.		

                                                                Jn 1.1

when all the terms are synonymous:

a	If MOUNT UP		
	b		to-the-heavens
		c	*his-height,*
		c'	*his-head*
	b'		to-the-clouds
a'	REACH		

                                                                Job 20.6

or when the two members are opposed:

a	WITH-ENTREATIES		
	b	*speaks*	
		c	the-poor
			and
		c'	the-rich
	b'	*answers*	
a'	WITH-HARSHNESS.		

                                                                Prov. 18.23

```
a      for I am a man
   b                  UNDER AUTHORITY
       c                  set,
       c'                 having
   b'                 UNDER ME
a'     soldiers.
```

Lk. 7.8

2.2.4.2.2. *Partial symmetry.* when two of the six terms correspond to one another in opposed position.

+ symmetry of the extreme terms:

```
= EVERY-THING
              .   THROUGH    HIM        was made
                                and
              .   WITHOUT    HIM        was made
= NOTHING.
```

Jn 1.3

(This figure is also known as 'inclusion', especially when the extreme terms are identical; note that inclusion does not imply a symmetry of the intermediate terms, like it is the case for the two examples cited).

+ symmetry of the median terms:

```
. He-gave                      their-land
          + AS-A-HERITAGE
          + AS-A-HERITAGE
. to-Israel                    his-people.
```

Ps. 135.12

```
+ Because-they-sell        for-silver
          - THE INNOCENT
                and
          - THE-POOR
+ for-a-matter             of-sandals.
```

Amos 2.6de

(When the median terms are identical, they are often called 'hook-words'; note that in this case as well the hook-word does not imply a symmetry of the whole).

When the six terms correspond to one another

either in the a b c / b' c' a' order:

+ YOU-SHALL-BREAK-THEM
:   *with-a-rod*   of-iron
:   like-a-vessel   *of-pottery*
+ YOU-WILL-DASH-THEM.

Ps. 2.9

or in the a b c / c' a' b' order:

: On-*the-lion*   and-the-adder
       +   YOU-WILL-TREAD
       +   YOU-WILL-TRAMPLE
: *the-young-lion*   and-the-serpent.

Ps. 91.13

: And-he-tore   *perpetually*
       + HIS-ANGER
         and
       + HIS-WRATH
: kept-himself   *for-ever.*

Amos 1.11fg

it is possible to consider the parallel terms as a whole:

(a b) C / C'(a'b')   and   A (b c) / (b'c') A'

In case of total or partial identity of the parallel terms:

+   WAIT   *FOR-THE-LORD*
:   be-strong
       and
:   take-courage
+ and-WAIT   *FOR-THE-LORD.*

Ps. 27.14

= ALL-YOU-SONS   *OF-JACOB*
: glorify-him;
: fear him
= ALL-YOU-SONS   *OF ISRAEL.*

Ps. 22.24

it is without doubt the symmetry of identical terms which, considered as a whole, should be remembered as particularly relevant.

Despite the fact that the extreme terms are in a loose relationship, the following segment can be considered to be of the A (b c) / (b' c') A' type:

```
+ HE-SETS
            :    the barren         of-house,
            :    mother            of-sons
+ HAPPY.
```

Ps. 113.9

+ symmetry of the central terms:

The last possibility of partial symmetry is that the central terms of each member be closely linked:

```
. Praise         THE-NAME        OF-THE-LORD,
. for-lofty      HIS-NAME        ALONE.
```

Ps. 148.13

The other terms of this segment could be related to one another, 'alone' with 'the Lord'[25] and 'praise' with 'lofty', that is to say 'worthy of praises', which would make it a parallel segment. It is also the case in the following example:

```
- He who is not         WITH ME         is against me,
        and
- who he does not gather WITH ME         scatters.
```

Lk. 11.23

So the six terms bimember segment (2×3 terms) completes a tour of all the figures of composition which can now be summarized in the following table:

---

25. It would be what M.J. Dahood calls 'Breakup of stereotyped phrases' (*Psalms* [AB, 17A; 1970], p. 413); e.g., Exod. 22.19; 1 Sam. 7.4; Isa. 2.11, 17.

Total symmetries	Partial symmetries		

PARALLELISM

initial terms	final terms

A
  B
    C

A			

	C		

A'
  B'
    C'

A'			

	C'	central terms	

B

B'

CONCENTRISM

extreme terms	median terms

A
  B
    C

A			

	C		

    C'
  B'
A'

A'			

	C'		

Inspired by the 'leading terms' and 'final terms' of Thomas Boys, the terminology adopted here was chosen for being both systematic and self-evident.

The terminology which was developed by exegesis over a century:

. inclusion	for	extreme terms
. hook-words	for	median terms

is clear but it is not *systematic*.

As for the Greek and Latin terminology of classical rhetoric which was used by the exegetes,[26] among others:

26. S. Glass, *Philologia Sacra*, coll. 1992–94; C. Souvay, *Essai sur la métrique des Psaumes*.

. *anadiplosis*	*reduplicatio*	for	median terms
. *epanalepsis*	*redditio*	for	extreme terms
	resumptio		
. *anaphora*	*relatio*	for	initial terms
. *epiphora*	*conversio*	for	final terms
epistrophè			

it is seldom clear for the modern reader.[27]

In all the examples of six terms bimember segments quoted above, total or partial symmetry linked the terms of their two members. For certain bimember segments however, symmetry is global and not term by term:

. Because-they-have-ripped-up		the-pregnant	of-Gilead,[28]
. that-they-might		enlarge	their-border.

Amos 1.13de

- And-the-stout	of-heart	amid-the-mighties,
- nude	shall-fly	in-that-very-day.

Amos 2.16ab

In other segments, the six terms are unequally distributed between the two members:

: Be	the-name	of-the-Lord	blessed,
: from-now		and-for-ever.	

Ps. 113.2

where the syntactical organization of the sentence allows us to separate it in two members: the subject–predicate group (4 terms), followed by a time complement (2 terms).

. I-will-send	fire	upon-the-wall	of-Gaza,
. and-it-shall-devour		her-palaces.	

Amos 1.7[29]

27. J. Molino and J. Tamine, *Introduction à l'analyse linguistique de la poésie* (Paris: PUF, 1982; Chapter 5, 'Répétitions et parallélismes') propose the following terminology:

. *répétitions en contact*	for	median terms
. *répétition en parenthèse*	for	extreme terms
. *répétition à distance*	including	initial terms
	and	final terms.

28. 'The pregnant' that is the 'pregnant women'.

29. See also Amos 1.10 (p. 267); 1.14ab (p. 268).

2.2.5. *Bimember Segment of More than Six Terms*

There are bimember segments of seven terms and more. The two
following examples, from Lk. 6.41-42, which count respectively eight
and ten terms, will give us an idea of the possible variety of the
constructions:

	a	*do you see*	
Why		b	the SPECK	that (is) in the eye *of your brother*
			and
		b'	the LOG	that (is) *in your own* eye
	a'	*you* do not *notice?*	

	a take out		first
	b the LOG	from the eye	*of you:*
Hypocrite,	*you will see clearly*	then
	b' the SPECK	which is in the eye *of your brother*
	a' to take it out.	

The interrogative 'why' is 'factored' because it counts for the second
as well as the first proposition. The same applies to the apostrophe,
'Hypocrite' of the second example.

The same applies also for the following segment:

	a	*the God Jacob*
	b	for his help,
HAPPY who (has)		and
	b'	his hope
	a'	*in the-Lord his God.*

Ps. 146.5

In the following segment:

+ O GOD,

. *break*	**the-teeth**	in-their-mouth;
. *tear-out*	**the-fangs**	of-the-young-lions

+ O LORD.

Ps. 58.7

the names of God are placed as extreme terms, four of the six other
terms being parallel to one another.

In Amos 1.3–2.16, five bimember segments count seven terms:

Some of them are relatively regular:

. I-will-send	fire	UPON-THE-HOUSE	*of-Hazael,*
. and it-shall-devour		THE-PALACES	*of-Ben-Hadad.*

Amos 1.4

| . because they-deported | in-a-total | deportation | to-Edom, |
| . and-did-not-remember | the-covenant | of-brothers. | |

Amos 1.9de

Others are much less so:

| . TRAMPLING | into-the-dust-of the-earth | the-head | *of-the-deprived,* |
| . and-the-way | *of-the-destitutes* | THEY-TURN-ASIDE[30] | |

Amos 2.7ab

| . And-a-man | and-his-father | go-into | the-maiden, |
| . to-profane | the-name | of-my-sanctity. | |

Amos 2.7cd

| . And-you-made-drink | *the-Nazirites* | wine, | | |
| . and-*to-the-prophets* | you commanded | saying: | 'Do not prophesy!' | |

Amos 2.12

Amos 2.13 is a bimember with nine terms:

| Behold, | Myself | I-will-press | beneath-you, | |
| like | presses | a-cart | very-full | of-sheaves. |

2.3. *The Trimember Segment.*

Although generally far less numerous than the bimember segments, there are also trimember segments. By the relationship between the members, we can distinguish four dispositions:

2.3.1. *ABC Type*

The three members are equally similar and different and there is no special relationship between two of these vis-à-vis the third one (abc type):

A	SING TO THE LORD	a new song!
B	SING TO THE LORD	all the earth!
C	SING TO THE LORD	bless his name!

Ps. 96.1-2

like an enumeration (with gradation, from top to bottom):

A	that-is	in-heavens	*above,*
	and		
B	that-is	on-earth	*below,*
	and		
C	that-is	in-the-waters	*below the-earth.*

Exod. 20.4

---

30. The Hebrew text which links the three words translated as 'into the dust of the earth' by the *maqqeph* (hyphen) considers them as a single term.

(the same preposition of the original had to be translated by 'in' and 'on').

with chronological progression:

A	And behold,	*you will conceive*	in your	WOMB,
B	and	*you shall bear*	a	SON,
C	and	*you will call*	his name	JESUS.

Lk. 1.32-33

or logical progression:

A	For	PRESSING	milk	produces curds,
B	and	PRESSING	the nose	produces blood,
C	and	PRESSING	anger	produces strife.[31]

Prov. 30.33

A	And who he lets fly	the arrow	shall not stand,
B	And who is swift	with his feet	shall not save himself,
C	And who he rides	the horse	shall not save his life.

Amos 2.15

where the gravity of the peril increases from member to member until death.

2.3.2. *AA'B Type*

The first two segments are closer to each other than they are to the third.

A		HE WILL BLESS	*the house of*	**Israel,**
A'		HE WILL BLESS	*the house of*	**Aaron,**
	B	HE WILL BLESS	those who fear	the Lord.

Ps. 115.12-13

A		*He raises up*	**to sit up,**
A'		and *he stoops*	**to see,**
	B	IN THE HEAVENS	AND ON THE EARTH.

Ps. 113.5-6

or, with an abbreviation:

A		WE WILL SEE	if *THE VINES*	**have buds,**
A'		— —	if **have opened**	*THE GRAPE BLOSSOMS,*
	B	— —	if **are in bloom**	the pomegranates.

Cant. 7.13

'vines' and 'grape blossoms' are together and are distinct from the 'pomegranates'.

---

31. 'Nose' and 'anger' are in a close relationship in the original: *'appayîm* (= 'anger') is the duel of *'ap* (= 'nose').

The two successive trimember segments of Psalm 146 belong to the same type:

A	THE LORD	*opens* (the eyes)	of the BLIND,
A'	THE LORD	*holds up*	the BOWED,
B	THE LORD	*loves*	the just.

Ps. 146.8

'Blind' and 'bowed' both designate cripples, which contrasts with 'the just', even if all three probably designate the same persons.

A	The Lord	*keeps*	THE SOJOURNERS,
A'	THE ORPHAN	AND THE WIDOW	he restores,
B	and the way of	the wicked	*he twists.*[32]

Ps. 146.9

It will have been noticed that there is a compensation in v. 9: 'the Lord', in A, which does not reappear in A' nor in B is compensated by the expansion of the complements, 'the orphan and the widow', 'the way of the wicked'.

A	And I will cut off	*who sits*	from Ashdod
A'	and *him that holds*	*the scepter*	from Ashkelon
B	and I will turn	my hand	on Ekron.

Amos 1.8abc

where 'who sits' is synonymous to 'him that holds the scepter'.

A	And I,	*I brought you up*	out of the land	of Egypt
A'	and	*I made you walk*	in the desert	forty years,
B		to inherit	the land	of the Amorite.

Amos 2.10

---

32. *The Jerusalem Bible* (London, 1966) has not understood this construction and replaced it with the following construction:

8	Yahweh restores sight to the blind,
	Yahweh straightens the bent,
9	Yahweh protects the stranger,
	he keeps the orphan and widow.
8c	Yahweh loves the virtuous,
9c	and frustrates the wicked.
10	Yahweh reigns for ever,
	your God, Zion, from age to age.

it seems to obtain stanzas of four members like the preceding ones (except for the first one, which cannot, even by force, enter into this straitjacket).

where the two principal coordinated propositions are followed by the final one. This is from the syntactical point of view. From the semantic point of view, however, this trimember should be considered to be of the ABA' type:

A	And I,	I brought you up out of	THE LAND	OF EGYPT,
B	and	I made you walk	in the desert	forty years,
A'		to inherit	THE LAND	OF THE AMORITE

with a starting point and a point of arrival, with a transition between the two; this construction is strengthened by the symmetrical repetition of 'the land', followed each time by a place name.

2.3.3 ABB' Type

The last two members are closer to one another than they are to the first:

A For	good	(is) the Lord,
B	EVERLASTING	(is) *his love*,
B'	FROM AGE TO AGE	(is) *his faithfulness.*

Ps. 100.5

A The Lord	will give him the THRONE	of David his father,	
B and he	WILL REIGN	over the house of Jacob	*for ever*,
B' and his	REIGN		*will not have an end.*

Lk. 1.31-33

A	And I will break	the bar	of Damascus,
B	and cut off	HIM THAT SITS	from Bikeat-Aven,
B'	and him that holds	THE SCEPTER	from Beth-Eden.

Amos 1.5abc

(to be compared to the symmetrical trimember, 1.8abc, quoted above in the preceding category).

A And I,	I destroyed	the Amorite	before them
B who	LIKE the height	*of the cedars*	his height,
B' and strong he		LIKE *the oaks.*	

Amos 2.9abc

A And shall lack	flight	for the swift,
B and the strong	shall not retain	his strength,
B' and the mighty	will not save	his life.

Amos 2.14

2.3.4. *ABA' Type*

The two extreme members are closer to one another than they are to central term, which results in a kind of concentrism,

when the central segment includes only one different term to the extreme members:

A		THE RIGHT HAND OF THE LORD	does valiantly,
	B	THE RIGHT HAND OF THE LORD	**is exalted**,
A'		THE RIGHT HAND OF THE LORD	does valiantly.

Ps. 118.15-16

when the relationship of identity is less obvious:

A		**there is none**	HOLY	*like*	THE-LORD.
	B	Yes, **there is none**			besides	YOU
A'		and **there is no**	ROCK	*like*	OUR-GOD.

1 Sam. 2.2

A And if	YOU	**love** *who* loves you,
B	what credit is that to you?	
A' For even	SINNERS	**love** *who* love them.

Lk. 6.32

2.3.5. *Mixed Constructions*

Certain trimember segments are difficult to classify in the preceding categories; some can be classified in two categories, depending on the envisaged point of view.

Such is Ps. 146.9 which was classified in the AA'B category (see above, §2.3.3):

A The Lord	KEEPS	*THE SOJOURNERS,*
A' *THE ORPHAN*	*AND THE WIDOW*	HE RESTORES,
and		
B the way	of the wicked	he twists.

because from the semantic point of view, 'keeps' and 'restores' designate favourable, positive actions, and 'sojourners', 'orphan and widow' form a series of unprivileged people, without support, who are often found together in many texts.

If we consider the syntactic constructions and the verbal modalities, however, the last two members are more similar to each other:

A The Lord	KEEPING	the sojourners,
B the orphan	and the widow	HE RESTORES,
and		
B' the way	of the wicked	HE TWISTS.

(this more literal translation respects the difference between the participle 'keeping' and the conjugated verbs 'he restores' and 'he twists'). Verse 7 of the same Psalm

He-makes	right	for-the-oppressed,
He-gives	bread	the hungry,
The Lord	frees	the-prisoners.

Ps. 146.7

can be classified in the AA'B category from the syntactic point of view, but can be classified in the ABA' category from the semantic point of view, if we consider that 'bread' is more concrete than justice and freedom, a distinction which is perhaps not relevant in biblical culture. From the morphological point of view, it is to be classified ABA', because in the original 'oppressed' and 'prisoners' are two passive participles, which is not the case of 'hungry'.

One will have noted that the trimember segment has not be dealt with as the bimember segment. When the latter has been analysed term by term, the study of the trimember segment has generally been more global by considering the symmetry between the members. Witness the use of the letters a, b, c, which (in the minuscule) designated the terms for the bimember segments and (in the majuscule) the members for the trimember segment. As if with the trimember segment one already went from one level to the next, superior to that of the bimember segment.

3. *The Piece*

The piece is the textual unit superior to the segment. As the segment comprises either three, two, or even one member, the piece is formed of either three, two, or even one segment. Which means that every segment does not necessarily enter, with one or two other segments, in the composition of a piece. The same way that certain members do not enter, with one or two other members, in the composition of a segment, but form in themselves 'unimember' segments, certain segments form in themselves pieces with similar status and function in the text as complex pieces, formed by two or three segments.

The pieces are classified according to how many members they comprise. The shortest piece comprises one member; the longest, three trimember segments, that is nine members; between the two extremes, all the different possibilities exist.

If one ponders the multiplicity of possible arrangements within the piece, one will understand why this exposition limits itself to the presentation of a few of them.[33] But, however great the number of possible arrangements may be, the two basic figures are always parallelism and concentrism.

3.1. *The Single Segment Piece*

In Psalm 146, the unimember segment of 4c has the status of a piece (see below, §5.2.2). In Psalm 113, four pieces comprise only one bimember segment: 1bc, 4, 5b-6a, 9ab (see below, §5.2.1).

As for Amos 1.3–2.16, sixteen segments have the status of pieces: eight bimembers (1.3de, 6de, 12ab, 13de; 2.1de, 5ab, 7cd, 16) and three trimembers (2.10, 14, 15).

3.2. *The Twin Member Piece*

: Thus showed me the Lord God:			
–	Behold,	a basket	of summer.

Amos 8.1

This piece is the size of a bimember segment. But the symmetry of this piece with that which is symmetrical to it (8.2c-3) within the framework of the passage to which it belongs, leads to the conclusion that it is comprised of two unimember segments, and not one bimember segment.[34]

3.3. *The Piece with Three Members*

: Thus he showed me:				
– and behold	the Lord standing on a wall		of	tin
– and	in his hand	(was)		tin.

Amos 7.7

This piece could have been considered a trimember segment. But the symmetry of this piece with the piece which is symmetrical to it

---

33. These examples are borrowed mostly from the three texts analysed during this methodological exposition. It would have been preferable if the choice was guided by the frequency of the arrangements. One will easily understand that at this stage of the research it is absolutely impossible.

34. P. Bovati and R. Meynet, *Le Livre du prophète Amos* (Rhétorique biblique, 2; Paris: Cerf, 1994), p. 313.

(7.8c-9) within the framework of the passage to which they belong, leads to the conclusion that it is formed of two segments (one uni-member and one bimember), not one trimember segment.[35]

One can see how the coherence of the superior level can determine the organization of the inferior level.

3.4. *The Piece with Four Members*

3.4.1. *Parallel Construction*

3.4.1.1. *Of the a a' b b' type*

The four members can form an enumeration, apart from the fact that they are synonymous two by two:

a	[6] The LORD	brings-to-life		and brings-to-death,
a'		he	brings-down to Sheol	and brings-up;
b	[7] The LORD	makes-poor		and makes-rich,
b'		he	brings-low	and brings-up.[36]

1 Sam. 2.6-7

The two segments can mark a logical (and chronological) progression:

a	He raises up	from the dust	the weak
a'	from the dung	he exalts	the poor
b	**to** set him	with princes	
b'	and a seat	of glory	inherits.

1 Sam. 2.8

The two segments can be complementary:

a	Because	he pursued	with the sword	his brother
a'		suffocating		his bowels;
b	and	he tore	perpetually	his anger
b'	and	his wrath	keeping	for ever.

Amos 1.11d-g

35. Bovati and Meynet, *Le Livre du prophète Amos*, p. 295.

36. The parallelism is more marked than in the original since all the verbs are in the *hiphil*; on the other hand, all are participles except the fourth 'he brings up'; for the analysis of the song of Hannah, see R. Meynet, 'Dieu donne son nom à Jésus; analyse rhétorique de Lc 1,26-56 et de 1Sam 2,1-10', *Bib* 66 (1985), pp. 39-72.

The second segment adds precision to the first: 'anger' (aa') is 'for ever' (bb').

a	Because they have rejected	the Law	of the	LORD
a'	and	his precepts	they have not kept;	
b	and	have misled	their	Lies
b'	which have followed	their fathers.		

Amos 2.4d-g

Having turned from the true God (aa'), they followed the false gods (their lies) of their fathers.

The second segment can explain the first:

a	Do not trust	in-princes	
a'	in-a-son-of-clay	in-which	no salvation:
b	departs	his-breath,	
b'	he-returns	to-its-clay.[37]	

Ps. 146.3-4

And similarly:

a	Happy	who has the God	of Jacob	for his help
a'		and his hope	in YHWH	his God
b	making	heaven and earth		
b'	and the sea	and all that (is) in them.		

Ps. 146.5-6

The four members can form a sort of enumeration:

a	Because they sell	for silver	*the innocent*
a'	and *the poor*	for a matter	of sandals
b	trampling	into the dust of the earth	the head of *the deprived*
b'	and the way	of *the destitutes*	they turn aside.

Amos 2.6d-7b

37. The two occurrences of 'clay' (a' and b') render the original play on words between 'Adam' in a' and *'ădâmâ* (= 'clay') in b'. The play on words could be rendered by the paronomasia 'homo' – 'humus'.

3.4.1.2. *Of the a b / a'b' type*

a And upon garments		*taken in pledge*	THEY-GO-TO-LAY
b	beside every	**altar**;	
a'	and the wine of	*the fined*	THEY-DRINK
b'	in the house of	**their gods**.	

Amos 2.8

This example shows particularly clearly how a less than obvious symmetry at a level of organization of the text (in this case segments; see above, end of §2.2.3) can turn out to be very significant at the superior level (in this case the piece).

3.4.2. *Concentric Construction*

Whether the members correspond to one another two by two, the first to the last and the second to the third:

a	Beginning of	*wisdom*	
b	the fear of	THE LORD	
	and		
b' the knowledge of		the HOLY (one)	
a'	(is)	*insight.*[38]	

Prov. 9.10

Or even:

a **YET**	**HE OPENS NOT HIS MOUTH**		
b	*like a lamb*	to the slaughter	IS LED
		and	
b'	*like a sheep*	before its shearers	IS DUMB
a' **AND**	**HE OPENS NOT HIS MOUTH**		

Isa. 53.7

Concentrism can be more marked:

a Be **THE NAME OF THE LORD**			
b	*blessed*		
c		FROM now	TILL ever
c'		FROM the rising of the sun	TILL its setting
b'	*praised* (be)		
a' **THE NAME OF THE LORD**			

Ps. 113.2-3

38. 'Saint' is in the plural in the original; the translation takes it as an elative plural.

Or even:

a			THE EARTH	
	b	gave his fruit		
		c **he blesses**	**us**	**God**
			OUR	**GOD**;
		c' **he blesses**	**us**	**God**
	b'	and they fear him		
a'		all the ends of	THE EARTH	

Ps. 67.7-8

The piece with four members is not only formed of two bimembers; it can also comprise, for example, one unimember and a trimember:

+ [1] Thus showed me the Lord God:

: Lo, he was forming locusts in the beginning of the shooting up of the latter growth
: and lo, the latter growth after the king's mowing
: [2] and it happened, when they had finished eating the grass of the earth,

Amos 7.1-2a

3.5. *The Piece with Five Members*

The piece with five members can be formed of a trimember segment and a bimember segment, or of two bimember segments and one unimember segment.

3.5.1. *A Trimember and a Bimember Segment*

The relationship between the two segments can be obvious:

+ And myself,	I DESTROYED	the Amorite	before them
. who	like the height	of the cedars	his height
. and strong	he (was)	like the oaks;	
+ and	I DESTROYED	his fruit	above
+ and		his roots	beneath.

Amos 2.9

where the only two verbs, identical, play the role of initial terms. The second segment follows the comparison introduced in the second member of the first segment.

Given the uneven number of members in this type of piece, it is not surprising to find that their construction is sometimes concentrical:

| a | *This-one* | came | for testimony |
| b | | TO TESTIFY IN FAVOUR OF THE LIGHT | |

| | | c | THAT all might believe through him. |

| a' | He was not | *that-one* | the light |
| b' | but | TO TESTIFY IN FAVOUR OF THE LIGHT | |

Jn 1.7-8

The second and last members are identical (the last one nevertheless adds 'but'). The first and fourth are in some ways opposed to one another: one says what 'this one' (John) does, and the other what 'that-one' (always John) is not. The third member of the first segment is therefore at the heart of the construction.

3.5.2. *Two Bimember Segments and One Unimember*

When the unimember segment is in the center, as in the following examples, the construction is concentric:

| a | THE GRASS WITHERS, | THE FLOWER FADES | |
| b | when the breath | of the Lord | blows upon it. |

| | c | **Surely, the people (is) grass.** |

| a' | THE GRASS WITHERS, | THE FLOWER FADES | |
| b' | but the word | of our God | will stand for ever. |

Isa. 40.7-8

The beginning of the Prologue of John (1.1-2) offers a good example of this construction:

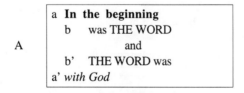

Jn 1.1-2

The third segment (A') reproduces the terms of the first (A): b''
reproduces in pronominal form at once b and b'.[39] At the centre,
between A and A', both expressing exactly the same idea in a different
form, namely a certain distinction between 'the word' and 'God', a
unimember segment enunciates the identity of nature between 'the
word' and 'God'.

3.6. *The Piece with Six Members*

The piece with six members can be formed of either two segments
(trimembers) or of three segments (either three bimembers, or one
trimember, one bimember and one unimember, in whichever order).

3.6.1. *Formed by Two Trimember Segments*

3.6.1.1. *In parallelism*

a And I tell you,		**ask**	and it will be	**GIVEN** you
b		SEEK	and you will	find
	c	*KNOCK*	and it will be	*open* to you.
a'	For everyone	**asks**		**RECEIVES**
b' and he who		SEEKS		finds
	c' and to him who	*KNOCKS*	it will be	*opened.*

Lk. 11.9-10

3.6.1.2. *In concentrism*

a	Though he will not	**GIVE** him
b	*getting up*	
	c	**because** he is his friend
	c'	**because** of his importunity
b'	*rising*	
a'	he will	**GIVE** him whatever he needs

Lk. 11.8

---

39. So the economy law is verified: when two symmetrical textual unities follow
one another, even from a distance, the second one is often shortened.

Or even:

a		Make-fat	the *HEART* of this people
	b	and their	EARS	make-heavy
		c	and their	**eyes**	shut;
		c'	lest they	see	with their **eyes**
	b'	and with their	EARS	they hear
a'		and with their	*HEARTS*	they understand.

Isa. 6.10

Or even, in another form:

a	and	SIX BRANCHES GOING OUT	of its sides:
	b	*three branches* and	*of the lampstand*	*out of the side one,*
	b'	*three branches*	*of the lampstand*	*out of the side two.*
	c	three cups like almonds on each branch with capital and flower, and		
	c'	three cups like almonds on each branch with capital and flower;		
a'	so for the	SIX BRANCHES GOING OUT	of the lampstand.

Exod. 25.32-33

3.6.2. *Formed by Three Segments*

3.6.2.1. *Three bimembers*
Like the trimember segments, the piece formed of three bimembers can be classified under four categories:

3.6.2.1.1. *Of the a b c type (or parallel).* Whether the two members of each of the three segments are synonymous:

a	Behold your God,				
a'	Behold the Lord GOD:				
	b	with	**might**	he comes,	
	b'	and	**his arm**	rules for him;	
	c	Behold,	HIS REWARD	with	him,
	c'	and	HIS RECOMPENSE	before	him.

Isa. 40.9-10

Or whether each of the three segments reproduce the same opposition:

a	The bows	of the MIGHTY	are broken
a'	the **feeble**	are girded	with strength;
b	the SATED	for bread	engage-themselves
b'	the **hungry**	are-fattened	of food;[40]
c'	the **barren**	**bears**	seven
c	the NUMEROUS	of children	is forlorn.

1 Sam. 2.4-5

where the same opposition is found between each member of each segment; one will note however the inversion of the order in c' c, which 'buckles' the series by ending with a negative the same way that the piece had started in a. Or whether the second members are very similar:

a	Get you up to a high mountain,		
	+ **O herald of good tidings**	to	SION
b	Lift up your voice with strength,		
	+ **O herald of good tidings**	to	JERUSALEM
c	Lift it up, fear not		
	+ **say**	to the	CITIES OF JUDA. . .

Isa. 40.9-10

3.6.2.1.2. *Of the a a'b type.*

+ [14] I will kindle fire	upon the wall	of Rabbah
+ and it shall devour	her palaces	
+ with shouting	in the day	of battle
+ with a tempest	in the day	of whirlwind;
. [15] and shall go	their king	in deportation
. he		and his princes altogether.

Amos 1.14-15b

The unity of this piece is thematic: the three segments enumerate the consequences of the sin of the Sons of Ammon, 'because they have ripped up the pregnant (women) of Gilead, so they may enlarge their border' (1.13de). The first two segments say what God will do (in the

---

40. For the translation of this member, see P.K. McCarter, *I Samuel* (AB, 8; Garden City NY: Doubleday, 1980) *ad loc.*

first person singular), the last what will happen to the leaders (in the third person singular).

3.6.2.1.3. *Of the a b b' type.*

+	You will bring them	and plant them
+	on the MOUNTAIN	*of your heritage,*
	: to the PLACE	*of your abode*
	: which you have made,	**O Lord**,
	: to the SANCTUARY,	**O Adonay**,
	: which have established	your hands.

Exod. 15.17

The last two segments develop the last member of the first segment: their first terms ('to the place' and 'to the sanctuary') reproduce the first term of the second member of the first segment, 'on the mountain'. Note that the second members of the last two segments start with two synonyms (initial terms) and that 'Lord' and 'Adonay' play the role of median terms between the last two segments. Similarly, 'of your heritage' and 'of your abode' play the role of median terms between the first and the second segments.

The following piece offers a peculiar parallel construction:

− 7		He RAISES UP	from the dust	*the weak*
−		from the dung	he EXALTS	*the poor*
	+ 8	to **SET** him	with **princes**	
	+	with the **princes**	of his people;	
− 9		he **SETS**	*the barren*	of home
	+	**mother**	**of children**	happy.

Ps. 113.7-9b

The last segment (v. 9) is parallel to the first two (vv. 7-8): indeed, the passage from humiliation (v. 7) to glorification (v. 8) is reproduced between the two members of v. 9. The first segment (v. 7) and the first member of the last segment (v. 9a) present the action of God in favor of two disadvantaged categories, 'the weak' and 'poor' (v. 7) and 'the barren' (v. 9a); note the complementarity between the masculine (v. 7), and the feminine (v. 9a). The second segment (v. 8) and the second member of the last segment (v. 9b) describe the final state of the categories saved by God: 'the weak' and 'the poor' are found with 'the princes', 'the barren' becomes 'mother of children'.

3.6.2.1.4. *Of the a b a' type (or concentric).*

a	I and this woman	dwell			IN the same	HOUSE,
a'	and		I gave-birth	*with her*	IN the	HOUSE.

Then on the third day	after my **childbirth**,
she also **gave-birth**	that woman.

a	And	we together without anybody *with us*	IN	the	HOUSE,
a'	only	we two	IN	the	HOUSE.

1 Kgs 3.17-18[41]

+ [2] I will send	fire	upon	***MOAB***	
+ and it shall devour	the palaces	of	***Kerioth***	
= and *will die*	amid uproar		***MOAB***	
= amid shouting	at the sound	of the horn		
+ [3] and I will cut off	the ruler	from the midst of	***him***	
+ and all his princes	*I will kill*	with	***him***.	

Amos 2.2-3b

The unity of this piece is due to the fact that it constitutes the ensemble of the consequences of the sin of Moab: 'because he burned the bones of the king of Edom into lime' (v. 2.1de). The two extreme segments say what God will do (in the first person singular; except v. 2b, the subject of which is neither God nor Moab, but 'fire'), whereas the central segment says what will happen to those chastised by God (in the third person singular); note the repetition of 'Moab' at the end of the first members of the first and second segments, and the symmetry of 'kill' and 'die' between the central segment and the last segment.

Concentrism can be much more pronounced and obvious:

---

41. For the rhetorical analysis of the judgment of Solomon in his entirety, see R. Meynet, *Initiation*, I, pp. 113-18; II, pls. 17.18.

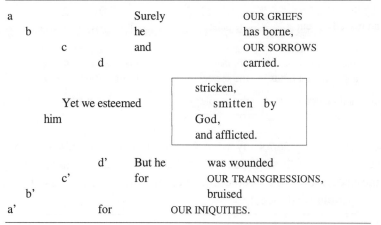

a				Surely	OUR GRIEFS
	b			he	has borne,
		c		and	OUR SORROWS
			d		carried.

	Yet we esteemed him	stricken, smitten by God, and afflicted.

		d'		But he	was wounded
		c'		for	OUR TRANSGRESSIONS,
	b'				bruised
a'				for	OUR INIQUITIES.

Isa. 53.4-5[42]

And also in the following piece:

+ [11] *And I raised up*	*from amid your sons*	***PROPHETS***
= and	from amid your young men	**NAZIRITES**.

Is it not indeed so, O sons of Israel?   Oracle of the LORD.

= [12] And you made drink	the **NAZIRITES**	wine
+ *and to the **PROPHETS***	*you commanded*	*'Do not prophesy'.*

Amos 2.11-12

3.6.2.2. Unimember + bimember + trimember. Amos 1.3–2.15 is composed of two pieces both formed by one bimember, one trimember and one unimember:

---

42. From the point of view of stichometry, it is clear that one has to cut this way:

Yet we,	esteemed him	stricken	(3 terms)
smitten	by God	and afflicted	(3 terms)

But the enumeration of three participles, of which only the second has a complement, leads to the proposed analysis.

+ ⁴ I will send a fire	upon the house	of	*Hazael*	
+ and it shall devour	the palaces	of	*Ben-Hadad*	
+ ⁵ and I will break	the bar	of	*DAMASCUS*	
+ and cut off	who sits	from	*Bikeat-Aven*	
+ and him that holds	the scepter	from	*Beth-Eden*	
= and shall be deported	the people	of	*ARAM*	to Kir.

Amos 1.4-5d

The first two segments say what God will do (in the first person singular; except for 'it shall devour' of 4b), the last one what will happen to the people of Aram (in the third person singular). It is also the case in the symmetrical piece:

+ ⁷ I will send a fire	upon the wall	of	*GAZA*
+ and it shall devour	her palaces		
+ ⁸ and I will cut off	who sits	from	*Ashdod*
+ and him that holds	the scepter	from	*Ashkelon*
+ and I will turn	my hand	on	*Ekron*;
= and shall perish	the remnant	of the	*PHILISTINES*,

Amos 1.7-8d

Note at the end of the members in the first two segments, the list of the cities of the Philistine pentapole (incomplete since Gat is missing), and at the end of the last segment the name of the people of the 'Philistines'.

3.7. *The Piece with Seven Members*

Here again, given the uneven number of members, the construction will often be concentric. For example:

. ⁴ Let praise you		THE PEOPLES,	God,
. Let praise you		THE PEOPLES,	all!
	for you	judge	
⁵ Let be glad	THE PEOPLES	with equity	
and sing-for-joy	and		
THE NATIONS	THE NATIONS	upon earth	
	you	guide.	
. ⁶ Let praise you		THE PEOPLES,	God,
Let praise you		THE PEOPLES,	all!

Ps. 67.4-6

Verses 4 and 6 are identical. Each of those two segments is formed by two almost identical members: only the last word of each member changes, 'God' and 'all', the first identifying the object of the verb, the second identifying its subject. The central segment (v. 5) is a tri-member. The first member reproduces vv. 4 and 6 with two verbs, ' be glad' and 'sing for joy', synonymous with 'praise', followed by the subject, 'the nations', synonymous with 'the people'. Two members then give the reasons for which God should be praised by the nations (they are introduced by 'for'); these two members are constructed in chiasm, with synonymous verbs at the extremities, 'judge' and 'guide', then 'the people' and 'the nations', another two synonyms which reproduce those of vv. 4, 5 and 6, each followed by an expansion ('with equity' and 'upon the earth'). The first member has been 'factored' because it is the main clause followed by the two causal clauses that it rules.

Also of concentric construction is 2 Cor. 11.23-25:

a	IN THE DEADS	*OFTEN*	
b	from the Jews	**forty lashes** less one	*I have received*
c		**three times**	*I have been beaten with rods*
		once	*I was stoned*
c'		**three times**	*I have been shipwrecked*
b'		**a night and a day** at sea	*I have been adrift*
a'	ON JOURNEYS	*OFTEN*	

3.8. *The Piece with Eight Members*

a		9	He was the light	(the) true (one)[43]
	b		that enlightens	every man
		c	COMING	*INTO THE WORLD.*
d		10	In the world	he was
e			and the world	through him was made
		f	**and the world**	**knew him not.**
	c'	11	*TO HIS OWN*	HE CAME
	f'		**and his own**	**received him not.**

Jn 1.9-11

The two members of the last segment (11) reproduce in the same order the last two members of the preceding trimember.

Such a construction, although not false, depends nonetheless on the preceding level and always keeps apart the segments that the piece brings together. It works insofar as one considers that 'every man' in the first segment stands for 'the world' in the second segment and for 'his own' in the third. It is not certain however that to interpret—according to the categories of Paul—'the world' as 'the pagans' and 'his own' as 'the Jews', would correspond to the vision of John. Each level has its own coherence which does not always coincide with the divisions and the organization of the other levels.

+ 9 He was	THE LIGHT	(the) true (one)
. that	ENLIGHTENS	**every man**
+	*COMING*	*into the world.*
10 In	**the world**	he was
and	**the world**	through him was made.
And	**the world**	KNEW HIM NOT:
+ 11	*to his own*	*HE CAME*
. and	**his own**	RECEIVED HIM NOT.

43. 'He' designs 'the Word' which is the subject of v. 1; for the analysis of the ensemble of the text, see R. Meynet, 'Analyse rhétorique du Prologue de Jean', *RB* 96 (1989), pp. 481-510.

This concentrism does justice to the veritable construction of the text. The last three members, forming themselves a small concentrical construction, are opposed indeed to the first three: the centre of the second side (11a) is found at the end of the first (9c) in almost identical form ('his own' is not identical to 'the world', but both have the same referent) and the two synonymous members 10c and 11b are opposed to 9b (the Word has not been 'known' nor 'received' by 'the world', by 'his own' which is 'every man' to whom it was destined). Here again there is a passage between the center (9b) to the extremities (10c and 11b). This 'law',[44] is here doubly demonstrated. As for 10ab in the center, it is a sort of corrective which aims at emphasizing that, if the Word has come in the world like the rest of the piece tells us, one should not forget that it was already there, since it is through Him that the world came to be. These are apparently two contradictory things which are being said at the same time.

3.9. *The Piece with Nine Members*

The three segments can be parallel with each other, member to member. For example:

+ [32]	And if you	LOVE	who love you,
– WHAT CREDIT IS THAT TO YOU?			
: For **even** *sinners*		love	who love them.
+ [33]	And if you	DO GOOD to	who did good to you,
– WHAT CREDIT IS THAT TO YOU?			
:	**Even** *sinners*	do the same.	
+ [34]	And if you	LEND to	those from whom you hope to receive
– WHAT CREDIT IS THAT TO YOU?			
:	**Even** *sinners*	lend to	sinners to receive as much again.

Lk. 6.32-34

44. N.W. Lund, *Chiasmus*, pp. 40-41 (see above, pp. 143-44).

The following example:

+ [7]	HE MAKES	right	for the oppressed
+	HE GIVES	bread	the hungry
:	*THE LORD* FREES		the prisoners
: [8]	*THE LORD* OPEN (the eyes) of		the blind
:	*THE LORD* HOLDS UP		the bowed
:	*THE LORD* LOVES		**the just**
: [9]	*THE LORD* KEEPS		the sojourners
+	the orphan	and the widow	HE RESTORES
+	but the way	**of the wicked**	HE TWISTS

Ps. 146.7-9

is concentric since the three members of the central segment begin
with 'the Lord' as well as the two members that frame it. Only the
first two members start with the verb, only the last two end by the
verb (these are conjugated whereas the others in the original are participles). This concentric construction does not prevent the opposition
between the last member and all the preceding ones (underlined by the
only coordinant of the piece); however one has to note that this last
member is opposed to the last member of the central segment ('the
wicked'—'the just') which indicates that all concerned by the first eight
members are the 'oppressed' just (according to the first member of the
piece), obviously not the 'wicked'.

4. *The Part*

As the segment is formed of three or two (or even one) members and
the piece is formed of three or two (or even one) segments, the part
counts three or two (or even one) pieces.

This means that the part can have as many as twenty-seven members: this would be the case with a part formed of three pieces each
composed of three trimember segments. Since the maximum number
of members of a piece is nine, one could think that the minimum number of members in a part would be ten members; but as some parts
have but one piece which is itself formed of one segment, either bimember or even unimember, there will therefore be parts which have
only one member. The criteria is therefore not the number of members, but the degree of complexity of the textual organization. The

same applies to the level of the text as to the other levels of organization of language. The moneme is not defined by the number of phonemes that constitute it: there are some which contain a great number of phonemes, such as the lexeme which is said to be the longest word in the French language—'anticonstitutionnellement'—which has no less than eighteen phonemes; but there are also some which have but one phoneme, such as the English article 'a'. The sentence is not defined by a predetermined number of monemes and the text is not defined by the number of its sentences. One knows of the bet that Voltaire had made with one of his friends to write the shortest possible letter: this friend had written to him, in Latin, the following words: *Eo rus* ('I am going to the country'), and Voltaire answered, in the same language: *I* ('Go').

So far, at the level of the segment and of the piece, it was possible to classify the different types according to the number of members that composed them. One will easily understand that at the level of the part, it is hardly conceivable to make an exhaustive catalogue of all the possible configurations: even if one retained a single example for each category (according to the number of their members), it would amount to twenty-seven examples. It is therefore necessary to limit oneself, to prevent this methodological exposition from growing out of proportion. The examples provided, essentially from the three texts that were retained at the beginning, will suffice to give an outline of what a part can be.

To render the complexity of certain texts, it is sometimes necessary to introduce an intermediary degree between the piece and the part: I will call 'sub-part' a textual unit which in itself has the same characteristics of the part (namely that it is constituted of one, two or three pieces) but that at the superior level is on a par with pieces with which it composes a part. We will see several examples of sub-parts in the text of Amos.

4.1. *The Part Which is Composed of One Piece*

It represents the same characteristics as the piece of which it is formed. Such a piece is identified as a part only at the superior level, when it is found that it is symmetrical to another part itself composed of two or three pieces.

In Psalm 113, the unimember segments 1a, 5a, 9c, have the status of parts (see below, §5.2.1).

In Psalm 146, besides the unimembers 6c, 10c and the trimembers 1, 2, 10ab, vv. 7-9 are a piece formed of three trimember segments which, being symmetrical to the part 3-6b, will have to be considered themselves as a part (see below, §5.2.2). One can nonetheless note that each of these two parts has nine members.

In Amos 1.3–2.16, sixteen pieces have the status of parts (or sub-parts);

+ with one segment
  - unimember: 1.3a, 5e, 6a, 8e, 9a, 11a, 13a, 15c; 2.1a, 3c, 4a, 6a, 16c.
  - bimember: 1.3bc, 6bc, 9bc, 11bc, 13bc; 2.1bc, 4bc, 6bc, 13.
+ with three segments
  - three bimembers: 2.11-12.

4.2. *The Part Composed of Two Pieces*

4.2.1. *Psalm 113.5b-9b*

+ 5b	He rises up	**to SIT UP**	
+ 6	and he stoops	to see	
+	in the heavens	and on the earth.	

– 7 He raises	from the dust	the weak	
– from the dung	he exalts	the poor,	
: 8	**to SET HIM**	with princes	
:	with the princes	of his people;	
– 9 he	**SETS** the barren	of home	
: mother	of children	happy.	

The first piece (5b-6) is the size of a trimember segment; the second has three bimembers. The most straightforward link between the two pieces is the triple recurrence of a verb of the same root: 'to sit' (5b) and 'to set' (8a, 9a). The double movement of raising (7: 'raises', 'exalts') and enthronement (8: 'set him with princes') of the second piece, articulated by the conjunction 'to', is found in the first piece under another shape: the same 'to' (5b) articulates two opposite movements, the elevation of Him who will sit as absolute king and the stooping towards the earth of him who rules in heaven. God is therefore at once above everything and very close to the small and weak, the immanence is stated along with the transcendence. The reign of God proclaimed at the beginning (5b-6) is spread to the poor that share it (7-8), as a heritage for the sons given by God (9). The calling of man is therefore to become king, in the image of he who is his Father. Thus can we understand the co-ordination between 'heaven' and 'earth' which end the first piece (6b): man who is from the earth, especially the one who is humiliated, who is in the 'dust' and 'dung', is exalted as God himself and comes, to a certain extent, to share what can be called the heavenly nature. Heaven and earth are not only embraced in one glance by God; the movement of exaltation brings man from earth to heaven.

4.2.2. *Amos 2.9-10*

+ ^{9}	And **MYSELF**,	I destroyed	*THE AMORITE* before them	
.		who like the height of the cedars their height		
.		he who was strong like the oaks;		
-		and I destroyed his fruit above		
-		and his roots beneath.		

= ^{10}	And **MYSELF**,	I brought you up out of the land of Egypt	
=		and made you walk in the desert forty years	
+		to inherit the land of *THE AMORITE*.	

I will not reproduce here the analysis of each piece, nor of each segment, since it has already been done at the inferior levels. Consequently, this rewriting only brings to light the relationship between the two pieces, and not those which are internal to each piece and even less to each segment.

The first piece (9) is formed of two segments (one trimember and one bimember), whereas the second (10) has only one trimember. The two occurrences of 'And myself' (9a and 10a) play the part of initial terms, while those of 'the Amorite' (9a and 10c) play the role of extreme terms.

4.2.3. *Luke 11.31-32*

+ [31] The queen of   **the South**   *will rise*   at the judgment
  with the men of   this generation
  – and judge them,

    : because she came from the ends of the earth
    to LISTEN TO   *THE WISDOM*   of   Solomon

        = and see, there is here more than   Solomon!

+ [32] The men of   **Nineveh**   *will get up*   at the judgment
  with   this generation
  – and judge it,

    : because
    THEY REPENTED at   *THE PROCLAMATION* of   Jonah,

        = and see, there is here more than   Jonah!

This part has two pieces (31 and 32); the first is formed of two tri-member segments (31abc and 31def), the second of one trimember (32abc) and one bimember (32de). The two pieces are parallel to one another. This part will enable the highlighting of two important points.

One will note at first that the second piece makes the economy of 'the men of' in 32b and especially 'she came from the ends of the earth' in 32d; thus, when the second segment of the first piece is a tri-member (31def), the second segment of the second piece is reduced to a bimember (32de). This phenomenon that Jousse called 'graphic ab-breviation' and it would be better to call 'economy', has already been noted at the level of the segment (see above, §2.2.3; in the following example, the economy will be marked even more strongly).

The second point is more important because it has crucial implica-tions for interpretation: the identity,[45] from one piece to the next, should not mask the oppositions. On the contrary, it is not an exagge-ration to say that the function of identity is to strengthen the dif-ferences (see above, §2.2.2.3.5). In such texts, one is often tempted to pay more attention to what is being repeated.[46] If the effect of

---

45. I will nonetheless note the variation, usual in Luke, between 'to rise' (31a: *egeirō*) and 'get up' (32a: *anistēmi*); see R. Meynet, *L'Evangile selon saint Luc*, II, pp. 258-59.

46. Such is, for example, the opinion of A. George. Speaking of double parables, such as Lk. 13.18-21; 14.28-32; Mt. 13.31-33, he says: 'We have here a

insistence created by the repetition is not to be neglected, it would be dangerous to stop at that. Here, it will be crucial to note the complementary oppositions woman–man ('the Queen'–'the men'), South–North ('South'–'Nineveh'), centrifugal–centripetal movement (the Queen of the South has come to Israel when Jonas had come out of Israel to go to Nineveh), king–prophet (the king 'Solomon' and the prophet 'Jonas') and mostly 'wisdom'–prophecy (that is 'proclamation'; opposition which reflects two of the three parts of the Bible: Law, Prophecy, Wisdom) and lastly hearing–execution with 'listen' and 'repented', two indispensable successive operations, since there is no real understanding without practise, without obedience.

4.2.4. *Luke 6.32-35*

The following example will show that economy can take very different forms:

+ ³² And if   you   **LOVE**   **who love you,**
 – what *CREDIT* is that to you?
 : For even *sinners* love   who love them.

+ ³³ And if   you   DO GOOD   to who did good to you,
 – what *CREDIT* is that to you?
  :   Even *sinners* do the same.

+ ³⁴ And if   you   *lend* to   those from whom you hope to receive
 – what *CREDIT* is that to you?
  :   Even *sinners* lend to   sinners to receive as much again.

- -

+ ³⁵   But   **LOVE**   **your enemies,**
+   and   DO GOOD
+   and   *lend*   expecting nothing in return;

       – and it   will be   great your *CREDIT*
       – and you   will be   the sons of the Most High,

             : for he is kind to *the ungrateful* and *the selfish.*

---

literary parallelism; it is very interesting to write them in corresponding lines: the same words are found at the same place [note, however, that he rewrites only what in Lk. 14.28-32 and 15.4-10 is parallel].

It is strictly parallel. It is a technique which enables the gaze to centre on the essential of the parable. What the parable means, is what is kept in parallel in both parables... The parallels help to discover what is the fundamental theme of the parable. This theme is what is parallel; the rest is decoration, imagery' (A. George, *Lecture de l'Evangile selon St Luc*, [Lyon: Profac, 1971], p. 53).

This part counts two pieces. The first piece (32-34), formed of three bimember segments, has already been analysed above (see p. 245); the second piece (35) is composed of one trimember (35abc), one bimember (35de) and one unimember (35f). The trimember 35abc reproduces the first members of each of the three segments of the first piece (32a, 33a, 34a, making nonetheless the economy of the complement in the second segment); then it is only two members (35de) that are opposed to the three identical second members of the first piece, 'What credit is that to you?' (32b, 33b, 34b); at last the final unimember (35f) opposes the action of God to the triple action of the sinners (third members of the segments of the first piece: 32c, 33c, 34c). The economy here is therefore conjugated with another arrangement of the members.

4.3. *The Part Composed of Three Pieces*

Given the uneven number of pieces that compose it, this kind of part, which is the most frequent, will often be of concentric composition.

4.3.1. *Psalm 113.1b-4*

+ 1b	PRAISE,	O servants	of	THE LORD,
+	PRAISE	*the name of*		THE LORD!
2		Be	*the name of*	THE LORD
	BLESSED			
3		.	from now	till ever;
		.	from the rising of the sun	till its setting,
	PRAISED (be)			
			the name of	THE LORD.
+ 4	*EXALTED*		above all nations	THE LORD
+			above the heavens	HIS GLORY.

This part has four segments organized in three pieces. Each of the extreme pieces (1bc and 4) is the size of a bimember segment; these segments are of parallel composition. The central piece (2-3) counts two bimembers organized in a concentric manner.

The same name of God, 'the Lord', is repeated five times, each time in a different position: in the position of final terms in the first piece (1bc), in the position of extreme terms (or to be more precise at the end of the extreme syntagms) in the second piece (2a and 3c), at the end of the first member of the third piece (4a); the fact that the name of 'the Lord' is not repeated at the end of 4b but is replaced with 'His glory' is a good example of what one can call a phenomenon of closure. 'Praise' is reproduced three times (1b, 1c, 3b) and his synonyms, 'blessed' (2b) and 'exalted' (3b), are found in the position of initial terms in the first piece, of central terms in the second piece, of unique initial term in the last piece. The two occurrences of 'the name of the Lord' (1c and 2a) play the part of median terms that staple the first two pieces together.

The identity between all these terms calls for a search for a relationship between all those left, a relationship which is not absolutely obvious at first glance. 'Servants' of the beginning is almost detailed and made explicit in the following pieces: it is the servants of all times ('from now till ever': 2c) and of all places ('from the rising of the sun till its setting': 3a), it is the servants of all time and space. The last piece (4) reproduces and extrapolates from this idea: all the nations are nations from the East to the West (and so are the nations of all times); and, at the end of the part, changing abruptly of plan, it is 'the heavens' (4b), and not only the earth, with the innumerable crowd of spirits and powers that people them: these too are 'servants of the Lord'. We now understand that 'His glory' comes to close the list formed of the five 'the Lord': to the invitation of the first piece, and to the wishes of the following, succeeds in conclusion the recognition of a reality which goes beyond all praise and whose existence imposes itself as a blinding self-evidence.

4.3.2. *Psalm 146.3-6*

– [3] Do not **TRUST**	**in princes,**	
– in *A SON OF ADAM*	in whom there is no	**SALVATION:**
= [4] (when) departs	his breath,	
= he returns to	his *adamah*.	

      <u>IN THAT DAY   PERISH HIS PLAN!</u>

+ [5] Happy who has	*THE GOD OF JACOB*	for his **HELP**
+ and his **HOPE**	**in the Lord his God:**	
= [6] he makes	heaven and *earth*	
= and the sea	and all that (is) in them.	

Two pieces, each formed of two bimember segments (3-4b and 5-6), frame a unimember segment (4c).

To the first segment of the first piece (3), corresponds the first segment of the second piece (5a): the extreme terms of one ('trust' and 'salvation') are opposed, by the same negation, to the median terms of the other to which they are synonyms to ('help' and 'hope'). Note that it is not a positive order which corresponds to the negative imperative of the beginning, but a beatitude. 'Princes' at the end of the first member (3a) is opposed to 'God' at the end of the last member (5b); 'sons of Adam' is therefore opposed to 'God of Jacob'.

The second segments (4ab and 6) give the reason for the prohibition (4ab) and the beatitude (6): the Lord is he who made all things, as the familiar enumeration indicates, the three parts of the world, strengthened by the adjunction 'and all that (is) in them', including man, 'the son of Adam' that God made in the beginning from clay, 'Adamah' from which he draws his name, into which he blew his 'breath' (4ab). Thus are put in opposition, not only the Maker and his creature, but mostly God who is the principle of life and man who, because of the disobedience of the first sin, is subjected to the law of death (one can note the similarity of the significatum of 'Adamah'—that is 'the soil', in 4b—and 'earth' in 6a).

These two segments are indeed not properly understood unless they are placed in the tradition common to the Psalm and with the tale of Genesis 2–3; that of creation of man from clay:

The the Lord God formed	ADAM	
(of) dust of the	ADAMAH;	
he breathed into his nostrils	a breath of	**life**
and Adam became	a **living**	being

Gen. 2.7

and of the curse that followed sin:

'In the sweat of your face you shall eat bread
till you return to the Adamah for out of her you were taken
for you are dust, and to dust you shall return'

Gen. 3.19

and Adam is thrown out of Eden, deprived of the tree of life from which he could eat 'and live forever' (Gen. 3.22).

It remains to explain why 'the Lord God' (5b) is called 'God of Jacob' in the preceding segment: the God of Jacob or God of Israel (see above, §2.2.2.3.4) is the God of the specific alliance that the

Maker made with a people chosen among all the nations; it is he who rules over Israel and it is on this unique king that the elected people must count. It therefore has to be defiant of 'princes'[47] that 3a speaks of, the powerful that govern them, must perhaps mostly be the foreign powers with which it is always tempted to conclude a pact.

The piece is focused at last on the unimember segment of 4c. One can object that this member is part of the preceding sentence which it follows. Would it not be more natural to consider that v. 4 is a trimember segment? The objection merits our attention. It is true that those three members end in a similar way (with the same third person suffix pronoun in the original) and one could even link 'in that day' to the end of the second member, which would amount to a very well-balanced trimember segment of concentric construction:

. Departs	**his**	breath
+ he returns to	**his**	Adamah in that day
. perish	**his**	plans

with, at the extremities, the same syntactic construction (verb + subject), different from that of the intermediary member. There are, however, three reasons to justify the choice that was made: two are internal, the third is external. The two members 4ab are exactly parallel to one another and symmetrical to the equally bimember segment 6ab. Besides, we will see later (§5.2.2) the importance of 'in that day' which is opposed to other expressions of the same type at once at the extremities and at the centre of the whole psalm. It is frequent—and it is the external reason—that the centre of a text is occupied by the end of its first half, an end which does not have its equivalent at the end of the second half and could therefore seem to be a sort of outgrowing or enlarging of the first half. This phenomenon has, besides, already been noted at the level of the bimember segment (see above, §2.2.3).

Lastly this part allows an important precision to be made. The identification of the concentric composition of a text does not mean that its dynamic should be ignored; concentrism does not automatically exclude progression, concentrism is not synonymous with statism.[48]

47. On the meaning of *nadîb*, translated by 'princes', see, for example, L. Jacquet, *Les Psaumes et le Coeur de l'homme: Etude textuelle, littéraire et doctrinale* (Gembloux: Duculot, I. Pss. 1–50; II. Pss. 51–100: 1977; III. Pss. 101–150, 1979), III, p. 260; see also pp. 704 and 310.

48. Contrary to the views of I. de La Potterie for whom statism is the first of the four objections that he gives in opposition to the concentric structures: 'Let us

Even in the texts where concentrism is much stronger, there is always a modification, an event shall we say, something that happens between the beginning and the end. An analysis which would not take it into account would indeed deserve the reproach of statism.

4.3.3. *Amos 2.6b-8*

Amos 1.3–2.16 has a great number of parts (several of which have two sub-parts). It would be too long and fastidious to present the composition of each of those units now. I will limit discussion to one example (Amos 2.6b-8); the others will be analysed at the following level, that of the passage.

– [6b]	*For*	*three*	*transgressions*		*of Israel*
+ *and*		*for*	*four*	*I will not come back;*	

– *for* they sell		for silver	the **innocent**
– and the **poor**		for a matter	of sandals,

. [7] trampling	into the dust of the earth		the head of **the deprived**
. and the way of	**the destitute**		*THEY TURN ASIDE;*

> and a man and his father go into the maiden
> to profane the **SANCTITY** of my name;

: [8] and upon	garments	**taken-in-pledge**	*THEY GO TO LAY,*
= beside	every	**ALTAR**,	

:	and	the wine of	**the fined**	they drink,
=	in	the house of their	**GODS.**	

This part has two sub-parts; the first (6bc) has a single bimember segment, the second (6d-8), which details the crimes that are mentioned in the first, has three pieces:

—The two bimembers of the first piece (6d-7b) are of analogous composition, with the direct objects in median terms: 'the innocent and the poor' in the first segment, 'the head of the deprived and the way of the destitute' in the second; note that 'innocent' and 'poor' are in the singular in the first segment, whereas 'deprived' and destitute' are in the

observe first that this structure is completely static: the second branch of the parable repeats the first. We cannot perceive any of the dynamism that animates the prologue: between the beginning and the end, no progression is found' ('Structure du Prologue de Jean', *NTS* 30 [1984], p. 356).

plural in the second and that the four terms of this list are homogeneous and practically synonymous.

—The last piece (8) also counts two bimembers that are totally parallel term by term; the alternation of the numbers (plural, singular) of the first piece is also found, but in reverse order ('garments' and 'wine').

—From one piece to the next, the verbs translated by 'turn aside' (7b) and by 'go to lay' (8a) are, in Hebrew, homonymous (*yaṭṭû*); (both share the same root and, despite the fact that the first is in the hiphil and the second in the qal, those two verbs have exactly the same significant); at the end of the members that frame the central piece, these two verbs play the part of median terms from a distance. 'Innocent' which is opposed to 'the fined'[49] play the function of extreme terms for the second sub-part.

—As regards the central piece (7cd), it is composed of only one bimember segment that is distinct from those that frame it because it is the only one which subject is lexicalized ('a man and his father') and the only one that has a final proposition (7c). The word 'sanctity' (7d: at the end of the segment) announces the cultual terms of the last piece, 'altar' and 'house of their gods' (8b and d: at the end of the segments). Thus the central piece has the function of linking the first piece and the last where it is no longer a question of injustice, but injustice linked to worship, and probably justified by it.[50]

The central segment is discussed more than any other of that part. First the expression 'a man and his father' is unique; if we take *'îš* in the distributive sense of 'each', it can signify 'any man and his father', or even 'any man like his father'. On the other hand 'father' can be understood, not so much as the genitor, but as the one responsible, the leader. The syntagm 'go into the maiden' has often been interpreted as indicating the fact of going to a woman's house to have sexual relations with her; but the verb translated as 'go', constructed with the

49. Indeed, the root *'nš* (to pay a fine) is used, in a judicial context, as a sanction for a wrong done to others (Exod. 21.22; Deut. 22.19). Someone who is 'fined' is therefore guilty. The opposition between the two terms is also found in Prov. 17.26: 'To impose a fine (*'nš*) on the innocent (*ṣaddîq*) is not right'.

50. W.R. Harper (*A Critical and Exegetical Commentary on Amos and Hosea*, [ICC; Edinburgh: T. & T. Clark, 1905, 1979], p. 48) has well perceived that this segment was the climax of the part: it is one of the reasons for which he proposes to move it to the end.

preposition *'el* ('into'), is never used to speak of sexual relations. Several commentators see in the feminine character a whore or a sacred whore. But in the Bible the word *na'ara* neither means a prostitute (*zōna*) nor a sacred prostitute (*qᵉdēša*), but simply 'the young girl'. If we include this character in the list of 'innocent', 'poor', 'destitute' and 'deprived' that are mentioned in the two preceding segments, it could mean the young domestic slave girl, indistinctly abused by the son and his father. If on the other hand we see in this segment a preparation for the two following segments, it would then be question of a feminine divinity, ironically designated by the prophet as 'the maiden', or more likely a woman who greets the pilgrims for a sacred meal (called *mrzḥ*)—not necessarily in the temple—and the expression would be a way to mock the pilgrims: instead of saying that they go to the temple, Amos would have chosen the provocative expression 'go into the maiden'.[51] It seems in any case that one should not dissociate the mention of the girl from the place where a man and his father go, the temple and its altars.

In conclusion, it would be useful to briefly recall the two particularly important points of methodology that the texts analysed here, and especially at the level of the part, have enabled us to make.

The textual units that are in a symmetrical relationship are not always at the same level; so, for example, to a piece formed of two bimember segments could correspond a piece formed of a single bimember segment; one member could have the status of sub-part (this is what the definitions of the segment, piece and part imply, each being composed of one, two or three units of the inferior level).

It is not unusual that the second piece of a part be abbreviated in comparison to the first; it is in truth but the extension on a superior level of the phenomenon of economy already noted at the level of the segment (see above, 2.2.3).

---

51. Similarly to what we could say about the young men who go to church, to meet their girlfriends rather than to pray.

5. *The Passage*

So far, that is for the three preceding levels, it was possible to say that the textual unity of each level was formed by three or two, or even one unit of the inferior level, at the cost of confusing, so to speak, the levels in placing on a par the units of different levels, for example having a part formed of one member and two pieces. It seems that this way of putting things—this system or model—allows the presentation of phenomena in a simple and coherent fashion. The first three levels work the same way by analogy with that of the phoneme, syllable and moneme: many monemes are formed of several syllables, but some of them have just one (like the two preceding monemes, 'just' and 'one'; similarly many syllables have two or three phonemes, but there are some that only have one (such as the article 'a', or the interjection 'O'); some monemes are therefore formed of one single phoneme syllable, then of one phoneme.

Beyond the part, this system does not operate any more and it seems that one has reached another stage: indeed, the passage, the sequence and the section are formed of one or more units of the level immediately below. Such has got to be the definition of these units.

As for the passage, its quantitative definition (a textual unit formed of one or more part) does not suffice. The part or parts that compose it form a coherent whole, from the point of view of form as well as meaning.

The passage is the first separable unit, which can be autonomous. It is a kind of minimal unit of reading or 'recitation'. This is particularly relevant and immediately obvious in the case where the passage is a parable or a story, of healing for example. One could not stop half way through, before the story had come to an end. The passage corresponds, if not always within the precise limits at least in principle, to what is called 'pericope' in liturgy.

As for the inferior levels, if the 'segment', the 'piece' or the 'part' have identifiable limits, they do not have real autonomy; the terms that describe them say, in a rather unambiguous way, that they belong to a superior whole. If they are identifiable as distinct, they are nonetheless inseparable from the whole. Their autonomy is that of the 'citation': they can be cut, to be integrated to another discourse in which they become segment, piece or part. One does not *cite* a passage, one *recites* it.

5.1. *The Passage Composed of One Part*

Psalms 113 and 146 are formed of several parts; there is not one passage in Amos 1.3–2.16 that is formed of a single part. The third Gospel, on the other hand, counts several passages composed of a single part, and it is not necessary to reproduce them here.[52]

5.2. *The Passage Composed of Several Parts*

Psalms 113 and 146 are passages formed respectively of five and seven parts. As for the first section of Amos (1.3–2.16), it counts eight passages.

5.2.1. *Psalm 113*

This passage counts five parts. At the extremities, two parts formed of a single unimember segment (the same 'Alleluia', translated 'Praise Yah!'). The two parts 1b-4 and 5b-9b were analysed as such above.[53] The central part has only one unimember segment that distinguishes itself from the two parts that frame it: on one hand it is the only interrogative sentence of the whole passage, on the other hand it makes the link between the two sides that constitutes the answer to the central question.

52. For example, the central passage of the sequence C1 (Lk. 10.17-20: see R. Meynet, *L'Evangile selon saint Luc*, I, p. 109; II, p. 128). One can even find shorter passages, especially at the center of sequences, such as the central passage of sequence D2 (Lk. 22.71; *ibid.*, I, p. 215; II, p. 228) that is formed of one segment; this segment can nonetheless be considered to be a passage since it is part of the composition of the sequence as such, on a par with longer and more complex passages (see also the central passage of sequence D3: Lk. 23.38; *ibid.*, I, p. 221; II, p. 233).

53. See §4.2.1, and §4.3.1.

¹ **PRAISE** YAH!

+ **PRAISE,**   O servants   of   YHWH,
+ **PRAISE**   the name   of   YHWH.

----

    ² Be   the name of   YHWH **BLESSED**
      . from now and for ever,

      .³ from the rising of the sun to its setting
      PRAISED be the name of   YHWH!

+ ⁴ **EXALTED** above *all nations,*   YHWH,
+ above *the heavens* HIS GLORY.

                 | ⁵ Who (is) like   YHWH   **OUR GOD?** |

+ He rises up to sit up
+ ⁶ and he stoops to see
+ in *the heavens* and on the earth.

      – ⁷ He raises from the dust the weak,
      – from the dung **he EXALTS** the poor.

            = ⁸ to set him with princes,
            = with the princes of HIS PEOPLE.

      – ⁹ He sets the barren of home
            = mother of children happy.

PRAISE YAH!

The central segment bears indeed two names, 'YHWH' like in each of the three pieces of the preceding part and 'our God' the possessive of which heralds that it is of 'his people' (8b) in the following part. The second part therefore gives a picture of YHWH as a universal God, in time (2), and space (3), of 'all nations' (4), while the fourth one describes him as the God of a particular people ('his people'), reaching towards all the oppressed, 'the weak' and 'the poor' (7) whom he elevates as a 'prince', 'the barren' to whom he gives 'children' that is a 'home'. 'The earth' (6) and the 'home' that the Lord is taking care of to raise and exalt them is thus the land and the house of Israel. However the two imperatives at the beginning (1), as well as the word 'servants', seem indeed to designate, at this level, the members of the elected people. So the other nations are also called to praise the name of YHWH (2-4) like and with the people of Israel (1).

The list of all the words that indicate praise of the greatness of YHWH in the second part, 'praise' (1b, 1c), 'blessed' (2a), 'praised' (3b), 'exalted' (4a), finds its counterpart in the fourth part with the series of verbs, of which God is now the subject and not the object, in particular 'he exalts' (7b) which is the same one as in 4a. So the fourth part enumerates the reasons for which God should be praised: because he saves the humble ones of his people. And it is not only Israel that is called to praise him (1) but also all the nations of all times and all places (2-4). The Lord who is above 'the heavens' (the two occurrences of the word, in 4b and 6b, play the part of median terms for the second and fourth parts) is at the same time the one who, on 'earth' (6b), takes care especially of the people that he has chosen among 'all the nations' (4a), that he 'exalts' (7b) like he himself is 'exalted' (4a), which makes him a prince (8) like he himself is the king that rules above all (5b).

5.2.2. *Psalm 146*

This passage is formed, not of five parts like the preceding one, but of seven.

The first part (1) is composed of one bimember segment, the second member of which reproduces the first but in the first person singular. The last part (10c) is composed of one unimember segment that repeats the first member of the initial segment but 'economizes' the second.

¹ Praise **YAH**!   Praise, my soul, **YHWH**!

. ² I will praise   **YHWH**   IN ALL MY LIFE,
. I will sing   **my God**   IN ALL MY DURATION.

– ³ Do not trust   in *princes*
– in *a son of Adam*   in whom there is no salvation:
      = ⁴ (when) departs his breath,
      = he returns to his Adamah,

            IN THAT DAY   perish his plans.

+ ⁵ Happy who has   **the God of Jacob**   for his help
+ and his hope in   **YHWH**   **his God**:
        = ⁶ he *MAKES*   heaven and earth
        = and the sea   and all that is in them.

        HE KEEPS TRUTH   FOR EVER.

+ ⁷ He *MAKES*   right for the oppressed,
+ he gives   bread the hungry,
+   **YHWH** frees the prisoners.

            + ⁸   **YHWH** opens (the eyes) of the blind,
            +   **YHWH** holds up the bowed,
            +   **YHWH** loves the just.

+ ⁹   **YHWH** keeps the sojourners,
+ the orphan   and the widow he restores
+ but the way of   *the wicked* he twists.

. ¹⁰ **He reigns**   **YHWH**   FOR EVER
. **your God**,   O Sion,   FROM AGE TO AGE.

Praise **YAH**!

Then, there are two parts the size of a piece formed of two bimember segments (2 and 10ab) where the divine names are reproduced 'YHWH' and 'my/your God'. The last terms are opposed: 'in (all) my life' and its synonym 'in (all) my duration', despite the extension to the entire life, indicates a limited time, as opposed to 'for ever'; 'from age to age' (which would be better translated by 'from generation to generation', but it would lengthen it and change the rhythm) means the same as its parallel 'for ever', but in a different way, through the indefinite succession of lives, of limited duration, of each man mentioned in v. 2.

The name 'YHWH' reappears five times in the 7-9 part; it is a subject like in 10. In the symmetrical part (3-6) it is an object like in v. 2. But one will note that v. 5, as well, reproduces not only 'YHWH his God' (this time in a single syntagm) but also calls him 'God of Jacob', which announces the name of 'Sion' of the end preceded by 'your God' (10b).

At the center of the passage, a very brief part, since it only has a unimember segment (6c) the verb of which is distinct from those that surround it: indeed, if it is a participle (in Hebrew), like in 6 and 7-9a, this participle is the only one to have an article. This segment ends with 'for ever' like in 10a, which confers it a particular importance. If one sees that 'in that day', at the center of the third part (4c), belongs to the series of syntagms that indicate time, we can see once more that the centre and the extremities are strategic places that often answer one another. The 'in that day', which is the day of the princes' death, is therefore in opposition with all the other indications of time: everything ends on that day, even the plans for the future ('in that day perish his plans'), which is not the case of the just whose flag is passed on in the following generations.[54] At the beginning of the third part (3a), 'princes' does seem to be opposed to the last word of the fifth part, 'the wicked' (9c). Those princes in which no one can trust, in whom salvation does not reside, who are not kings chosen by God, but are mere sons 'of Adam' (3b), may they be foreign kings or bad princes of Israel. The same word 'princes' is more directly opposed to 'reigns' (10a): God alone exerts true kingship, that which consists in saving 'the justs' (8c) 'oppressed' (7a) by 'the wicked' (9c). God is not only king because he has 'made' everything (6) but also because he 'makes right for the oppressed' (7a): the two occurrences of this same verb link the two parts 3-6 and 7-9 together (they play the part of median terms); they show God as creator (6) and saviour (7).

---

54. Thus 6c finds its place and function in the psalm and does not have to be considered a burden (E. Beaucamp, *Le Psautier* [Paris: Gabalda, 1979], p. 303).

5.2.3. *Amos 1.3-5*

---

³ Thus says the LORD:

– **'For**	three	transgressions	of	***DAMASCUS***
+ and for	four,	I will not come back;		

– **because** they had threshed with (threshing) sledges of iron
– the (land of) **GILEAD**,

+ ⁴ I will send a fire		upon the house	of	***Hazael***
+ and it shall devour		the palaces	of	***Ben-Hadad***
+ ⁵	and I will break	the bar	of	***DAMASCUS***
+	and cut off	him that sits	from	***Bikeat–Aven***
+	and him that holds	the scepter	from	***Beth–Eden***
= and shall be deported		the people	of	ARAM to Kir',

says the LORD.

The formulas of introduction (3a) and conclusion (5e) of the oracle are considered as parts, despite the fact that they are the size of uni-member segments.

The oracle itself (3b-5d) constitutes the second part; its two sub-parts (3bc and 3d-5d) start with the same words (first translated by 'For' in 3b, and by the conjunction 'because' in 3d) and thus serve the part of initial terms.

The first sub-part (3bc) only counts one bimember segment.

The second sub-part (3d-5d) is formed of two pieces which reproduce and develop the precedent two members of the preceding sub-part:

1. the first piece (3de) counts only one bimember segment denouncing the crime (despite the fact that the verb is at the third person plural, the subject refers to 'Damascus');

2. it follows a long piece (4-5d) which, like 3c, heralds the punishment: this piece counts three segments,

a. one bimember concerning the fire of the royal house (4),

b. one trimember heralding the taking of the capital and the fall of the monarchy (5abc),

c. and finally one unimember predicting the deportation of the people (5d; this last segment distinguishes itself from the preceding ones because it has 'people' for subject).

'Hazael' and 'Ben-Hadad',[55] at the end of the members of the first segment (4) as well as 'him that sits' and 'him that holds the scepter' in the following trimember (5bc) also designate the king; given the parallelism of the three members 5abc, it is possible to understand 'the bar' in a metaphorical sense, since the king is, among other things, the one defending his city against the assaults of his enemy.

5.2.4. Amos 1.6-8

This passage shares the same construction as the preceding one. The members 7a and 8abc end with four of the five names (like in Zeph. 2.4) of the Philistine pentapole;[56] Gat is missing (mentioned in 6.2) perhaps because this city was destroyed (2 Kgs 12.18; 2 Chron. 26.6), or because it is included in 'the remnant of the Philistine'. The 'total deportation' of 6d and the extermination of the Philistine to their 'remnant' (8d) serve as an inclusion for the sub-part 6d-8d.

---

[6] Thus says the LORD:

– 'For	three	transgressions of	*GAZA*
+ and for	four,	I will not come back;	

- -

– **because** they	deported	*in a total deportation*	
– to deliver them		to **EDOM**,	
+ [7] I will send a fire	upon the wall	of	*GAZA*
+ and it shall devour	her palaces		
+ [8] and cut off	him that sits	from	*Ashdod*
+ and him that holds	the scepter	from	*Ashkelon*
+ and I will turn	my hand	on	*Ekron*;
= and shall perish	*the remnant*	of the	*PHILISTINES*',

says the Lord GOD.

---

55. Hazael, officer of Ben Hadad II, assassinated his master and reigned in his place in the second half of the ninth century (2 Kgs 8.15); famous for his cruelty (2 Kgs 8.12), he waged war on Israel on several occasions (2 Kgs 8.28-29; 9.14-15; 10.32-33; 13.3-7, 22-25). His son, Ben Hadad III (c. 797–773 BCE) continued to fight Israel (2 Kgs 13.3), but was beaten several times (2 Kgs 13.24-25).

56. The land of the Philistine, or Philistia, is situated at the south west of Israel. Philistia was not organized as a centralized state, but formed an ensemble of five city-states commonly knowned as 'the Philistine pentapole' (Josh. 13.3; Judg. 3.3); Gaza was its most important city.

5.2.5. *Amos 1.9-10*

⁹ Thus says the LORD:

– 'For	three	transgressions		of	***TYRE***
+ and for	four,	I will not come back;			

– **because** they delivered up	mass deported	people to	EDOM
– and did not remember	the covenant	of brothers,	
+ ¹⁰ I will send a fire	upon the wall	of	*Tyre*
+ and it shall devour	her palaces'.		

This passage is shorter than the preceding ones: it is comprised of only two parts, the formula of introduction (9a) and the words of the oracle (9b-10); the formula of conclusion of the oracle, at the end of the preceding oracles, is not reproduced here. Like in the preceding oracles, the second part has two sub-parts: the first (9bc) is identical to that of the preceding oracles, the second (9d-10b) has two pieces: the first (9de) is a bimember reporting the particular crime of Tyre; while the second one (10), is composed of a single bimember segment, heralding the fire.[57]

5.2.6. *Amos 1.11-12*

This oracle is of the same general construction as the preceding one. In the first piece of the second part, describing the crime (11d-g), the second segment marks a progression compared to the first: the anger described in 11de is said to be without end in 11fg.[58] The piece announcing the punishment (12) does not repeat the name of 'Edom' but names two of its localities, at the end of the members.

---

57. It would seem better to avoid resorting to the sub-part for this passage: the two bimember segments 9d-10 can indeed be considered as one piece (and not as a sub-part formed of two pieces each comprised of one bimember segment); 9bc would then be a piece as well. That would not change the fact that the oracle forms a part and that the ensemble 9-10 is of the size of a passage. The option retained is determined by the will to harmonize the analysis of all the oracles.

58. One is bound to ask why the last three segments (11d-12) have not been considered simply as one piece (of the a a'b type). The preferred solution (one first piece describing the crime in 11d-g and one second piece heralding the punishment) aims at a maximum coherence in the description of the whole of the oracles, as we will see below.

[11] Thus says the LORD:

– 'For	three	transgressions	of	*EDOM*
+ and for	four,	I will not come back;		

| – because | he pursued | with the sword | his brother |
| – | suffocating | | his bowels, |

| – and | he tore | perpetually | his anger |
| – | his wrath | keeping | for ever, |

| + [12] I will send | | a fire | upon | *Teman* |
| + and it shall devour | | the palaces | of | *Bozrah*'. |

5.2.7. *Amos 1.13-15*

[13] Thus says the LORD:

– 'For	three	transgressions	of	*THE AMMONITES*
+ and for	four,	I will not come back;		

| – because they have ripped up | the pregnant of | GILEAD |
| – that they might | enlarge | their border, |

| + [14] I will kindle a fire | upon the wall of | *Rabbah* |
| + and it shall devour | her palaces | |

| + with shouting | in the day | of battle |
| + with a tempest | in the day | of whirlwind |

| = [15] and shall go | their king | into deportation |
| = he   and | his princes | altogether', |

says the LORD.

This passage reproduces the complete structure of the first two oracles (against Damascus and Gaza). The piece describing the punishment (14-15b) is of the AA'B type, because the first two segments (14) enunciate what God will do to the fortresses ('I will kindle a fire' in the first person), whereas the third (15ab) predicts the ultimate consequence of the punishment ('and shall go', in the third person) against men.

5.2.8. *Amos 2.1-3*

2,[1] Thus says the LORD:

– 'For	three	transgressions of		*MOAB*
+ and for	four,	I will not come back;		

- - **because** they burned   the bones   of the king of   EDOM
- - to (make from them) lime,

+ [2] I will send	a fire	upon	*MOAB*
+ and it shall devour	the palaces	of	*Kerioth*
= and shall die	amid uproar		*MOAB*
= amid shouting	at the sound	of	the horn
+ [3] and I will cut off	the ruler	from the midst of	*him*
+ and all his princes	I will kill	with	*him*',

says the LORD.

This passage much resembles the preceding one. The last piece of the central part (2-3b) is composed of three bimembers, but instead of being of the AA'B type (like in the preceding part in 1.14-15b), it is of ABA' type: the extreme segments begin with a verb in the first person singular, while the central segment begins with a verb in the third person. The link between the crime (1de) and the punishment (2-3b) is particularly well marked here, since the fire of God answers the action of the burning of Moab. One will note that the correspondence between the crime perpetrated on 'the king' of Edom and the punishment that is inflicted upon 'the ruler' (and the 'princes') of Moab.

5.2.9. *Amos 2.4-5*

4 Thus says the LORD:

– 'For	three	transgressions	of	*JUDAH*
+ and for	four,	I will not come back;		

- - **because** the have rejected the law of the LORD
- - and his precepts they have not kept,
- - and have misled them their Lies
- - which have followed their fathers,

+ 5 I will send a fire upon *JUDAH*
+ and it shall devour the palaces of *Jerusalem'*.

This oracle is exactly of the same construction as the fourth (1.11-12); but the name of the land of 'Judah' is reproduced in 5a like in 4b, before the name of its capital 'Jerusalem' is mentioned in 5b. In the piece denouncing the crime (4d-g), the extreme members have four terms, while the others have only three terms; 'Lies' at the end of the first member of the second segment (4f) is opposed, if only by its plural, to 'Lord' at the end of the first member of the first segment (4d).

5.2.10. *Amos 2.6-16*

For Psalms 113 and 146, the analysis did not stop at their composition alone, it led to some remarks of interpretation; but the two operations were not separated. The first seven passages of Amos 1.3–2.16 (§5.2.3 to 5.2.9) have provided but a description of their composition. For the last passage of the section—which is longer and more complex—the distinction should be made between the two operations, the 'Composition' (tables and descriptive explanation) and 'Interpretation'.

5.2.10.1. *Composition*

The formulas of introduction and conclusion of oracles ('Thus says the Lord': 6a and 'Oracle of the Lord': 16c) find an echo at the heart of the passage: the last member of the central segment, 'Oracle of the Lord' (11c), reproduces the last part (16c). These are the only occurences of the word 'Lord'.[59]

5.2.10.1.1. *The Pronouns.* At the extremities, part 6b-8 and 14-16a are in the third person (plural in one, singular in the other, but the singular indicates categories composed of many individuals).

The parts that frame the center (9-10 and 13) are in the first person singular, underlined three times (9a, 10a, 13a) by the use of 'myself' ('ᾱνōκî): 'I destroyed' in 9a and c, 'I brought you up' in 10a, 'I made you walk' in 10b on one hand, and 'I will press you beneath' on the other in 13a.

In the central part (11-12), the first person singular of the first segment (11ab; like in the preceding part) is opposed to the second person plural of the last segment (12; it is the only occurence of the second person plural in this passage).

5.2.10.1.2. *Vocabulary.* Parts 6b-8 and 14-16 do not share a common lexic; however the list of the strong and the swift on the end is opposed to that of the weak at the beginning; 'nude' in 16c recalls 'garments' of 8a (those who dispossessed others will be dispossessed in turn).[60]

59. Note that the central segment of the second part (7cd) ends on the mention of the 'name' of the Lord and that the second part ends with 'their gods' (8d).

60. One could also note the double occurence of the homonymous verb, translated by 'they turn aside' and 'they go lay' in the second passage (7b and 8a), and, in the penultimate passage, the double occurence of 'will not save his life' (14c and 15c).

⁶ **THUS SAYS the** L<small>ORD</small>:

> 'For three transgressions of ISRAEL   and for four, I will not come back;
> > because they sell for silver the **innocent**
> > and the **poor** for a pair of sandals;
> ⁷ they that trample into the dust of the earth the head of the **deprived**
> and *turn aside* the way of the **destitute**;
>
> > > and a man and his father go into the maiden
> > > to profane the sanctity of my name;
>
> ⁸ because they *go to lay* upon garments they have **taken in pledge**
> beside every altar;
> > and they drink the ***WINE*** of those they have **fined**
> > in the house of their gods.

> ⁹   And **MYSELF**, I destroyed the Amorite before them
> > who like the height of the cedars their height
> > he who was strong like the oaks;
> > and I destroyed his *fruit* above and his roots BENEATH.
> ¹⁰ And **MYSELF, I brought you up** out of the land of Egypt
> > and made you walk in the desert forty years
> > to inherit the land of the Amorite.

> ¹¹ *And I raised up from amid your sons prophets*
> > *and from amid your young men nazirites.*
> I<small>S IT NOT INDEED SO</small>,   O <small>SONS OF</small> I<small>SRAEL</small>?   **ORACLE of the** L<small>ORD</small>.
> > ¹² *And you made drink the Nazirites* ***WINE***
> *and to the prophets you commanded: "You shall not prophesy'.*

> ¹³   Behold, **MYSELF will press you** BENEATH
> > like presses the *sheaves* a cart very full.

> + ¹⁴ And flight shall lack to the **swift**
> > — and the **strong** shall not retain his strength
> > — and the **mighty**   *will not save his life.*
> > . ¹⁵ And the bowman shall not stand
> > . and the foot-soldier **swift** shall not save himself
> > and the horseman *shall not save his life*
>
> + ¹⁶ and he who (is) **stout** of heart amid the **mighties**
> > nude shall fly in that day,'

ORACLE of the L<small>ORD</small>.

Parts 9-10 and 13 oppose two actions of God who 'brought up' his people from Egypt and who will 'press' him; 'beneath' is repeated in the two parts (9d and 13a).[61] The words 'fruit' (9d) and 'sheaves' (13c) both refer to the agricultural word, and more precisely to harvests. Besides, note the repetition of an element of comparison, 'like' (9b and 13b).

The 'wine' is found at the end of the second part and at the end of the central part (8c and 12a), therefore in final terms of those two parts; not only do they themselves drink a wine which does not belong to them (in the beginning), they give it to drink to the Nazirites who have vowed not to drink it (in the centre).

Also note that the only two occurrences of 'Israel' appear at the beginning (6b) and in the central segment of the central part (11c) and that the only two occurrences of 'oracle of the Lord' provide the link between this central segment and the last part of the passage (16c).

5.2.10.1.3. *The Characters*
Weak and strong. At the beginning, part 6b-8 describes the crimes of Israel against the weak of the land. By correlation, at the end, part 14-16 announces that whoever uses his strength to oppress the weak, will be weakened in turn by an enemy stronger than himself: the six occurrences of the terms designating the strong at the end (the 'swift' of 14a and 15b, 'strong' and 'mighty' of 14bc, 'stout' among 'the mighties' of 16a) seem to reflect the six terms that, at the beginning, designate the weak: 'innocent' and 'poor' in 6de, 'deprived' and 'destitute' in 7ab, people in debt ('taken in pledge' and 'fined') in 8.

God and his people. At the extremities, God is absent. At the beginning (6-8), God seems present, but in fact his name is prophaned and it is the reign of the other gods; at the end (14-16), God, his strength and his salvation, has disappeared. On the other hand, in the parts that frame the centre, God is present: in 9-10, he destroys the Amorite to give its heritage to Israel; in 13, he crushes his own people (who suffer the fate of the Amorite in turn!).

In the central part (11-12), the action of God (who manifests his presence in the engagement of the Nazirites in the war and through

---

61. Note the play on words between 'Amorite' (*'emorī*) at the beginning and at the end of the third passage (9a, 10c) and 'sheaves' (*'āmîr*) at the end of the fifth (13b).

the word of the prophets) is destroyed by the sons of Israel. Therefore this central part reproduces, around the question of 11c, the two sequences of the first half of the passage, but in reverse order: benefit + fault (11ab + 12), instead of fault + benefit (6b-8 + 9-10).

5.2.10.2. *Interpretation*
5.2.10.2.1. *Crime and Punishment.* The partition between crime and punishment that structures the oracles against the nations can also be used to understand the oracle against Israel; there is indeed in this oracle a direct relation between two types of actions, that of the accused, Israel, which are unjust and those of the judge, God, who is just. The justice of God is manifested in the fact that the punishment fits the crime.

Most of the usual interpretations of this sequence are based on this simple relationship between crime and punishment. Indeed, for reasons of literary criticism, the central verses (9 to 12) are considered editorial: there are also, according to different authors, other parts of the text that are judged inauthentic, but the majority agrees in recognizing in the central verses a vocabulary, a style, and themes which do not belong to Amos, but would be of deuteronomistic redaction. These verses being held as secondary, ergo less important, are neglected when interpreting the thought of Amos.[62]

The figure of the text, such as tradition has transmitted it, is concentric: if the couple crime–punishment occupy the extremities of the sequence (crime at the beginning in 6-8 and punishment at the end in 14-16), what is found between the two parts are the elements which do not exactly agree with the partition between crime and punishment: in vv. 9-10, God intervenes in the first person to recall a series of actions which are not punitive; in vv. 10-13, the 'you' obviously refers to those who are targeted by the 'they' of the denunciation of the crime (6-8) and by the announcement of the punishment (14-16), but it confers on these verses a very strong sense of address to the reader; finally the interrogation of v. 11 does not only concern what was said

---

62. As it has already been said concerning the series of six oracles against the nations, far from having to be considered as negative, these editorial interventions are to be held as the 'authentic' interpretation of the prophet Amos. It is perhaps necessary to go as far as to say that, without this interpretation, we are left with very little of the genuine Amos, but with another interpretation, a singularly impoverished reconstruction.

immediately beforehand—namely that God has sent prophets and Nazirites—and is not only a request of approval by God to the reader; it concerns the whole of the text and calls for the recognition of all forms of sins denounced since the beginning as well as the just and necessary character of what is to follow.

If the centre of the whole oracle is a question (11c), it also means that there is something there to understand. The effort of intelligence —of wisdom—required from the hearer, constitutes the mediation of his agreement. It is only if one 'sees' how, in a few words, God, by the intermediary of his prophet, interprets truly the whole of a history, that one can say: 'He told me all that ever I did' (Jn 4.39) and adhere and believe in his Word, that is, convert. What the reader is invited to understand is the problem of the relation between crime and punishment, because the announced punishment seems disproportionate to the denounced crime. To speak straight, it seems that the key of the interpretation of this oracle is the following: the extreme gravity of the sin of Israel is linked to the fact that its injustice is hidden; worse still, it is perverse.

5.2.10.2.2. *The Crime*. All the commentators agree in recognizing that Amos denounces acts contrary to justice, but the exact nature of these crimes is not altogether clear, and, at first sight, they do not seem to be as bad as to deserve such a severe condemnation. One should see that these acts are merely symbolic and serve to unravel the root of the behaviour of Israel and the nature of the evil to which it adheres.

Legal Acts. Several of the acts denounced seem legal, that is conform to the law, or to the interpretation of this law, in all cases to customs that are not disapproved by it. The institution of lending includes, according to the law, the sanction that allows a debtor, who is unable to repay his loan, to be sold (6c), or that which belongs to him, his garments for example, be taken in pledge (8a). Despite being ruled and limited by the law,[63] the taking in pledge is absolutely legitimate, and one might imagine that the creditor has the right to use it, as a partial and temporary compensation of the damage incurred. The

---

63. The coat taken in pledge must be given back at nightfall because the poor should be able to protect himself from the cold to sleep (Exod. 22.25-26; Deut. 24.10-13).

wine of those who were fined (8c) also refers to a penal procedure conform to the law.[64]

It is true that Amos wants to show that the law is not truly observed: the innocent is sold for a minimal debt, the garments taken in pledge, which one lies on, should be given back at nightfall, the fine should be the compensation of a loss and not an excuse for getting drunk. However, Amos does not speak about the crimes which are the most contrary to the law: neither homicide, theft, adultery, nor idolatry. But what is worse is that injustice hides under a veneer of legality.

Endorsed by the Judges. Judicial action, which should defend the weak, is unfortunately subordinated to economic interest and abuse of power. In a more or less direct manner, Amos refers to judicial decisions, publicly taken by tribunals. The sale of a man, above all, but also the sequestration of the garments and fining, were public acts which had to be accomplished with the guarantees of the law, such that on one hand the execution could be speeded up and on the other that cancelling of the charges could also be pronounced. Besides, the expression 'they turn aside the way of the destitute' (7b) should be interpreted in a legal sense, like the turning aside of the judicial proceedings instituted by the destitute. The injustice committed against the poor is economic, since from the start it is a question of 'silver'. It is the privilege of the rich, the powerful, but it has to rely on legality in order to receive social assent: it has to be approved by the official interpreters of the law, the magistrates who, in Israel, were identified with authority, namely the leaders, the ancients, the king.[65]

Sanctified by Religion. Even more decisive than the legitimization by the judicial powers, the religious element gives its assent, definitely legitimizing the actions of the Israelites. In the cult, the name of God

---

64. The root *'nš* ('to be fined') indicates a compensatory punitive measure (Prov. 17.26; 19.19; 21.11; 22.23 = 27.12) conformed to the law and regulated by the judges (Exod. 21.22; Deut. 22.19); its practice is attested even in international relations (2 Kgs 23.33 = 2 Chron. 36.3). Obviously, the legal procedure can be unjustly applied to the innocent (Prov. 17.26).

65. In the tale of the grapevine of Nabot (1 Kgs 21), the king (or the queen, to be precise) uses the 'ancients and notables' of the city to invent a trial: the judicial condemnation of Nabot allows the king to legally take possession of the so-coveted vine.

confers an appearance of sanctity, perfection, supreme justification, to those who come to the sanctuary. It is true that in the denunciation of the sins of Israel, in vv. 6-8, a long list of synonymous terms refers to the poor and needy, but the central segment (7cd) takes the attention from a purely sociological and judicial aspect to the cultural and religious sphere, when the Holy Name of God is evoked, soon to be followed by the mention of the altars of the temple (8b.d).

Because of the specificity of the vocabulary, it seems that the ensemble of denunciation of the sin is placed in the religious context of pilgrimage. The itinerary goes from the city or village, at the doors of which the commercial and judicial activities take place, where the pilgrim has procured himself the 'silver' of the tithe and the 'sandals' for the trip; it then leads the pilgrim on the 'dust' that he will 'trample' by going to the temple; when he has reached his goal, after having taken his sandals off, he will 'lay' with the 'maiden' on 'garments taken in pledge' and make merry by 'drinking the wine'.[66]

This image of the pilgrimage allows us to discern the perversity of these actions. Instead of 'going towards' God in his temple, one 'goes into' 'the maiden'. It seems that by systematically playing on words, Amos refers to sexual license that was practised during feast days in sanctuaries: what draws one to the temple, is not the desire to 'worship' God (*l^ehallel*), but the 'maiden', which consequently 'profanes' (*l^ehallel*) the sanctity of God's name.[67] Instead of 'prostrating' to adore

---

66. The link between the 'silver' of the tithes and the 'wine', in the context of a cultic feast, is explicitly indicated in Deut. 14.25-26 (also 12.17-19; 14.22-23); the law of Deuteronomy, in a way analogous to Num. 18.21-32, asks that in such circumstances one should not neglect the Levite (Deut. 14.27) who, having no property (Deut. 18.1-2), is associated with the categories structurally poor of the orphan and the widow (Deut. 14.29; 16.11, 14). To celebrate the weaning of her child, Ann, mother of Samuel, brought to Siloh 'three bullocks, and one ephah of flour, and a bottle of wine' (1 Sam. 1.24); it is thus possible to deduct from this that the celebratory aspect of the religious festival required eating (meat) and drinking (wine) in a sacred place (1 Sam. 1.14-15)—'beside every altar', would Amos say; see, in the same line, 1 Sam. 10.3 (pilgrimage to Beth-El). Amos does not speak of the religious feast as an occasion to share with the poor, but as one for celebrating the exploitation of the lower classes.

67. The conjunction *l^ema^aan*, translated by 'in order to', usually indicates the finality of an action; however, it is also used to designate consecutiveness (Joüon, 169g). One would thus have a turning around of the finality of going to the temple, culminating in the profanation of the sanctity of God's Name.

or 'inclining' themselves to humble themselves, 'they go to lay'.
Despite the fact that Amos does not use the verb 'to sleep (with)', *škb*
the sexual connotation seems clear; if the idea of sacred prostitution is
not the most probable, Amos certainly refers to what happened during
festivals, even religious ones, during which the rejoicing led to expressions of vital exuberance, to the point of licentious excess which in
such an atmosphere might seem legitimate.[68] So the altars are no
longer places of sacrifice but of pleasure, and instead of the libation
being spilled in the honor of God,[69] the wine is drunk by those who
have brought it. At last, the fact that the relationship to God is substituted with the relationship with 'the maiden' appears that much
worse when cultic prescriptions require sexual abstinence for those
who are to meet the sanctity of God.[70] This custom is not only a taboo,
it signifies that life is not something that man gives by himself, but
that it is given by God.[71] The fact that 'a man and his father' go
together towards the girl, would be an aggravating circumstance: if
this sin is understood as a case of incest, it belongs to the category of
the 'sexual' wrongs, but it mostly stresses the perversion of the relationship to the origin, the confusion of the individual that does not
recognize the difference between the one who gives life and the one
who receives it; if on the contrary one understands the word 'father'
in a larger sense of 'leader', the sin would be that those responsible
would tolerate, or would fail to forbid these practises and favour the
cultic perversion in order to preserve their own interests.

The Perversion of History. As it appears in the legislative traditions,
pilgrimage is linked to three agricultural feasts, unleavened bread,

---

68. See Prov. 7.14-18. The relationship between 'wine' and 'love', a common
theme in many literatures, is also present in the Bible: see, for example, Joel 4.3;
Prov. 31.3-4; Cant. 2.4; 5.1; 7.10; 8.2; Est. 1.10-11; Jdt. 12.12-13, 20.

69. The rituals followed in the sanctuaries in the eighth century are not known
with any accuracy; it seems however plausible that the libation of wine, a common
religious act in Antiquity and documented in biblical ceremonial (see Exod. 29.40;
Lev. 23.13; Num. 28.14; 15.5, 7, 10; Deut. 32.38; Hos. 9.4), was a common
enough practice at the time of Amos.

70. For example, Exod. 19.15; 1 Sam. 21.5. Sexual relations incur an impurity
(Lev. 15,18) which constitutes a hindrance to the exercise of the cult (Lev. 22.3).

71. It is the same, by analogy, for fasting and abstinence from wine: it funda-
mentally means that only God can give sustenance and joy.

harvests and ingatherings;[72] the first aim of the celebration of these pilgrimages is the action of grace on the occasion of harvesting. The first of these three feasts, that of the unleavened bread, is linked in the Law to the coming out of Egypt;[73] the saga of victory over the enemy is probably the backdrop of these pilgrimages. And that would explain the passage from the denunciation of sins (6-8) to the reminding of the benefits of God (9-10). The sense of this reminding is not limited to noticing the ingratitude of Israel; in reducing Exodus (the coming out of Egypt, object of the pride of Israel in 3.1 and 9.7) to the story of the destruction of the Amorite, Amos would unravel the perversion of Israel. To recall that God had radically destroyed what was strong, in favour of his people who were then weak, would be a way of denouncing the sin of Israel which had perverted the sense of its own history, since it is now the powerful who crush the weak. Moreover, they have twisted the action of God itself, insofar as the invocation of the name of God seems to give reason to the actual powers, when the name of God is called holy because it presses down the strong and brings up the weak.[74] This reminding of the total destruction of the Amorite also implies a threat: if Israel behaves like the Amorite, like the pagan nations for whom only the exercise of strength counts, then it will be crushed like they were.

However the denounced perversion by the prophet is not yet complete. Amos also mentions another action of God after the story of Exodus and the conquest, and another action of Israel which negates the action of God. When before, the actions of Israel (6-8) and those of God (9-10) seemed juxtaposed, at the heart of the sequence they are clearly correlated (11-12). God inspires Nazirites and prophets: these are two realities that perpetuate in Israel the memory of an authority, a strength, a referent irreducible to human interpretation and to individual designs. The prophet bears the word of God and interprets his will, the Nazirite testifies that there is no veritable strength and courage outside God. The perversion of the Israelites lies in corrupting the Nazirites in making them follow their own logic, in binding them to a

---

72. See Exod. 23.14-17; 34.18-23; Deut. 16.1-17; Lev. 23.4-8, 16-21, 34-36.

73. It will be much later that the two other feasts are linked to historical events of the history of Israel, the gift of the Law at Sinaï for the feast of weeks or pentecost, and the sojourn in the desert for Sukkôt, the feast of ingatherings.

74. See the Magnificat (Lk. 1.46-55); see R. Meynet, *L'Evangile selon saint Luc*, II, pp. 24-28.

known source of strength, that which procures wine; even worse, in shutting the prophets up, the authorities substitute themselves to the supreme authority of God who had ordained the prophets to speak.[75] The perversion thus reaches its climax, since no one ever speaks any more, since there is no more room for criticism and contestation.[76] This is the society that Amos addresses, a society where, from the king–priest–prophet triad, only the first two subsist: the authority of the king is no longer referred to another authority which surpasses and controls it and speechless sacrality is reduced to commerce, that of economical exchanges and consumption (6, 8), that of prostitution (7).

5.2.10.2.3. *Judgment and Salvation*

At the beginning of v. 13, the expression 'Behold, myself' introduces the announcement of the punishment.[77] It is therefore the second half of the sequence that is devoted to punishment. It is noticeably shorter than the first half. The action of God against Israel is presented as the punishment through two images.

The Cart. The image of the cart (v. 13) is ambiguous. That one sees a cart so full of sheaves that it splits the ground under its wheels, like an earthquake would, or a cart used to flail the grain, these interpretations have a pronounced eschatological tonality in common: it is the end that is announced. Besides, the image of the full cart evokes the accumulation of riches which is synonymous with death; the oppression of the poor whose head is trampled into the dust of the earth finds here its counterpart, or its punishment, by its pressure and crushing under riches. In the context of the pilgrimage at the times of harvest, this image could represent a sort of ironic turning around: the benediction of abundant harvests to sustain life turns into a cursing of death. If, as was the case in the oracle against Damascus, it is an image of flailing, it would bear a warlike connotation which would prepare the following passage.

---

75. The refusal of the prophet is the refusal of all the history of Israel as divine action; that is why it provokes the end.

76. See Amos 5.13; the same thing is expressed further down, in the shape of a narrative in 7.10-17.

77. Like in many prophetic texts; see P. Bovati, *Ristabilire la giustizia: Procedure, vocabolario, orientamenti* (AnBib, 110; Rome: Biblical Institute Press, 1986), p. 73.

The Flight. In the war[78] that God makes on his rebellious people, is revealed the powerlessness of military might (14-16):[79] strength does not save, weapons and agility are useless.[80] Only the weak seem to be able to flee, only will the one who is naked be saved, he who has relinquished all weapons and protection (16). This is in opposition no doubt to those who had seized the garments that protected the body of the poor.

Thus the sequence ends on this image of nudity, a sort of unveiling of the perverse and hidden sin of Israel. As if the intervention of God was to destroy what veils sin, namely the institutions themselves, temple and kingship, which became the fundamental threat insofar as, instead of being the instruments of justice, they are the locus of its perversion. This nudity signifies the situation of shame destined, 'in that day', to the leading class of Israel, a humiliating defeat which will reveal the injustice towards the poor and the manipulation of religion. God will reveal Himself as the just judge insofar as he will not spare his own people.

6. *The Sequence*

The sequence is the unit superior to the passage. It encompasses one or several passages.

The two psalms studied so far were one passage long. On the other hand, Amos 1.3–2.16 has three sequences.

6.1. *The Sequence Composed of Only One Passage*

As we will see in the following paragraph, both the oracle against Judah (Amos 2.4-5) and the oracle against Israel (Amos 2.6-16) have the status of sequence in the composition of the first section of the book of Amos.

---

78. War was already evoked by the destruction of the Amorite, and by the mention of the Nazirites.

79. Flight signifies defeat in battle; as such, it reveals a divine judgment (see Lev. 26.17, 36-37; Deut. 28.25). The humiliating aspect of flight (2 Sam. 19.4) is even more underlined when one has to abandon everything (Judg. 4.15, 17). In fleeing, one hopes to save ones life, but sometimes flight—as Amos says (2.14-16; 9.1-4)—is without hope (Jer. 25.35; 46.5).

80. See Isa. 30.16-17.

6.2. *The Sequence Composed of Several Passages*

The first six oracles of the book of Amos form a single sequence, organized in three sub-sequences. Each sub-sequence will first be presented, then the whole of the sequence.

6.2.1. *The Oracles against Damascus and Gaza (Amos 1.3-8)*

6.2.1.1. *Composition*

The addressees are 'Damascus' (3b) and 'Gaza' (6b): note however the mention of other localities, Ashdod, Ashkelon and Ekron in the oracle against Gaza (8), Bikeat-Aven and Beth-Eden in the oracle against Damascus (5). In relation to Israel, Damascus is the enemy of the North, whereas the Philistines are the enemy of the South.

The particular crimes (3d and 6d) are different but both end with the name of a people: but, when 'Galaad' is a victim of the crime of Damascus, 'Edom' is its beneficiary and accomplice (the victim is not named in the second oracle).

The beginning of punishments (4 and 7) are very similar, but the first targets the king of Damascus ('Hazael', 'Ben-Hadad') and his palaces, whereas the second targets the city and the palaces of Gaza; note the abbreviation by pronominalization in 7b in comparison with 4b. The rest of the punishment (5a-d and 8a-d) is also very similar (one trimember in 'I' first, followed by one unimember in 'he'); the syntagms 'I will cut off him that sits from' and 'him that holds the scepter from' are reproduced identically in 8ab as in 5bc, but not in the same position (these lexical repetitions are proper to those oracles); in the first case, the city (5a), then the king (5bc) and at last the people (5d) are concerned, whereas in the second case the list of cities, begun in 7a continues in each of the three members of the segment of 8abc, to end in a global manner in 8d with the name of the 'Philistines'. Each oracle ends with the name of the guilty tribe in question, 'Aram' in 5d and the 'Philistines' in 8d (which recalls the names of the cities at the beginning of each passage, 'Damascus' in 3b and 'Gaza' in 6b); the final segments of the oracles, 5d and 8d, despite using different words, have the same syntactical construction (apart from the expansion 'to Kir' in the first case).

'Shall be deported' in 5d and 'they deported' of 6d play the role of median terms, but, when deportation is part of punishment in the first case, it constitutes the crime in the second case (this correspondence is proper to this couple of oracles).

At last the formulas of conclusion of oracles (5e and 8e) are slightly different, the second including a final development with the adjunction *'adōnāy.*

6.2.1.2. *Interpretation*

What seems to be denunced in the aggressions of Damascus and the Philistines is that they were not only very violent but mostly systematic, if not limitless. The threshing with sledges of iron denotes the ferocity of the military operations but also the technical efficacy of a relentless exploitation. To be more explicit, the deportation operated by the Philistines is qualified as 'total': as if leaving nothing which would offer the hope of a new beginning behind.

---

[3] **Thus says the** L<small>ORD</small>:

– '*For* three transgressions of *DAMASCUS*
   + and for four, I will not come back;

– *because* they had threshed with (threshing) sledges of iron
– the (land of) GILEAD,

   + [4] I WILL SEND A FIRE UPON THE HOUSE   of   Hazael
   + WHICH SHALL DEVOUR THE PALACES   of   Ben-Hadad

   + [5]   and I will break the bar   of   *Damascus*
   +   and **cut off him that sits**   from   Bikeat–Aven
   +   and **him that holds the scepter**   from   Beth–Eden

   = *and shall be*   **deported**   *the people*   *of*   ARAM *to Kir*',
   says the L<small>ORD</small>.

---

[6] **Thus says the** L<small>ORD</small>:

– '*For* three transgressions of *GAZA*
   + and for four, I will not come back;

– *because* they   **deported** in a total deportation
– to deliver them to   EDOM,

   + [7] I WILL SEND A FIRE UPON THE WALL   of   *Gaza*
   + WHICH SHALL DEVOUR HER PALACES

   + [8]   and **cut off him that sits**   from   Ashdod
   +   and **him that holds the scepter**   from   Ashkelon
   +   and I will turn my hand   on   Ekron;

   =   *and shall perish*   *the remnant*   *of the*   *PHILISTINES*,'
   says the Lord G<small>OD</small>.

It is for this reason that Damascus and Gaza will be punished so harshly: once the capital taken and the dynasty extinguished, the people of Aram will be taken back to the place of its origins, its conquests and its empire being thus cancelled (1.5d); the punishment of the Philistines seems even more radical, since it is not said that they will be taken back to their place of origin but that they will perish without trace (1.8d). According to the *lex talionis*, the sanction is proportionate to the crime.

The stress which is put on the kings and governors (5bc + 8ab), on their palaces and fortified towns (4b + 7ab), underlines the official character of the crimes commited. Indeed the violence which is exercised is not the result of private individuals or groups, but that of the highest authorities. The crime is the more severe that it rests on the perversion of power which politically justifies the resort to force.

6.2.2. *The Oracles against Tyre and Edom (Amos 1.9-12)*

6.2.2.1. *Composition*

The essential resemblance point between the list of crimes is that 'brother' of 11d (doubled by 'all pity' of 11e) reproduces 'brother' of 9e;[81] but one should also note the almost perfect character of the crimes: the deportation to Edom is 'total' in 9d, the wrath of Edom is kept 'for ever' in 11d. The major difference lies in the fact that the crime counts only one bimember in the first case (9de), but two in the second case (11de and fg).

The announcement of the punishment (10 and 12) is very similar; 'the wall' of 10a, however, is not reproduced in 12a, whereas 10b is abbreviated by pronominalization; only 'Tyre' is named in 10, because it is a city-state, whereas for the land of Edom, it is two of its localities that are mentioned in 12.

Edom is mentioned twice: it is not only the culprit mentioned in the second passage (11b), but also the accomplice, or in any case the beneficiary, of the crime of Tyre in the first passage (9d).

---

81. 'Keeping' of 11g can be put in relation with 'remember' of 9e (in identical position, in the last member of the piece devoted to the crimes), because these two verbs are used in parallel (Ps. 103.18; 119.55) with the Law or the commandments for object: 'not to remember the covenant' would be linked to 'keeping [his wrath] for ever'.

⁹ **Thus says the LORD**:

- '*For* three transgressions   of   *TYRE*
  + and for four, I will not come back;

- *because* they delivered up mass deported people   to   EDOM
- an did not remember the covenant of   BROTHERS,

         + ¹⁰ I WILL SEND A FIRE UPON THE WALL   of   *Tyre*
         + WHICH SHALL DEVOUR HER PALACES'.

---

¹¹ **Thus says the LORD**:

- '*For* three transgressions   of   *EDOM*
  + and for four, I will not come back;

- *because* he pursued with the sword his   BROTHER
- casting of all pity,

- having torn his anger perpetually
- and his wrath keeping for ever,

         + ¹² I WILL SEND A FIRE UPON   *Teman*
         + WHICH SHALL DEVOUR THE PALACES   of   *Bozrah*'.

6.2.2.2. *Interpretation*

Again, it is the neighbours of Israel, from the north then the south, whose crimes are denounced. Their victim is not directly mentioned, but it is probably the whole of Israel who is not only their neighbour but, more to the point, their brother.

The progression is doubly underlined from one oracle to the next: on one hand, the brotherly relation is stronger between Edom and Israel, since—according to the patriarchal traditions in any case—they are brothers by blood, not only by covenant; on the other, not only is the pitiless character of its enmity totally stressed, since it is mentioned that its wrath is forever (11fg), but also death (11de) is a crime more serious and definitive than deportation (9d). The crime of Edom reaches its climax in the fact that, besides being a sinner, it is designated as the accomplice of Tyre, benefiting from the deportation that the latter is responsible for (9d).

When Tyre is accused of not having been faithful to the covenant, of not 'remembering', Edom on the other hand will be punished for not having been able to forget its 'wrath' and its 'anger', for 'keeping' it 'perpetually' and 'for ever'. The two attitudes are symmetrical and meet each other. Indeed, when the alliance between brothers is sealed to establish a close union, the deportation on the other hand separates and takes apart. The same holds for 'mercy', this sentiment which unites those who were born from the same womb; the 'pursuit with the sword' illustrates on the contrary a will for contact which does not concern life, but the seeking of death.

6.2.3. *The Oracles against Ammon and Moab (Amos 1.13–2.3)*

6.2.3.1. *Composition*
The sons of Ammon and Moab are neighbours, both of them east of the Jordan, the first in the South of Galaad, the second in the North of Edom.

The crimes (13de and 1de) are complementary: both sought the destruction of their enemies, from before their birth ('they have ripped up the pregnant women') as far the Ammonites are concerned, and beyond the death of their king ('they burned the bones of the King of Edom to lime') for the Moabites.

The announcements of the punishment (14-15b and 2-3b) have both three bimembers, although they are arranged differently; the first segments are very similar ('Rabbah' and 'Kerioth' are names of cities); 'shouting' is repeated in the second segments (14c and 2d; linked to 'tempest' in 14d and to 'uproar' in 2c), 'princes' in the second members of the last segments (15b and 3b; with 'King' in 15b and 'Ruler' in 3a); both pieces end on two synonyms, 'altogether' and 'with him' (15b and 3b). Note that the two occurrences of 'King' (15a and 2d) play the role of median terms.

The formulas of conclusion of the oracle (15c and 3c) are identical.

[13] **Thus says the LORD**:

– '*For* three transgressions		of	***THE AMMONITES***
+ and for four, I will not come back;			

– *because* they have ripped up the pregnant women		of	**GILEAD**
– that they might enlarge their border,			

+ [14] I WILL KINDLE A FIRE UPON THE WALL		of	Rabbah
+ WHICH SHALL DEVOUR HER PALACES			

+ with	**SHOUTING**	in the day of battle
+ with	**a tempest**	in the day of whirlwind

= [15] *and shall go their KING into deportation*		
= *he and his PRINCES*	***altogether***',	

says the LORD.

2.[1] **Thus says the LORD**:

– '*For* three transgressions		of	***MOAB***
+ and for four, I will not come back;			

– *because* they burned the bones of the *KING*		of	**EDOM**
– to (make from them) lime,			

+ [2] I WILL SEND A FIRE UPON Moab			
+ WHICH SHALL DEVOUR THE PALACES		of	Kerioth

= *and shall die amid*	**uproar**	*Moab*
= *amid*	**SHOUTING**	*at the sound of the horn*

+ [3] and I will cut off the *RULER* from its midst		
+ and all his *PRINCES* I will kill	***with him***',	

says the LORD.

6.2.3.2. *Interpretation*

Each of the two people has attacked its neighbour, the Ammonites their northern neighbour, the Moabites their southern neighbour. Their crime is extremely serious. Indeed not only did they kill, but they have set themselves against life, beyond its own limits: the ones went as far as to kill the beings even before their birth, the others went as far as to make the remnants of the king of Edom disappear after his death. In killing the children yet to be born with their mothers, the sons of Ammon sought to destroy future itself; in burning the bones of the king of Edom, Moab tried to end royal descent forever.

One can note a certain progression in the sanction: indeed, while the chiefs of the Ammonites are deported, those of Moab are killed, and not only their rulers but the whole people. Whatever the case may be, the acts of war are punished by acts of war and the clamour of battle answers to the silence to which the victims were reduced.

6.2.4. *The Oracles against the Nations (Amos 1.3–2.3)*

6.2.4.1. *Composition*
6.2.4.1.1. *The relationship between the first and the last sub-sequence.* The name of 'Galaad' and 'Edom' recur, in similar positions, in the denunciation of the crime, first Galaad in 1.3c and in 1.13c, and Edom in 1.6c and in 2.1c. One should note that if Galaad is always the victim, of Damascus in the first oracle, of the sons of Ammon in the fifth oracle, the role of Edom is ambivalent: it is the victim of Moab in the last oracle, but it is the accomplice and beneficiary of the crime of Gaza in the second oracle.

The 'Monarch' of 1.5b and 1.8a, coupled with 'him that holds the scepter' in 1.5c and 1.8b, herald 'their king' and 'the ruler' of 1.15a and 2.3a, coupled with 'his princes' of 1.15b and 2.3b. The words 'cut off' occur twice in the first sub-sequence (1.5b, 8a), once in the last sub-sequence (2.3a).

The couple deportation–execution is found in the same order: 'shall be deported' in 1.5d and 'shall go in deportation' in 1.15a; 'shall perish' in 1.8d and 'I will kill him' in 2.3b (preceded by 'shall die' in 2.2b); the punishment of these two couple of nations is therefore parallel, probably with a progression in the gravity of the punishment, death being more 'terminal' than deportation.

---

[3] THUS SAYS the LORD:
: 'For three transgressions of   DAMASCUS   and for four, I will not come back;
- because they had threshed with (threshing) sledges of iron   GILEAD,
    [4] I WILL SEND A FIRE UPON THE HOUSE of Hazael
    WHICH SHALL DEVOUR THE PALACES of Ben-Hadad
        +[5] and I will break the bar of Damascus
        + and **cut off**   *the monarch*   from Bikeat–Aven
        + and him that holds   *the sceptre*   from Beth-Eden
         . and the people of Aram shall be *deported* to Kir', SAYS the LORD.

⁶ THUS SAYS the LORD: --

: 'For three transgressions of   GAZA   and for four, I will not come back;

- because they ***DEPORTED MASS PEOPLE*** to ***DELIVER*** them   to   **EDOM,**

     ⁷ I WILL SEND A FIRE UPON THE WALL of Gaza

     WHICH SHALL DEVOUR HER PALACES

         + ⁸ and I will **cut off**   *the monarch*   from Ashdod

         + and him that holds   *the sceptre*   from Ashkelon

         + and I will turn my hand on Ekron

                 . and shall *perish* the remnant of the Philistines',   SAYS the Lord

                                                                     GOD.

---

⁹ THUS SAYS the LORD:

: 'For three transgressions of   TYRE   and for four, I will not come back;

- because they   *DELIVERED*   *MASS PEOPLE*   to   **EDOM**

- and did not remember the covenant of   BROTHERS,

     ¹⁰ I WILL SEND A FIRE UPON THE WALL of Tyre

     WHICH SHALL DEVOUR HER PALACES'.

¹¹ THUS SAYS the LORD: --

: 'For three transgressions of   EDOM and for four, I will not come back;

- because he pursued with the sword his   BROTHER

- suffocating   HIS BOWELS

     because his anger tore perpetually   and his wrath kept for ever,

     ¹² I WILL SEND A FIRE UPON Teman

     WHICH SHALL DEVOUR THE PALACES of Bozrah'.

---

¹³ THUS SAYS the LORD:

: 'For three transgressions of the   AMMONITES and for four, I will not come

                                       back;

- because they have ripped up   the PREGNANT WOMEN   of   **GILEAD**

- that they might enlarge their border,

     ¹⁴ I will kindle A FIRE UPON THE WALL of Rabbah

     WHICH SHALL DEVOUR HER PALACES

         .. with shouting in the day of battle   with a tempest in the day of whirlwind

         = ¹⁵ and shall go   ***their king***   in *deportation*

         = he and   ***his princes*** altogether',   SAYS the LORD.

2.¹ THUS SAYS the LORD: --

: 'For three transgressions of   MOAB   and for four, I will not come back;

– because they burned to (make of them) lime the bones of the king of   **EDOM**

     ² I WILL SEND A FIRE UPON Moab

     WHICH SHALL DEVOUR THE PALACES of Kerioth

         .. and Moab shall die amid uproar   amid shouting at the sound of the horn

         = ³ and I will **cut off**   ***the ruler***   from its midst

         = and all   ***his princes***   I will *kill* with him', SAYS the LORD.

6.2.4.1.2. The relationship between the central sub-sequence and the other two sub-sequences. The two oracles of the central sub-sequence are distinct from the other four: on one hand, the gravity of the crimes is explicit (treason and revenge), on the other, the chastisement is notably briefer; finally the formula of conclusion of the oracle is missing.

Like in the other two other sub-sequences, the couple deportation–death is found, but no longer in the punishment but in the crimes: the fault of Tyre is to have 'deported' (9c), that of Edom is to have 'pursued *with the sword* his brother' (11c). The position of Edom is nevertheless abnormal, not in the second passage of the sub-sequence, but in the first.

The second and third oracles are linked together by the repetition of 'mass people' (lit. 'in a total deportation') and of 'to deliver' in 6c and 9c, in the position of median terms of the first two sub-sequences. The link between the fourth and fifth oracles is less obvious; however, 'bowels' (literally 'womb' in the plural) in 11d seems to herald the 'pregnant women' in 13d, that is in the position of median terms of the last two sub-sequences. In both cases, one will have noticed that those median terms are found in a similar position, at the beginning of the denunciation of the crimes: 6d, 9d, 11e, 13d.

6.2.4.2. Interpretation
6.2.4.2.1. The Nations as seen by Israel. The first way of interpreting the text is to identify with the historical audience at the time of Amos: it is indeed to the people of Israel that the oracles of the prophet refer to (1.1). One can imagine they assembled at Bethel during a festival celebration (2.8).

Geographical proximity. The text is marked with continual geographical references concerning the territories and the cities, the position of which are significant in relation to Israel. The six incriminated nations are all found at the borders of Israel.

It might appear that the first four countries surround Israel like cardinal points:[82] Damascus in the north (-east) inland, Gaza in the south (-west) next to the Mediterranean; Tyre in the north (-west) on the mediterranean, and Edom in the south (-east) inland. It would therefore be a crossed system, according to the following figure:

---

82. Like in Zeph. 2.4-15: Philistines in the west, Moab and Ammon in the east, Ethiopia in the south and Assur in the north.

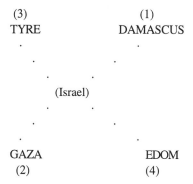

On the other hand, this representation could well be nothing more than a projection of our own geographical categories and that the only relevant point of the construction is the north–south opposition;[83] more so that this opposition is also found in the following couple, the sons of Ammon–Moab.[84] This recurrence would aim to indicate the totality: from the north to the south the same crime is perpetrated and, consequently, the same sanction should be applied.[85]

Proximity by relation. The people mentioned do not only have a relationship of spacial proximity with Israel; they are also part of its history and the traditions interpreting it. The repetition of the word 'brothers' (1.9, 11), at the centre of the sequence, invites one to consider the relationship of kinship, affinity, and alliance that Israel nurtures with its neighbours.

The oracles coming in pairs, it is necessary to look for the characteristics of each couple of nations. Aram and the Philistines, at the beginning of the sequence, are strangers, traditional enemies of Israel.[86] The last two people are cousins of Israel: Lot, the father of Moab and Ammon, son of Haran, the brother of Abraham, was therefore the nephew of Abraham. Tyre and Edom, at the centre, are also much

83. But Isaiah, in Judas, places 'the Syrians before, and the Philistines behind' (9,11).

84. The order of the two people in the oracles against the nations is Moab–Ammon in Jer. 48–49; Zeph. 2.8-9, but Ammon–Moab in Ezek. 25.

85. North and south indicate the totality in Amos 9.7 (Philistines–Aram); 6.2 (Kalné, Hamat–Gat); 6.14 (Lebô–Hamat–Araba).

86. They will therefore be represented together in Isa. 9.11 (and also Ezek. 16.57).

closer to him: the first is in brotherly alliance with Israel (see 1 Kgs 5.26 and 9.13); Edom (that is Esau) is even closer to Israel (that is Jacob), since they are brothers by blood, being both sons of Isaac.

From this point of view, the sequence is of concentric construction, since the central sub-sequence is the culminating point of the progression. As in all centres of concentrism, it is not only its climax but also its key: the presence of the brothers at the centre does not only indicate ultimate treason for Tyre and Edom, but it also reveals that all peoples are brothers and that violence is fratricide.

Israel the victim? From hearing this first proclamation by Amos, the Israelites can do nothing but rejoice: in punishing the nations that are their adversary, the irrevocable verdict of God (1.3, 6, 9, etc.) vindicates the victim, that is Israel. This aspect is worth considering, in a precise way, in the text.

Galaad is named twice, in symmetrical position, as a victim of Damascus its northern neighbour in the first oracle (3c), and as a victim of the Bene-Ammon its southern neighbours in the fifth oracle (13c). Situated on the other side of the Jordan, the territory of the Galaad is a part of Israel, the most exposed and the most difficult to defend from the attacks of other people.

The victim of Edom is not named, but it is clearly designated as its brother (11c): it is probably Israel.

The victims of Gaza and Tyre are not formally identified. As far as the Philistines are concerned, the complementary parallelism which links the oracle that concerns them with the one that is addressed to Damascus can easily lead the readers of Amos into believing that they are the victims of both nations. It is not excluded that, in the same movement, the Israelites saw themselves as the victim of Tyre.[87]

So, until the penultimate oracle, the recipient could think that the victim was Israel all along. But the last oracle lifts the veil of ambiguity, since the victim of Moab is not Israel but Edom (1c).[88] The choice of Edom as the final victim could not be better. Indeed, Edom had already been named three times before the last oracle: according to the fourth oracle, it is not only guilty of a crime but of the worst crime, since it sought to kill its own brother, and what is more, its

87. See Joel 3.6.
88. That is perhaps why Moab the eldest is not named before Ammon, its younger brother, as it should, but after.

twin. And to add even more to its guilt, it is named in the second and third oracle as the accomplice and beneficiary of the crime of Gaza and Tyre. But it is nonetheless the last victim!

The clever surprise thus created is full of teachings. Israel might be tempted, like any other nation, to see itself as the only victim of all the other nations. The prophet, very subtly, dissipates this illusion of ethnocentrism. If the worst enemy of Israel, its brother-in-arms, which has been involved in the crimes of many others, is also a victim, then Israel is no longer the only victim of the exactions committed by the nations. It would be too simple! It means that the victim could be anyone, any nation when it is considered by its neighbour, no longer as a brother, but as an object of coveting and exploitation. The fact that each victim is in all cases the neighbour, on the other side of a frontier which divides but also unites, marks the respect that should be given to limits. When the frontier no longer signifies the identity of the other as well as one's own, when it ceases to be the membrane which enables exchanges, it can but be transgressed by the stronger. In destroying his brother or selling him as a slave, the aggressor does not only negate the other as a brother, but he renounces his own quality of brother, he destroys himself. War between nations does not make victors or vanquished, it only makes victims.

6.2.4.2.2. The nations as seen by the prophet Amos.[89] In comparison with the other collections of oracles against the nations (see Isa. 13–23; Jer. 46–51; Ezek. 25–32; etc.), the text of Amos distinguishes itself by its brevity and mostly by the accentuated schematism with which the crime and punishment are portrayed.

The same crime. One can assert with confidence that, for Amos, the international domain is marked with an impressive uniformity: all the nations commit the same type of crimes (always called *peša'*) and all do so repeatedly ('for three transgressions... and for four'). Each nation as a proper name, possess its own territories and cities; but their behaviour is substantially the same: each of them makes *war* on its neighbour.[90]

---

89. This concerns the ultimate redactor of the book of Amos, not the historical figure to which the prophecy was attributed. In general, secondary literature negates the authenticity of the first two chapters, for reasons of literary form or historical inconsistencies. There is, however, no lack of authors to support their authenticity.

90. The word 'war' is not mentionned by Amos in the denunciation of the

War obeys a double motivation. The first is economic in nature: one attacks one's neighbour to pillage him. This is especially true of the first three oracles:[91] Damascus holds Galaad as a field to be ploughed (1.3), Gaza and Tyre are specialized in the trade of slaves (1.6, 9).[92]

The second motivation of war is political: indeed, what is targeted in a military expedition is not only plunder, but also the affirmation of the domination of someone else's territory ('that they might enlarge their border' in 1.13). In the text of Amos, this aspect is particularly highlighted in the last three oracles, against Edom, Ammon and Moab. The intention of Tyre towards its brother is to kill him (1.11), as the Ammonites have done with the pregnant women of Galaad (1.13) and the Moabites with the dynasty of the kings of Edom (2.1). This specificity of the violence, towards the suppression of the other, is not there in the first three oracles; it is nonetheless necessary to illustrate the unlimited will to hold power which regulates the international relations.

In the central sub-sequence (1.9-12), the crime common to all the nations is interpreted for its judicial value, or better still according to the law which regulates, or should regulate, international relations. The concept of 'brotherhood' (1.9, 11) and that of 'covenant' (1.9), which is correlated to the first, provokes the opposite of war; the 'law' of the covenant asks that the relations between nations should be inspired by mutual aid (and not by injustice, such as it is denounced in the deportations: 1.9); and that, in case of tension and controversy, wrath should be quelled in order to leave room for understanding and reconciliation (the opposite of homicidal fury: 1.11).

In conclusion, all steal, all kill, and break their words given to uphold the covenant.

---

crimes, but only in the announcement of the punishment (1.14); however, it is obvious that the acts to which the prophet refers to, are military campaigns. The history of a nation is often told as a succession of wars, of conquests and defeats, as an illustration of the saying *homo homini lupus*.

91. This does not mean, strictly speaking, that economically-driven wars are necessarily the privilege of Damas, Gaza and Tyre. According to the laws of textual composition (and therefore of 'economy'), what is said of Damascus and Gaza is also valid for Ammon and Moab, which constitute the corresponding sub-sequence (the similarities between the punishment of the two extreme sub-sequences confirm this hypothesis). Similarly, the crime of Tyre brings some light to that of Edom (these passages are linked by their identical structure).

92. Deportation has a clear economic connotation since the slaves are specifically 'delivered' to Edom.

The same punishment. In order to put an end to a repeated and universal crime, God intervenes in an irrevocable verdict ('I will not come back')[93] which falls equally on all. The universality of judgment is manifested not only in the fact that all the nations are hit (from the north to the south), but also by the fact that everything, within the nation itself, suffers the punishment: the list of cities and the couple 'monarch'–'people' (1.5, 8), in the first sub-sequence, are in this sense particularly relevant to illustrate that no 'remnant' (1.8) can escape the divine judgment.

As befits the just judgment of God, punishment fits the crime according to the *lex talionis*. The punishment is realized through war (see 1.14), in which the culprits suffer an irrevocable and definitive defeat without reprieve. This is expressed explicitly in the sentence, repeated in each oracle: 'I will send a fire upon. . . ' (1.4, 7, 10, etc.); it is indeed the burning of cities, generally capitals, which marks the end of all military resistance.[94] The military aspect is specified in the fact that the fire hits the walls (1.7, 10, 14)[95] and the palaces (1.4, 7, 10, 12, 14; 2.2), that is, fortified buildings which no doubt served a defensive purpose in cities; the breaking of the bar (1.5), the metaphor of the 'whirlwind' (1.14 in parallel with the word 'battle') and the sound of the horn (2.2) belong to the semantic field of war. It is the same for the deportation of population (1.5, 15)[96] and the putting to death of the sovereigns or the ruling classes (1.5, 8; 2.3),[97] which were dispositions that victors took to prevent further hostilities.

The economic aspect of war, the pursuit of financial gain through war (already mentioned above) is here punished with the destruction by fire of 'palaces' and 'houses' (1.4, 7. etc.); for Amos, the 'palace' is

93. One can probably see an opposition between the multiple crimes commited by the nations (three/four) and the 'one' word of divine punishment (word which, because it is not cancelled by another, is the more irrevocable). To be more precise, the divine word without reprieve ends a series of crimes which has gone too far.

94. Think of the fall of Jerusalem which saw the burning of the temple and palaces, associated with the destruction of the walls (2 Kgs 25.9-10).

95. One can note that the 'walls' are mentioned only once in each of the three sub-sequences.

96. Deportation, as punishment, is explicitly mentioned in the first of the two oracles of the extreme sub-sequences.

97. The execution of sovereigns is explicitly mentioned in 2.3, in conclusion of the sequence; in this verse, the verb 'kill' is used in parallel with 'cut off' (also found in 1.5, 8, in identical position) to which we attribute the same signification.

no doubt a symbol of wealth (see 3.9, 10, 11; 6.8).

The political aspect of war, its hegemonic goal is immediately sanctioned by the sentence of the Lord; the text insists much on this point, especially in the extreme sub-sequences, where the judgment or punishment is more developed. 'The monarch' is punished, that is 'him that holds the sceptre' (1.5, 8), the 'king' (1.15), the 'ruler' (2.3) as well as the 'princes' (1.15; 2.3): their will to have power and domination over other territories, which expresses itself through war on other nations, is annihilated forever.

In killing and exiling cruelly,[98] whoever went to war has transgressed the law of the nations, betrayed treaties, renounced the relationship of brotherhood which should rule the relations between nations (1.9, 11). By his ruling, God establishes justice, imposes law and order on the earth. He judges the judges of the earth.[99]

All three sequences of Amos belong to the same literary genre, that of the prophetic oracle. Of course, one will distinguish in the last oracle (against Israel) elements which are distinct from one another in their content: the reminding of the blessings of 2.9-10b is not on the same level as the announcement of the punishment in 2.13. But these elements are but the components of the same literary genre, the oracle of misfortune.

98. In each of the oracles of the extreme sub-sequences, the punishment ends with deportation (1.5d and 1.15a), and death (1.8d and 1.2b, 3b). In the first sub-sequence, the deportation is the punishment for dealing death (1.3c) and conversely death is the punishment for deportation (1.6c); this switching of crime and punishment is not the same in the last sub-sequence since, if the deportation of 1.15 punishes the death given in 1.13c, death in 2.2b-3b does not punish deportation (2.1c). In the central sub-sequence, the same switching between deportation and death is also found, but only in the denunciation of the crime (1.9c and 1.11cd), since punishment is reduced to fire. Deportation and death are therefore as much crimes as they are punishments. Which might mean that God uses the crimes of some to punish the others. But it mostly means that all the nations are involved indiscriminately in violence and sin, and on the other hand that it is God who rules history by dealing with them each according to their own works.

99. The formula used by Amos—particularly the use of the preposition *'al* ('for' / 'because'), the word *peša* ('crime')—interprets history as the execution of a divine ruling without remit. This ruling is justly addressed to the authorities who should have kept the law; the 'monarch', in 1.5, 8, is the one who is also a judge; the 'ruler', in 2.3—at the end of the sequence—is precisely the judge (*šōpēṭ*).

Sometimes the passages of a sequence belong to different genres and the difference in genres can be relevant in the construction of the sequence. The sequence B4 of the Gospel of Luke (5.17–6.11), for example, has three passages distributed concentrically:

A healing-controversy	5.17-29
B CONTROVERSY	5.30-35
PARABLE	5.36-39
B' CONTROVERSY	6.1-5
A' healing-controversy	6.6-11

The sequence C7 (Lk. 18.31–19.45) has seven passages organized concentrically as well:[100]

A PROPHECY	18.31-34
B story	18.35-43
C story	19.1-10
PARABLE	19.11-28
B' story	19.29-36
C' story	19.37-40
A' PROPHECY	19.41-45.

7. *The Section*

In turn the sequences are organized in sections (and sub-sections), in the same way that passages are grouped in sequences (and sub-sequences). The three sequences of Amos analysed above form a single section (Amos 1.3–2.16).

7.1. *Composition*

The first two chapters form a section of concentric composition: to the oracles against the six nations of the first sequence corresponds the great oracle against Israel which forms the last sequence. At the center, the oracle against Judah serves as a link between the other two sequences:

Oracles against six nations	Oracle against Judah	Oracle against Israël

---

100. For more detail, see R. Meynet, *L'Evangile selon saint Luc*, or for this last example, *idem*, *Initiation*, pp. 85-131.

7.1.1. *The Links between the Three Sequences*

All these oracles start exactly the same way: 'Thus says the Lord: For three transgressions of X and for four, I will not come back'. Each oracle then develops the two elements of this introductory formula: the denunciation of injustice and announcement of a sanction. These similarities are obviously aimed at establishing a relationship between all the nations. The offences are indeed different, but are all called 'crimes'. The sanctions are not exactly the same for all, but are all equally chastised by war.

7.1.2. *The Links between the Sequences at the Extremes*

The resemblance is stronger between the oracles against the six nations that surround Israel; these form a block which has its own consistency and needs therefore to be distinguished from the rest of the section. The first sequence should nonetheless be considered in relation with the other great block which mirrors it at the end of the section, the oracle against Israel. The title of the Book (1.1-2) clearly announces that the words of Amos are addressed to Israel; the first section does not only aim at organizing a confrontation between each of the eight nations concerned, but between the ensemble of foreign nations on one hand and Israel on the other. The function of this relationship is precisely to say something specific about Israel and to further emphasize its sin.

The two extreme sequences are noticeably longer than the central passage.

The two extreme sequences start with the same formula as each of the six oracles of the first sequence. This initial formula therefore puts Israel on the same footing as the six nations of the first sequence.

7.1.2.1. *The Similarities between the Nations and Israel.* One can note the points of similarity between the crime of Israel and those which are imputed to the nations ('For three transgressions [. . .] and for four'); it should be the same for the sanction which is common to all ('I will not come back').

Resemblance in the crime. Whether it is Israel or the foreign nations, it is always violence that is exerted against men, victims of injustice. But, when the violent action is perpetrated against one's neighbours in the case of the nations,[101] for Israel the crime is committed within the

101. These strangers are neighbours, more or less related or linked by relation-

boundaries of the country, against the members of the same people, by a group against another group of the same fellow citizens.[102] The economic interest which motivates the nations to occupy the territory of others, to deport and to 'deliver' human beings, leads some in Israel to 'sell' the innocent poor, to despoil him and to take away his wine. The reader will not indeed recognize in these crimes the manifest cruelty of massacres following military expeditions, but the prophet sees in it a cruelty more perverse still, since the lack of mercy against the poor is camouflaged by the judicial apparatus and by religious celebrations.

The conflictual relationship between Israel and another people (Egypt first, but mostly the Amorite) is represented in the last sequence as the founding event of Israel (2.9-10). However, what we have here is not a justification of violence: in the liberation from the land of Egypt and in the destruction of the Amorites, it is not the triumph of the strong over the weak which is revealed; it is, on the contrary, the prodigy—accomplished by God—of the victory of those unarmed over 'whose height was like the height of cedars, and who was as strong as oaks'. Such was the 'judgment' of God in the past; and so will also be divine punishment against any form of violence in the future.

In the first sequence, Israel is also represented, in its relations with other nations, as a victim of the violence of its neighbours, as the 'weak' oppressed by a 'more powerful' nation.[103] But, in the light of its past history (the victory over the Amorites), and in that of its current history (the oppression of the poor), all the first sequence takes on a new signification: God intervened in order to punish, via criminal nations, the crime of Israel. This—as Amos will explicitly say in 4.10—should have encouraged Israel to convert; but having failed to achieve its ends, the irrevocable verdict of the Lord will hit Israel as harshly as it did the surrounding nations.

ships of alliance; but they are always defined by a proper name which signifies their difference in relation to one another.

102. One can deduce from the text that the oppressors belong to the upper class, administrators of the justice and laden with the burden of the political life of the nation; it is nonetheless interesting to note that, from a strictly literary point of view, those responsible for the injustice are not qualified precisely: which is a way of signifying that Israel is a victim of itself.

103. Indeed, Galaad is mentioned twice (1.3, 13), but Israel is probably also the victim in the other oracles, in the exception however of the last.

Resemblance in the punishment. In the last sequence, Amos does not repeat the formula of condemnation by fire that is rife in the first (1.4, 7, 10, 12, 14; 2.2). If—as already said—fire represents total war culminating in defeat without remit, since no walls, palaces, or bolts on doors resists fire, it follows that the same punishment is predicted for Israel (2.14-16): it will be war, and no defence or weapons will prevent the defeat of Israel and his shamefull flight. The end is for all, for Israel as well as for the nations.[104]

7.1.2.2. *The Specificity of Israel*

Specificity in the crime. In the long description of the crime of Israel, some exegetes have seen the three, four—or even seven—violations which had not been dealt with in the denunciation of the crimes of the nations. In fact, it is not so much a list of acts different from one another, but the description of the one crime of injustice hidden under the mask of judicial procedure and ritual celebration (2.6-8). Such is the characteristic of the conduct of Israel, which renders its crime the more subtle, and intolerable—so much more serious that the people of God, in its crime, contradicts the meaning of its own origins (2.9-10). On the other hand, not only Israel refuses to convert, but it also obliges the Nazirites and the prophets to change their lifestyle (2.11-12). The gift of God which gives to Israel its own face is thus submitted to a logic of continued and repeated injustice.

---

104. The concept of the end is expressed by the verb *'bd* ('to fail', 'perish') which also signifies 'to die' (Deut. 7.20; 2 Sam. 1.27; Isa. 41.11; etc.); this verb appears in the first sequence to express the disappearance of 'the remnant of the Philistines' (at the end of the first sub-sequence: 1.8); and again, in the third sequence, to indicate that flight will be denied Israel (2.14). From the point of view of the rhetorical construction, the first sub-sequence of the first sequence (1.3-8) has a special relationship with the last two parts of the third sequence (2.13-16). Besides the repetition of the verb *'bd*, an agricultural metaphor is repeated: 'threshed with sledges of iron' (1.3) corresponds the chariot full of threshes—or, according to another interpretation, the sledges that crush the threshes—(2.13). The mention of iron (1.3) is almost certainly an allusion to the military equipment described in 2.15; it is a sign of strength which is mentioned repeatedly in 2.14-15. Should we be exhaustive, one could also note the relationship of paronomasia between the first nation named *'arām* (1.5d) and the last, *'emōrî* (2.9a and 10c), as well as the similarities between the syntagms, 'Beth-Eden' ('House of Pleasure') at the beginning of the first passage (1.5c) and 'House of their God' at the beginning of the last (2.8d).

Specificity of the punishment. It would be strange—and unjust—if God treated more favourably a nation which not only proved as sinful as the others, but whose responsibility is even greater than theirs. The recipient of the words of Amos, who had listened with pleasure to the oracles of the first sequence, has to listen in shame to his own accusation. To the question: 'Is it not indeed so, O people of Israel?' (2.11), he is obliged to answer in the positive.

The punishment will substantially be identical, but, if Israel confesses its sin, the punishment that it will suffer will have a different signification. In the shame of the flight (2.16), a form of salvation will appear.

7.1.3. *The Function of the Oracle against Judah*[105]

The oracle against Judah provides the link between the other two sequences. Other than the similarity of form which makes it similar to the oracles of the first sequence and the specific link of kindred which links it with Israel, one should note the relationship that this short central passage has with the centres of the sequences that surround it.

Its form is close to that of the two central oracles of the first sequence, since these three oracles end with the segments which announce the punishment by 'fire' (2.5 as 1.10 and 12); the verb 'keep' is repeated in 1.11g and in 2.4e.

The oracle against Judah does not have the same form as the centre of the last sequence (2.11-12); however, one should note the relationship between 'the Law of the Lord' (4d), rejected by Judah, and the 'prophets' (11a, 12b) sent by the same Lord, also rejected by Israel.

The three centres, those of the first and the third sequence as well as the center of the whole section (the oracle against Judah) correspond to one another. They place in a series:

—on one hand 'brother' (1.9, 11), 'fathers' (2.4) and 'sons' (2.11),
—on the other the 'covenant' (1.9), 'the law' (2.4) and 'the prophets' (2.11-12).

7.2. *Biblical Context*

The book of Amos provides the first example of a collection of *oracles against the nations*; this ensemble is sufficiently wide and organized to have inspired the writing of similar collections in the other prophetic

105. See above, §5.2.9.

books. However, Amos is the only one to present the oracles against the nations at the beginning of his book; Isaiah, Ezekiel and Zephaniah place them in a more or less central position (Isa. 13–23; Ezek. 25–32; Zeph. 2.4-15), whereas Jeremiah[106] and Joel situate them at the end of their book (Jer. 46–51; Joel 3.1-14).

The particularity of these collections, namely the fact that these prophecies of condemnation are addressed to nations other than Israel, often leads interpreters to consider them as separate chapters, without any precise relations with the rest of the book which is aimed at the principal recipient of the prophetic word, the people of the Lord.[107] It is anyway accepted that the oracle against an enemy nation prepares the announcement of salvation for Israel,[108] the same way that the words of solace to Israel prepare the punishment of its enemies.[109] Such a correlation is indeed found in Amos 9.11-12; but, as far as chs. 1–2 are concerned, the perspective is totally reversed: the punishment of the nations does not prepare the salvation of Israel, it is on the contrary a premonitory sign of its own chastisement.[110]

Only Amos 1–2 follows a rigorous literary scheme, common to all the nations.[111] Also it is only in Amos that the fault ascribed to the

106. It is a question of the disposition of the Massoretic Text; it is well known that the Greek text of LXX placed the series of oracles against the nations after ch. 25, that is at the centre of the book, thus conforming to the order of the other two great prophets, Isaiah and Ezekiel.

107. The little attention which is given to the relationship between the oracles against the nations and the other literary ensembles of the different books is due, or at least encouraged by, the considerations of literary critics: exegetes generally think, not only that there have been various additions and manipulations in the course of time, but that the very idea of the collection is the fruit of a posterior redaction, and is therefore without any value for someone who deals with the 'authentic' text.

108. See for example Isa. 14.1-2; Jer. 46.27-28; 50.4-7, 16-20, 33-34; 51.34-36; Ezek. 28.24-26.

109. See Isa. 40.15-26; 43.14; 45.14-17; 47.1-15; Jer. 30.8, 16; Ezek. 36.2-7; etc.

110. This is also the point of view of Zephaniah who has the oracles against the nations (2.4-15) followed by a prophecy of condemnation held against Jerusalem. Jeremiah also announces a condemnation for all, but in the reverse order: Jerusalem first, then all the nations (Jer. 25.8-13, 18-26) will drink from the cup of the wrath of God.

111. The structure of the oracle against the nations remains substantially the same; however, in the course of time it is modified, through displacement, substitution, elimination of the elements.

nations exclusively concerns violence in the context of international relations. And last, it is only in Amos that the relationship between Israel and the nations, clearly regulated by the rhetorical structure of the text, is placed as the spearhead of the interpretation.

7.3. *Interpretation*

7.3.1. *The Sin of all the Nations: The Ultimate Sin*

All the nations with–out exception are guilty. All are accused not only of having committed multiple crimes, but also and mostly of having committed the ultimate sin. Gaza (1.6) and Tyre (1.9) are both accused of having 'carried into exile entire communities': their crime is therefore not limited to a few razzias, but targets entire populations. When the Ammonites are accused of having 'ripped open pregnant women in Gilead' (1.13), it is not so much the cruelty of this crime which is blamed but the will to carry to its ultimate conclusion the destruction of an entire population: in killing at once the women and the children they carry, it is the future of an entire nation that is radically suppressed. By another sort of merism which unites the Moabites with their brothers the Ammonites, the same will of total annihilation pushes Moab to eradicate the very bones of the king of Edom (2.1): indeed, they are not content with his death, but their dark design leads them to trespass the threshold of life, in order to radically eradicate even the mere possibility of a future for the people of Edom. This will of accomplishing the crime to its bitter end is also represented at the centre of the first sequence: it is indeed underlined that the wrath and relentlessness of Edom are without end and last forever (1.11).

As far as Israel is concerned, the same idea of completion of sin is strongly marked, although in a different way. Israel is also guilty of a perfect crime, as a matter of speech, which starts from the city and ends in the temple, implying the different levels of social life, political, judicial, and cultic (2.6-8).

It is the same for Judah (2.4), insofar as its disobedience of the Lord's Law is not temporary but has lasted since the beginning: the sons carry on the behaviour of their fathers.

7.3.2. *The Sin of the Nations: 'Forgetting the Covenant*

The different crimes of the nations surrounding Israel and Judah are all in the context of warfare. In the international field, each nation is defined by the fact that it occupies a specific territory, that it possesses cultural particularities, that it is regulated by specific laws, and that it enjoys sovereignty. It is precisely that which, in the fist six oracles, is presented as transgressed: each nation is accused of having committed a crime against another nation, of having undermined the identity of the other. International relations are regulated through alliance treaties, or founded on ancestral customs. The fundamental law of those relations is that each nation should be respected within its own frontiers. The frontier plays the part of a legal boundary which defines a nation in relation to another: it is within the frontiers of a nation that a population lives, different from the neighbouring people, with its own economic, administrative and political autonomy. The transgression of frontiers undermines the life of individuals and nations, not only their physical life but also their political existence.

The crime of the nations can be seen in two ways. The first level of interpretation is that of violence: aggression, the use of force, iron and the sword, are the sign of the will to unjustly dominate another and exterminate him.

The second level of interpretation is that of disloyalty in relation to an agreement. The very word of covenant is explicitly used at the centre of the sequence (1.9) and, in the oracles against Tyre and Edom, the mention of the betrayal of the covenant is indicated by the use of the word 'brother' (1.9, 11). The concept of brotherhood is in strict relation with alliance treaties, which bind two individuals or nations situated at the same level. It is not only violence, the mere oppression of a neighbour, it is the confidence on which a treaty is built that is thus betrayed. Indeed, there are ethnic relationships of varying degrees between certain nations, but it is not so much the relationship which is built on blood links that is in question here. The prophet is more bent on showing that each nation has betrayed its own word, in failing to recognize the other as an equal and in exerting an arbitrary violence against him, this being clearly expressed in the formula: 'they have forgotten the covenant'. The treaties do not last; what is maintained on the other hand is 'wrath'.

7.3.3. *The Sin of Israel: 'You Commanded the Prophets, saying, You Shall not Prophesy!'*

In Israel as in the nations, injustice is manifested on two levels. The first is that of domination of the strong over the weak: the victims are poor or innocents who cannot defend themselves. The centre of the oracle against Israel, however, expresses what truly constitutes its sin: the root of all their faults is infidelity to the word and the fact that they refused to listen to the prophets. These refer to a superior authority, that of God, who requires obedience to his word. The crime of the Israelites resides in their seeking to give themselves another law, and to impose their own will on the prophets.

At the heart of the sequence against the six foreign nations, the word 'brother' appears twice (1.9, 11); at the heart of the sequence against Israel, the word 'son' repeated with the synonym 'young ones', is then reproduced in the central question: 'Is it not indeed so, O sons of Israel?' (2.11). 'I raised up some of your sons to be prophets': this sentence can be referred to Deut. 18.18 where God promises to raise among the sons of Israel a prophet like Moses. So, if the relationship between the nations are to be regulated through faithfulness to a mutually-given word between brothers, in Israel the relations between father and son are subject to a superior word, which comes out of the mouth of God. The Law, which is transmitted from father to son, is what enables the son to go into life accepting obedience, in reference to a superior gift. What is transmited to the sons, because of sin, is not the Law of God, this law which reveals the paternity of the Lord manifested through his freing his people from Egypt and in making it the heir to the land of the Amorites; what is unmasked, is the presumption of the leaders who impose their will in doing away with the authority of God.

7.3.4. *The Sin of Judah: 'They have Rejected the Law of the Lord'*

The oracle against Judah is very specific in what concerns its crime. There is no question of injustice in the relationship between men or between nations. The only thing mentioned is that they have betrayed the Law of God, completed by an allusion to idolatry, 'the lies after which their fathers walked'. One should note that the idols are not represented according to the traditional categories of vanity, but according to categories of the word: it is lies that are substituted for the Law of God. The word 'Law' calls for the word 'covenant' (1.9); indeed, there is no treaty that is not regulated by a series of rules defining it and giving it the status of law. This signifies that Judah, in 'rejecting' the Law, 'has not kept' the covenant towards God, has betrayed a treaty, and followed lies. In their rebellion, the pagan nations express the propagation of violence, fruit of greed and envious pride; in the fact that they 'keep their wrath forever' (1.11), they reveal the refusal of reconciliation which leads to the renewal of the covenant. They follow false ideals (which is suggested indirectly by Amos), identical to those that Judah follow (which is explicitly under-lined by Amos), those 'forgotten gods' which are power and wealth.[112]

The prophet speaks of 'lies' followed by the 'fathers' (2.4): there-fore another figure of authority appears, the father, who, instead of leading into the ways of obedience to the will of God, leads into rebel-lion (see 2.7 and 2.11-12). However, Amos does not accuse the fathers, but the sons, whom he reproaches having followed the way of their fathers, instead of obeying the Law spoken by the Lord. Judah thus reveals, in front of all the nations, that the heart of rebellion is the refusal to obey God, the refusal of his paternity, of his sover-eignty.

This oracle reveals the true roots of sin, the sin which is at the source of all the injustice in the world, as much social injustice as international injustice. Judah can recognize that it is the refusal of the Law of God that is the principle of injustice. According to literary criticism, the oracle against Judah, the heart of the whole section, is held as secondary; the same way that the heart of the first sequence (the oracles against Tyre and Edom) is; as well as the heart of the last sequence against Israel (concerning the prophets and the Nazirites). As it turns out, it is specifically these three hearts that constitute the key to the fundamental interpretation of the picture which is painted by the prophet. What is there in the redaction of Judah is the reading made in Sion and Jerusalem: the unveiling of the meaning of all injustice deployed in the world. Indeed, in Israel as well, the sin is not limited to harming one's neighbour but also to opposing God and his word. However, it is being said explicitly and synthetically in Judah: the principle of all evil is disobedience to the Law of God.

The first two chapters of Amos could be compared to the first three chapters of the letter of Paul to the Romans. Indeed, the first section of the book of Amos paints a picture of history according to which all nations are sinful. The root of this common sin is idolatry, the refusal to recognize God as God, which is the source of all injustice. The con-sequence will be the total destruction and all will be equally subjected

---

112. See J.L. Sicre Díaz, *Los dioses olvidados: Poder y riqueza en los profetas preexílicos* (Madrid: Ed. Christiandad, 1979).

to an irrevocable punishment. The fire that burns is the image that expresses annihilation best. Deportation, in parallel with death, is not a punctual punishment; it represents the death of a nation since, when moved outside its boundaries, it is no longer recognized as such. With the disappearance of the rulers, it is the symbol of the political autonomy of the nation that vanishes. It is therefore the end of the nations that is announced.

For Israel, the sanction is represented differently, but it will also be faced with war, and even the strong among the brave will not escape. There is nonetheless a sign of hope for it, with the final character who runs naked. The general tone remains nevertheless pessimistic. War is a sign of injustice, but it is at the same time a sign of the judgment of God against injustice.

This text, one of the first written pages of the tradition of Israel, speaks (already!) of the end. However, it is not given to the reader to see what the judgment of God opens to. In the third section, the visions of Amos speak of earthquakes, and it is only in the final page (9.11-15) that the future of reconstruction and life will appear. But it will be necessary to go through fire first.

8. *The Book*

Lastly, the ensemble of the sections form one 'book'. As far as the Gospel of Luke is concerned, I have shown elsewhere how its four sections form a structure, one book;[113] it is necessary to add immediately that the third Gospel is but one of two books written by Luke. Those two books form a diptych in which each part brings light to the other.

As for Amos, it is a convention in Christian tradition to hold it as one book, despite its small dimensions; in the Jewish tradition, on the contrary, it forms, with the other 'small prophets', a single book traditionally called *T^ere 'Aśar* ('the twelve'). It is not only each of these three sections which are structured, but also the whole—the book—that they form.[114]

Whether there are two books of Luke or two aspects of one work,

---

113. Meynet, *L'Evangile selon saint Luc*, I, pp. 247-54 (Italian trans.: *Il vangelo secondo Luca*, pp. 705-16).

114. Bovati and Meynet, *Le Livre du prophète Amos*, pp. 381-405 (Italian ed.: *Il libro del profeta Amos*, pp. 411-36).

the book of the prophet Amos, or the book of Twelve ('small prophets'), the 'book' is but one of the levels of textual organization. The
biblical text does not stop there. Luke has written two books which
are themselves part of the New Testament, the twenty-seven books of
which are related to the twenty-seven books of the Old Testament.[115]
Finally, what the Greek call 'the books' (*ta biblía*) and what the
modern languages have translated with the singular 'Bible' form one
Book.

The reader will understand that a methodological exposition like
this one has to be limited. It is out of the question to expose here the
structure of an entire book. It has already been done elsewhere for the
Gospel of Luke, and the book of Amos.

115. See P. Beauchamp, *Parler d'Ecritures saintes* (Paris: Seuil, 1987), pp. 51-
52.

Chapter 7

THE SITUATION OF RHETORICAL ANALYSIS
IN THE FIELD OF EXEGESIS

Rhetorical analysis is often introduced as an exegetical method.[1] It seems to me now more appropriate to consider it one of the operations of exegesis. This does not diminish its importance—on the contrary. Indeed, if it is considered a method, this means that it represents only one possibility among many: the exegete could choose, among all the methods (and approaches) that are available on the market of exegesis, this one or another, according to personal taste. On the other hand, if seen as one of the operations of the exegetical work, on a par with textual criticism, morphological or syntactic analysis, lexicographical research, and others, it becomes as necessary as they are. Which, far from diminishing its value, gives it a much more important status.

One should add immediately that exegetes have always practised this operation. It is indeed impossible to comment on a whole book at once; it is necessary to segment and explain, verse by verse—or even word by word—pericope by pericope. But one has to admit that it is usually done in an empirical manner, and the various partitions are rarely justified. Rhetorical analysis, on the other hand, provides necessary criteria to operate a segmentation of the text, at the different levels of its organization.

To pretend that rhetorical analysis is one of the necessary operations of the exegetical work amounts to saying in the same breath that it is not the only one. Whichever operation we might choose, it will nonetheless be necessary to start with textual criticism; one could

1. This is how it is described in the document of the Pontifical Biblical Commission, *The Interpretation of the Bible in the Church*; and it was my position in the French edition of this book where the first version of this chapter is entitled 'The Four Steps of Rhetorical Analysis' (as well as in the Italian edition).

not avoid studying grammatical problems, or do the lexicographical inquiries required. In the writing of a commentary, the headings will vary according to the importance that one will give to each operation.

In my commentary on Luke, I have chosen three headings only: 1. 'Composition'; 2. 'Interscriptural References' ('Biblical Context' in the Italian edition); 3. 'Interpretation'; certain questions of literary criticism, grammar and lexicography were dealt with, when necessary, in the footnotes. In our commentary of Amos, on the other hand, we have dealt with those questions under one heading entitled 'Text'. In the book I am writing on the Passion and Resurrection of the Lord in the first three Gospels, I am planning on a fifth heading, necessitated by the subject matter, called: 'Synoptical Comparison'.

Even if rhetorical analysis can have an influence on other operations (as will be seen in the conclusion), they nevertheless have to be made independently from it. The following pages propose a few thoughts on a way—my own—of presenting the results of rhetorical analysis.[2]

1. *Writing the Text*

The writing—or 'rewriting'—which, by an appropriate typographical disposition, aims at visualizing the rhetorical disposition of the text at different levels, is of crucial importance for whoever conducts the analysis as well as for the reader. Without speaking of the priceless benefits that the manipulation brings in enabling the incorporation of the text through the eyes but also through the hand, rewriting implies an objectivization that does not allow approximation. It forces one, in the proper meaning of the expression, to place all the words of the text without omission of a single word.

It is necessary to recall that this placing, and pagination, can only be done on the original. Translations, even literal ones, necessarily deform the text, in that they mask or destroy the rhetorical figure.

Since the analysis is based on the original text, except if one addresses a very narrow audience of specialists, it is necessary to translate. Like any translation, the translation which is destined for

2.   This is not the place to explain the procedures necessary to conduct a rhetorical analysis; see R. Meynet, *'E ora, scrivete per voi questo cantico'. Introduzione pratica all'analisi retorica*. I. *Detti e proverbi* (Retorica biblica, 3; Roma: Edizioni Dehoniane, 1996), which provides fourteen exercises—and a fifteenth one—complete with corrections.

rhetorical analysis, and therefore to a rewriting, will be functional, insofar as it will be done with the function aimed at in mind: to respect—as far as the structure of the host language permits—the composition of the original, beyond the limits of grammatical correctness if necessary, as long as comprehension remains possible. It seems preferable to choose a translation which is difficult to understand in the rewriting, even if it is necessary to provide explanations in the commentary, rather than risk a deformation which would prejudice the original text.

In fact, instead of speaking of a translation in the singular, it would be more appropriate to speak of several translations. The translation will indeed depend on the level of analysis of the text: it will be the more literal if one works on the most elementary levels, those of the segment, the piece or the part; less necessarily so when working on the level of the passage or the sequence, except for the relevant lexical (and syntactic) recurrences relevant to the respective levels. One should not be surprised if the translations of the first two chapters of Amos were somewhat different according to the level of analysis.

It remains to analyse, as briefly as possible, the rules of rewriting. Rewriting is an art which, like the *calligrammes* of Apollinaire, shares characteristics with poetry and drawing. But, like all art, it implies a technique. Which can and has to be described in order to be intelligible, to oneself as well as to others. Here are the leading principles and tools.

What to Rewrite?
The text, all of the text, nothing but the text. 'All the text' means that it is necessary to be defiant of points of suspension: experience proves that what is omitted is almost invariably what is the most important. 'Nothing but the text' means that any form of subtext is to be avoided; the use of the letters, a b c / a' b' c' and so on, is reserved for the level of the segment. On the other hand certain signs (full stops, addition marks, equal marks, etc.) will be very useful to visualize certain symmetries, as we will see below.

In What Order?
In the order of the text, line after line, regardless of the blanks to be left between words. The only exception to this rule is when something is factored: for example, when the central piece of a speech is introduced with a short sentence of narrative, the speech will be framed

and the sentence of narrative will be justified, on one or more line, on the left of the frame (see, e.g., p. 23, v. 42b-e).

How Often?

If an exhaustive study is envisaged, as many times as the text has levels. What was done for Psalms 113 and 146, wholly rewritten at every level of their composition, segments, pieces, sub-parts, parts and passages. Why every time? Because it is impossible to visualize all the levels with a single rewriting. If attempted, one would obtain a muddle where the keenest eye would not find its way. Only what is relevant to the level studied should be visualized. When entering the higher levels, it is necessary to forget the symmetries of the preceding levels.

In practice, it would be too cumbersome, for the reader, and especially for the editor, to be tied to such a requirement for all the texts, especially if they are long. Generally, it is possible to limit oneself—and it is what was done for the commentaries of Luke and Amos—to two (or three) rewritings, for the passage and the sequence (and subsequence).[3] When necessary, partial rewritings are given during the description of the text.[4]

Where?

It is very simple: the reader should be able to refer to the rewriting when reading the explanations provided for it, without having to turn the pages at every step. One should add that each figure has to appear on a single page, and not on two.[5] If the principle is simple, its realization is far less so.

In my first two publications,[6] the figures were published in a loose sheet volume; the inconvenience was the difficulty in keeping these sheets in order and the ease with which they were lost (or stolen in public libraries!).

---

3.   The same spirit of economy explains the omission, in this volume, of the rewriting of parts and sub-parts for the first seven oracles of Amos 1.3–2.16.

4.   See, for example, *Le Livre du prophète Amos*, p. 169, where the bimember segments of Amos 5.7 and 5.8abc are rewritten, besides the rewriting of the whole passage 5.7-13 on p. 168.

5.   Which occurs often in Lund's *Chiasmus in the New Testament*; in the present work, we have made sure that this fault would not be reproduced.

6.   *Quelle est donc cette Parole?* (1979) and *Initiation à la rhétorique biblique* (1982).

For my commentary of Luke in French,[7] I wanted to remedy this inconvenience in gathering all the figures in one bound volume: the inconvenience is that the reader has to manipulate two volumes at once, which is not very convenient, given the imposing size of those two volumes (21 cm × 24 cm).

Finally, I have arrived,[8] thanks to the progress of word-processing, at the solution of one volume where the figure and its description (under the title 'composition') are found both in succession, the figure on the even page and the explanations on the odd page (or reversely). If this greatly facilitates the comfort of the reader, it must be said that the work of the copy editor is far more complicated. And since it is very difficult, if not impossible, to convince the publishers of the necessity of certain constraints of pagination, it is safer to let the author do the job himself! The problem is to convince the publisher. Things become even more complicated when publishing in a periodical: even if one has succeeded to convince that the figures composed by the author should be reproduced as such, it is necessary to check that they are not cut in half and spread over two pages, especially not recto–verso, and it is almost impossible to get the explanations facing the figure.[9] A professional page editor has difficulty agreeing to leaving half a page blank, which is nonetheless necessary if one wants to respect the principle enunciated above.

How to Rewrite?
The principle is to conform to the principle of organization of the text. Everything can be summed up this way: to highlight the identities and the oppositions of the text through a set of identities and typographical differences. Hence the following tools:

a set of different characters, avoiding nonetheless too great a diversity. Three should be plenty,[10] on the condition that their difference is

7. *L'Evangile selon saint Luc* (1988).

8. *Il vangelo secondo Luca* (1994); P. Bovati and R. Meynet, *Le Livre du prophète Amos* (1994); idem, *Il libro del profeta Amos* (1995).

9. For example, I am very sorry that my last article was not reproduced as I had prepared it: some rewritings are cut and printed on two, or even three pages; see 'Composition et genre littéraire de la première section de l'Epître aux Galates', in J. Schlosser (ed.), *Paul de Tarse: Congrès de l'ACFEB (Strasbourg, 1995)* (LD, 165; Paris: Cerf, 1996), pp. 51-64.

10. Personally, I try to limit myself to two styles: Times (with serif) and Helvetica (without serif); I sometimes use Palatino. The characters with shadows are

well marked. If one plays with oppositions between 'bold' and 'fine', 'upper case', 'small upper case' and 'lower case', which increases the variety. The relations between symmetrical elements are written using the same characters.

vertical alignments: the elements to be put in relation with one another are aligned vertically, may they be words or textual units. In this last case, I will speak of margins.

lines: frames are distinct from horizontal lines. The frames around symmetrical textual units will have the same width. Lines (continual or intermittent) separate without isolating them, the units of inferior levels, inside a frame. One can also play on the width of the frames or lines as an indicator of repeated symmetry.

special characters: / + / – / - / = / , / : / :: / * /.[11] They precede symmetrical lines (words, syntagms, members or segments). Although they repeat the indication of the vertical alignments, they are nonetheless useful to signal or underline relationship.

screen: lastly, one can use, as a redundant tool, screens of various density. It goes without saying that an exposition will never replace, especially on this point, a careful scrutiny of reality.

2. Describing the Text

The ideal would be a rewriting so well done that it would speak for itself, without commentary or explanation. Experience proves, however, that it is almost always indispensable for it to be accompanied with a text which serves as a justification as well as a guide. This commentary should strictly be limited to the description of the formal characteristics of the text.

The description does not have to be linear, if the composition is not. It should adopt the form of the text, that is, follow its symmetries. If the text is of concentrical composition, one has the choice between two movements: to start from the extremities and go towards the centre, or reversely.

---

also useful; on the other hand, one should avoid characters with relief which are too pale, especially when printing.

11. Most of the time, those signs will not have the symbolic value in a pagination; however, one might be tempted to use, for example, the opposition between + and – to underline the opposition between positive and negative segments.

3. *Interpreting the Text*

The interpretation is not exterior or in addition to the rhetorical analysis; it is its culmination. As a personal operation of appropriation, the interpretation is obviously marked by the personality of its author; but it is also the fruit of anterior stages of analysis; which will give it, if it is well done, some guarantee of objectivity. The principle is to say in the language of the interpreters, in the categories of the culture to which they belong and according to their own logic, what rhetorical analysis enabled them to understand of the text.

If necessary, when the text refers, explicitly or not, to other texts of the Bible, reference will be made to the text or the series of texts to which it belongs. This is especially valid for the analysis of texts of the New Testament which quote so often those of the Old; but this stage is often necessary to bring to light, or to simply understand, the texts of the Old Testament in comparison to one another. The text of reference belongs indeed to the context of the text studied.

The same way that formal analysis obeys certain laws, interpretation does not operate outside certain rules. It is certainly more difficult to enunciate these laws, or the procedures of interpretation, than to describe the rules of the formal organization of the text. The result of formal analysis does not immediately give the meaning of the text; if it precedes it, a great deal of thinking remains nevertheless to be done in order to express the content of the text and its message. Some will even say that the transition from one operation to the next can only be done at the price of an 'interpretative jump' which is difficult, or even impossible, to codify. The thinking, and in the first instance the description, of what goes on between formal analysis and interpretation remains to be done, for the most part. I will nevertheless allow myself to propose what I think is one of the major rules, if not the fundamental law, of interpretation. It is the first draft of an effort of thematization of what has been my practise in the analysis of these texts.

If the application of these principles, even on the rhetorical level that concerns us here, is far from being always easy, its principle is very simple. And it follows from the basis of formal analysis. In Chapter 5, it was said that the relationship between linguistic elements which mark the composition of the texts is of two kinds, of identity and opposition. When formal analysis shows that two textual units are in relation, these two units appear either very similar or completely different from one another. In the first case, one must discover the difference, in the second the resemblance. This is already true on the most elementary level, of the segment or bimember. When two members seem to say the same thing, in other words, what Lowth calls 'synonymous' distychs, the difference between the two members will perhaps be as significant as their similarity.[12] On the contrary, when the two members seem very different, or even totally heterogeneous, their resemblance will probably be more significant than their differences.

With a few methodological thoughts made during the analysis of the four term bimember segment (above, §2.2.2.3.5), I proposed the enigma of the 'parables of mercy' in ch. 15 of the Gospel of Luke. Because the answer to this enigma had already been given at the end of the Foreword (pp. 34-36), there is no point in repeating it here: the reader will have to refer to it, as if to make an inclusion!

12. See the criticism of the synonymic parallelism of Lowth by Jebb. A criticism which agrees with that of J.-H. Herder in the last century: *Histoire de la poésie des Hébreux* (trans. A. de Carlowitz; Paris: Didier, 1855), pp. 22-23, and that of J. Kugel, *The Idea of Biblical Poetry*, pp. 96-97, would reproduce.

Chapter 8

THE FRUITS OF RHETORICAL ANALYSIS
FOR BIBLICAL EXEGESIS*

'No good tree bears bad fruit, nor again does a bad tree bear good
fruit; for each tree is known by its own fruit' (Lk. 6.43-44). There
remains a questions to be asked: what fruit does the operation that we
are describing bears? At the end of my commentary of the Gospel of
Luke, I devoted a few pages to the 'benefits of the rhetorical method'.[1]
I will attempt here, with further examples, to build on these few
pages. Notwithstanding the fact that I was not the first—by far—to
show that rhetorical analysis is useful for exegesis: the predecessors to
whom the whole of the first part of this book is devoted were the first
to discover the fruits of this new methodology: 1. for textual criticism; 2. for translation; 3. for the interpretation of texts.[2] I will start
with a problem that the preceding authors did not bring to light particularly well, namely that of the delimitation of the literary units, in
other words the problem of a more scientific definition of the notion
of 'context'. The fruits of rhetorical analysis for the domain of translation and textual criticism will then be exposed.

1. *Delimitation of Literary Units*

It seems that the first fruit of rhetorical analysis is to provide genuine
scientific criteria to delimit the literary units, at the different levels of
their organization.

---

* This chapter reproduces the conference paper I gave at the Seminar of the
New Testament's Roman exegetes on December 1 1994, and then published with the
title: 'I frutti dell'analisi retorica per l'esegesi biblica', *Greg.* 77 (1996), pp. 403-36.
   1. *L'Evangile selon saint Luc*, II, pp. 261-64.
   2. See above, pp. 52-53 (Lowth), p. 59 (Schöttgen), p. 61 (Bengel), pp. 65-66
(Jebb), pp. 98-99, 104-107, 108, 125-26 (Boys), pp. 142, 152 (Lund).

1.1. *At the Lower Levels*

This is true for *the first level*, that of the segment (unimember, bimember or trimember). The 'parallelism of the members' is obvious in the poetical texts but it is also found—in my opinion—in the texts in prose. Here is a bimember segment:

| Love | the enemies of | you, |
| do good to | those who hate | you. |

(Lk. 6.27)

How is it possible to recognize a unit in this segment? Knowing the form of the parallelism of the members, it is recognizable here between several elements: verbal syntagms + synonymous complements. However, if the beginning of the segment is without ambiguity, because this is where the list of commandments edicted by Jesus starts in the speech of the plain in Luke 6, the other limit is unsure, namely the end of the segment, as long as the limits of the following unit is found, namely the second segment:

| Bless | those who curse | you, |
| pray for | those who abuse | you. |

(Lk. 6.28)

In this segment as well, it is easy to recognize a synonymous parallelism between the two members; this synonymity, term by term, and in the same order, provides a first criterion for the internal coherence of the whole of the segment. The other criterion lies in the resemblance, and also the difference, between two bimember segments:

: Love	the enemies of	you,
: do good to	those who hate	you.
- Bless	those who curse	you,
- pray for	those who abuse	you.

Resemblance is obvious: same syntactic structure, partial synonymity, between the four verbs as well as between the four complements. One should not underestimate the *differences*: in the first member, only two characters appear, the disciples ('you who listen') and the enemies; in the second segment, however, another character appears, He in the name of whom blessing is done in the first member, the Lord God, who is not named but who is presupposed by the two verbs and also by the first complement ('those who curse you').

We nonetheless ignore the question of whether this last segment is a bimember: indeed, the two members taken into consideration could be but the first two members of a trimember segment. In carrying on the analysis, we will see that it is not a trimember, since a clear change occurs (Lk. 6.29):

| To him who strikes you | on the cheek, | *offer* | | also the other; |
| and of him who takes | your cloak, | also your coat | | *do not withhold.* |

Here again are two bimember segments, parallel to one another, very different from the preceding ones, and with their own form of parallelism; moreover, these two segments are not juxtaposed like the last two but are coordinated by 'and'. Let us end with the following two segments (Lk. 6.30):

| To every one begs from | you, | *give*; |
| and of him who takes | yours, | *do not ask.* |

It is unnecessary to explain the relations existing between these two segments, any more than the link between the two pairs of segments:[3]

+ To him who strikes you	on the cheek,	**offer**	also the other
– AND OF HIM WHO TAKES	your cloak,	also your coat	*do not withhold.*
+ To every one	begs	from you,	**give**
– AND OF HIM WHO TAKES	yours,		*do not ask.*

The conclusion that one can draw from the examination of these segments is that to operate the segmentation of units one needs to: 1. Recognize the textual forms (here the *parallelismus membrorum*); this knowledge enables one in turn to recognize, in the *continuum* of the text, the internal relationships of each unit (here between the two members of the segment), namely the internal coherence of this minimal literary unit. 2. Recognize a literary unit, which depends on the identification of the contiguous units; in other words, one cannot be sure of the coherence of a unit until the coherence of the unit surrounding it can be recognized.

I have used so far the term 'form' to speak of the *parallelismus membrorum*. One could also use that of 'figure'. These terms indicate relationships between elements which 'form' together a coherent whole in which these formal elements in relation to one another have a

---

3.   I left this analysis as it was in my article (referred to on p. 329 n. *), but the new analysis given above (pp. 202-203) is better; see also R. Meynet, '*E ora, scrivete per voi questo cantico*', pp. 54, 56, 108.

semantic function. Like in a drawing, the different lines that can be
identified as separate nonetheless contribute to a whole, to 'form' a
significant 'figure'. In a more complex ensemble of lines, one can recognize different forms or figures: the lines are attributed to, or rather
one will recognize that they belong to, one or another figure. In other
words, one will identify the relevant context of each line. To carry on
with the examples of Lk. 6.27-30, to have identified the first segment
means that the immediate context of the first member was identified,
at the first level of textual organization; therefore, to have understood
the relationship between the two members means that the second member, 'do good to those who hate you', enables the understanding of the
meaning of the first member, 'Love your enemies'; moreover, 'to do
good' is a kind of definition of the verb 'to love'.

Beyond the segment, the problem of the grouping of segments in
units of the superior level appears. We have already seen how the six
segments quoted above are linked two by two, in three 'pieces'.

1.2. *Delimitation of the Pericopes*

There is no more time to spend on these inferior levels; let us go to
the level of the pericope (the 'passage' according to my terminology).
This will furnish another example of the application of the criterion
of coherence, above all formal, or the 'regularity of composition' of
each passage.

There is no difficulty in determining the beginning of the beatitudes
of Matthew (5.3; see the rewriting following). The real problem lies
at the end of the passage: in general it ends with v. 12. Considered
from a different point of view, the problem lies in the internal organization of vv. 3-12, or, in other words, the question of the number of
beatitudes in Matthew: seven according to the preference of the first
evangelist for this number, eight if one counts the number of those
that begin the same way ('Blessed [. . .], for [. . .]'), or nine if one
considers the number of occurrences of the word 'Blessed'. Do vv. 3
and 10—because of the identity of their second member: 'for theirs is
the kingdom of heaven'—play a role of inclusion for a unit which
includes vv. 3 to 10? Or, on the contrary, do those two occurrences
serve the purpose of initial terms for two distinct units (2-9 and 10-
11)? To summarize, one can say that the question of the limits of
passages is linked to that of internal composition.

[3] **BLESSED** the poor in spirit

        for theirs is THE KINGDOM OF HEAVEN!

[4] **BLESSED** those who mourn

        for they shall be comforted!

[5] **BLESSED** the meek

        for they shall inherit the earth!

[6] **BLESSED** those who hunger and thirst

        for righteousness

        for they shall be satisfied!

[7] **BLESSED** the merciful

        for they shall be granted-mercy!

[8] **BLESSED** the pure in heart

        for they shall see God!

[9] **BLESSED** the peacemakers

        for they sons of God shall be called!

[10] **BLESSED** the persecuted   *for righteousness*

        for theirs is THE KINGDOM OF HEAVEN!

[11] **BLESSED** are you when men revile you and persecute
and utter all kinds of evil against you [falsely] on my account
[12] Rejoice and be glad, for your reward (is) great in heaven!
For so men persecuted the prophets before you.

The only criterion for the division is that which allows—or rather allows one to recognize—a regular composition for each of these two passages. After having attempted several divisions, I think I am in a position to say that only a division between v. 9 and v. 10 enables the recognition of a regular composition as much of the first unit (3-9) as of the second (10-12). It is impossible to give here a detailed demonstration; I will show only the composition of the beatitude of the persecuted:

+ [10] **Blessed**   THE PERSECUTED   because of righteousness

    – FOR theirs is the kingdom **OF HEAVEN!**

+ [11] **Blessed** are you

    when they revile   *you*

    and PERSECUTE

    and utter all evil against   *you*   because of me.

+ [12] **Rejoice** and **be glad,**

    – FOR your reward (is) great **IN HEAVEN!**

+ For so   THEY PERSECUTED   *the prophets before you.*

Note the recurrence, at the extremities and in the centre, of the same verb 'to persecute', with the repetition in a symmetrical position of 'for [...] heaven'; and besides, the unity of the content, persecution, which is avoided, at least explicitly, in the preceding verses.

It is most of all important to show the regularity of the first passage, formed by the first seven beatitudes, in the slightly different order of the Codex Bezae which allows a construction even more regular than in the text chosen by Nestlé-Aland (this prepares the third point of this exposition on the benefits that rhetorical analysis can bring to textual criticism).

+ [3] BLESSED the poor in spirit		for theirs is the kingdom of HEAVEN!	
- [5] BLESSED the meek		for they shall **inherit** the earth!	

[4] BLESSED	those who mourn		for they shall *be comforted*!
[6] BLESSED	those who hunger and those who thirst	for righteousness	for they shall *be satisfied*!
[7] BLESSED	the merciful		for they shall *be granted-mercy*!

+ [8] BLESSED the pure in heart		for GOD	they shall see!
- [9] BLESSED the peacemakers		for **son of God**	they shall be called!

Note the three verbs in the passive tense at the end of the second members of the central piece (4, 6, 7), the symmetry between 9 and 5 where 'son' recalls 'inherit', between 8 and 3 where 'heaven' has to be seen as a synonym of 'God', the shape of the first member of the central beatitude which is different from the other six. The criticism generally addressed to this analysis is that one should not divide the beatitudes into two pericopes. At this level, they need to be distinguished; the link between all the beatitudes is operated at the superior level.

At this level, the central role of the beatitude of the persecution appears. Note briefly the more saliant facts:

1. 'heaven' recurs at the extremities of the central passage (10b and 12b) and at the extremities of the sequence (3 and 16c; since 10b reproduces word for word 3b, one could look for the relation between 12b and 16c);

2. 'son of God' (9) and 'your father' (16c) play, with 'see' (8, 16b) the role of final terms for the extreme passages;

3. 'righteousness' (6 and 10a) is reproduced at the centre of the first passage and at the beginning of the second.[4]

---

[3] *Blessed* the poor in spirit,	**for theirs is the kingdom of**	*HEAVEN*!
[5] *Blessed* the meek,	for they shall inherit the earth!	

: [4] *Blessed* those who mourn   for they shall be comforted!

[6] *Blessed* those who | hunger and for *righteousness*, for they shall be satisfied! thirst

: [7] *Blessed* the merciful,   for they shall be granted-mercy!

. [8] *Blessed* the pure in heart,   for they shall *SEE* God!

. [9] *Blessed* the pure in heart,   for they shall be called **SONS** of God!

---

[10] *Blessed*   the persecuted for *righteousness*,

for theirs is the kingdom of   *HEAVEN*!

[11] *Blessed* are you

when men revile you and persecute

and utter all kinds of evil against you on my account.

[12] Rejoice and be glad,

for your reward is great in   *HEAVEN*!

For so men persecuted the prophets before you.

---

[13] You, you are   the salt   of the earth.

–But if salt lost its taste,

–how shall its saltiness be restored?

= It is no longer good for anything

= except to be thrown out

= and trodden under foot by men.

----

[14] You, you are   the light   of the world.

- A city cannot be hid

+ on a hill located.

- [15] Nor do men light a lamp   and put it under a bushel

+ but on a stand   and it gives light to all in the house.

= [16] Let so shine the light of you before men

= that they may *SEE* your good works

= and give glory to your **FATHER** who is in   *HEAVEN*.

---

4.   This is a good example of the law no. 4 of Lund (see above, p. 144).

This example shows how a text is organized on several levels: indeed, the beatitude of the persecution (central passage) is in close relation with the preceding one (first passage), but it is also in relation with the two images of salt and light (third passage). Moreover, this analysis calls for the recognition of a specific position, and therefore function, to the beatitude of the persecuted. I will come back to this point when dealing with interpretation from composition.

There is another criterion besides that of internal coherence of the passage for the identification of its limits: the coherence or regularity of the superior level, namely the 'sequence', or structured ensemble of several 'passages'.

The seventh sequence of the third section of Luke provides another illustration of this second criterion: it is composed of seven passages, organized concentrically (see illustration following). The problem of the limits between passages does not exist for the first side of the sequence (the first three passages and the beginning of the fourth); on the other hand, for the second side (the end of the central passage and the last three passages), the editions of the Greek text, the translations and the commentaries propose very different divisions. With the realisation that these passages form a sequence whose organization, among many other marks of composition, is indicated through indications of movement towards a location forming a very regular system, we have a very strong criterion of segmentation. To which it is necessary to add, as a confirmation of the criterion of coherence at the level of the sequence, the preceding criterion, of the regularity of the internal coherence of each of the seven passages (it is impossible to expose it here).[5]

5. See R. Meynet, *L'Evangile selon saint Luc*, I, pp. 176-83; II, pp. 179-90.

we are going up to	JERUSALEM	
ANNOUNCEMENT OF THE PASSION OF JESUS		18.31-34

he was drawing near to	*JERICHO*	
THE BLIND MAN CURED		18.35-43
he was passing through	*JERICHO*	
THE RICH MAN JUSTIFIED		19.1-10

he was near to	JERUSALEM	
THE PARABLE OF THE KING		19.11-28
getting up to	JERUSALEM	

he was drawing near to. . .	*THE MOUNT OF OLIVES*	
THE ENTHRONING OF THE KING		19.29-36
he was drawing near to. . .	*THE MOUNT OF OLIVES*	
THE ACCLAMATION OF THE KING		19.37-40

he was drawing near to. . .	THE CITY	
ANNOUNCEMENT OF THE PASSION OF JERUSALEM		19.41-46
entering into	THE TEMPLE	

1.3. *Delimitation of the Superior Units*

To have identified a sequence is not enough. One cannot be sure that they have found a sequence before identifying the preceding and the following one, and so on and so forth, up to the limits of the superior unit, namely the section; and the limits of the section will not be identified until the establishment of the structure of the whole book. This is, obviously, only if the presupposition that a book is composed and well composed holds true.[6] For now, I have precisely analysed two books only, the Gospel according to Luke and, with Pietro Bovati, the book of Amos.[7] The reader will understand that I am not in a position to present here, even less to demonstrate, the composition of a whole book. It will, on the other hand, be possible to give a rapid overview of the structure of a section, for example, the central section of the book of Amos.[8]

6. On this first presupposition, see Meynet, 'Présupposés de l'analyse rhétorique', pp. 72-75; above, pp. 169-72.

7. P. Bovati and R. Meynet, *Le Livre du prophète Amos* (1994); *idem*, *Il libro del profeta Amos* (1995).

8. Bovati and Meynet, *Il libro del profeta Amos*, p. 117.

| B1: A trap | for | | the Sons of Israel | 3.1-8 |

| B2: Multiply | **the wealth** | *will not save* | the Sons of Israel | 3.9–4.3 |

| B3: Multiply | *the sacrifices* | *will not save* | the Sons of Israel | 4.4-13 |

| B4: DIRGE | ON THE | | VIRGIN OF ISRAEL | 5.1-17 |

| B5: *A cult* | *perverted* | *will not save* | the House of Israel | 5.18-27 |

| B6: **A wealth** | *perverted* | *will not save* | the House of Israel | 6.1-7 |

| B7: The poison | | of | the House of Israel | 6.8-14 |

According to our analysis, the second section of Amos (3–6) counts seven sequences, organized in a concentric manner:

1. The extreme sequences (B1 and B7) are brief and play the role of introduction and conclusion; they both enunciate a threat.

2. The sequences B2 and B6 deal only with riches.

3. The sequences B3 and B5 deal only with cult.

4. The sequences B2 and B3 denounce the multiplication (or riches, and cultic acts).

5. The sequences B5 and B5 denounce perversion (of the cult, and riches).

6. As for the central sequence (B4), which articulates the denunciation of injustice and a debased cult, they announce the end of Israel.

7. Whereas all the first side (B1 to B3) is addressed to the 'Sons of Israel' and all the second side (B5 to B7) to 'the House of Israel', the central sequence targets the 'Virgin of Israel'.

2. Interpretation

2.1. Interpretation of a Passage

From within the pericope, rhetorical organization already helps to identify the symmetries, oppositions and identities, which enable the identification of structuring relationships between the elements, relationships which indicate the way to a better understanding of the message. I do not want to keep referring to the same example over and over again, for example, the very demonstrative parable of the prodigal son (Lk. 15).[9]

Let me take a passage from Luke (5.17-26; see following illustration). After the introduction (17), the story is organized in a concentrical way around two couples of questions: that of the scribes and pharisees (21) and that of Jesus in answer to their arguments (22-23). The fact that the centre is occupied by a question (a group of questions in this case) is a confirmation that it was well identified, because it is a case, among many, of what we can call 'the law of the question in the centre'.[10]

---

9. See Meynet, *L'Evangile selon saint Luc*, II, pp. 736-37; 'L'analyse rhétorique, une nouvelle méthode pour comprendre la Bible', *NRTh* 116 (1994), pp. 641-57; see above, pp. 32-36.

10. See other examples above, pp. 91-92, and esp. pp. 260-61, 270-72; see also Meynet, *L'Evangile selon saint Luc*, II, p. 261; 'Le cantique de Moïse et le cantique de l'Agneau (Ap 15 et Ex 15)', *Greg.* 73 (1992), pp. 19-55; 'L'enfant de l'amour (Ps 85)', *NRT* 112 (1990), pp. 843-58; Bovati and Meynet, *Le Livre du prophète Amos*, e.g. pp. 81, 84, 108, 211, 222, 335.

+ [17] *It happened, on one of those days,*   *that he WAS*   *TEACHING*

: *and*   *were sitting*   *pharisees*   *and*   *teachers-of-the-law*
: *who*   *had come*   *from every village*   *of Galilee and Judea and Jerusalem*

+ *and a power of the Lord*   *WAS there so that he*   *HEAL.*

. [18] And behold	men	bringing	on a bed	
.	a	man	who was	paralysed,
	– sought to		bring him in	and lay him BEFORE HIM.
. [19] But finding no way to		bring him in	because of the crowd,	
.			coming up on the roof,	
	– through the tiles		they let him down	
			with the bed into the midst	BEFORE JESUS.

[20] *When he saw their* ***faith****, he said:*

'Man,   **YOUR SINS ARE FORGIVEN YOU**'.

| [21] *And the scribes and the pharisees began to QUESTION SAYING:* | 'Who is this that speaks blasphemies?
 Who   can   **FORGIVE SINS**
 but God only?' |
| [22] *Jesus perceiving their QUESTIONINGS answering SAID:* | 'Why do you question in your hearts?
 [23] Which is easier, to say: **YOUR SINS ARE FORGIVEN YOU**
 or to say: *RISE* and walk?' |

[24] *But you may* ***know*** *that*
the Son of man has authority on earth to   **FORGIVE SINS'**,

. he said	to the paralysed:	'I say to you, *RISE,*
– take up	your bed	and go home.'
. [25] Immediately,	*RISING*	before them,
– taking up	that on which he *LAY,*	he went home, GLORIFYING GOD.
. [26] *Amazement*	seized them all	
–		and they GLORIFIED GOD
. and were filled	with *awe,* saying:	
–		'We have seen strange things today'.

The centre of a concentrical composition has been recognized as the keystone,[11] or the heart,[12] of a text since the beginning of the nineteenth century. This does not mean that it is the most important element, from the, so to speak, quantitative point of view! I often use the image of the *menorah*, the seven branches candlestick: if the central arm is the most important, it is because it holds all the other ones together, which guarantees the cohesion of the whole: should another branch be taken away, the *menorah* would be unbalanced, but it would remain a *menorah*; if, on the other hand, the central arm be taken away, the candlestick would be destroyed and only scattered pieces would remain.

What is the organizing function of the questions of 21-23 for the whole of the passage, or—to say it differently—how does the text respond to these questions, or how does the centre articulate the various parts of the text?[13] The problem lies in knowing who can forgive: God alone, or also Jesus? As the questions of Jesus already suggest (22-23) in answering those of the scribes and pharisees (21), the answer will be: both, in other words Jesus as God. In the second question (23), Jesus explains the link between recovery and forgiveness, or between power over disease and over sin. At the beginning of the passage (17d), the narrator takes position on this problem: 'and a power of the Lord was there so that he could heal'. Therefore, according to the narrator, recovery flows from the power of God. At the end of the text, after the recovery, all the characters think the same: when the paralytic is restored to health and 'all praise God' (25b, 26b), they recognize that the healing was done by God. They share the same opinion as the scribes and pharisees, and they say the truth when they say that only God can forgive sins.

However, the text also says that Jesus possesses the same power: already at the beginning (17d), the subject of the verb 'heal' is Jesus: in this sentence of introduction, the narrator prepares the way for the answer to the central questions. Then Jesus will say the same thing, when, in v. 20, he uses a perfect passive (divine passive?): 'Man, your

11. See above, p. 122.
12. See above, pp. 146-47.
13. Which will enable me to improve the interpretation of this passage that I gave in my commentary (see *L'Evangile selon saint Luc*, II, p. 72).

sins are forgiven you'. And yet the scribes and the pharisees understand correctly that he who forgave was indeed Jesus, and the acknowl-
edgment of Jesus in v. 24 does not leave the shadow of a doubt of his
'authority'. Even the people know—or better, believe—that Jesus can
heal: otherwise, they would not have brought the paralytic 'before
Jesus' (twice: 18c, 19c).

Such is the central problem, the heart of the passage. The speech is
eminently christological. At this point the reader is invited to think
and to deepen his reflexion in the light of other texts: how can two
seemingly contradictory affirmations be reconciled? If this authority
is at the same time God only and yet also belongs to Jesus, the only
way to hold together the two terms of the antinomy is to situate them
in the reality of filiation: 'All things have been handed over to me by
my Father' (Lk. 10.22). Jesus has this authority because he received it
in the quality of Son of God.

Another example, the tale of the circumcision of John the Baptist
(Lk. 1.57-66), shows how a formal symmetry can highlight an unsus-
pected significant relationship:

If the composition of this passage is exact, vv. 59a and 64 are in
symmetrical position: bearing in mind the texts on the circumcision of
the lips (Exod. 6.12, 30), the ears (Jer. 6.10), and the heart (Deut.
10.16; 30.6; Lev. 26.41; Jer. 4.4; 9.24-25; Rom. 2.25-29; Col. 2.11),
a relationship between those two segments appears obvious, not only
formal, but also meaningful: to the circumcision of the child corresponds the circumcision of the ears and lips of the father. It is at the
moment when Zachariah shows that he believes in the words of the
angel Gabriel, in giving to his son the name that he had foretold, that
from deaf and dumb as he was, he recovers at once both hearing and
speech.

+ [57] Now the time came for Elizabeth
                - to be delivered
                . and she gave birth to a son.
+ [58] And the NEIGHBORS and kinsfolk HEARD
                  - that the LORD had shown great mercy   WITH HER,
                  . and they rejoice-with her.

        [59] And the eighth day
        they came to circumcise the child.

: They were *NAMING* him	after the *name* of his father, Zechariah.
[60] Answering, his mother said:	**'No, he shall be called John'.**
: [61] They said: 'None of your kindred	is *CALLED* by this *name'.*
: [62] They made-signs to his father	how he would him to be *CALLED*.
[63] Asking for a tablet, he wrote:	**'John is his name'.**
: And they all marveled.	

        [64] And immediately his mouth was opened and his tongue,
        and he spoke blessing God.
+ [65] And fear came on all their NEIGHBORS,
                      . and through all the hill country of Judea
                      . all these things were talked about.
+ [66] And all who HEARD them, laid them up in their hearts:
                      . saying: 'What then will this child be?'
                      . for the hand of the LORD was   WITH HIM.

2.2. *Interpretation of the Superior Units*

The fruits represented so far are not to be disdained, but the most important fruit of rhetorical analysis is without doubt the ability to read together several passages and to bring to light effects of meaning which, too often, escape a piecemeal reading. Rhetorical analysis reads together different passages, because it recognizes that they were composed to this effect. As the word itself reveals, 'com-prehend' is to 'apprehend together', which amounts to understanding the relationships. It is necessary first of all to understand the relations of linguistic relationships, or symmetries, of all sorts, without being limited however to a purely formal analysis. All the technical work is targeted

towards bringing to light the relationships of contents, as we have seen
in the preceding stage, especially with the example of John and
Zachariah. For rhetorical analysis, *form is the gateway to meaning*.

One of the most representative examples is that of the 'editing' done
either by Mt. 20.20-34 or by Mk 10.35-52 with the demand of the
sons of Zebedee and the healing of the blind of Jericho (two blindmen
in Matthew), around the speech on service. Since I have already used
this example several times,[14] I do not want to use it again here. I will
not reproduce the magnificent example of the sequence C7 of Lk.
18.31–19.46 either.[15]

Let me take a double example instead which will show how
rhetorical analysis proposes a new way of approaching the study of
synoptical Gospels. The second sequence of Easter of the Lord Jesus
(the Passion and Resurrection) is devoted to the trial of Jesus. Between
Matthew and Mark, the material is practically the same; however,
Matthew adds several episodes. There is no need to go into detail; it
will be enough to show—without demonstration—how they have organized the material and what the repercussion of these two different
compositions on interpretation is.[16]

In Mt. 26.57–27.26, the trial is organized in two stages, the Jewish
phase (26.57-75) and the Roman phase (27.3-26), articulated by a
short piece (27.1-2) of 'transition'.

FALSE WITNESSES ACCUSE		*JESUS*	26.57-61
Before the High Priest, Jesus declares himself **CHRIST**			62-68
PETER WITNESSES AGAINST		*JESUS*	69-75

The Sanhedrin deliver Jesus to the Governor	27.1-2

JUDAS WITNESSES IN FAVOUR OF		*JESUS*	3-10
Before the Governor, Jesus declares himself	**KING OF THE JEWS**	11-14
PILATE WITNESSES IN FAVOUR OF		*JESUS*	15-26

14. See above, pp. 27-31.

15. See pp. 296-97.

16. See R. Meynet, *Passion de notre Seigneur Jésus Christ* (LiBi, 99; Paris:
Cerf, 1993), pp. 101-41.

The titles given to each passage aim at underlining the symmetry, either within each sub-sequence (16.57-75 and 27.3-26), or between the two sub-sequences. A special note for the pericope of the denial of Peter (26.69-75) which belongs to the Jewish phase of the trial, where Peter is placed in parallel with the false witnesses.

In Mk 14.53–15.20 (see the illustration following), the composition is very different. The first thing to note is the fact that the last passage, entitled 'The Soldiers Mock Jesus' ('the crown of thorns' in the Bible of Jerusalem: 15.16-20), belongs to the sequence of Mark; in Matthew, it belongs to the following sequence. The result is that—if this analysis is correct—the denial of Peter does not belong, like in Matthew, to the Jewish phase of the trial, but it stands alone, at the heart of the sequence. From the interpretative point of view, one can say that Mark organized the trial of Jesus in three distinct phases: the Jewish phase (14.53-65), the Pagan phase (15.1-20) and at last—or centrally—the 'Christian' phase.

Jesus is led	to the High Priest		14.53-54
THE HIGH PRIESTS			
	look for a witness		55-64
to kill	Jesus		
The servants	*of the High Priest*	*MOCK JESUS*	65
	DENIAL AND REPENTANCE OF PETER		66-72
Jesus is led	to the Governor		15.1
THE HIGH PRIESTS			
	look for a way		2-15
to crucify	Jesus		
The soldiers	*of the Governor*	*MOCK JESUS*	16-20

The basic logical movement seems to be the same in the two Gospels. In Matthew: if the heathen are guilty of the death of Jesus, the Jews are even more so. This is underlined in the diverse episodes proper to Matthew, especially when Pilate washes his hands while the whole people take on the blame for the condemnation to death of

Jesus. This logic should not be understood as anti-semitism, but as the reiteration of a habitual theme in the prophets of Israel. If Matthew is the Gospel of the Hebrew communities of Syria–Palestine, one understands his behaviour: for them, as for the other Jews, the world is divided in two: the Jews and the heathen. The Jews are worse than the heathen; their fault is greater because they are the elect, to which the Messiah was destined.

In Mark, the logic is similar, but it is threefold: if the heathen are guilty, and if the Jews are even more so for the same reasons as in Matthew, the disciples, represented by their chief, are even more guilty than both. If Mark was written in Rome, it is clear that the Christians from then on formed a group distinct from the Jews as well as from the heathen. The reflexion has made progress. In this sense, Mark represents a state of the church posterior to that of Matthew, perhaps not in time, but certainly from the point of view of the development of the history of the Church.

With this example, it is clear how rhetorical analysis deals with the synoptical problem: it is obviously interested in the comparison of pericopes, but at this level already, it also considers not only the small differences, but particularly those of composition; it is even more interested, however, in the architecture of sequences. To make a simplistic comparison, it is more interested in sentences than the words that compose them, more in syntax than morphology.

I will end this second part with a return to the decisive fruits of rhetorical analysis: it enables the scientific definition of the notion of 'context'. I do not want to reproduce here what has already been said on this matter, because I hope the examples used so far are clear enough and also because I have already written about it at length.[17] I will only reproduce two examples:

1. If my analysis is correct, the context of the passage of the 'crown of thorns' is indeed different in Matthew and Mark: in the first Gospel, it is the first passage of the third sequence of the Passion, whereas in Mark, in contrast, it is the last passage of the second sequence. As in the syntagm 'Gospel of Luke', if the graphic context of the /s/ is composed by the two preceding letters (go) and by the following three (pel), the context of the /g/ is composed of only the following five letters (ospel) and that of the /l/ of the five preceding letters (gospe); although the /s/ is closer to the /o/ of 'of' than it is to the /g/ of 'gos-

17. See 'Présupposés de l'analyse rhétorique', pp. 107-108; above, p. 181.

pel', and that in the speaking chain it is in contact with the /o/ of 'of', it does not belong to the same unit. It goes the same for the syntactic level of the sentence, and at the rhetorical level for the various levels of the composition of the text.

2. In the example of the sequence C7 of Luke (see above, pp. 296-97), at the level of the sequence, the context of the last passage is not the following passage, because it belongs to the following sequence (C8); inside the sequence C7, the context of the last passage (Lk. 19.41-46) is not in the first place the passage immediately preceding, but the one further apart, namely the first passage of the sequence (Lk. 18.31-34), because their content and their form are very similar (see the illustration, opposite page; see my commentary, I, pp. 179-80).

It is indeed the same problem that is present, at the syntactic level, in the sentence often quoted on this subject:[18]

> because I hear of your love
> and of the faith
> which you have toward the Lord Jesus
> and all the saints   (Phlm. 5).

The syntactic context of the last syntagm is not the preceding one, but the first ('your love towards all the saints, and your faith towards the Lord Jesus'):

> + because I hear of *your love*
>   – and of the FAITH
>   – which you have toward THE LORD JESUS
> + and *all the saints*.

---

18. For example, J. Jebb, *Sacred Literature*, p. 345 (above, p. 88).

+ ³¹ Taking with him the Twelve,   he   **SAID** to them:
: 'Behold, we are GOING UP to   JERUSALEM,
+ and will be accomplished   all that is   *WRITTEN*
: by the prophets of   THE SON OF MAN.

. ³² He will be delivered   *TO THE GENTILES*,
. and will be mocked,
. and shamefully treated,
. and spit upon
. ³³ and, scourging him, they will kill him
- and on the third DAY he will rise'.

= ³⁴ But they   *understood*   none of these things;
– and   this **SAYING** for them   *was HID*
= and they   *did not grasp*   what was **SAID**.

+ ⁴¹ When he DREW NEAR, seeing   THE CITY,
+ he wept over   it,   **SAYING**:

= ⁴² '*Would you understand,*   IN THIS DAY, even you what is for   PEACE!
– But this *is HID*   NOW   from your   *EYES*.

∗ ⁴³ For the DAYS shall come upon you
. when they will cast up   *YOUR ENEMIES* a bank about you,
. and surround you
. and hem you in on every side;
. ⁴⁴ and dash you and your children within you
. and they will not leave one stone upon another in you,

= because *you did not know*   THE TIME   of your   VISITATION'.

+ ⁴⁵ And,   ENTERING   THE TEMPLE,
+ he began to   drive out   the sellers, ⁴⁶   **SAYING**:
                                            'It is   *WRITTEN*:
+ "My house   shall be   a house of prayer.
+ But you   have made it   a den of robbers"'!

3. *Translation*

In this chapter I will approach only two questions: (1) the translation of certain words the recurrence of which have a rhetorical function; (2) the order of the words and the syntactic constructions.[19]

3.1. *Respect of the Functional Lexical Recurrences*

When the lexical recurrences have a rhetorical function in the composition of a text, they have to be respected. G. Mounin, one of the greatest specialists of translation, writes, on the subject of rhetorical analysis:

> This work, already so rich, makes room at last for a final revolutionary question, a very uncomfortable one. If these rhetorical structures exist—and for the most part they do—, if they construct, at least on important points, a stylistic approach to meaning in the gospels, they should be translated. It is the whole current theory of translation of the Bible in the vernacular that is being questioned; and for reasons neither of false reverence, nor pseudo-theological, but for reasons that bear on the function of the structures of the text itself, on its functioning.[20]

In all the translations of the parable of the prodigal son (Lk. 15.11-32; see the illustration, below) that I have looked at, the four recurrences of the verb *didōmi* are never translated by the same verb. It is a shame, because it indicates—with other obvious literary facts—the construction of the text (and they are not indifferent for its interpretation).

---

19. On the contribution of rhetorical analysis for the translation of the Bible, see the opinion of a great specialist of translation, Georges Mounin, in the preface to R. Meynet, *Quelle est donc cette Parole?*, A, p. 9; see also, by the same author: 'Biblical Rhetoric and Faithful Translation', *BT* 30 (1979), pp. 336-40; 'Traduction', *Encyclopaedia Universalis* (Paris: Encyclopaedia Universalis, 1985), p. 141.

20. G. Mounin, Preface to R. Meynet, *Quelle est donc cette Parole?*, p. 9.

¹¹ He said: There was a man who had two sons. ¹² The younger said to
the father: 'Father,   **GIVE** me the share of property that falls to me.'
And the father divided his living between them. ¹³ Not many days later, gathering *all*, **the
younger son took his journey into a far country** and there he squandered his
property in loose living. ¹⁴ When he had spent *all*, a great famine arose in that country, and
he began to be in want. ¹⁵ So he went and joined himself to one of the citizens of that
country, who sent him into his fields to feed swine.

----

¹⁶ And he would gladly have fed on the pods that the swine *ate*;
     AND NO ONE   **GAVE** him. ¹⁷ Then he came to himself and said:
'*How many* SERVANTS of my father abound in bread but I perish here with hunger!

----

¹⁸ I will arise and go to my father, and I will say to him: "Father, I have sinned against
heaven and against you; ¹⁹ I am no longer worthy to be called your son. Treat me as one of
your hired servant".'
²⁰ And he arose and came to his father. But while he was yet at a distance, the father saw
him and had compassion, and ran and embraced him and kissed him. ²¹ And the son said to
him: 'Father, I have sinned against heaven and against you; I am no longer worthy to be
called your son. . . '.

²² The father	= 'Bring quickly,	the best robe	and put them on him,
said to the	**GIVE**	the ring for his hand	and shoes on his feet.
SERVANTS:	= ²³ Bring	the fatted calf	and kill him.

Let us eat, and MAKE MERRY,
²⁴ *for this my son was dead, and is alive again,   he was lost, and is found.'*
And they began to MAKE MERRY.

²⁵ The elder son was in the field. As he came and drew near to the house, he heard music
and dancing; ²⁶ he called one of the servants and asked what this meant. ²⁷ The servant said
to him: "Your brother has come back and your father has killed the fatted calf, because he has
received him safe and sound." ²⁸ But he was angry and refused to go in. The father came out
and entreated him. ²⁹ But he answered his father:

'Lo, these *many* years *I* HAVE SERVED you and I never disobeyed your command,
     YET YOU NEVER   **GAVE** me a kid that I make merry with my friends.
³⁰ But when this SON OF YOURS came, who *has eaten* your living with harlots,

----

you kill for him the fatted calf.'
³¹ The father answered to him: 'Son, **you are always with me**
and all that is mine   **IS YOURS**;
³² but it was fitting to MAKE MERRY and be glad,
for this your brother was dead, and is alive again,   he was lost, and is found'.

Another example: if—as I think I have demonstrated—the three pericopes of Lk. 7.18-50 constitute a single sequence, one should translate the three occurrences of the verb *charizomai* (7.21, 42, 43) by the same verb; this is so much more remarkable that they are the only occurrences of this verb in Luke and that, on the other hand, in Lk. 7.20-21 as well as in the scene of the pharisee Simon (7.36-50), they are specific to Luke. This symmetry is nonetheless never respected in the seven English translations that I have looked at: for example, the RSV translates the first: 'and on many that were blind *he bestowed* sight' (7.21) and the other two by '*to forgive*' (7.42-43); the translation *Phillips Modern English* translates the first occurrence by 'he *restored* sight', the second by 'he *generously cancelled* both *of their debts*' and the third by 'the one who *has been* more *generously treated*'! This is also the case for all the French translations seen, for the Hebrew translation of UBS (1991), for the Arabic translation of Dar el Machreq (Beirut, 1989); on the other hand, the Italian translation of the CEI is the most faithful since it translates the first occurrence by: 'e *donò* la vista a molti ciechi' (7.21) and the other two by: '*condonò* il debito a tutti e due' (7.42) and 'Suppongo quelle a cui *ha* condonato di più' (7.43).

Another example: the two parables of Luke 16 in Greek start with the same expression:

16.1: Ἄνθρωπός τις   ἦν πλούσιος ὃ εἶχεν οἰκονόμον, καὶ. . .
16.19: Ἄνθρωπός δέ   τις ἦν πλούσιος καὶ ἐνεδιδύσκητο. . .

Especially when we have seen that these parables are symmetrical, at the extremities of the same sub-sequence, why translate them differently? For example, the NEB:

16.1: *There was*   A RICH MAN   *who* had a steward. . .
16.19: *There was*   **once** A RICH MAN,   *who* dressed. . .

but especially the *Living Bible* which should have respected this characteristic of the living oral style:

16.1:   A   RICH MAN   hired. . .
16.19: *There was*   A **certain**   RICH MAN, Jesus said, who was. . .

The RSV translates the two propositions the same way:

16.1: *There was*   A RICH MAN   *who*   had a steward. . .
16.19: *There was*   A RICH MAN,   *who*   was clothed. . .

3.2. *Respect of the Order of Words and the Syntactic Constructions*

It is always better to respect the order of words, and the syntactic constructions, especially when they are relevant. One example will suffice; in Lk. 8.39 is read:

Ὑπόστρεφε	εἰς τὸ οἶκόν σου
καὶ **διηγοῦ**	ὅσα σοι ἐποίησεν ὁ θεός
καὶ ἀπῆλθεν	καθ᾽ ὅλην πόλιν
κηρύσσων	ὅσα ἐποίησεν αὐτῷ

Why not respect the parallelism which is so marked in these two segments? The RSV translates:

Return	*to your home,*	and DECLARE
	how much God	has done for you.
And he went away,	PROCLAIMING	*throughout the whole city*
	how much Jesus	had done for him

changing the order of syntagms. It would be without doubt more respectful of the original form to translate:

Return	*to your home,*	and DECLARE
	how much God	has done for you.
And he went away	*throughout the whole city*	PROCLAIMING
	how much Jesus	had done for him

It is true that the translation of the RSV is dictated by its interpretation of the syntactic structure of the second member: indeed, it makes 'throughout the whole city' the complement of 'proclaiming' and not of 'he went away'. One can think that it is necessary to privilege the order of syntagms, to the cost of modifying somewhat the syntactic relations, as I have done in my commentary on Luke;[21] an English equivalent of my translation would be:

Return	*to your home,*	to DECLARE
	how much God	has done for you.
And he went away	*throughout the whole city*	to PROCLAIM
	how much Jesus	had done for him

However, the reproach that one could make to this translation is to put too much stress on the parallelism.

---

21. *L'Evangile selon saint Luc*, I, pp. 81-82.

4. *Textual Criticism*

At last, rhetorical analysis can benefit textual criticism. This fruit is not new. More than two centuries ago, in 1753, R. Lowth published his *De sacra poesi Hebraeorum praelectiones academicae Oxonii habitae*;[22] in his nineteenth lesson, he gave the description of the famous *parallelismus membrorum*. Lowth, and Michaelis, had realized the use of the parallelism of the members for the critica textus:[23] it allows the corrections of the mistakes of the copyists, to verify and confirm a correction offered by a manuscript or an antique version.[24] Lowth and Michaelis had nevertheless been preceded on this path by C. Schöttgen: the latter, twenty years earlier, had given, in his *Horae Hebraicae et Talmudicae*[25] a long *dissertatio* devoted to *exergasia*. The third chapter of this dissertation is entitled: 'Of the Use of *Exergasia Sacra*'; the *exergasia* first allows the better understanding of the meaning of certain words; it is also useful to interpret more easily and more safely the difficult and corrupted texts. Schöttgen has devoted another dissertation to discuss the case of Gen. 49.10 (seventh *dissertatio*). Several other authors have later underlined the advantage of this method.[26]

It is not enough to affirm, even in basing one's affirmations on the authorities of the past; it is necessary to illustrate this fruit of rhetorical analysis with examples drawn from one's own experience and research. It seems that rhetorical analysis can provide new criteria that can help to choose between different variants, especially to decide if part of the text should be considered as an omission or an addition. I will give a few examples of these two problems, without discussing them in depth for lack of time.

---

22. Oxford, 1753.

23. See the addition of Michaelis to the nineteenth lesson in the second edition of Lowth's work, 1763, pp. 96-105.

24. R. Lowth, *Isaiah*, p. xxxvii.

25. Dresden and Leipzig: apud Hekelii, 1733.

26. For example, J.F. Scheusner, *De parallelismo sententiarum egregio subsidio interpretationis grammaticae* (Leipzig, 1781); T. Boys, *A Key to the Book of the Psalms*, p. 162; N.W. Lund, *Chiasmus in the New Testament*, pp. 282-83; A. Vaccari, 'De utilitate parallelismi poetici ad intelligentiam Sacrorum librorum', *VD* 1 (1920), pp. 188-89.

4.1. *Choosing Between Different Options*

If parallelism exists, not only in poetical texts, but even in the texts in prose, one could think that between the different variants one could be chosen for respecting the parallelism. A single example: Nestlé-Aland (27th edition) preferred the following text for Lk. 24.47:

καὶ κηρυχθῆναι ἐπὶ τῷ ὀνόματι αὐτοῦ μετάνοιαν
εἰς ἄφεσιν ἁμαρτιῶν εἰς πάβτα τὰ ἔθνη.

Numerous manuscripts have καὶ; instead of εἰς at the beginning of the second line. The structure of the piece offers good arguments for choosing this last variant:

[46] He said to them: "Thus it is written that

:	*the Christ*	should suffer		
	– and	rise	from the DEAD	on the third day
: [47] and	*in his name*	should be preached		repentance
	– and	forgiveness	of SINS	to all nations.

The parallelism of the two sentences should be underlined, with the second members both starting with καὶ,[27] instead of:

[46] He said to them: "Thus it is written that

:	*the Christ*	should suffer		
	– and	rise	from the DEAD	on the third day
: [47] and	*in his name*	should be preached		repentance
	– **to**	forgiveness	of SINS	**to** all nations.

However, this criterion should be used with care, since in the texts where there is no textual problem, the parallelism is not always stressed much.[28]

4.2. *Texts to be Considered as an Addition (to be Omitted)*

The manuscript attestation at the end of Lk. 11.42 is equivocal. Let us see first the Lukan composition, without this text, that I would be tempted to consider as a harmonizing addition.

The speech to the pharisees is composed of two very regular parts. The first part (39b-41) which starts with an apostrophe (39bcd) is of concentrical construction. The central bimember segment (40) is, as it

---

27. The three verbs complementing 'it is written' are infinitives in Greek and cannot have several coordinated subjects.

28. See R.Meynet, *Il vangelo secondo Luca*, pp. 732-33.

often occurs in biblical texts, a question.[29] Then four members correspond to one another two by two: first those that start with the synonyms translated 'but', followed by 'your inside' and its equivalent 'that is inside' and which oppose 'extortion and wickedness' to 'alms'; then there are, at the extremes, two other segments with 'you cleanse' and 'is clean'. The chiasm of the central segment (40) accentuate the concentrical construction of this sub-part.

	the outside of the cup and of the dish, YOU CLEANSE			
	: but *your inside* is full *OF EXTORTION AND WICKEDNESS*			
39b Now		Who	*made*	
you	40 You fools!	the outside		
Pharisees,		the inside also		
		did he not	*make?*	
	: 41 But	*that is within*	give it	*FOR ALMS*
	and behold, everything for you			IS CLEAN.

+ 42	But *WOE* to you, **Pharisees**,			
	- *for* you tithe	mint and rue,	and every herb,	
	: and neglect	justice	and the love of God.	
+ 43	*WOE* to you, **Pharisees**,			
	- *for* you love	the best seat	in the synagogues	
	- and	salutations	in the market places.	
+ 44	*WOE* to you			
	. *for* you are	like graves	which are not seen	
	. and men	walk over them	without knowing it.	

The second part (42-44) counts three bimembers the first members of which are identical (with abbreviations); the second members start with 'for' and the third with 'and'; 42b and c are antithetical, 43b and c are synonymous and 44b and c are complementary. These three segments reproduce the opposition 'exterior'–'interior' of the first sub-part: the first opposes the exterior duties, 'tithe' of the aromatic plants, to the internal duties, 'justice and love of God', the third opposes again interior, that is the death of the pharisees, and the exterior which hides it; as for the second segment, its two members indicate the external appearances. The figure formed by these oppositions is concentrical:

29. See for example, Ps. 113, pp. 260-61 (v. 5); Am. 2.6-16, pp. 270-72 (v. 11c); See also the list of examples in Luke in Meynet, *L'Evangile selon Saint Luc*, II, p. 261.

External	42a
INTERNAL	42b
External	43a
External	43b
INTERNAL	44a
External	44b

The great majority of the manuscripts end v. 42 with: 'These you ought to have done, and that to not neglect':

---

42 But woe to you Pharisees,

– for	*you tithe*	***mint and rue and every herb,***	b
+ and	NEGLECT	**justice and the love of God**.	c
–	***These***	you ought to *have done*,	d
+ and	**that**	to not NEGLECT!	e

In fact, only D and Marcion delete this text; the specialists who believe in the existence—and the importance—of the 'western text' would have an argument in favour of their thesis. One understands why a sentence could have been introduced in this place: 42d calls to 42b and 42e calls to 42c. However, to retain it would destroy the rigorous parallelism of the three maledictions. The presupposition—to which we arrived when seeing how the texts are most of the time well composed—is that the most regular text is preferable.

The solution of the manuscript b of *Vetus Latina* which places the sentence after v. 41 is, from the rhetorical point of view, very convincing: it would thus become the center of 39b-44. But this central statute would confer on it a more important value that does not seem to correspond to the meaning of the whole of the text: Jesus seems to want to insist on what the scribes and pharisees are omitting, rather than on the necessary link between the legal practise and their spirit.

Verse 40, proper to Luke, could in truth be the equivalent of the contested sentence: 'These you ought to have done, and that to not neglect'. This sentence would be considered as a harmonizing addition that reproduces Mt. 23.23 (except from the last verb: *pareínai* in Luke, *aphiénai* in Matthew).[30] Besides, as Lk. 11.40 is at the centre of 39-41, the incriminated sentence is also at the centre of Mt. 23.23-24 (see rewriting below).

---

30. Several manuscripts share the same verb for Luke and Matthew.

This criterion is discussed in the manual of Vaganay–Amphoux, in a paragraph entitled 'Te recourse to literary criticism': 'To examine the *context*, we will choose the lesson which is in agreement with the particular tendencies of the book. For that, we will have to consider what is commonly called the practise of the writer, namely: his vocabulary, his language, his style, the manner of quoting and of *composing*, [the emphasis is mine] etc. Attention will have to be paid to the questions of rhythm, to the process of "oral style" (M. Jousse), perhaps better preserved in one lesson than other, which facilitates the memorisation of a didactic speech in the societies of oral culture.'[31]

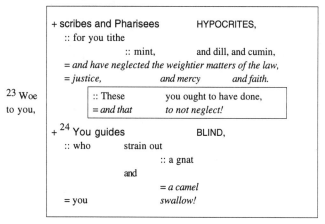

4.3. *Text to be Considered as an Omission (to be Kept)*

I will take the first example from the Old Testament. We know that Psalm 145 is an alphabetically acrostic poem (see illustration following). Yet there is a small irregularity in this formal structure of the alphabetical acrostic: in the Massoretic Text, the segment starting with nun is missing.

31. L. Vaganay, *Initiation à la critique textuelle du Nouveau Testament*, 2nd edn, completely rethought by C.-B. Amphoux (Paris: Cerf, 1986), p. 126.

I will extol you, my God and *King*, and BLESS your NAME **for ever and ever**.
² *Every* day I will BLESS you, and *praise* your NAME **for ever and ever**.

+ ³ Great is the Lord, and highly to be praised, and his greatness in unsearchable.

⁴ One age to an age shall laud your WORK, and they shall declare your prowesses.

− ⁵ The honour, the glory of your majesty, and the account of your wonders I will meditate.
− ⁶ And they shall say your terrible power, and your greatnesses I will recount.

⁷ They shall celebrate the fame of your abundant goodness, and sing your righteousness.

+ ⁸ Gracious and merciful is the Lord, slow to anger and great in faithfulness.

+ ⁹ Good is the Lord to **all**, and his compassion is OVER **all** HIS WORKS.

= ¹⁰ All your WORKS, Lord, shall thank you, and all your faithful shall BLESS you.

− ¹¹ They shall say the glory of your *KINGDOM*
  · of your prowesses
  they shall tell, ¹² to make known to the sons of Adam
  · your prowesses
− and the glory and the splendor of your *KINGDOM*.

= ¹³ Your *KINGDOM* is a kingdom of *every* **time**, your dominion for *all* **age and age**.

+ ¹³ᵇ [Veracious God in his words, faithful IN **all** HIS WORKS]

:: ¹⁴ The Lord upholds **all** who are falling, he raises up **all** who are bowed down.

− ¹⁵ Their eyes to you, **all** trust, and you give them their food in due season.
− ¹⁶ You open your hand, and you satisfy of *every* living one as he desires.

+ ¹⁷ Just the Lord in **all** his ways, and faithful IN **all** HIS WORKS.

− ¹⁸ Near the Lord to **all** who invoke him, to **all** who invoke him in truth.
− ¹⁹ He does the will of who fears him, he hears their cry and saves them.

:: ²⁰ The Lord preserves **all** who love him, but **all** the wicked he will destroy.

²¹ My mouth will say the *praise* of the Lord
  and **all** flesh will BLESS his holy NAME
  for ever and for ever.

This segment is found in a Hebrew manuscript, in the Septuagint, in the Syriac version and in the scroll of Psalms of Qumran. Several modern translations have integrated it in their text.[32]

Apart from external criteria, those of the manuscript attestations, one can use internal, structural, criteria; the first is the perfection of alphabetism. But one can add a further criterion: the regularity of the literary composition. This last criterion is nothing more than a more or less elaborate form of recourse to parallelism: more elaborate, or broadened, since the criterion of the *parallelismus membrorum* is limited to the level of the segment, whereas the criterion in question is on the level of the whole psalm. It is impossible to analyse here the composition of Psalm 145 to demonstrate that the verse nun has to be integrated to the poem for reasons of literary structure, or rhetorical analysis.[33]

The other examples are taken from the New Testament, and more precisely from Luke. It is impossible to discuss them in detail. It will suffice to say that the incriminated sentences are exactly at the centre of a composition. In the first example (Lk. 2.39-40):

---

[39] When they have performed everything, according to **the law of the Lord**

    . they returned into   Galilee,

    . to their own city,   Nazareth,

[as it was said by the prophet: | *"NAZARENE*   he will be **CALLED"**.]

    . [40] The child grew   and became strong

    . filled   with wisdom

and **the favour of God** was upon him.

---

32. In English, for example, the RSV; in French, Dhorme, Osty, BJ, TOB; in Arabic, the translation of Dar el-Machreq, Beirut, 1989; the Italian translation of the CEI on the contrary did not include it in its text and only mentions it in a note.

33. I have to be content with a reference to my study: 'Le Psaume 145'.

Apart from the symmetry of the conclusion of this sequence with its introduction (2.21-24), the fact that the adjunction is in the centre is a positive argument, since it is often the case that quotations of the Old Testament be at the centre of a composition of the New, as Lund had already observed.[34]

The other example is that of Lk. 23.17 which plays the role of hinge between the two parts of the Roman phase of the trial of Jesus. It is clear that these two parts are to be considered as one passage, since—among other things—their respective centres correspond to one another: 'I did not find this man guilty of any of your charges against him' (23.14e) and 'I have found him not guilty of death' (23.22e).

Note besides that the last member of the centre of the last part ('I will chastise him, and release him': 22f) reproduces the end of the first part ('Therefore, I will chastise him, and release him': 16), because it is a good example of Lund's law no. 4. Yet, the texts are so often of concentric composition that we could be tempted to consider v. 17 as integral part of the Lukan text. However, this rhetorical argument is only an argument among others. To be brief, another argument against the theory which makes Lk. 23.17 a harmonizing addition, is the precise comparison of this verse with its parallels in Matthew and Mark. The verse in Luke is so different from the other two that it is difficult to understand how it could be a harmonization:

Lk. 23.17:   ἀνάγκεν δὲ εἶχεν ἀπολύειν αὐτοῖς κατὰ ἑορτὴν ἕνα.
              Now there was necessity to release to them at the feast any one.
Mk 15.6:   Κατὰ δὲ ἑορτὴν ἀπέλυεν αὐτοῖς ἕνα δέσμιον
              Now at the feast he used to release to them any one prisoner,
              whom they asked.
Mt. 27.15:   κατὰ δὲ ἑορτὴν εἰώθει ὁ ἡγεμὼν
              ἀπολύειν ἕνα τῷ ὅν ἤθελον.
              Now at the feast the governor was accustomed
              to release for the crowd any one prisoner, whom they wanted.

---

34. *Chiasmus in the New Testament*, p. 41; it is his law no. 5 (see above, pp. 144-43).

¹³ Pilate, calling the chief priests, the rulers and the people,
¹⁴ said to them:

+ 'You brought me this man
  - as one who was perverting the people
      : and behold, I have examined him   *before you*:

      I did not find this man guilty of any of your charges against him.

      : ¹⁵ neither did   HEROD, for he sent him back *before us*.
  - Nothing deserving death has been done by him.
+ ¹⁶ Therefore, **I will chastise him, and release him.**'

[¹⁷ NOW HE WAS OBLIGED TO RELEASE SOMEONE AT THE FESTIVAL.]

¹⁸ They all cried out together:

+ 'Take   **THIS**
+ and release   ***Barabbas***'.
  : ¹⁹   ***That one*** *had been thrown into prison*
                   for an insurrection in the city *and for murder*.
– ²⁰ Again   Pilate *CRIED* to them   that he wanted to release Jesus.
  . ²¹ *But they*   *CRIED*   saying: '*Crucify, crucify him!*'.

²² A third time, he said to them:

      'Why, what evil has he done?
          I have found him not guilty of death.
      I will chastise him, and release him'.

  . ²³ *But they* insisted with great *CRIES* asking that he should be *crucified*,
                           and prevailed their *CRIES*.
– ²⁴ And   Pilate decided   that their demand should be granted.
  : ²⁵ He released
  :
                   that one *who had been thrown into prison*
                   for an insurrection and murder whom they asked for.
+ And   **JESUS**, he delivered up to their will.

To conclude the presentation of this last fruit of rhetorical analysis,
one can cite C. Amphoux once more: 'the major preoccupation of the
years to come may not be documentary, but literary'.³⁵

35. *Initiation à la critique textuelle*, p. 253.

Conclusion

When you ask a peasant to present the fruits of his field, it is always a hardship for him. How can he communicate his enthusiasm for them in so little time? He either chooses one, maximum two, obviously among the best, in having to the guest. Or he tries to present them all, but without time to do them justice. I have tried to conciliate these two possibilities, in the hope of not having provoked the nausea of the reader, but in having whetted his appetite, by indicating in which texts he can find those fruits, if and when he wants to taste them. I am well aware that the few examples that I have just provided are not sufficient to evaluate the potential of an entire field.

It is obvious that the criteria provided by rhetorical analysis for textual criticism, even if they can be interesting, are secondary fruits. On one hand, the aim of the methodology has never been to establish the text; on the other, in textual criticism, the criteria of composition cannot be the first. The same holds for the services that rhetorical analysis can provide for translation: even if it can be very useful, it is not the principal objective of this type of research. Textual criticism and translation are exegetical operations which have each their own procedures. If exegesis can be described as an ensemble of diverse operations which have to follow their own rules, one should not forget that the object of research, that is the text, is one; which amounts to saying that there is a sort of interdependence between the different exegetical operations and that the results of one of them can affect another.

There are two main fruits of rhetorical analysis. The first is to provide scientific procedures and criteria—linguistic ones—for *the delimitation of literary units* at various levels of organization of the text; it follows that the notion of 'context', fully employed in exegesis but often empirically, also acquires a truly scientific definition. At last, the principal fruit of rhetorical analysis is *to provide the conditions for an interpretation* which allows one to 'com-prehend', that is to grasp the significant relations between the literary units, at the different levels of structuration of the text, as if they had been 'com-posed' by the authors themselves.

CONCLUSION

When Greek rhetoric took shape more than two millennium and a half ago, followed by the Romans and their heirs in the western world up to the modern day, biblical rhetoric began to be discovered and described in its proper characteristics only two and a half centuries ago.

Despite the fact that predecessors were found and that he refers himself to Rabbi Azarias dei Rossi, Robert Lowth, the poetry lecturer at Oxford, is considered the father of poetical analysis of the Bible: of his *Lessons on the Sacred Poetry of the Hebrews*, published in 1753, was retained his 'parallelism of the members' which he classifies under synonymous, antithetic, and synthetic parallelism. A few years before in Germany, Johann-Albrecht Bengel signaled, laterally, the existence in the New Testament, of a double figure, the chiasm, direct and inverted (the parallel and concentric structures).

But Bengel and Lowth were only precursors. In 1820, taking inspiration from the intuitions of Bengel and mostly on the discovery of Lowth, John Jebb prolonged his observations of the latter to the New Testament. His major contribution was the discovery, on a large scale, of the inverted parallelism (the *chiasmus inversus* of Bengel), namely the concentric structure. Jebb organized the numerous examples he provided according to their length: distych, quatrains, stanzas of five or six verses, and more. In 1824 and 1825, Thomas Boys spread the discovery of Jebb to whole texts, epistles and psalms, and from poetry to prose. Boys is the first to attempt to establish a catalogue, already rich, of marks of composition, 'leading terms' and 'final terms' in particular.

Almost entirely covered by the great wave of historical criticism, the enquiries of rhetorical type would carry on, but more slowly than before and often on avenues encumbered by the categories of Graeco-Roman rhetoric: in Germany with, among others, David Müller, Johannes Zenner, in England with John Forbes and Ethelbert Bullinger, and in France with Albert Condamin, Marcel Jousse, in the

United States at last, and more productively, with George B. Gray and the Frenchman, Charles Souvay.

It was not before the American, Nils W. Lund, in the 1930s and 40s, that rhetorical analysis renewed the links with the great founders of the preceding century. The great merit of Lund was to give new impetus to research on the way to an empirical description, free from the false guide of Graeco-Roman rhetoric, in particular the stanza theory. Lund is the first to show clearly how biblical rhetoric is distinct from Greek rhetoric. He is also the first to attempt to establish a catalogue of proper organization of laws of the biblical texts. The current explosion of research certainly takes its origin with his efforts.

At the term, provisional by definition, of this bi-centenary story, the need to tidy up the rhetorical workshop was greatly felt: it was necessary to inventory, test, sort, and label and file the tools thus accumulated by the pioneers. It was also necessary to show that the texts are organized on several levels, from the segment to the book. From the start, it was obvious that the Hebraic verse was composed of either three, two, or even one member; the projection of this observation at the levels immediately superior gives vigour and flexibility to the system. A univocal and transparent terminology was needed to designate on one hand the textual units at the different levels of their organization (members, segments, pieces, parts, passages, sequences, sections, book), on the other the various marks of composition (initial, final, extreme, median and central terms). And at last, it was necessary to further the art of rewriting, to ease the visual identification of the symmetries.[1]

There remains a question which has often been asked for a long time, which I would not avoid at the end of this book. A serious question, since it concerns the very existence of the said 'biblical' rhetoric. Is it more fitting to speak of Hebrew rhetoric, biblical rhetoric, semitic rhetoric, or even more broadly of oral rhetoric?

Hebrew or Biblical Rhetoric

One will recall that the professed aim of Lowth was to prove that the characteristics of the poetical books of the Hebrew Bible were also found in the prophets. The discourse of Jebb was then to broaden the

---

1. The reader probably felt the need to write over, or even colour, the rudimentary rewritings of the first half of this work, which have always been reproduced without modifications.

field of application to the New Testament, and that of Boys to the texts
in prose, those of the Old Testament as well as those of the New. It is
now an established fact that the Greek texts, of the Old Testament as
well as the New, even if they could have been influenced, more or
less, by Greek rhetoric, belong very clearly to the laws of composition of another rhetoric, which we are in the position to call biblical.

Hebrew and Greek Rhetoric

Lund opposed Hebraic rhetoric which he found in use in the Greek
texts of the New Testament, to classical rhetoric, that of the Greek and
Romans.

However, one should note that, in order to analyse and describe the
texts of the Bible, the founders of rhetorical analysis of the eighteenth
century used the tools, and terminology, of classical rhetoric. Thus
Schöttgen[2] calls the first part of his dissertation *De Exergasia Sacra*:
'*de exergasia in genere*'. He first defines *exergasia*, after all the rhetoricians, as the 'conjunction of two whole sentences sharing the same
meaning', and he then lists all the diverse appellations of this phenomenon: *expolitio, isocolon, pleonasmus, tautologia*. If this parallelism has, since antiquity, received these various names, it is because
they are in Greek and Latin texts and are not proper to biblical literature.[3]

In the following century, Jebb provided a number of Greek and
Latin examples of chiasm (of crossed symmetries); he gives the
diverse classical appellations of this figure of style: *hustereusis, chiasmus, synchysis, epanodos*.[4] But he also immediately stressed the specificity of Biblical rhetoric: 'Some are disposed to maintain that it is
purely classical; and it does *sometimes* occur in Greek and Latin
authors; but it is so prevalent, and so peculiarly marked, in the Sacred
Volume, that it may be justly accounted a Hebraism; and, as I am disposed to believe, a feature of Hebrew poetry'.[5]

---

2.   *Horae Hebraicae et Talmudicae*, I, pp. 1263-64.
3.   See J. Welch, 'Chiasmus in Ancient Greek and Latin Literatures', in *Chiasmus in Antiquity*, pp. 250-68; see also J.D. Denniston, *Greek Style Prose* (Oxford:
Clarendon Press, 1952).
4.   *Sacred Literature*, pp. 69-70.
5.   *Sacred Literature*, p. 65. More recently, the existence of these forms was
found in texts of Graeco-Roman antiquity, but also in the Renaissance. See E.M.
Duval, 'Panurge, Perplexity, and the Ironic Design of Rabelais's Tiers Livre',

Semitic Rhetoric

If it is at all possible to find some of the figures of biblical rhetoric in the texts of Graeco-Roman antiquity, it is mostly in the other semitic literature that they are predominant. Recently, Ugaritic texts[6] have been studied from the rhetorical point of view by J.W. Welch.[7] Despite the fact that this study is only in its infancy, the results are very demonstrative. A single example will be enough to illustrate this point: the rewriting of KTU 1.2.IV (UT 68; apart from the intro-duction and the conclusion the text of which is damaged: see p. 357)[8] shows, without the need of any explanation, the parallel construction of lines 7-15 and 16-26 of our rewriting and the concentric composi-tion of lines 2-6 and 28-31.[9]

Even more ancient, the Akkadian texts,[10] also show construction along the same lines:[11] as in the Ugaritic texts, the parallelism of the members is also very strong. Four short texts (of the size of a part),[12] of identical function, the proclamation of the divine name, allow us to

Renaissance Quarterly 35 (1982), pp. 381-400; Duval refers to A. Fowler, *Tri-umphal Forms: Structural Patterns in Elizabethan Poetry* (Cambridge: 1970), which in turn summarizes the demonstrations of C. Whitman for the *Iliad*, P. Maury for the *Eglogues* of Virgil, and B. Otis for the *Eneid*.

6.   Ugarit was an important center of old Phoenicia, beyond the northern border of Lebanon, in actual Syria. The ugaritic texts found belong to the thirteenth or fourteenth century before Christ. They are the oldest testimonies of the west semitic.

7.   'Chiasmus in Ugaritic', *UF* 6 (1974), pp. 421-36; reproduced and developed in J.W. Welch (ed.), *Chiasmus in Antiquity*, pp. 36-49.

8.   This text was analysed, independently, with the same conclusion by J. Welch, *Chiasmus in Antiquity*, p. 39; Welch only gives the general articulation and the editing, slightly eroneous, of our lines 1-6 (p. 38): he integrates our line 7 to the concentric figure of 2-6 in considering that 1 and 7 are the extremities of the figure, whereas in fact 7 corresponds to 16, as initial terms of two parallel units 7-15 and 16-26.

9.   The translation of the illustration was done thanks to the cooperation of Jean-Michel de Tarragon of the Ecole biblique of Jerusalem.

10.   Akkadian, with its Babylonian and Assyrian variations, was spoken and written from 2500 before Christ.

11.   Condamin ends his *Poèmes de la Bible* with the presentation of a few Babylonian and Assyrian stanzas (pp. 268-76).

12.   Text 1: in *RA* 22 (1925), p. 170. Text 2: in the same periodical *RA* 75 (1981), p. 230. Text 3: in *RA* 75 (1981), p. 126. Text 4: in *RA* 75 (1981), p. 108. All these translations have been verified and improved thanks to the kind cooperation of P. Marcel Sigrist of the Biblical School of Jerusalem.

see the operation of the passage from parallelism to concentrism (see
p. 358). The first text is totally parallel, 'the goddess' praised in the
first piece is named, at the same position and with the same syntactic
function, in the second piece; in the second text, the name of the goddess is found between two parallel pieces, the composition of the
whole becoming concentric; same phenomenon in the third text, but
with a frame which strengthens the concentrism (note the word
'heroic' which adorns the name of the goddess Ishtar at the center
which corresponds to the two adjectives with which the extremities
start);[13] finally the last text offers a concentric construction of the
same type as the preceding one. Even if the number of Akkadian texts
studied from the point of view of rhetorical analysis is limited,[14] there
is no doubt that they obey rules analogous to those of the biblical
texts.

On the other hand, in much more recent texts than those of the
Bible, those of the Arabo-Islamic tradition, similar phenomena are
also found. Among many other texts of the Muslim tradition (*Hadîth-s*
or deeds of the Muhammed or his followers) analysed during a seminar of the Institute of Islamo-Christian Studies of the University Saint-
Joseph of Beirut,[15] two short texts (see p. 359) will be enough to show
their kinship of construction with those of the Bible: for an identical
content, the first is of concentric composition, the other of parallel
composition.

Oral Rhetoric
It has been long since it was found that the parallelism of the members
was not exclusive to the Bible or to the semitic world, but that it is
found in several poetic traditions,[16] in particular in China,[17] and in

13. Another example of the third law of Lund. The symmetry of the two extreme
members bring to light the meaning of the last line; the correction proposed by
B. von Groneberg, 'Philologische bearbeitung des Agugaya-hymnus', *RA* 75
(1981), p. 126 (read na instead of la) is therefore to be discarded. It is another example of the importance given to rhetorical phenomena.
14. See R.F. Smith, 'Chiasm in Sumero-Akkadian', in *Chiasmus in Antiquity*,
pp. 17-35.
15. R. Meynet, L. Pouzet, N. Farouki and A. Sinno, *Tarîqah al-taḥlîl al-balāġî
wa l-tafsîr* (Rhetoric and Hermeneutic Method: Analysis of Texts of the Bible and of
the Muslim Tradition) (Beirut, 1993); we thank our colleagues for having allowed us
to reproduce the analysis of these two texts.
16. See R. Jakobson, 'Grammatical Parallelism and its Russian Facet', *Language*

many popular productions of oral civilizations.[18] Even before Lowth, Cajanus and Julsenius had already noted that parallelism governed Finnish folkloric poetry as well as that of the Bible.[19] Since then, the same observations were spread to other people of oral tradition, Ostiaks and Vogouls, Turks, Mongols,[20] Russians.[21] All these studies, however, remain most of the time on the level of the most elementary units, segments and pieces, and concern parallel constructions only. As for the extent of the phenomenon, 'our information about the distribution of parallelism in the folklore of the world and its character in various languages is still sparse and fragmentary'.[22]

Despite belonging to the Greek tradition, the homeric poems also have orality to answer to: the analysis of the famous description of the shield of Achilles, the last one hundred and fifty verses of Song xviii of the *Iliad*, show that, if parallelism of the members is weaker than in biblical poetry, probably because of the constraints of the metres, the construction of each passage as well as that of the whole seems nonetheless very similar to the construction of semitic texts.[23] Should we attribute this kinship to orality? Or to the geographic proximity, insofar as the homeric texts would have their origins in Asia Minor? Nothing, it seems, in the current state of research, would allow us to conclude.

These few openings prove that, if the field of investigation is not totally virgin territory, it remains that the work of clearing has barely started and that many treasures await discovery. As for biblical exegesis, the little that was done so far leaves us hopeful of further harvests, for a better understanding of the Word of God.

---

42 (1966), pp. 399-429 (reproduced in *Selected Writings*, III: *Poetry of Grammar and Grammar of Poetry*) [The Hague, Paris and New York: Mouton, 1981], pp. 98-135; we make reference to this edition).

17. R. Jakobson, 'Grammatical Parallelism', pp. 100-102.

18. R. Jakobson, 'Grammatical Parallelism', p. 103.

19. E. Cajanus, *Linguarum ebraeae et finnicae convenentia* (Åbo 1697); D. Julsenius, 'Oratio de convenentia linguae Fennicae com Hebraea et Graeca', *Schwedisch bibliotek* I, 1728.

20. R. Jakobson, 'Grammatical Parallelism', pp. 104-106.

21. R. Jakobson, 'Grammatical Parallelism', pp. 106-107.

22. R. Jakobson, 'Grammatical Parallelism', p. 103.

23. R. Meynet, 'Analyse rhétorique du Bouclier d'Achille', *Strumenti critici* 59 (1989), pp. 93-115.

UGARITIC TEXT   KTU 1.2.IV

AND KHOTAR-KHASIS ANSWERS: 1

+ I say to you	O Prince	**BAAL** I repeat to you O Rider of the Clouds	2
. This is your enemy	O	**BAAL**	3
. This is your enemy	you will strike him		4
. You will slaughter	your adversary		5
+ You will reclaim	your eternal kingship	your perpetual sovereignty	6

KHOTAR FASHIONS TWO MACES   AND HE PROCLAIMS THEIR TWO NAMES: 7

. Your name is YAGRUSH		YAGRUSH overthrows	**Yam**	8
. Overthrows Yam from his throne		**Nahar** from the seat of his domination		9
. May you fly from the hand of	**BAAL**	like a sparrowhawk through his fingers		10
. Strike the SHOULDER of the Prince	**Yam**	between the TWO ARMS the Judge	**Nahar**	11
: The mace flies from the hand of	**BAAL**	like a sparrowhawk through his fingers		12
: Strikes the SHOULDER of the Prince	**Yam**	between the TWO ARMS the Judge	**Nahar**	13
: Strong	is	**Yam**	he does NOT falter	14
: his articulations do NOT weaken		his face is NOT undone		15

KHOTAR FASHIONS TWO MACES   AND HE PROCLAIMS THEIR TWO NAMES: 16

. Your name is AYYAMUR		AYYAMUR expels	**Yam**	17
. Expels Yam from his throne	**Nahar**	from the seat of his domination		18
. May you fly from the hand of	**BAAL**	like a sparrowhawk through hisfingers		19
. Strike the SKULL of the Prince	**Yam**	between the TWO EYES the Judge	**Nahar**	20
That may fall	**Yam**	and crumple to the ground		21
: The mace flies from the hand of	**BAAL**	like a sparrowhawk through his fingers		22
: Strikes the SKULL of the Prince	**Yam**	between the TWO EYES the Judge	**Nahar**	23
: He falls	**Yam**	and crumples to the ground		24
: His articulations weaken		his face is undone		25
Baal drags and dismembers	**Yam**	he kills off the Judge	**Nahar**	26

BY (his) NAME, AKHTART CALLS (him):   27

+ Scatter him O very powerful	**BAAL** scatter him O Rider of the Clouds		28
. Because he is our prisoner	the Prince	**Yam**	29
he is our prisoner	the Judge	**Nahar**	30
+ May he leave [. . .]	may scatter him the powerful **BAAL**		31

AKKADIAN TEXTS

1.

| + Sing | **the goddess,** | the most imposing | of the goddesses |
| . Be glorified | the mistress of the people, | the greatest | of the Igugu. |

| + Sing | **ISHTAR,** | the most imposing | of the goddesses |
| . Be glorified | the mistress of the people, | the greatest | of the Igugu. |

2.

| + Combat is her feast | to bound into the fray |
| . As soon as she seizes the fire | the warriors among the fiercest tremble, |

ISHTAR

| + Combat is her feast | to bound into the fray |
| . As soon as she seizes the fire tremble. | the warriors among the fiercest |

3.

+ **Impetuously**   [her   DEEDS]
    : the strongest of the gods and the most vigorous
       – to make her might resplendent
         . she always stands majestically

ISHTAR   the heroic

    : the strongest of the gods and the most vigorous
       – to make her might resplendent
         . she always stands majestically
+ **Elevated** are   her great   DEEDS.

4.

+ **I glorify**

                    the greatest among the gods
                    the heroic
                    the eldest daughter of   Ningal
        :   her might!

I praise   her name   ISHTAR!

                    the greatest among the gods
                    the heroic
                    the eldest daughter of   Ningal
        :   her might
+ **I repeat!**

ISLAMIC TEXT,   Saḥîḥ 24,26

[. . .] the Prophet said:

'When from the house of	a woman her husband	nourished (a poor) without extravagance,
=	**to her**	**her reward**
:	*to him*	*equally*

	+ TO THE STEWARD	the same

:	*to him*	*because*	*he earned it*
=	**to her**	**because**	**she dispensed of it**'.

[. . .] the Prophet said:

'When from her house	a woman	has dispensed food without extravagance,
=	**to her**	**her reward**
	and	
:	*to the husband*	*because he earned it*
	and	
+	TO THE STEWARD	the same'.

BIBLIOGRAPHY

In addition to the titles quoted in the work, this bibliography counts some references to rhetorical studies that were called upon in the course of the research. The bibliography of J. Welch (ed.) (*Chiasmus in Antiquity*) only gives the titles of books (pp. 272-86); but he also provides an index where research including articles on Egyptian, Sumerian–Akkadian, Ugaritic and Mormon texts is included (pp. 287-97) and also on the Bible (following the order of the biblical books; pp. 297-352); this index reproduces and completes that of A. di Marco (*Il chiasmo nella Bibbia*).

Alonso Schökel, L., *Estudios de poetica hebrea* (Barcelona: Juan Flors, 1963).
Alonso Schökel, L., and A. Strus, *Nomen–Omen: La stylistique sonore des noms propres dans le Pentateuque* (AnBib, 80; Rome: Biblical Institute Press, 1978).
—'Salmo 122: Canto al nombre de Jerusalén', *Bib* 61 (1980), pp. 234-50.
Angénieux, J., 'Structure du Cantique des Cantiques', *ETL* 41 (1965), pp. 96-142.
—'Les différents types de structure du Pater dans l'histoire de son exégèse', *ETL* 46 (1970), pp. 40-77.
Astruc, J., *Conjectures sur les mémoires originaux, dont il paroit que Moyse s'est servi pour composer le Livre de la Genèse, avec des remarques, qui appuient ou qui éclaircissent les Conjectures* (Brussels: Chez Fricx, 1753).
Auffret, P., *Hymnes d'Egypte et d'Israël: Etudes de structures littéraires* (OBO, 34; Fribourg/ Göttingen: Editions universitaires, 1981).
—*La Sagesse a bâti sa maison: Etudes de structures littéraires* (OBO, 49; Göttingen: Vandenhoek & Ruprecht, 1982).
—'Note sur la structure littéraire de Lc 1,68-79', *NThS* 24 (1977–78), pp. 248-58.
—'Pivot Pattern: Nouveaux exemples', *VT* 28 (1978), pp. 103-104.
Avishur, Y, 'Studies of Stylistic Features Common to the Phoenician Inscriptions and the Bible', *UF* 8 (1976), pp. 1-22.
—*Stylistic Studies of Word-Pairs in Biblical and Ancient Semitic Literature* (Kevelaer: Butzon & Bercker, 1984).
Azarias, R., *Meor Enajjim* ('The light of the eyes') (Mantova, 1573).
Bailey, K.E., *Poet and Peasant & Through Peasant Eyes: A Literary Approach to the Parables in Luke* (Grand Rapids, MI: Eerdmans, 1983).
Baker, A., 'Parallelism: England's Contribution to Biblical Studies', *CBQ* 35 (1973), pp. 429-40.
Barre, L.M., 'Recovering the Literary Structure of Psalm XV', *VT* 34 (1984), pp. 207-10.
Basset, S.E., 'Husteron Proteron Hômericôs (Cicero, Att. 1,16,1)', *HSCP* 31 (1920), pp. 39-62.
Beaucamp, E., *Le Psautier* (Paris: Gabalda, 1979).
Beauchamp, P., *Création et Séparation: Etude exégétique du chapitre premier de la Genèse* (Bibliothèque de sciences religieuses; Paris: Aubier Montaigne, 1969).

—'Quelques faits d'écriture dans la poésie biblique', *RSR* 61 (1973), pp. 127-38.

—*Parler d'Ecritures Saintes* (Paris: Seuil, 1987).

Bengel, J.A., *Gnomon novi testamenti* (Tubingen: Io. Henri Philippi Schranii, 1742); ET (trans. C.T. Lewis and R. Vincent; 2 vols.; Philadelphia, 1860–62).

Berlin, A., *The Dynamics of Biblical Parallelism* (Bloomington, IN: Indiana University Press, 1985).

Bertman, S., 'Symmetrical Design in the Book of Ruth', *JBL* 84 (1965), pp. 165-68.

—'Structural Symmetry at the end of the Odyssey', *GRBS* 9 (1968), pp. 115-23.

Black, E., *Rhetorical Criticism: A Study in Method* (New York: Macmillan, 1965).

Blayney, B., *Jeremiah and Lamentations* (Oxford: 1784; London: Thomas Tegg & Son, 3rd edn, 1836).

Bligh, J., *Chiastic Analysis of the Epistle to the Hebrews* (Heythrop College Oxon: The Athenaeum Press, 1966).

Boadt, L., 'The ABBA Chiasm of Identical Roots in Ezechiel', *VT* 25 (1975), pp. 693-99.

Boismard, M.-E., and A. Lamouille, *La Vie des évangiles: Initiation à la critique des textes* (Initiations; Paris: Cerf, 1980).

Boccacio, P., 'I termini contrari come espressioni della totalità in ebraico', *Bib* 33 (1952), pp. 179-80.

Bonamartini, U., 'L'epesegesi nella S. Scrittura', *Bib* 6 (1925), pp. 424-44.

Booth, W.C., 'The Revival of Rhetoric', in M. Steinman, Jr (ed.), *New Rhetorics* (New York: Charles Scribner's Sons, 1967), pp. 2-15.

Bossuyt, Ph., and J. Radermakers, *Jésus, Parole de la grâce selon Saint Luc* (Brussels: Institut d'Etudes Théologiques, 1981).

Boulton, N., *The Anatomy of Poetry* (London: Routledge, 1953).

Bovati, P., *Ristabilire la giustizia: Procedure, vocabolario, orientamenti* (AnBib, 110; Rome: Biblical Institute Press, 1986); ET *Re-Establishing Justice: Legal Terms, Concepts and Procedures in the Hebrew Bible* (JSOTSup, 105, Sheffield: JSOT Press, 1994).

Bovati, P., and R. Meynet, *Le Livre du prophète Amos* (Rhétorique biblique, 2; Paris: Cerf, 1994).

—*Il libro del profeta Amos* (Retorica biblica, 2; Rome: Edizioni Dehoniane 1995).

Boys, T., *Tactica Sacra: An Attempt to Develop, and to Exhibit to the Eye by Tabular Arrangements, a General Rule of Composition Prevailing in the Holy Scriptures* (London: T. Hamilton, 1824).

—*A Key to the Book of Psalms* (London: L.B. Seeley & Sons, 1825).

Briggs, C., *Biblical Study* (New York, 1883).

—'Hebrew Poetry', *Hebraica* 2 (1885–86), pp. 164-70.

—*General Introduction to the Study of the Holy Scripture* (New York: Charles Scribner's Sons, rev. edn, 1900).

—*The Book of Psalms* (ICC; Edinburgh: T. & T. Clark, 1952).

Bryant, D.C., 'Rhetoric: Its Function and Scope', in J. Schwartz and J. Rycenga (eds.), *The Province of Rhetoric* (New York: Donald Press Co, 1965), pp. 3-36.

—*The Rhetorical Idiom* (Ithaca: Clarendon Press, 1925; New York: Cornell University Press, 1958).

Bullinger, E.W., *A Key to the Psalms being a Tabular Arrangement, by which the Psalms are Exhibited to the Eye according to a General Rule of Composition Prevailing in the Holy Scripture by the Late Rev. Thomas Boys*, (London, 1890).

—*The Book of Job* (London: Eyre & Spottiswoode, 1903).

Burke, K., *A Rhetoric of Motives* (Englewood Cliffs, NJ: Prentice-Hall, 1950).

Burney, C.F., *The Poetry of our Lord: An Examination of the Formal Elements of Hebrew Poetry in the Discourses of Jesus Christ* (Oxford: Clarendon Press, 1925).

Bussby, F., 'Bishop Jebb: A Neglected Biblical Scholar', *ET* 60 (1948–49), p. 193.

Caquot, A., *et al.*, *Textes ougaritiques* (LAPO; Paris: Cerf, 1974).

Cajanus, E., *Linguarum ebraeae et finnicae convenentia* (Abo, 1697).

Ceresko, A.R., 'The A:B::B:A Word Pattern in Hebrew and North-Western Semitic with Special Reference to the Book of Job', *UF* 7 (1975), pp. 73-88.

—'The Function of Chiasmus in Hebrew Poetry', *CBQ* 40 (1978), pp. 1-10.

—'A Rhetorical Analysis of David's "Boast" (1 Sam 17:34-37): Some Reflections on Method' *CBQ* 47 (1985), pp. 58-74.

Clark, D.J., 'Criteria for Identifying Chiasm', *LB* 5 (1975), pp. 63-72.

Clifford, R.J., 'Rhetorical Criticism in the Exegesis of Hebrew Poetry', in P. Achtemeier (ed.), *Society of Biblical Literature 1980 Seminar Papers* (Chico, CA: Scholar Press, 1980), pp. 21-28.

Clines, D.J.A., *et al.*, *Art and Meaning: Rhetoric in Biblical Literature* (JSOTSup, 19; Sheffield: JSOT Press, 1982).

Collins, J.J., 'Chiasmus, the "ABA" Pattern and the Text of Paul', in *Studiorum Paulinorum Congressus Internationalis Catholicus* (AnBib, 17-18; Rome: Biblical Institute Press, 1963), pp. 575-83.

Collins, T., *Line-Forms in Hebrew Poetry: A Grammatical Approach to the Stylistic Study of the Hebrew Prophets* (Rome: Biblical Institute Press, 1978).

Condamin, A., 'Un chant d'imprécation (Ps CVIII, ebr. 109)', *Revue Théologique Fran-çaise* (1901), pp. 246-52.

—'Les chants lyriques des prophètes, Strophes et choeurs', *RB* (1901), pp. 1-26.

—*Le Livre d'Isaïe* (Paris: Victor Lecoffre, 1905).

—*Le Livre de Jérémie* (Paris: Gabalda, 1920).

—*Poèmes de la Bible, avec une introduction sur la strophique hébraïque* (Paris: Beauchesne, 1933).

Coulot, C., 'Propositions pour une structuration du livre d'Amos au niveau rédactionnel', *RevSR* (1977), pp. 169-86.

Craven, T., 'Artistry and Faith in the Book of Judith', *Semeia* 8 (1977), pp. 75-101.

Culley, R., 'Structural Analysis: Is it Done with Mirrors?', *Int* 28 (1974), pp. 167-71.

Dahood, M., 'A New Metrical Pattern in Biblical Poetry', *CBQ* 29 (1967), pp. 574-79.

—'Chiasm in Job', in H.N. Bream (ed.), *A Light unto my Path* (Philadelphia: Temple University Press, 1974), pp. 119-30.

—'The Chiastic Breakup in Isaiah 58.7', *Bib* 57 (1976), pp. 105.

—'Chiastic Word Patterns in Hebrew', *CBQ* 38 (1976), pp. 303-11.

—*Psalms* (AB, 16, 17, 17A; Garden City, NY: Doubleday, 1965–66, 1968, 1970).

Denniston, J.D., *Greek Style Prose* (Oxford: Clarendon Press, 1952).

Des Places, E., *La Religion grecque* (Paris: A. & J. Picard, 1961).

—*Une Formule platonicienne de récurrence* (Collection d'Etudes anciennes; Paris: Les Belles Lettres, 1929).

Devey, J., 'The Literary Structure of the Controversy Stories in Mark 2:1–3:6', *JBL* 92 (1973), pp. 394-401.

Dhorme, E., *La Poésie biblique* (Paris: Grasset, 1931).

Di Marco, A., *Il chiasmo nella Bibbia: Contributi di stilistica strutturale* (Torino: Marietti, 1980).

Du Contant de La Molette, *Traité sur la poésie et la musique des Hébreux* (Paris: Moutard, 1781).

Duval, E.M., 'Panurge, Perplexity, and the Ironic Design of Rabelais's Tiers Livre', *Renaissance Quarterly* 35 (1982), pp. 381-400.

Ehlen, A.J., *The Poetic Structure of a Hodayah from Qumran* (Harvard PhD Dissertation, 1970).

Ernesti, J.C.T., *Lexicon technologiae Graecorum rhetoricae* (Leipzig, 1795).

Exum, J.C., 'The Structure of Paul's Speech to the Ephesian Elders (Acts 20.18-35)', *CBQ* 29 (1967), pp. 233-36.

—'A Literary and Structural Analysis of the Song of Songs', *ZAW* 85 (1973), pp. 47-79.

—'Aspects of Symmetry and Balance in the Samson Saga', *JSOT* 19 (1981), pp. 3-29.

—'Of Broken Pots, Fluttering Birds and Visions in the Night: Extended Simile and Poetic Technique in Isaiah', *CBQ* 43 (1981), pp. 331-52.

Fédry, J., 'L'Afrique entre écriture et oralité', *Etudes* 346 (1977), pp. 581-600.

Fenton, J.C., 'Inclusio and Chiasmus in Matthew', *StEv* 73 (1959), pp. 174-79.

Fessard, G., 'Une nouvelle psychologie du langage. Le Style oral, du P. Marcel Jousse', *Etudes* 192 (1927), pp. 145-62.

Fitzgerald, R.P., 'The Place of Robert Lowth's De Sacra Poesi Haebraeorum in Eighteenth Century Criticism' (PhD Dissertation, University of Iowa, 1964).

Fleisch, H., 'Etudes de psychologie linguistique' [on M. Jousse, *Le style oral*], *RevPhil* (1931), pp. 623-41; (1932), pp. 147-83.

Fokkelman, J.P., *Narrative Art and Poetry in the Books of Samuel: A Full Interpretation Based on Stylistic and Structural Analyses* (SSN, 20; Assen: Van Gorcum, 1981).

Fontanier, P., *Les Figures du discours* (Paris: Flammarion, 1968 [1818–30]).

Forbes, J., *The Symmetrical Structure of Scripture: Or the Principles of Scripture Paralleism Exemplified in an Analysis of the Decalogue, the Sermon on the Mount and other Passages of the Sacred Writings* (Edinburgh: T. & T. Clark, 1854).

—*Analytical Commentary on the Epistle to the Romans Tracing the Train of Thought by the Aid of Parallelism* (Edinburgh: T. & T. Clark, 1868).

Fowler, A., *Triumphal Forms: Structural Patterns in Elizabethan Poetry* (Cambridge, 1970).

Freedman, D.N., 'Archaic Forms in Early Hebrew Poetry', *ZAW* 72 (1960), pp. 101-107.

—'On Method in Biblical Studies: the OT', *Int* 17 (1963), pp. 308-18.

—'The Structure of Job 3', *Bib* 49 (1968), pp. 503-508.

—'The Structure of Psalm 137', in H. Goedicke (ed.), *Near Eastern Studies in Honor of W.F. Albright* (Baltimore: The John Hopkins University Press, 1971), pp. 187-205.

—'Acrostics and Metrics in Hebrew Poetry', *HTR* 65 (1972), pp. 367-92.

Freedman, D.N., Preface to G. Gray, *The Forms of Hebrew Poetry* (New York: Ktav, repr. 1972 [1915]).

—'Pottery, Poetry and Prophecy: An Essay on Biblical Poetry', *JBL* 96 (1977), pp. 5-26.

—'Psalm 113 and the Song of Hannah', *ErIs* 14 (1978), pp. 56-69.

—*Pottery, Poetry and Prophecy: Studies in Early Hebrew Poetry* (Winona Lake, IN: Eisenbrauns, 1980).

Freedman, D.N., and C.F. Hyland, 'Psalm 29: A Structural Analysis', *HTR* 66 (1973), pp. 237-56.

Gaechter, P., 'Semitic Literary Forms in the Apocalypse and their Import', *TS* 8 (1947), pp. 547-73.

Galbiati, E., *La struttura letteraria dell'Esodo* (Rome: Alba, 1956).

Garcia Lopez, F., *Analyse littéraire de Deutéronome V–XI* (Rome: Biblical Institute Press, 1978).

Geller, S.A., *Parallelism in Early Biblical Poetry* (HSM, 20; Missoula, MT: Scholars Press, 1979).

George, A., *Lecture de l'Evangile selon St Luc* (Lyon: Profac, 1971).

Gevirtz, S., *Patterns in the Early Poetry of Israel* (Chicago: University of Chicago Press, 1963).

Girard, M., 'L'unité de composition de Jn 6, au regard de l'analyse structurelle', *EeT(O)* 13 (1982), pp. 79-110.

—*Les Psaumes: Analyse structurelle et interprétation*. I. *Ps 1–50* (Montreal: Bellarmin; Paris: Cerf, 1984).

—*Les Psaumes redécouverts: De la structure au sens*. II. *Ps 51–100*, III. *Ps 101–150* (Montreal: Bellarmin, 1994).

Glass, S., *Philologia Sacra* (Leipzig, 1725).

Glasson, T.F., 'Chiasmus in St Matthew VII, 6', *ET* 68 (1956–57), p. 302.

Goulder, M.D., 'The Chiastic Structure of the Lucan Journey', *SE* II, (1964), pp. 195-202.

Gray, G.B., *The Forms of Hebrew Poetry* (London, 1915; New York: Ktav, 1972).

Greenwood, D., 'Rhetorical Criticism and Formgeschichte: Some Methodological Considerations' *JBL* 89 (1970), pp. 418-26.

Groneberg, B. von, 'Philologische Bearbeitung des Aguhaya-hymnus', *RA* 75 (1981), pp. 107-34.

Hakham, A., *T^erē 'Aśar* (Jerusalem: Mossad Harav Kook, 1973).

Henry, A., *Eloquence et poésie des livres saints* (Paris: Lecoffre, 1849).

Harper, W.R., *A Critical and Exegetical Commentary on Amos and Hosea* (ICC; Edinburgh: T. & T. Clark, 1905, 1979).

Herder, J.G., *The Spirit of Hebrew Poetry* (trans. J. Marsh; Burlington: Edward Smith, 1833).

—*Histoire de la poésie des Hébreux* (trans. A. de Carlowitz; Paris: Didier, 1855).

Holladay, W.L., 'Chiasmus: The Key of Hosea XII,3-6', *VT* 16 (1966), pp. 53-64.

—*The Architecture of Jeremiah 1–20* (Lewisburg, PA: Bucknell University Press, 1976).

Holman, J., 'The Structure of Psalm CXXXIX', *VT* 21 (1971), pp. 298-310.

Holmgren, F., 'Chiastic Structure in Isaiah LI,I-II', *VT* 19 (1969), pp. 196-201.

Honeyman, A.M., '*Merismus* in Biblical Literature', *JBL* 71 (1952), pp. 11-18.

Hurvitz, A., 'Chiasmus anachronicus', in B. Uffenheimer (ed.), *Lingua Hebraica Biblica* (Univ. Tel-Aviv, 1972).

Jacquet, L., *Les Psaumes et le Coeur de l'homme: Etude textuelle, littéraire et doctrinale* (Gembloux: Duculot, I. Ps 1–50; II. Ps 51–100: 1977; III. Ps 101–150, 1979).

Jakobson, R., 'Grammatical Parallelism and its Russian Facet', *Languages* 42 (1966), pp. 399-429; reprinted in *Selected Writings*. III. *Poetry of Grammar and Grammar of Poetry* (The Hague/Paris/New York: Mouton, 1981), pp. 98-135.

—*Essais de linguistique générale* (Paris: Seuil, 1963).

—*Questions de poétique* (Paris: Seuil, 1973).

Jakson, J.J., and M. Kessler, *Rhetorical Criticism: Essays in Honor of James Muilenburg* (Theological Monograph Series, 1; Pittsburgh: Pickwick, 1974).

Jakson, M., 'Rhetorical Criticism and Jer VII,1–VIII,3', *VT* 30 (1980), pp. 20-26.

Jeanne d'Arc, Sr, *Les Pélerins d'Emmaüs* (Paris: Cerf, 1977).

Jebb, J., *Sacred Literature Comprising a Review of the Principles of Composition Laid Down by the Late Robert Lowth, Lord Bishop of London in his Praelectiones and*

Isaiah: And an Application of the Principles so Reviewed, to the Illustration of the New Testament in a Series of Critical Observations on the Style and Structure of that Sacred Volume (London: Cadell & Davis, 1820).

—*Correspondence with Alexander Knox* (ed. C. Forster; 2 vols., Philadelphia, 1834).

Jeremias, J., 'Chiasmus in den Paulusbriefen', *ZNW* 49-50 (1958), pp. 145-56.

Jousse, M., 'Le Style oral rythmique et mnémotechnique chez les verbo-moteurs', *ArPh* 2.4 (Paris 1925); reprinted *Le Style oral* (Paris: Fondation Marcel Jousse/Flammarion, 1981).

—*Rythmo-mélodisme et rythmo-typographisme pour le Style oral palestinien* (Paris: Librairie orientaliste Paul Goethner, 1952).

—*L'Anthropologie du geste* (Paris: Gallimard, 1974).

—*La Manducation de la parole* (Paris: Gallimard, 1975).

—*Le Parlant, la Parole et le Souffle* (Paris: Gallimard, 1978).

Julsenius, D., 'Oratio de convenentia linguae Fennicae com Hebraea et Graeca', *Schwedisch bibliotek* I, 1728.

Kennedy, G.A., *New Testament Interpretation through Rhetorical Criticism* (Chapel Hill/London: University of North Carolina Press, 1984).

Kessler, M., 'A Methodological Setting for Rhetorical Criticism', *Semitics* 4 (1974), pp. 22-36.

Kikawada, I.M., 'The Shape of Genesis 11.1-9', in Jakson and Kessler (eds.), *Rhetorical Criticism: Essays in Honour of J. Muilenburg*, pp. 18-32.

—'Some Proposals for the Definition of Rhetorical Criticism', *Semitics* 5 (1977), pp. 67-91.

Koenig, E., *Stilistik, Rhetorik, und Poetik in Bezug auf die biblische Literatur* (Leipzig: Dieterich, 1900).

Koester, F., 'Die Strophen oder der Parallelismus der Verse der Hebraischen Poesie', *TSK* (1831), pp. 40-114.

Krasovec, J., *Der Merismus im Biblisch-Hebraïschen und Nordwestsemitischen* (BibOr, 30; Rome: Biblical Institute Press, 1977).

Kugel, J.K., 'On the Bible and Literary Criticism', *Prooftexts* 1 (1981), pp. 217-36.

—*The Idea of Biblical Poetry: Parallelism and its History* (New Haven/London: Yale University Press, 1981).

Labat, R., *et al.*, *Les Religions du Proche-Orient asiatique* (Paris: Fayard, 1970).

Lamarche, P., *Zacharie IX–XIV: Structure littéraire et messianisme* (EBib; Paris: Gabalda, 1961).

—'Structure de l'Epître aux Colossiens', *Bib* 56 (1975), pp. 453-63.

Lamarche, P., and C. Le Dû, *Epître aux Romains V–VIII: Structure littéraire et Sens* (Paris: Editions du CNRS, 1980).

La Potterie, I. de, *Exegesis quarti evangelii. Prologus S. Johannis* (teaching notes, Roma, 1974–75 and 1979–80).

—'Structure du Prologue de Jean', *NTS* 30 (1984), pp. 254-81.

Lausberg, H., *Handbuch der literarischen Rhetorik: Eine Grundlegung der Literaturwissenschaft* (I–II; Munich: Max Hueber, 1960); Spanish trans. *Manual de retòrica literaria* (I–III; Madrid: Gredos, 1966).

—*Elemente der literarischen Rhetorik* (Munich: Max Hueber, 1949); Italian trans. *Elementi di retorica* (Bologna: Il Mulino, 1969).

Léon-Dufour, X., 'Trois chiasmes johanniques', *NTS* 7 (1960–61), pp. 249-55.

Linton, O., 'Le parallelismus membrorum dans le Nouveau Testament; simples remarques', in *Mélanges bibliques en hommage au R.P. Béda Riguaux* (Gembloux: Duculot, 1970), pp. 489-507.

Lohfink, N., *Lectures in Deuteronomy* (Rome: Biblical Institute Press, 1968).

Lohr, C.H., 'Oral Techniques in the Gospel of Matthew', *CBQ* 23 (1961), pp. 403-35.

Lowth, R., *De sacra poesi Hebraeorum praelectiones academicae Oxonii habitae* (Oxford, 1753); ET *Lectures on the Sacred Poetry of the Hebrews* (ed. C.E. Stowe; trans. G. Gregory; Andover, 1829); French trans. *Leçons sur la poésie sacrée des Hébreux traduites pour la première fois en français du latin du Dr Lowth* (trans. M. Sicard; 2 vols.; Lyon, 1812; Avignon: Segin aîné, 2nd edn, 1839); *Cours de poésie sacrée par le Dr Lowth traduit pour la première fois du latin en français* (trans. F. Roger; Paris, 1813).

—*Isaiah: A New Translation with a Preliminary Dissertation and Notes* (London: J. Dodsley & T. Cadelle, 1778).

Lund, N.W., 'The Presence of the Chiasmus in the Old Testament', *AJSL* 46 (1929–30), pp. 104-28.

—'The Presence of Chiasmus in the New Testament', *JR* 10 (1930), pp. 74-93.

—'The Influence of Chiasmus upon the Structure of the Gospels', *AThR* 13 (1931), pp. 27-48.

—'The Influence of Chiasmus upon the Gospel According to Matthew', *AThR* 13 (1931), pp. 405-33.

—'The Literary Structure of Paul's Hymn to Love', *JBL* 50 (1931), pp. 260-76.

—'Chiasmus in the Psalms', *AJSL* 49 (1933), pp. 281-312.

—*Outline Studies in the Book of Revelation* (Chicago: Covenant Book Concern, 1935).

—*Chiasmus in the New Testament: A Study in Formgeschichte* (Chapel Hill: University of North Carolina Press, 1942); repr. *Chiasmus in the New Testament: A Study in the Form and Function of Chiastic Structures* (Peabody, MA: Hendrickson, 1992).

—'The Significance of Chiasmus for Interpretation', *CrozQ* 20 (1943), pp. 105-23.

—*Studies in the Book of Revelation* (Chicago: Covenant Press, 1955).

Lund, N.W., and H.H. Walker, 'The Literary Structure of the Book of Habakkuk', *JBL* 53 (1934), pp. 355-70.

Lunbom, J.R., *Jeremiah: A Study in Ancient Hebrew Rhetoric* (SBLDS, 18; Missoula, MT: University of Montana, 1975).

Malatesta, E., 'The Literary Structure of John 17', *Bib* 52 (1971), pp. 190-214.

—*The Epistles of St John: Greek Text and English Translation Schematically Arranged* (Rome: Gregorian University Press, 1973).

Mallon, E.D., 'A Stylistic Analysis of Joel 1.10-12', *CBQ* 45 (1983), pp. 537-48.

Martinet, A., *Eléments de linguistique générale* (Paris: Armand Colin, 1960); ET *Elements of General Linguistics* (trans. E. Palmer; London: Faber & Faber, 1964; London/Chicago: Faber & Faber/University of Chicago Press, 1966).

Martini, C.-M., *Novum Testamentum e Codice Vaticanus Graeco 1209* (Vatican: Bibl. Apost. Vat., 1968).

McCarter, P.K., *1 Samuel* (AB, 8; Garden City NY: Doubleday, 1980).

Meek, Th.J., 'The Structure of Hebrew Poetry', *JR* 9 (1929), pp. 523-50.

Metzger, B., *The Text of the New Testament: Its Transmission, Corruption and Restoration* (Oxford: Clarendon Press, 1964).

Meynet, R., *Quelle est donc cette Parole? Lecture 'rhétorique' de l'Evangile de Luc (1–9 et 22–24)* (LD, 99 A and B; Paris: Cerf, 1979).

—'Au coeur du texte, Analyse rhétorique de l'aveugle de Jéricho selon Saint Luc', *NRT* 103 (1981), pp. 693-710.

—'Deux paraboles parallèles; analyse rhétorique de Lc 15,1-32', *Annales de Philosophie de la Faculté des Lettres et des Sciences Humaines* de l'Université Saint-Joseph (Beyrouth) 2 (1981), pp. 89-105.

—*Initiation à la rhétorique biblique: Qui donc est le plus grand?* (Initiations; Paris: Cerf, 1982).

—'Qui donc est le plus fort? Analyse rhétorique de Mc 3,22-30; Mt 12,22-37; Lc 11,14-26', *RB* 90 (1983), pp. 334-50.

—'Les dix commandements, loi de liberté, analyse rhétorique d'Ex 20,2-17 et de Dt 5,6-21', *MUSJ* 50 (1984), pp. 405-21.

—'Dieu donne son nom à Jésus; analyse rhétorique de Lc 1,26-56 et de 1Sam 2,1-10', *Bib* 66 (1985), pp. 39-72.

—*L'Evangile selon Saint Luc: Analyse rhétorique.* I. *Planches*, II. *Commentaire* (Paris: Cerf, 1988); Italian trans. *Il vangelo secondo Luca* (Retorica biblica, 1; Roma: Edizioni Dehoniane, 1994).

—'Le Bouclier d'Achille', *Strumenti critici* 59 (1989), pp. 93-115.

—'Analyse rhétorique du Prologue de Jean', *RB* 96 (1989), pp. 481-510.

—*L'Analyse rhétorique, une nouvelle méthode pour comprendre la Bible: Textes fondateurs et exposé systématique* (Initiations; Paris: Cerf, 1989); Italian trans. *L'analisi retorica* (Biblioteca biblica, 8; Brescia: Queriniana, 1992).

—'L'enfant de l'amour (Ps 85)', *NRT* 112 (1990), pp. 843–58.

—'Histoire de l'analyse rhétorique en exégèse biblique', *Rhetorica* 8 (1990), pp. 291-320.

—'Le psaume 145', *Annales du Département des lettres arabes (Institut de lettres orientales)*, Festschrift Maurice Fyet, 6B (1991–92), pp. 213-25.

—'Le cantique de Moïse et le cantique de l'Agneau (Ap 15 et Ex 15)', *Greg* 73 (1992), pp. 19-55.

—'A Análise retórica. Um novo método para compreender a Bíblia', *Brot.* 37 (1993), pp. 391-408.

—*Passion de Notre Seigneur Jésus Christ selon les évangiles synoptiques* (Lire la Bible, 99, Paris: Cerf, 1993).

—'"Celui à qui est remis peu, aime un peu" (Lc 7,36-50)', *Greg* 75 (1994), pp. 267-80.

—'Quelle rhétorique dans l'Epître aux Galates? Le cas de Ga 4,12-20', *Rhetorica* 12 (1994), pp. 427-50.

—'Un nuovo metodo per comprendere la Bibbia: l'analisi retorica', *CivCatt* (1994), III, pp. 121-34.

—'L'analyse rhétorique, une nouvelle méthode pour comprendre la Bible', *NRT* 116 (1994), pp. 641-57.

—'Présupposés de l'analyse rhétorique, avec une application à Mc 10,13-52', in C. Coulot (ed.), *Exégèse et Herméneutique: Comment lire la Bible?* (LD, 158; Paris: Cerf, 1994), pp. 69-111.

—'Pour comprendre proverbes et énigmes (Pr 1,1-7; 10,1-5; 26,1-12)', in P. Bovati and R. Meynet (eds.), *Ouvrir les Ecritures: Mélanges Paul Beauchamp* (LD, 162; Paris: Cerf, 1995), pp. 97-119.

—*Lire la Bible* (Dominos, 92; Paris: Flammarion, 1996).

—'I frutti dell'analisi retorica per l'esegesi biblica', *Greg.* 77 (1996), pp. 403-36.

—'Al-taḥlīl al-balāġī, ṭarīqa ǧadīda li-'idrāk ma'ānī al-kitāb al-muqaddas', *Al-Machriq* 70 (1996), pp. 391-410.

—*'E ora, scrivete per voi questo cantico': Introduzione pratica all'analisi retorica*. 1. *Detti e proverbi* (Retorica biblica, 3, Roma: Edizioni Dehoniane, 1996).

—'Composition et genre littéraire de la première section de l'Epître aux Galates', in J. Schlosser (ed.), *Paul de Tarse. Congrès de l'ACFEB (Strasbourg, 1995)* (LD, 165; Paris: Cerf, 1996), pp. 51-64.

—see P. Bovati.

Meynet, R., N. Farouki, L. Pouzet, and A. Sinno, *Tarîqah al-taḥlîl al-balāĝî wa l-tafsûr: Taḥlîlât nuṣûṣ min al-kitâb al-muqaddas wa min al-ḥadît al-nabawî* (*Méthode rhétorique et herméneutique: Analyse de textes de la Bible et de la Tradition musulmane*) (Beirut: Dar el-Machreq, 1993); French rev. edn *Rhétorique sémitique. Textes de la Bible et de la Tradition musulmane* (Patrimoines. Religions du Livre; Paris: Cerf, 1998).

Milligan, W., *Lectures on the Apocalypse* (London, 3rd edn, 1892).

—*The Book of Revelation* (New York: Expositor's Bible, 1902).

Minguez, D., *Pentecostés: Ensayo de Semiotica narrativa en Hch 2* (AnBib, 75; Rome: Biblical Institute Press, 1976).

Mirsky, A., 'The Origin of the Anadiplosis in Hebrew Literature', *Tarbiz* 28 (1958–59), pp. 171-80.

Molino, J., and J. Tamine, *Introduction à l'analyse linguistique de la poésie* (Paris: Presses Universitaires de France, 1982).

Mortara Garavelli, B., *Manuale di retorica* (Milan: Bompiani, 1988, 5th edn, 1991).

Moulton, R.G., *The Literary Study of the Bible* (Boston, 1889).

Mounin, G., 'Biblical Rhetoric and Faithful Translation', *BT* 30 (1979), pp. 336-40.

—'Rhétorique', *Encyclopaedia Universalis* (Paris: Encyclopaedia Universalis, 1989), t. 20, pp. 10-14.

—'Traduction', *Encyclopaedia Universalis* (Paris: Encyclopaedia Universalis, 1989), t. 22, pp. 829-31.

—'Une rhétorique biblique?', *Critique* 475 (1986), pp. 1198-1203.

Mueller, D.H., *Die Propheten in ihrer ursprünglicheren Form* (Vienna: Hoebder, 1896).

Muilenburg, J., 'A Study in Hebrew Rhetoric: Repetition and Style' (VTSup, 1; Leiden: E.J. Brill, 1953), pp. 97-111.

—'Form Criticism and Beyond', *JBL* 88 (1969), pp. 1-18.

Murphy, R.E., 'The Structure of the Canticle of Canticles', *CBQ* 11 (1949), pp. 381-91.

Newman, L.I., and W. Popper, *Studies in Biblical Parallelism* (3 vols.; Berkeley: University of California Press, 1918).

Nida, E.A., 'Rhetoric and the Translator: with Special Reference to John 1', *TPBT* 33 (1982), pp. 324-28.

Nielsen, E., *Oral Tradition: A Modern Problem in Old Testament Introduction* (Studies in Biblical Theology; London: SCM Press, 1954).

Norden, E., *Die antika Kunstprosa* (2 vols.; Leipzig/Berlin: Teubner, 1918).

Pairault, C., 'Le prophète Marcel Jousse', *Etudes* 359 (1983), pp. 231-43.

Patte, D. and A., *What is Structural Exegesis?* (Philadephia: Fortress Press, 1976, 1978).

Pautrel, R., 'Les Canons du mashal rabbinique', *RSR* (1936), pp. 5-45; (1938), pp. 264-81.

Pesch, R., 'Zur konzentrischen Struktur von Jona 1', *Bib* 47 (1966), pp. 577-81.

Pontifical Biblical Commission (The), *The Interpretation of the Bible in the Church* (Rome: Libreria Editrice Vaticana, 1993).

Porten, B., 'The Structure and Theme of the Solomon Narrative (I Kings 3–11)', *HUCA* 37 (1967), pp. 93-128.

Bibliography

369

Radday, Y.T., 'Chiasm in the Biblical Narrative', *BetM* 20-21 (1964), pp. 47-72.
—'Chiasm in Samuel', *LB* 9-10 (1971), pp. 21-31.
—'Chiasm in Tora', *LB* 19 (1972), pp. 12-23.
—'Chiasm in Joshua, Judges and Others', *LB* 3.27-28 (1973), pp. 6-13.
—'Chiasm in Kings' *LB* 31 (1974), pp. 52-67.
—'Le chiasme dans le récit biblique', *NCah* 38 (1974), pp. 44-55.
Radermakers, J., *Au fil de l'Evangile selon saint Matthieu* (Heverlee/Leuven: Institut d'Etudes Théologiques, 1972).
—*La bonne nouvelle de Jésus selon saint Marc* (Brussels: Institut d'Etudes Théologiques, 1974).
Renaud, B., *Structure et attaches littéraires de Michée IV–V* (Paris: Gabalda, 1964).
Robinson, T.H., *The Poetry of the Old Testament* (London: Gerard Duckworth, 1947; repr. 1969).
—'Basic Principles of Hebrew Poetic Form', in J.C.B. Walter Baumgartner *et al.* (eds.), *Festschrift Albert Bertholet* (Tübingen: Mohr, 1950), pp. 438-50.
—'Hebrew Poetic Form: The English Tradition', *VTSup* 1 (1953), pp. 128-49.
Rossi (Rabbi Azarias de Rubeis, or dei Rossi): see Azarias.
Rousseau, F., 'La structure de Mc 13', *Bib* (1975), pp. 157-72.
—'Les structures littéraires du Benedictus (Lc 1,68-79)', *NTS* 32 (1986), pp. 268-82.
Sanders, E.P., 'Chiasmus and the Translation of I Q Hodayot VII, 26-27', *RdQ* 23 (1968), pp. 427-31.
Scheusner, J.F., *De parallelismo sententiarum egregio subsidio interpretationis grammaticae* (Leipzig, 1781).
Schöttgen, C., *Horae Hebraicae et Talmudicae* (Dresden and Leipzig: apud Hekelii, 1733); ET of the Seventh Dissertation in Lundbom, *Jeremiah*, pp. 121-27.
Scott, R., and B. Brock, *Method of Rhetorical Criticism: A Twentieth-Century Perspective* (New York: Harper & Row, 1972).
Scott, W.S., *Five Approaches of Literary Criticism* (New York: Collier Books, 1962).
Segalla, G., 'Giovanni 7–9: una struttura chiasmatica?', *StPat* 27 (1980), pp. 605-60.
Seux, M.-J., *Hymnes et prières aux dieux de Babylonie et d'Assyrie* (LAPO; Paris: Cerf, 1976).
Sicre Díaz, J.L., *Los dioses olvidados: Poder y riqueza en los profetas preexílicos* (Madrid: Ed. Christiandad, 1979).
Simoens, Y., *La Gloire d'aimer: Structures stylistiques et interprétatives dans le Discours de la Cène (Jn 13–17)* (AnBib, 90; Rome: Biblical Institute Press, 1981).
Sloan, T.O., 'Restoration of Rhetoric to Literary Study', *ST* 16 (1967), pp. 91-97.
Smalley, W.A., 'Recursion Patterns and the Sectioning of Amos', *TPBT* 30 (1979), pp. 118-27.
Smith, R., 'Chiasm in Sumero-Akkadian', in Welch (ed.), *Chiasmus in Antiquity*, pp. 17-35.
Souvay, C., *Essai sur la métrique des Psaumes* (St-Louis: Séminaire Kenrick, 1911).
Standaert, B., *L'Evangile selon Marc: Composition et genre littéraire* (Zevenkerken/ Brugge: Stichting Studentenpers Nijmegen, 1978).
Steele, R.B., *Chiasmus in Sallust, Caesar, Tacitus and Justinus* (Minnesota: Northfield Press, 1891).
—'Chiasmus in the Epistles of Cicero, Seneca, Pliny and Fronto', in *Studies in Honor of Basil L. Gildersleeve* (Baltimore: The Johns Hopkins University Press, 1902), pp. 339-52.

Stock, A., 'Chiastic Awareness and Education in Antiquity', *BTB* 14 (1984), pp. 23-27.

Stummer, F., *Sumerisch-akkadische Parallelen zum Aufbau altestamentlicher Psalmen* (SGKA, 11.1/2: 1922).

Tannehill, R.C., 'The Magnificat as Poem', *JBL* 93 (1974), pp. 263-75.

Thiering, B., 'The Poetic Forms of the Hodayot', *JSS* 8 (1963), pp. 189-209.

Tidiman, B., 'La structure en chiasme et le livre d'Ezéchiel', *Hokma* 28 (1985), pp. 48-67.

Topel, L.J., 'A Note on the Methodology of Structural Analysis in Jn 2.23–3.21', *CBQ* 33 (1971), pp. 211-20.

Tromp, N.J., 'Amos V 1-17: Towards a Stylistic and Rhetorical Analysis', *OTS* 23 (1984), pp. 56-84.

Tschang, T.M., *Le Parallélisme dans les vers du Cheu King* (Paris: Geuthner, 1937).

Vaccari, A., 'De utilitate parallelismi poetici ad intelligentiam Sacrorum librorum', *VD* 1 (1920), pp. 188-89.

—'Cassiodoro e il pasûq della Bibbia ebraica', *Bib* 40 (1959), pp. 309-21.

Vaganay, L., *Initiation à la critique textuelle du Nouveau Testament* (2nd edn, completely rethought by C.-B. Amphoux; Paris: Cerf, 1986).

Van Dyke Parunak, H., 'Transitional Techniques in the Bible', *JBL* 102 (1983), pp. 525-48.

Vanhoye, A., *La Structure littéraire de l'Epître aux Hébreux* (Paris: Desclée de Brouwer, 1963, 1976).

—*Traduction structurée de l'Epître aux Hébreux* (Rome: Biblical Institute Press, 1963).

—'Les indices de la structure littéraire de l'Epître aux Hébreux', *SE* II (1964), pp. 493-509.

—'La composition de Jn 5,19-30', in *Mélanges bibliques en hommage au R.P. Béda Riguaux* (Gembloux: Duculot, 1970), pp. 259-74.

—'Discussions sur la structure de l'Epître aux Hébreux', *Bib* 55 (1974), pp. 349-80.

—'Structure du Benedictus', *NTS* 12 (1976), pp. 382-89.

—'L'interpretazione della Bibbia nella Chiesa: Riflessione circa un documento della Commissione Biblica', *CivCatt* (1994), III, pp. 3-15.

Vanni, U., *La struttura letteraria dell'Apocalisse* (Rome: Herder, 1971).

Waard, J. de, 'The Chiastic Structure of Amos V,1-17', *VT* 27 (1977), pp. 170-77.

—'The Structure of Qohelet', in *Proceedings of the Eighth World Congress of Jewish Studies* (Jerusalem: World Union of Jewish Studies, 1982), pp. 57-64.

Waard, J. de, and J.W.A. Smalley, *A Translator's Handbook on the Book of Amos* (Stuttgart: United Bible Society, 1969).

Walker, H.H., and N.W. Lund, 'The Literary Structure of the Book of Habakkuk', *JBL* 53 (1934), pp. 355-70.

Walsh, J.T., 'Genesis 2:4b–3:24: A Synchronic Approach', *JBL* 96 (1977), pp. 161-77.

—'Jonah 2.3-10: A Rhetorical Critical Study', *Bib* 63 (1982), pp. 219-29.

Watson, W.G.E., 'The Pivot Pattern in Hebrew, Ugaritic and Akkadian Poetry', *ZAW* 88 (1976), pp. 239-53.

—*Classical Hebrew Poetry: A Guide to its Techniques* (JSOTSup, 26; Sheffield: JSOT Press, 1984).

Welch, J.W., 'Chiasmus in Ugaritic', *UF* 6 (1974), pp. 421-36.

—'Chiasmus in Ancient Greek and Latin Literatures', in *idem* (ed.), *Chiasmus in Antiquity*, pp. 250-68.

Welch, J.W. (ed.), *Chiasmus in Antiquity* (Hildesheim: Gerstenberg, 1981).

Wichelns, H.A., 'Some Differences between Literary Criticism and Rhetorical Criticism', in R.F. Howes (ed.), *Historical Studies of Rhetoric and Rhetoricians* (Ithaca, NY: Cornell University Press, 1961), pp. 217-24.

Wilder, A.N., *The Language of the Gospel: Early Christian Rhetoric* (New York: Harper & Row, 1964).

—*Early Christian Rhetoric: The Language of the Gospel* (Cambridge, MA: Harvard University Press, 1971).

Willis, J.T., 'The Structure of the Book of Micah', *SEÅ* 34 (1969), pp. 5-42.

—'The Structure of Micah 3–5 and the Function of Micah 5.9-14 in the Book', *ZAW* 81 (1969), pp. 191-214.

Willis, J.J., 'The Song of Hannah and Ps 113', *CBQ* 35 (1973), pp. 139-54.

Wolff, H.W., *Anthropologie des Alten Testaments* (Munich: Kaiser, 1973); ET *Anthropology of the Old Testament* (Philadelphia: Fortress Press, 1974).

—*Dodekapropheton*. 2. *Joel und Amos* (BK, 14.2; Neukirchen: 1969); ET *Joel and Amos* (Philadephia: Hermeneia, 1977).

Wright, A., 'Numerical Patterns in the Book of Wisdom', *CBQ* 29 (1967), pp. 524-38.

—'The Riddle of the Sphinx: The Structure of the Book of Qohelet', *CBQ* 30 (1968), pp. 313-34.

—'The Structure of the Book of Wisdom', *Bib* 48 (1967), pp. 165-84.

—'Numerical Patterns in the Book of Wisdom', *CBQ* 29 (1967), pp. 524-38.

Wuellner, W., 'Where is Rhetorical Criticism taking us?', *CBQ* 49 (1987), pp. 448-63.

Zenner, J.K., *Die Chorgesänge im Buche der Psalmen: Ihre Existenz und ihre Form* (Freiburg: Herder, 1896).

GLOSSARY OF TECHNICAL TERMS

1. *Linguistic Terms*

Apart from the terms of traditional grammar, known by all, such as 'preposition', 'main' or 'subordinate' clause ('causal', 'temporal', 'conditional'), 'verb', 'adjective', 'pronoun', a few terms of modern linguistics have been used here, for the commodity of the exposition:

SEMANTIC FIELD
Domain of signification which regroups a class of terms; the semantic field of 'seating' comprises 'the chair', 'the armchair', 'the stool', 'the sofa', 'the couch', 'the bean bag' and so on.

EXPANSION
'Every element added to an utterance which does not modify the mutual relationships and the function of the pre-existing elements' (A. Martinet, *Elements of General Linguistics*, §§4-30, p. 119). Generic term: the epithet adjective is an expansion of the noun, all the complements, of noun or verb, are also expansions, the adverb is an expansion of the noun, verb or adjective.

FUNCTIONAL
For 'functional moneme': 'moneme which serve to indicate the function of another moneme' (Martinet, *Elements*, §§4-12, p. 104). Generic term which comprises prepositions as well as conjunctions.

LEXEME
(Or 'lexical moneme'): 'lexical monemes are those which belong to unlimited inventories' (Martinet, *Elements*, §§4-19, p. 110); 'those monemes... are listed in the lexicon and not in the grammar' (Martinet, *Elements*, §§1-9, p. 25). Examples: 'table', 'to come', 'great', 'always'.

MODIFIERS
Grammatical determinants of lexemes (e.g. modes, voices, person, number of verbs; gender, number, and so on of substantives).

MONEME
Significant unit (called 'unit of the first articulation'; see Martinet, *Elements*, §§1-9, pp. 24-25); there are lexical monemes or lexemes and grammatical monemes or morphemes.

MORPHEME
The morphemes (or 'grammatical monemes' or 'tool-words') are monemes which belong to limited inventories (pronouns, prepositions, conjunctions, articles, modalities, etc.).

PHONEME
Distinctive phonic unit (called 'of the second articulation'; see Martinet, *Elements*, §§1-9, pp. 24-25).

PREDICATE
'The predicative moneme is the element around which the sentence is organized, the other constituent elements marking their function by reference to it' (Martinet, *Elements*, §§4-29, p. 119). In an independent verbal clause, the verb plays the role of predicate.

REFERENT
The object that is designated in situation by a moneme; e.g., in 'He began to teach in their synagogues' (Lk. 4.15), the referent of the pronoun 'he' is Jesus.

SIGNIFICANT
Phonic form of a linguistic sign.

SIGNIFICATUM
Meaning or value of a linguistic sign.

SYNTAGM
Any combination of monemes; a syntagm which starts with a preposition is called 'prepositional syntagm'.

2. *Rhetorical Terms*

2.1. *Terms Designating the Rhetorical Units*

Very often, in works of exegesis, the terms 'section', 'passage', and mostly 'piece' and 'part', are not used univocally. Here is the list of terms which, in the present methodological exposition, designate the textual units at each successive level.

2.1.1. The 'inferior' levels (or not autonomous levels): apart from the first, the units of inferior levels are all formed of ONE, TWO, or THREE units of the preceding level.

TERM
The minimal unit; it usually corresponds to a lexeme.

MEMBER
The member is a syntagm, or group of 'terms' linked together through close syntactic relationships; the 'member' is the minimal rhetoric unit.

SEGMENT
The segment counts one, two or three members; and there are *unimember* segments (the term of Greek origin would be 'monostychs'), *bimember* segment segments (or 'distychs') and *trimember* segment (or 'tristychs').

PIECE
The piece counts one, two or three segments.

PART
The part counts one, two or three pieces.

2.1.2. The 'superior' levels (or autonomous levels): they are all formed of either ONE or SEVERAL units from the preceding level.

PASSAGE
(The equivalent of the 'pericope' of exegetes): the passage is formed of one or several parts.

SEQUENCE
The sequence is formed of one or more passages.

SECTION
The section is formed of one or more sequences.

BOOK
Last, the book is formed of one or more sections.

It is sometimes necessary to recourse to intermediary levels such as 'sub-part', 'sub-sequence' and 'sub-section'; these intermediary units have the same definition as that of the part, sequence and section.

2.2. *Terms Designating the Rhetorical Function of Symmetrical Elements*

INITIAL TERMS
Identical or similar terms or syntagms that mark the beginning of symmetrical textual units; the *anaphora* of classical rhetoric.

FINAL TERMS
Identical or similar terms or syntagms that mark the end of symmetrical textual units; the *epiphora* of classical rhetoric.

EXTREME TERMS
Identical or similar terms or syntagms that mark the extremities of a textual unit; the 'inclusion' of traditional exegesis.

MEDIAN TERMS
Identical or similar terms or syntagms that mark the end of a textual unit and the beginning of the unit which is symmetrical to it; the 'hook-word' or 'staple-word' of traditional exegesis.

CENTRAL TERMS
Identical or similar terms or syntagms that mark the centres of two symmetrical textual units.

2.3. *Other Terms*

ABBREVIATION
Phenomenon of economy which makes that a linguistic element of a
first unit is not repeated in the symmetrical unit.

BIPOLAR
The bipolar opposition is that which puts in relation two complementary terms that indicate a whole; for example, 'heaven and earth'.

CHIASM
Figure of composition where four elements in relation two by two
respond to one another in an alternate way: A B / B'A'.
The chiasm is distinct from 'concentrism' by the absence of a central
element.

CONCENTRISM
Figure of composition where the elements, at least five, are disposed
in a concentric fashion around a central element (which can be a unit
of any levels of textual organization): A B C D E /x/ E'D'C'B'A'

ECONOMY
See 'abbreviation'.

PARALLELISM
Figure of composition where the elements in relations two by two are
disposed in a parallel fashion: A B C D E / A'B'C'D'E'
When two parallel units frame a unique element, parallelism will be
referred to to designate the symmetry between those two units, but the
whole will be considered (the superior unit) as concentric.

PARONOMASIA
Phonic relationship between two terms which have a different
meaning.

INDEXES

INDEX OF REFERENCES

OLD TESTAMENT

Rhetorical Analysis

INDEX OF AUTHORS

JOURNAL FOR THE STUDY OF THE OLD TESTAMENT
SUPPLEMENT SERIES